THE FEDERAL RESPONSE TO

HURRICANE KATRINA

LESSONS LEARNED

FEBRUARY 2006

For sale by the Superintendent of Documents, U.S. Government Printing Office
Internet: bookstore.gpo.gov   Phone: toll free (866) 512-1800;   DC area (202) 512-1800
Fax: (202) 512-2250 Mail: Stop IDCC, Washington, DC 20402-0001

ISBN 0-16-075600-6

THE WHITE HOUSE

WASHINGTON

February 23, 2006

The President of the United States
The White House
Washington, DC 20500

Dear Mr. President:

Pursuant to your direction, I most respectfully submit for your consideration: *The Federal Response to Hurricane Katrina: Lessons Learned.*

You often remind us that your most solemn obligation as President is to protect the American people. And every day and night, millions of men and women throughout the Federal government—both civilian and military—work to achieve that objective. Given the dangerous world in which we live, they do an outstanding job.

Despite all we do, however, Hurricane Katrina was a deadly reminder that we can and must do better, and we will. This is the first and foremost lesson we learned from the death and devastation caused by our country's most destructive natural disaster: No matter how prepared we think we are, we must work every day to improve.

When you addressed the Nation from Jackson Square, New Orleans, on the evening of September 15, 2005, you ordered a comprehensive review of the Federal response to Hurricane Katrina so we as a Nation could make the necessary changes to be "better prepared for any challenge of nature or act of evil men that could threaten our people." At your direction, we assembled a team of experienced professionals dedicated to this mission. In addition, we enjoyed a tremendous partnership with each of your Cabinet Secretaries; without their commitment to this process the Report would not have been possible.

As part of the review, we visited the hurricane-ravaged Gulf Coast during mid November 2005. We met with government officials, business and community leaders, and volunteers amidst the rubble of what had been their homes, schools, and places of worship. Their courage and fortitude in the face of tragedy was inspirational. And while we were determined to learn the lessons to improve our future disaster response, it was clear that for residents of the Gulf Coast, survival and hope still came a day at a time. We were struck by the decency and compassion of those we met and moved by their continuing emotion and pain. As you know, it is hard for those who have not witnessed first hand the hurricane's destruction and its human toll to fully comprehend the importance of your charge that we prepare to respond more effectively to our fellow citizens in their times of greatest need.

This Report then is a tribute to those who have served and those who have suffered. We remember those who lost their lives and all still affected by this tragedy. Though we can never replace their unfathomable losses, we have an obligation to continue helping those still suffering to recover and rebuild their lives.

Though there will be tragedies we cannot prevent, we can improve our preparedness and response to reduce future loss and preserve life. And while we will work diligently to implement immediate improvements, it is important to recognize that the true transformation envisioned in this Report will require a sustained commitment over time by the Federal government as well as by State and local governments that have essential duties in responding to disasters. The Report and recommendations are submitted in the hope of ensuring that the harsh lessons of Hurricane Katrina need never be learned again.

Thank you for the privilege and the honor of leading this review.

Sincerely,

Frances Fragos Townsend
Assistant to the President for Homeland Security
and Counterterrorism

TABLE OF CONTENTS

FOREWORD

On August 23, 2005, Hurricane Katrina formed as a tropical storm off the coast of the Bahamas. Over the next seven days, the tropical storm grew into a catastrophic hurricane that made landfall first in Florida and then along the Gulf Coast in Mississippi, Louisiana, and Alabama, leaving a trail of heartbreaking devastation and human suffering. Katrina wreaked staggering physical destruction along its path, flooded the historic city of New Orleans, ultimately killed over 1,300 people, and became the most destructive natural disaster in American history.

Awakening to reports of Katrina's landfall on the Gulf Coast the morning of Monday, August 29, American citizens watched events unfold with an initial curiosity that soon turned to concern and sorrow. The awe that viewers held for the sheer ferocity of nature was soon matched with disappointment and frustration at the seeming inability of the "government"—local, State, and Federal—to respond effectively to the crisis. Hurricane Katrina and the subsequent sustained flooding of New Orleans exposed significant flaws in Federal, State, and local preparedness for catastrophic events and our capacity to respond to them. Emergency plans at all levels of government, from small town plans to the 600-page National Response Plan—the Federal government's plan to coordinate all its departments and agencies and integrate them with State, local, and private sector partners—were put to the ultimate test, and came up short. Millions of Americans were reminded of the need to protect themselves and their families.

Even as parts of New Orleans were still under water, President Bush spoke to the Nation from the city's historic Jackson Square. He stated unequivocally, that "[f]our years after the frightening experience of September the 11th, Americans have every right to expect a more effective response in a time of emergency. When the federal government fails to meet such an obligation, I, as President, am responsible for the problem, and for the solution."[1]

In his address, the President ordered a comprehensive review of the Federal response to Hurricane Katrina so we as a Nation could make the necessary changes to be "better prepared for any challenge of nature or act of evil men that could threaten our people."[2] The President's charge has resulted in the material and conclusions of this Report—*The Federal Response to Hurricane Katrina: Lessons Learned.*

WHAT WENT WRONG

In general terms, the challenges to our collective response to Hurricane Katrina are not difficult to identify. Hurricane Katrina, its 115-130 mph winds, and the accompanying storm surge it created as high as 27 feet along a stretch of the Northern Gulf Coast from Mobile, Alabama, to New Orleans, impacted nearly 93,000 square miles of our Nation—roughly an area the size of Great Britain. The disaster was not isolated to one town or city, or even one State. Individual local and State plans, as well as relatively new plans created by the Federal government since the terrorist attacks on September 11, 2001, failed to adequately account for widespread or simultaneous catastrophes.

We were confronted by the pictures of destroyed towns and cities, each with their own needs. Smaller cities like Waveland, Mississippi, were completely devastated by Hurricane Katrina and required smaller scale yet immediate search and rescue efforts as well as large volumes of life saving and sustaining commodities. New Orleans, the largest affected city—which dominated much of what Americans saw on their televisions—suffered first from the initial impact of Katrina and then from the subsequent flood caused by breaches in its 350 mile levee system. Over an estimated eighteen-hour period, approximately 80 percent of the city flooded with six to twenty feet of water, necessitating one of the largest search and rescue operations in our Nation's history.

SCOPE AND METHODOLOGY

The President made clear that we must do better in the future. The objective of this Report is to identify and establish a roadmap on how to do that, and lay the groundwork for transforming how this Nation—from every level of government to the private sector to individual citizens and communities—pursues a real and lasting vision of preparedness. To get there will require significant change to the status quo, to include adjustments to policy, structure, and mindset.

While the Report notes that disaster preparedness and response to most incidents remains a State and local responsibility, this review did not include an assessment of State and local responses. The President specifically requested that we review the response of the Federal government. Where actions at the State and local level had bearing on Federal decisions or operations, they are included in order to provide full context. We note that although incident response remains a State and local responsibility, we must strengthen Federal support for their efforts and be better prepared for the Federal response to a catastrophic event. Furthermore, we were mindful of how simple and lucid a situation can appear with the clarity of hindsight. And so, judging in retrospect the decisions made and actions taken in the midst of a major disaster, without consideration of that fuller context, would have been a disservice to all. The scope of the review did not focus on recovery operations that continue to this day. Those important efforts are ongoing and require our continued commitment. Instead, the review's emphasis centers on identifying systemic vulnerabilities and gaps in our response and "fixing government."

The Report is organized in a manner to give the reader the most comprehensive and clear understanding possible of what happened during the Federal response to Hurricane Katrina. It begins with a discussion of the magnitude and complexity of the response challenge by discussing "Katrina in Perspective"—providing an historical comparison both of the hurricane itself and the resultant flood. Only by understanding what the storm was, and was not, can an appropriate and measured assessment of the response take place. A National Preparedness "Primer" on the current Federal framework is then provided to give the reader an understanding of how the current system was supposed to function. This chapter points out some fundamental confusion in the Federal planning and identifies potential shortcomings in the applicability of our plans to catastrophic widespread incidents.

Two major chapters of the Report follow with an analytical, narrative chronology that provides a detailed account of Hurricane Katrina. The first discusses the storm's development in the days "Pre-Landfall," and the next chronicles both the "Week of Crisis" from August 29 through September 5, and concludes with the transition from response to recovery. We note for the reader that the narrative is not meant to be a comprehensive, definitive account of all that transpired, and future information inevitably will shed additional light. We then present a detailed chapter on "Lessons Learned." Here, we describe the seventeen most critical challenges that were problematic before, during, and after Hurricane Katrina's landfall.

We conclude with the most important chapter: "Transforming National Preparedness." It describes the imperative and remedies for fixing the problems that Hurricane Katrina exposed. The foundations of the recommended reforms result in two immediate priorities: We must institutionalize a comprehensive National Preparedness System and concurrently foster a new, robust Culture of Preparedness.

The Report also contains several appendices, including 125 specific recommendations distilled from a four-month review. These recommendations are written for policy makers and emergency managers and contain more technical information not appropriate for the narrative. We have also included some stories of successes and heroic efforts we encountered by responders, volunteers, agencies, and public officials that must not be overlooked.

CONCLUSION

During a visit to the Gulf Coast, President Bush put our efforts in perspective, saying, "[o]ne of the lessons of this storm is the decency of people, the decency of men and women who care a lot about their fellow citizens, whether they be elected officials or just folks on the ground...trying to make somebody else's life even better than it was before. So we learned some lessons about how to respond, and we're going to change. But some of the lessons shouldn't change, and that is the decency and character of the American people."

Hurricane Katrina prompted an extraordinary national response that included all levels of government—Federal, State, and local—the private sector, faith-based and charitable organizations, foreign countries, and individual citizens. People and resources rushed to the Gulf Coast region to aid the emergency response and meet victims' needs. Their actions saved lives and provided critical assistance to Hurricane Katrina survivors. Despite these efforts, the response to Hurricane Katrina fell far short of the seamless, coordinated effort that had been envisioned by President Bush when he ordered the creation of a National Response Plan in February 2003.[3]

Yet Katrina creates an opportunity—indeed an imperative—for a national dialogue about true national preparedness, especially as it pertains to catastrophic events. We are not as prepared as we need to be at all levels within the country: Federal, State, local, and individual. Hurricane Katrina obligates us to re-examine how we are organized and resourced to address the full range of catastrophic events—both natural and man-made. The storm and its aftermath provide us with the mandate to design and build such a system.

We hope that this Report marks the beginning of a truly transformational state of preparedness throughout all levels of our Nation. Hurricane Katrina will undoubtedly be regarded by history as one of the most destructive, costly, and tragic events our Nation has ever endured. Yet with collective determination, unity of effort, and effective organizational change, the true legacy of Katrina can be that of a catalyst that triggered a real and lasting improvement to our national preparedness.

CHAPTER ONE: KATRINA IN PERSPECTIVE

Hurricane Katrina was one of the worst natural disasters in our Nation's history and has caused unimaginable devastation and heartbreak throughout the Gulf Coast Region. A vast coastline of towns and communities has been decimated.

—President George W. Bush, September 8, 2005[1]

Terrorists still plot their evil deeds, and nature's unyielding power will continue. We know with certainty that there will be tragedies in our future. Our obligation is to work to prevent the acts of evil men; reduce America's vulnerability to both the acts of terrorists and the wrath of nature; and prepare ourselves to respond to and recover from the man-made and natural catastrophes that do occur. The magnitude of Hurricane Katrina does not excuse our inadequate preparedness and response, but rather it must serve as a catalyst for far-reaching reform and transformation. To do this, we must understand Hurricane Katrina in its proper context.

HURRICANE KATRINA AMONG OTHER DISASTERS

Hurricane Katrina was the most destructive natural disaster in U.S. history.[2] The overall destruction wrought by Hurricane Katrina, which was both a large and powerful hurricane as well as a catastrophic flood, vastly exceeded that of any other major disaster, such as the Chicago Fire of 1871, the San Francisco Earthquake and Fire of 1906, and Hurricane Andrew in 1992.[3]

Hurricane Katrina's devastating effects were felt before the storm even reached the Gulf Coast on August 29, 2005. In the Gulf of Mexico, Hurricane Katrina battered the offshore energy infrastructure and forced the evacuation of more than 75 percent of the Gulf's 819 manned oil platforms.[4] Two days before landfall, U.S. energy companies estimated that the approaching storm had already reduced Gulf of Mexico oil production by more than a third.[5]

Seventy-five hurricanes of Katrina's strength at landfall—a Category 3—have hit the mainland United States since 1851, roughly once every two years.[6] Yet Katrina was anything but a "normal" hurricane. First, Katrina was larger than most. Hurricane Camille, a Category 5 storm that devastated the Gulf Coast in 1969,[7] had top wind speeds that exceeded those of Katrina upon landfall, but Camille's hurricane force winds only extended seventy-five miles from its center,[8] whereas Katrina's extended 103 miles from its center.[9] As a result, Hurricane Katrina's storm surge affected a larger area than did Hurricane Camille's.[10] In all, Hurricane Katrina impacted nearly 93,000 square miles across 138 parishes and counties.[11] The extreme intensity that Hurricane Katrina reached before landfall on the Gulf Coast, as well as its size, meant that its storm surge was consistent with a more powerful storm. In fact, the National Hurricane Center concluded that the height of Hurricane Katrina and Camille's respective storm surges were comparable to each other.[12]

Hurricane Katrina's winds and a storm surge that crested up to twenty-seven feet high dealt a ferocious blow to homes, businesses, and property on the coast and for many miles inland.[13] This storm surge overwhelmed levees all along the lowest reaches of the Mississippi River and the edges of Lake Pontchartrain.[14] The consequences for New Orleans, which sits mostly below sea level, were dire. Significant levee failures occurred on the 17th Street Canal, the Industrial Canal, and the London Avenue Canal. Approximately 80 percent of the city was flooded.[15]

The flooding destroyed New Orleans, the Nation's thirty-fifth largest city.[16] Much as the fire that burned Chicago in 1871 and the earthquake and fire that leveled San Francisco in 1906 destroyed the economic and cultural centers of an entire region, so too did Hurricane Katrina destroy what many considered to be the heart of the Gulf Coast. The destruction also called to mind the Galveston Hurricane of 1900, which thoroughly devastated the town of Galveston, Texas. At the time, Galveston was an economic and cultural center of Texas and was the State's fourth largest city.[17]

Even beyond New Orleans, Katrina's span of destruction was widespread. Indeed, one of the gravest challenges presented by this particular disaster was the vast geographic distribution of the damage. Towns and cities, small and large, were destroyed or heavily damaged up and down the Gulf Coast and miles inland. From Morgan City, Louisiana, to Biloxi, Mississippi, to Mobile, Alabama, Hurricane Katrina's wind, rain, and storm surge demolished homes and businesses. Large parts of the coastal areas of these States were devastated. As Mississippi Governor Haley Barbour stated, "The 80 miles across the Mississippi Gulf Coast is largely destroyed. A town like Waveland, Mississippi, has no inhabitable structures—none."[18]

Hurricane Katrina contradicts one side of an important two-part trend. For at least a century, America's most severe natural disasters have become steadily *less* deadly and *more* destructive of property (adjusted for inflation).[19] Figure 1.1 depicts this trend. Yet, Hurricane Katrina not only damaged far more property than any previous natural disaster, it was also the deadliest natural disaster in the United States since Hurricane San Felipe in 1928. The dark blue bars in the figure below show the decreasing number of deaths caused by natural disasters in the period from 1900 – 2005. The light blue bars show the increasing amount of damage caused by these same natural disasters adjusted to third quarter 2005 dollars.[20]

Figure 1.1 U.S. Natural Disasters that Caused the Most Death and Damage to Property in Each Decade, 1900-2005, with 2004 Major Hurricanes Added[21]Damage in Third Quarter 2005 Dollars

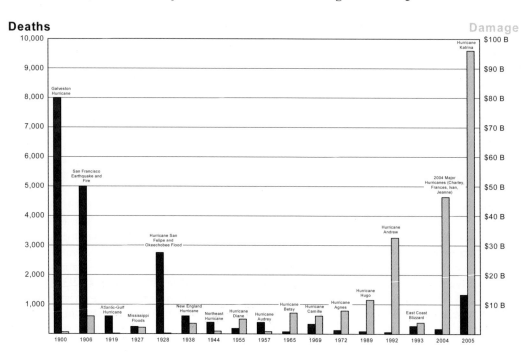

MEASURING HURRICANE KATRINA: THE PATH OF DESTRUCTION

Estimating disaster damage is not an exact science, and, in the case of Hurricane Katrina, it is further complicated by ongoing recovery efforts. Estimates vary but, considering property damage alone, Hurricane Katrina is America's first disaster—natural or man-made—to approach the $100 billion mark (See Table 1.1).[22]

Table 1.1 Estimated damage from Hurricane Katrina and the New Orleans Flood[23]

Housing	$67 billion
Consumer durable goods	$7 billion
Business property	$20 billion
Government property	$3 billion
Total	**$96 billion**

Hurricane Katrina devastated far more residential property than had any other recent hurricane, completely destroying or making uninhabitable an estimated 300,000 homes.[24]

This far surpasses the residential damage of Hurricane Andrew, which destroyed or damaged approximately 80,000 homes in 1992.[25] It even exceeds the combined damage of the four major 2004 hurricanes, Charley, Frances, Ivan, and Jeanne, which together destroyed or damaged approximately 85,000 homes.[26] Figure 1.2 charts the effects of Hurricane Katrina against other major hurricanes in recent U.S. history, comparing homes damaged or destroyed, property damage, and deaths.

Figure 1.2: Hurricane Katrina Compared to Hurricanes Ivan, Andrew, and Camille[27]

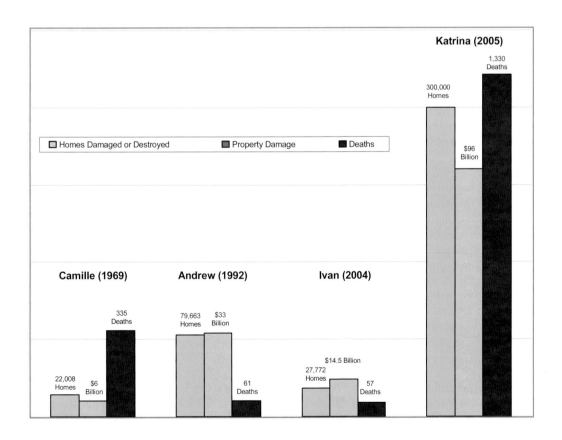

Hurricane Katrina's damage was extensive. The storm destroyed so many homes, buildings, forests, and green spaces that an extraordinary amount of debris was left behind—118 million cubic yards all told.[28] In comparison, Hurricane Andrew created 20 million cubic yards of debris.[29] The debris from Katrina, if stacked onto the space of a football field, would reach over ten and a half miles high.[30]

Hurricane Katrina's effects on the economy have yet to be fully reckoned. The worst consequences were local: between August and September, the unemployment rate doubled from 6 to 12 percent in the most affected areas of Louisiana and Mississippi.[31] In Louisiana, Mississippi, and Alabama, salaries and wages fell by an estimated $1.2 billion in the third quarter of 2005.[32] But short-term, economic ripples reached the entire country through the rising cost of gasoline. The approach of the storm forced the temporary shutdown of most crude oil and natural gas production in the Gulf of Mexico. In the immediate wake of Hurricane Katrina, gasoline prices rose sharply nationwide.[33] The combined effects of Hurricane Katrina and Hurricane Rita, which made landfall on the border between Texas and Louisiana early on September 24, 2005, were such that, between August 26, 2005, and January 11, 2006, 114 million barrels of oil production capacity were left unused, equivalent to over one-fifth of yearly output in the Gulf of Mexico.[34]

The storm devastated the regional power infrastructure. In Louisiana, Mississippi, and Alabama, approximately 2.5 million power customers reported outages.[35] By contrast, Hurricane Ivan denied 1.8 million customers power.[36]

Communications suffered as well. The storm crippled thirty-eight 911 call centers, disrupting local emergency services,[37] and knocked out more than 3 million customer phone lines in Louisiana, Mississippi, and Alabama.[38] Broadcast communications were likewise severely affected, as 50 percent of area radio stations and 44 percent of area television stations went off the air.[39]

Much more than any other hurricane, Katrina's wrath went far beyond wind and water damage. In fact, Hurricane Katrina caused at least ten oil spills, releasing the same quantity of oil as some of the worst oil spills in U.S. history. Louisiana reported at least six major spills of over 100,000 gallons and four medium spills of over 10,000 gallons.[40] All told, more than 7.4 million gallons poured into the Gulf Coast region's waterways, over two thirds of the amount that spilled out during America's worst oil disaster, the rupturing of the *Exxon Valdez* tanker off the Alaskan coast in 1989.[41]

The wave of destruction created environmental and health hazards across the affected region, including standing water, oil pollution, sewage, household and industrial chemicals, and both human and animal remains. The storm surge struck 466 facilities that handle large amounts of dangerous chemicals, thirty-one hazardous waste sites, and sixteen Superfund toxic waste sites, three of which flooded. The surge also destroyed or compromised 170 drinking water facilities and dozens of wastewater treatment facilities.[42]

Most terrible of all and most difficult to measure, however, were Hurricane Katrina's human effects.

MEASURING THE IMMEASURABLE: THE HUMAN TOLL

When the winds and floods of Hurricane Katrina subsided, an estimated 1,330 people were dead as a result of the storm.[43] The vast majority of the fatalities—an estimated 80 percent—came from the New Orleans metropolitan area; Mississippi suffered greatly as well, with 231 fatalities.[44] Many of the dead were elderly or infirm. In Louisiana, approximately 71 percent of the victims were older than sixty, and 47 percent of those were over seventy-five.[45] At least sixty-eight were found in nursing homes, some of whom were allegedly abandoned by their caretakers.[46] Of the total known fatalities, there are almost two hundred unclaimed bodies remaining at the Victim Identification Center in Carville, Louisiana.[47] As awful as these horrifying statistics are, unfortunately they are not the end of the story. As of February 17, 2006, there were still 2,096 people from the Gulf Coast area reported missing.[48]

For the survivors, the aftermath of Hurricane Katrina has been characterized by a mixture of grief, anxiety, and frustration. Around 770,000 people were displaced—the largest since the Dust Bowl migration from the southern Great Plains region in the 1930s.[49] After Hurricane Katrina, housing options often arrived slowly to those who could not return to their ruined homes; by the end of October, there were still more than 4,500 people staying in shelters. The numbers of evacuees residing in such transient emergency shelters had dropped significantly by January 2006, and families have slowly begun to find permanent housing.[50]

Moreover, many victims found it difficult to reconstruct their shattered lives. In many cases, they had either lost or forgotten basic documents, such as insurance information, birth certificates, and marriage licenses, which would later prove essential to rebuilding their lives.[51] Most of the evacuees did not have access to their medical records, which increased the risk of complications when receiving medical treatment.[52] For those who returned to their homes in the Gulf region, basic services were still wanting. By January, 85 percent of public schools in Orleans parish had still not reopened; in the metropolitan area, approximately two-thirds of the retail food establishments, half of the bus routes, and half of the major hospitals remained closed.[53] For Katrina's victims, a sense of "back to normal" still seems far away.

Of the 1.1 million people over the age of sixteen who evacuated in August 2005, approximately 500,000 of those evacuees had not returned home by late December. For the evacuees who have not returned to their homes, jobs have been scarce. Their unemployment rate was just below 28 percent in November and over 20 percent in December. The former evacuees who did return to their homes in the Gulf region had better access to work with an unemployment rate of 12.5 percent in November, which fell to 5.6 percent in December.[54] In July, before Katrina hit, the unemployment rate in the most affected areas of Louisiana and Mississippi had been 6 percent.[55]

By any measure, Hurricane Katrina was a national catastrophe. Similar to the images of grief and destruction on September 11, 2001, the images of suffering and despair from Hurricane Katrina are forever seared into the hearts and memories of all Americans. Those painful images must be the catalyst for change.

CHAPTER TWO: NATIONAL PREPAREDNESS — A PRIMER

Disaster response in America traditionally has been handled by State and local governments, with the Federal government playing a supporting role. Limits on the Federal government's role in disaster response are deeply rooted in American tradition. State and local governments—who know the unique requirements of their citizens and geography and are best positioned to respond to incidents in their own jurisdictions—will always play a large role in disaster response. The Federal government's supporting role respects these practical points and the sovereignty of the States as well as the power of governors to direct activities and coordinate efforts within their States. While we remain faithful to basic constitutional doctrine and time tested principles, we must likewise accept that events such as Hurricane Katrina and the terrorist attacks of September 11, 2001, require us to tailor the application of these principles to the threats we confront in the 21st Century. In later chapters, as we discuss the breakdowns in delivering Federal support and capabilities in response to Hurricane Katrina, the need for a flexible Federal response and a larger Federal role in catastrophic contingency planning becomes clear.[1]

FEDERALISM

The Founders created a constitutional framework in which each State, upon ratification of the Constitution, ceded some of its powers to the Federal government to create one united yet limited central government.[2] The Constitution sets forth the specific and delegated powers that delineate Federal and State roles. It tells us which branches and offices will be part of the Federal government, what powers they may exercise, and what limitations constrain them.[3] The Constitution also respects State powers by reserving those powers not given to the Federal government to the States or to the people.[4] Our Federal system provides a structure to enable coordination between the United States government and State governments to create a balance that respects the sovereignty of both entities.

The United States has long operated on the general premise that governments exist to do those things that individuals, alone or in free and voluntary association (*e.g.*, families and charities), are not best positioned to do for themselves, such as ensuring public safety and providing law enforcement. Following these principles, the Founders created the Federal government to do those things that States cannot or should not do individually, such as defending the Nation, conducting foreign relations, and ensuring open and free interstate commerce.[5]
Accordingly, State and local governments assume the first and foremost line of defense against civil disturbance and threats to public safety. The Federal government guarantees its assistance to protect the States in their existence as representative republican governments from the external threat of invasion or attack, and against internal subversion or rebellion.[6] Federal laws reinforce the concept that the Federal government should respect State sovereignty. For example, section 331 of the Insurrection Act requires the State legislature or, in its absence, the State governor, to make a formal request of the Federal government before the President may send in Federal troops to assist State efforts to restore order.[7]

The role of the Federal government in disaster response has evolved significantly throughout the past 200 years.[8] In 1803, in what is widely seen as the first instance of Federal intervention in a disaster scenario, Congress approved the use of Federal resources to assist the recovery of Portsmouth, New Hampshire, following a devastating urban fire.[9] Between 1803 and 1950, the Federal government intervened in over 100 incidents (earthquakes, fires, floods, and tornados), making Federal resources available to affected jurisdictions.[10] These interventions were limited and were delivered in an *ad hoc* manner without an established Federal role or coordinated response plan.[11] The Federal government also quickly recognized the role that private non-profit organizations can play. In 1905, Congress chartered the American Red Cross as a charitable organization to provide disaster relief support during crises. The value of this decision was demonstrated a year later, when the Red Cross provided key assistance during the San Francisco Earthquake and Fire of 1906.[12]

During the Great Depression, the approach of the Federal government became more proactive. For example, Congress endowed the Bureau of Public Roads with the authority to provide continuous grants to States for the repair of disaster-damaged infrastructure and charged the Army Corps of Engineers with the task of mitigating flood-related threats.[13] This piecemeal legislative approach was eventually replaced by the Civil Defense Act of 1950—the first comprehensive legislation pertaining to Federal disaster relief.[14]

In 1952, President Truman issued Executive Order 10427, which emphasized that Federal disaster assistance was intended to supplement, not supplant, the resources of State, local, and private sector organizations.[15] This theme was echoed two decades later in President Nixon's 1973 report, "New Approaches to Federal Disaster Preparedness and Assistance." The report clearly stated that, "Federal disaster assistance is intended to supplement individual, local and state resources."[16]

Today, the centerpiece legislation for providing Federal aid in disaster relief, the Robert T. Stafford Disaster Relief and Emergency Assistance Act (Stafford Act), reinforces the principle that response efforts should first utilize State and local resources.[17] The Stafford Act establishes a process for State governors to request assistance from the Federal government when an incident overwhelms State and local resources.[18] To provide and coordinate Federal aid to the people and the State and local governments impacted by a disaster using all Federal agencies, the Act authorizes the President to issue major disaster or emergency declarations, and to appoint a Federal Coordinating Officer (FCO) to coordinate the administration of Federal relief. The Stafford Act is frequently invoked in disaster and emergency response. Since 1974, an average of thirty-eight major disasters have been declared annually. In 2004, a near record disaster season, the President issued sixty-eight major disaster declarations and seven emergency declarations.[19]

In a 21st Century world marked by catastrophic terrorism and natural disasters, the Federal government must build upon our foundation of disaster relief and prepare for the larger role we will be called upon to play in response to a catastrophic event.

DISASTER RESPONSE STRUCTURE

After the terrorist attacks on September 11, 2001, the Federal government realized that additional measures were needed to ensure effective coordination with State and local governments and took steps to alter how it responds to emergencies. In the *National Strategy for Homeland Security*, issued in July 2002, President Bush called for a major initiative to build a national system for incident management and to integrate separate Federal response plans into a single, all-discipline[20] incident management plan. The President proposed that the initiative be led by the yet-to-be-created Department of Homeland Security (DHS).[21] In creating DHS in November 2002, Congress included the initiative as part of the Secretary of Homeland Security's responsibilities.[22] The Homeland Security Act was officially signed into law by the President on November 25, 2002.[23] On March 1, 2003, DHS assumed operational control of the nearly 180,000 employees from portions of 22 departments, agencies, and offices that were combined to constitute the newly created Department.[24]

In February 2003, the President issued Homeland Security Presidential Directive 5 (HSPD-5). Homeland Security Presidential Directives are presidential orders that establish national policies, priorities, and guidelines to strengthen U.S. homeland security. In HSPD-5, the President specifically directed the Secretary of Homeland Security to: (a) create a comprehensive National Incident Management System (NIMS) to provide a consistent nationwide approach for Federal, State, and local governments to work effectively together to prepare for, respond to, and recover from domestic incidents, regardless of cause, size, or complexity, and; (b) develop and administer an integrated *National Response Plan* (NRP), using the NIMS, to provide the structure and mechanisms for national level policy and operational direction for Federal support to State and local incident managers.[25]

HSPD-5 further directed the heads of all Federal departments and agencies to adopt the NIMS, use it in their individual domestic incident management activities, participate in the NRP, and assist the Secretary of Homeland Security in its development and maintenance.[26] The NIMS and the NRP were completed in 2004 and provide the foundation for how the Federal government organizes itself when responding to all disasters, including Hurricane Katrina.

The National Incident Management System

The *National Incident Management System* (NIMS) establishes standardized incident management protocols and procedures that all responders—Federal, State, and local—should use to conduct and coordinate response actions. It sets forth a "core set of doctrine, concepts, principles, terminology and organizational processes to enable effective, efficient, and collaborative incident management at all levels" of government.[27] The NIMS provides a common, flexible framework within which government and private entities at all levels can work together to manage domestic incidents of any magnitude.[28] In March 2004, the Secretary of Homeland Security approved the NIMS and sent a memorandum to officials at all levels of the government asking for continued cooperation and assistance in further developing and implementing the NIMS.

The central component of the NIMS is the Incident Command System (ICS). The ICS was developed and refined over many years by incident commanders at the Federal, State, and local levels and was being successfully implemented throughout the country prior to being included in the NIMS.[29] The ICS provides a means to coordinate the efforts of individual responders and agencies as they respond to and help manage an incident. The ICS organization, the structure and size of which can be tailored to the complexity and size of any given incident, comprises five major functional areas—Command, Planning, Operations, Logistics, and Finance/Administration.[30] This system grew out of the challenges of interagency coordination experienced when fighting wildfires in western states.

ICS requires that a command system be established from the onset of incident operations, thereby ensuring a unified command and the efficient coordination of multi-agency and multi-jurisdictional efforts.[32] Recognizing that most incidents are managed locally, the command function under ICS is set up at the lowest level of the response, and grows to encompass other agencies and jurisdictions as they arrive. Some incidents that begin with a single response discipline (e.g., fire or police department) within a single jurisdiction may rapidly expand to multi-discipline, multi-jurisdictional incidents requiring significant additional resources and operational support.[33] The concept of unified command is both more important and more complicated when local, State, and Federal commanders are required to coordinate their efforts. ICS clarifies reporting relationships and eliminates confusion caused by multiple, and potentially conflicting, directions and actions. The *National Response Plan* requires senior officials from multiple levels of government to come together at a single location to establish a common set of objectives and a single incident plan. This group, referred to as the "Unified Command," provides for and enables joint decisions on objectives, strategies, plans, priorities, and public communications.[34]

> ### *Unity of Command vs. Unified Command* [31]
>
> Unity of command: The concept by which each person within an organization reports to one and only one designated person. The purpose of unity of command is to ensure unity of effort under one responsible commander for every objective.
>
> Unified command: An application of the Incident Command System used when there is more than one agency with incident jurisdiction or when incidents cross political jurisdictions. Agencies work together through the designated members of the Unified Command, often the senior person from agencies and/or disciplines participating in the Unified Command, to establish a common set of objectives and strategies and a single incident action plan.

The National Response Plan

Adopted by the Federal government in December 2004, the NRP is an all-hazards plan that establishes a single, comprehensive framework for managing domestic incidents across all levels of government and across a spectrum of activities that includes prevention, preparedness, response, and recovery.[35] It provides the structure and mechanisms for coordinating Federal support to State and local incident managers and for exercising Federal authorities and responsibilities incorporating the NIMS structure.

The NRP is based on a number of fundamental precepts. Consistent with the traditions and customs that have developed under American federalism, the NRP is built on the premise that incidents are generally handled at the lowest jurisdictional level possible.[36] Local authorities provide the initial response capabilities to every incident, including man-made and natural disasters, and when overwhelmed, request assistance from neighboring jurisdictions. When incidents are of such a magnitude that these resources are overwhelmed, resources are requested from the State, which draws on its own internal emergency response capabilities or requests assistance from neighboring States through mutual-aid agreements. Many large and devastating events are handled this way without any Federal assistance.[37] When Federal response assistance is required, the NRP employs a systematic and coordinated approach to incident management at the field, regional, and Federal agency headquarters levels, establishing protocols for such activities as reporting incidents, issuing alerts and notification, coordinating response actions, and mobilizing resources.[38] Though the NRP generally seeks to preserve the primary role of State and local bodies as first responders, it does recognize some events will be so catastrophic that they will require a greater proactive Federal government response (as discussed in further detail in the "Planning a Proactive Federal Response" section of this chapter).[39] However, while the NRP recognized the need for a proactive Federal response in a catastrophe, no final plan has been put in place to make this operational.

What Triggers the NRP

The NRP "covers the full range of complex and constantly changing requirements in anticipation of or in response to threats or acts of terrorism, major disasters, and other emergencies."[40] It applies to "all Federal departments and agencies that may be requested to provide assistance or conduct operations in the context of actual or potential Incidents of National Significance."[41] The NRP is also designed to be flexible and scalable: "Consistent with the model provided in the NIMS, the NRP can be partially or fully implemented in the context of a threat, anticipation of a significant event, or the response to a significant event."[42] The NRP can be used to selectively implement specific components in unique situations or can be fully implemented to bring to bear the full efforts and resources of the Federal government.

However, the specific triggers for the *National Response Plan* and its various components are unclear. In HSPD-5, the President instructed the Secretary of Homeland Security to coordinate the Federal government's resources utilized in response to or recovery from terrorist attacks, major disasters, or other emergencies *if and when any one of the following four conditions applies*:

(1) A Federal department or agency acting under its own authority has requested the assistance of the Secretary;

(2) The resources of State and local authorities are overwhelmed and Federal assistance has been requested by the appropriate State and local authorities;

(3) More than one Federal department or agency has become substantially involved in responding to the incident; or

(4) The Secretary has been directed to assume responsibility for managing the domestic incident by the President.[43]

The NRP bases the definition of Incidents of National Significance (INS) "on situations related to" these HSPD-5 criteria.[44] However, the NRP lacks sufficient clarity regarding when and how an event becomes an INS. There are two dimensions to this issue. First, it is unclear whether satisfaction of one or more of the stated criteria is sufficient for an INS to exist, or whether additional considerations must apply. Second, the NRP is unclear as to whether the Secretary must formally declare an INS or, alternatively, whether an INS is triggered automatically when one or more of these criteria are satisfied, including when the President declares a disaster or emergency under the Stafford Act. With respect to Hurricane Katrina, when the Secretary of Homeland Security formally declared the event to be an INS on Tuesday, August 30, 2005, arguably an INS already existed, because two of the four HSPD-5 criteria noted above had already been satisfied.[45]

The lack of clarity on the second issue is illustrated by two seemingly inconsistent NRP provisions; the Scope and Applicability section states that the Secretary is responsible for declaring an INS,[46] which supports an interpretation that an INS cannot be in effect without a declaration by the Secretary, while the Planning Assumptions section states that "all Presidentially declared disasters and emergencies under the Stafford Act are considered Incidents of National Significance,"[47] which supports a conclusion that the President's issuance of an emergency declaration for Louisiana on August 27, 2005, put an INS into effect.

Most importantly, however, regardless of how an INS is defined or whether an INS must be formally declared by the Secretary or not, the NRP fails to articulate clearly which specific actions should be taken and what components should be utilized under the NRP as a result of an INS coming into effect. As a practical matter, many of the NRP's functions and structures were already being utilized at the time that the Secretary declared an INS.[48]

Since the NRP was adopted in December 2004, many parts of the Plan had been used to various degrees and magnitudes for thirty declared Stafford Act events to coordinate Federal assistance.[49] Yet, an INS had never formally been declared prior to Tuesday, August 30, 2005—during the Hurricane Katrina response. The lack of clarity discussed above caused confusion. The process and the operational consequences of declaring an INS should be further defined and clarified.[50]

NRP Concept of Operations

When applied together, the components of the NRP should provide for a unified command structure to serve as the local, multi-agency coordination center for the effective and efficient coordination of Federal, State, local, tribal, nongovernmental, and private-sector organizations with primary responsibility for incident-related prevention, response and recovery actions.[51] In many cases, this takes place at a Joint Field Office (JFO). The JFO co-locates the Principal Federal Official (PFO) and Federal Coordinating Officer in situations not involving multiple FCOs.[52] In HSPD-5, the President designated the Secretary of Homeland Security as the "principal Federal official for domestic incident management."[53] The NRP allows the Secretary to delegate his responsibility, defining a PFO "as the Federal official designated by the Secretary of Homeland Security to act as his/her representative locally to oversee, coordinate, and execute the Secretary's incident management responsibilities under HSPD-5 for Incidents of National Significance."[54] The FCO, a position created by the Stafford Act, manages Federal resource support activities and is responsible for coordinating the timely delivery of Federal disaster assistance resources to affected State and local governments, individual victims, and the private sector.[55] At the regional level, a Regional Response Coordination Center (RRCC) coordinates disaster response activities until a JFO can be established.[56]

At DHS headquarters, the Homeland Security Operations Center (HSOC) coordinates "incident information-sharing, operational planning, and deployment of Federal resources" together with its component element at the Federal Emergency Management Agency (FEMA) headquarters, the National Response Coordination Center (NRCC), a "multiagency center that provides overall Federal response coordination for Incidents of National Significance and emergency management program implementation."[57] Strategic-level coordination and resolution of resource conflicts unresolved by the NRCC occurs at the Interagency Incident Management Group (IIMG), an interagency body housed at DHS headquarters.[58]

The coordination of the Federal response—to include capabilities and resources—occurs at the field, regional, and Federal agency headquarters levels through the Emergency Support Function (ESF) framework. ESFs are organized groups of government and private sector entities that provide support, resources, and services. An ESF is staffed by specialists from multiple Federal departments, agencies, and the private sector. The purpose of the ESFs is to integrate skills and capabilities that reside in disparate organizations to coordinate support to State and local response agencies, including both physical resources and staff. The ESFs are structured so that resources and capabilities that are required to assist State and local officials in response and recovery operations can be handled by the appropriate Federal agency. A detailed break-down of each ESF by function and the primary Federal department or agency charged with leading each ESF can be found in Table 2.1.[59]

Table 2.1 Emergency Support Functions

	ESF	Primary Department or Agency
ESF #1	Transportation	DOT
ESF #2	Communications	DHS (IAIP/NCS)
ESF #3	Public Works and Engineering	DOD (USACE) and DHS (FEMA)
ESF #4	Firefighting	USDA (Forest Service)
ESF #5	Emergency Management	DHS (FEMA)
ESF #6	Mass Care, Housing, and Human Services	DHS (FEMA) and American Red Cross
ESF #7	Resource Support	GSA
ESF #8	Public Health and Medical Services	HHS
ESF #9	Urban Search and Rescue	DHS (FEMA)
ESF #10	Oil and Hazardous Materials Response	EPA and DHS (U.S. Coast Guard)
ESF #11	Agriculture and Natural Resources	USDA and DOI
ESF #12	Energy	DOE
ESF #13	Public Safety and Security	DHS and DOJ
ESF #14	Long-Term Community Recovery and Mitigation	USDA, DOC, DHS (FEMA), HUD, Treas, and SBA
ESF #15	External Affairs	DHS (FEMA)

FEDERAL EMERGENCY MANAGEMENT AGENCY

President Carter created FEMA through a 1978 reorganization plan that merged several elements of the Federal response into one agency.[60] In 2003, FEMA became a component of the newly created Department of Homeland Security. Within the Department, FEMA is the primary agency charged with coordinating Federal assistance during disasters.[61] Pursuant to its responsibilities under the NRP, FEMA has primary responsibility for emergency response and recovery coordination.[62] It maintains the NRCC and, as the Federal government's chief steward of disaster response, FEMA also continuously monitors for potential disasters and mobilizes resources when it anticipates Federal assistance will be requested. This occurs frequently during the hurricane season.

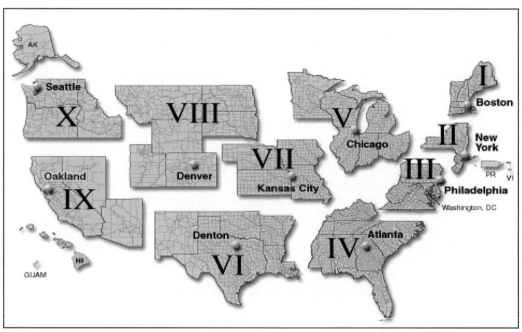

FEMA is not, however, the operational provider of most Federal response support. It is a small organization that primarily manages the operational response, relief, and recovery efforts of the rest of the Federal government.

FEMA does not, for instance, provide mass care or transportation after a disaster. Instead, pursuant to the NRP structure, FEMA tasks the Departments of Health and Human Services, Defense, and Transportation, as well as the American Red Cross, to perform these operations. Generally, State and local officials and first responders identify necessary missions and required commodities which FEMA—through its organizational structure, coordination practices, and administrative support—will assign to a Federal department or secure from the private sector. The organization exists primarily to coordinate other Federal agencies and departments during emergency response and recovery—acting as an honest broker between departments and agencies, providing a command structure, and serving as the single point of entry for State and local officials into the Federal government. It does not have its own critical response assets, such as buses, trucks, and ambulances.

The operational teams that FEMA is responsible for administering, such as the Urban Search and Rescue (US&R) teams, are State and local first responders from around the country that volunteer to be activated, deployed, and reimbursed by FEMA for their help during response activities. FEMA enforces standards, certifications, and qualifications for participation in such programs and provides funding for equipment and training.

To handle national needs, FEMA operates ten regional offices and two area offices that work directly with States in planning for disasters, developing mitigation programs, and meeting needs when disasters occur (see Figure 2.1).[63] Each of the offices maintains full-time staff who work with Federal, State, and local partners year-round. Additionally, each office can draw upon civilian reservist personnel to support the response when a Presidential major disaster or emergency declaration is issued.[64] When State governments request Federal assistance, FEMA deploys personnel to the appropriate regional office and the incident area. Also, the regional office controls the RRCC, from which FEMA coordinates its assistance.[65] Because Hurricane Katrina was advancing toward Louisiana (Region VI), and Florida, Mississippi, and Alabama (Region IV), both FEMA regions conducted response and recovery operations.[66]

PLANNING A PROACTIVE FEDERAL RESPONSE

Under the Stafford Act, requests for major disaster declarations must be made by the Governor of the affected State. The Governor's request must be based on "a finding that the disaster is of such severity and magnitude that effective response is beyond the capabilities of the State and the affected local governments and that Federal assistance is necessary."[67] Emergency declarations can be made in the same manner or, in limited circumstances, can be made by the President unilaterally.[68]

The system for providing Stafford Act assistance, set forth in the NRP and FEMA regulations, reflects the American system of federalism, allocating roles and responsibilities between levels of government by utilizing a layered system that requires local governments to first request assistance from their State. States, in turn, must use their own resources, if available, before requesting Federal assistance. As a prerequisite to major disaster assistance under the Stafford Act, a requesting Governor must "take appropriate response action under State law and direct execution of the State's emergency plan."[69] Similarly, State emergency operations plans are based on this layered system. For example, the State of Louisiana Emergency Operations Plan states that "[t]he initial actions . . . are conducted by local government. Local authorities will exhaust their resources, and then use mutual aid agreements with volunteer groups, the private sector and/or neighboring parishes."[70] When local and State governments require additional resources, they generally call upon neighboring jurisdictions and other States through mutual assistance agreements and through the Emergency Management Assistance Compact (EMAC), a Congressionally ratified agreement[71] that provides form and structure to interstate mutual aid, and through which States make available to each other in time of crisis their emergency response assets, such as National Guard troops.[72]

Traditionally, it is only after local, State, and mutual assistance resources are depleted, or prove insufficient, that the Federal government is requested to help. The Louisiana Emergency Operations Plan further explains that, "State assistance will supplement local efforts and federal assistance will supplement State and local efforts when it is clearly demonstrated that it is beyond local and State capability to cope with the emergency/disaster."[73] Should State and affected local governments become overwhelmed, the President may declare either a major disaster or emergency through his authorities under the Stafford Act.

After a Stafford Act declaration, FEMA, on behalf of the Federal government, receives State requests for assistance and fulfills them by tasking other Federal departments or agencies with the appropriate expertise or resources to meet the specific needs. This is often referred to as a "pull" system for Federal assistance because local and State governments must identify needs and make specific requests for assistance before the Federal government can deliver—they "pull" assistance from the Federal government. Equally important to understanding the current "pull" system is the method in which Federal assistance is delivered to those in need—relying on the State as an intermediary between the Federal government and any other entity. In many cases, the Federal government will satisfy a State request by providing commodities or assets to the State. In so doing, the Federal government is helping the State meet the needs of their local governments and first responders, as well as various operational components of the State. The Federal government does not always directly deliver its assistance to local governments or others in need. The State's role has been compared to retail sales in terms of organization, delivery, and management. Under this description, the Federal government's role is comparable to wholesale. This generally works well and should continue in the majority of instances.

However, in some instances the State and local governments will be overwhelmed beyond their ability to satisfy their traditional roles in this system. Indeed, in some instances, State and local governments and responders may become victims themselves, prohibiting their ability to identify, request, receive, or deliver assistance. This is the moment of catastrophic crisis—the moment when 911 calls are no longer answered; the moment when hurricane victims can no longer be timely evacuated or evacuees can no longer find shelter; the moment when police no longer patrol the streets, and the rule of law begins to break down.

> **Emergency vs. Major Disaster:** Under the Stafford Act, the President can designate an incident either as an "emergency" or a "major disaster." Both authorize the Federal government to provide essential assistance to meet immediate threats to life and property, as well as additional disaster relief assistance. The President may, in certain circumstances, declare an "emergency" unilaterally, but may only declare a "major disaster" at the request of a Governor that certifies the State and affected local governments are overwhelmed. Under an "emergency," assistance is limited in scope and may not exceed $5 million without Presidential approval and notification to Congress. In contrast, for a major disaster, the full complement of Stafford Act programs can be authorized, including long term public infrastructure recovery assistance and consequence management.

During the development of the NRP, such a catastrophic scenario was considered and planning for such an eventuality began. The NRP includes a Catastrophic Incident Annex which "establishes the context and overarching strategy for implementing and coordinating an accelerated, proactive national response to a catastrophic incident."[74] The intent behind this Annex was to plan for a case in which the Federal response posture would switch, upon a declaration by the Secretary of Homeland Security of a *catastrophic incident*, from the traditional "pull" system to one that includes a proactive "push" system, moving assets to the affected areas without waiting for State requests. Under the current Catastrophic Incident Annex, however, the general operating presumption is that Federal pre-deployed resources remain at staging areas until requested by the State and local incident command authorities. Thus, this Annex provides for proactive deployment of resources to the area, but the actual employment of the resources depends to a good degree on requests from State or local authorities and very often their participation in delivering the aid to those in need.

The *National Response Plan* defines a *catastrophic incident* as:

> Any natural or man-made incident, including terrorism, that results in extraordinary levels of mass casualties, damage, or disruption severely affecting the population, infrastructure, environment, economy, national morale, and/or government functions. A catastrophic event could result in sustained national impacts over a prolonged period of time; almost immediately exceeds resources normally available to State, local, tribal, and private sector authorities in the impacted area; and significantly interrupts governmental operations and emergency services to such an extent that national security could be threatened.[75]

Because it was recognized that a proactive Federal response can create strains on Federal resources and presents practical challenges for Federal responders not familiar with the terrain or infrastructure in a disaster area, the NRP Catastrophic Incident Annex required that a "more detailed and operationally specific NRP Catastrophic Incident Supplement . . . be approved and published independently of the NRP Base Plan and annexes."[76] The Catastrophic

Incident Supplement (CIS) is meant to address the "resource and procedural implications of catastrophic events to ensure the rapid and efficient delivery of resources and assets, including special teams, equipment, and supplies that provide critical life-saving support and incident containment capabilities."[77] The draft CIS by its current terms only applies to short notice or no notice events. On August 29, at the time Hurricane Katrina hammered into the Gulf Coast, the draft CIS had not been finalized and promulgated. It began final circulation for approval as part of the regular Federal staffing process shortly after Katrina made landfall.[78]

Ultimately, when a *catastrophic incident* occurs, regardless of whether the catastrophe has been a warned or is a surprise event, the Federal government should not rely on the traditional layered approach and instead should proactively provide, or "push," its capabilities and assistance directly to those in need. When the affected State's incident response capability is incapacitated and the situation has reached catastrophic proportions, the Federal government alone has the resources and capabilities to respond, restore order, and begin the process of recovery. This is a responsibility that must be more explicitly acknowledged and planned for in the NRP, and we must resource, train, and equip to meet this obligation when such a contingency arises. It is also important that we work with State and local governments to ensure they are better prepared to respond immediately, until Federal resources can arrive.

MOVING FORWARD

Hurricane Katrina was the most destructive natural disaster in U.S. history. However, there is no question that the Nation's current incident management plans and procedures fell short of what was needed and that improved operational plans could have better mitigated the Hurricane's tragic effects. As President Bush acknowledged from Jackson Square in New Orleans, "the system, at every level of government, was not well-coordinated, and was overwhelmed in the first few days."[79] A true national preparedness system should ensure that all levels of government effectively work together to keep the American people safe and secure at home.

CHAPTER THREE: HURRICANE KATRINA — PRE-LANDFALL

Hurricane Katrina is now designated a category five hurricane. We cannot stress enough the danger this hurricane poses to Gulf Coast communities. I urge all citizens to put their own safety and the safety of their families first by moving to safe ground.

—President George W. Bush, August 28, 2005[1]

HURRICANE SEASON FORECAST

On May 16, 2005, Brigadier General David L. Johnson (ret.), Director of the National Oceanic & Atmospheric Administration (NOAA), National Weather Service (NWS), released the 2005 Atlantic hurricane outlook to kick off National Hurricane Preparedness Week. In its report, NOAA assessed a 70 percent chance of an above-average hurricane season, predicting twelve to fifteen Atlantic tropical storms, with seven to nine becoming hurricanes and three to five of those becoming major hurricanes (equivalent to Categories 3, 4, and 5 on the Saffir-Simpson scale). [2] NOAA also noted that the previous year had been "extremely active," with fifteen Atlantic tropical storms, including nine that developed into hurricanes.[3] That same day, Max Mayfield, Director of the National Hurricane Center (NHC), cautioned, "[l]ast year's hurricane season provided a reminder that planning and preparation for a hurricane do make a difference. Residents in hurricane vulnerable areas who had a plan, and took individual responsibility for acting on those plans, faired [sic] far better than those who did not."[4]

> **Hurricane Season:** The official Atlantic hurricane season takes place each year between June 1 and November 30, with peak hurricane activity generally occurring between mid-August and mid-October.
>
> In an average year, ten tropical storms develop in the Gulf of Mexico, Caribbean Sea, or Atlantic Ocean; six of these storms become hurricanes. In a typical three-year span, five hurricanes hit the United States mainland; two are designated major (Category 3 – 5) hurricanes. The southeastern United States is the region most vulnerable to a hurricane strike. The States most likely to be hit by a major hurricane are Florida, Texas, and Louisiana.
>
> —National Oceanic and Atmospheric Administration, *Hurricanes: Unleashing Nature's Fury* and *U.S. Mainland Hurricane Strikes by State*

The first two months of the 2005 hurricane season confirmed NOAA's predictions, with a record seven Atlantic tropical storms developing in June and July.[5] Two of these storms developed into major hurricanes, including Hurricane Dennis, "an unusually strong July major hurricane that left a trail of destruction from the Caribbean Sea to the northern coast of the Gulf of Mexico."[6] Dennis prompted mandatory evacuations in the lower Florida Keys and major disaster declarations in Alabama, Florida, and Mississippi.[7] Louisiana Governor Blanco declared a state of emergency.[8] While Cuba ultimately received the worst of the damage inflicted by Dennis, the NHC still estimated U.S. damages in excess of two billion dollars.[9]

On August 2, 2005, NOAA released an updated 2005 Atlantic hurricane season outlook that projected the formation of an additional eleven to fourteen tropical storms, with seven to nine becoming hurricanes, including three to five major hurricanes. Based on the developments in June and July, NOAA revised its assessment to a "95 to 100

Saffir-Simpson Hurricane Scale	
Category	Winds
1	74 – 95 mph
2	96 – 110 mph
3	111 – 130 mph
4	131 – 155 mph
5	Greater than 155 mph

* To be a Tropical Storm, winds must be between 39-73 mph.

percent" chance of an above-normal 2005 Atlantic Hurricane season. It reported that "the atmospheric and oceanic conditions favoring hurricane formation that were predicted in May are now in place. These conditions, combined with the high levels of activity already seen, make an above-normal season nearly certain." Moreover, while there already had been "considerable early season activity," NOAA emphasized that the next three months constituted the peak of hurricane season.[10] NHC Director Mayfield explained, "Knowing precisely where a hurricane will strike and at what intensity cannot be determined even a few days in advance." He urged that "residents and government agencies of coastal and near-coastal regions should embrace hurricane preparedness efforts and should be ready well before a tropical storm or hurricane watch is posted."[11] With four more months remaining in hurricane season, the NOAA outlook proved an ominous forecast.

KATRINA'S BEGINNINGS

August 23, 2005

On Tuesday, August 23, the NWS reported Tropical Depression Twelve had formed over the Bahamas from the remnants of Tropical Depression Ten.[12] The NHC released the first in what would be a series of sixty-one advisories over the next seven days reporting on and tracking the development of the storm.[13]

The Federal government began monitoring the storm as a potential hurricane shortly after the NWS announced Tropical Depression Twelve had formed. Federal department and agency Emergency Operation Centers (EOC)—bases used to coordinate and direct response activity—began to closely monitor NWS bulletins and incorporate them into their own updates and situation reports.

The U.S. Northern Command (USNORTHCOM), the military command charged with defending the U.S. homeland and providing military support to civil authorities, also began monitoring the Tropical Depression at its Operations Center in Colorado Springs, Colorado, on August 23.[14]

August 24, 2005

On Wednesday, August 24, the Tropical Depression strengthened into a Tropical Storm and was given the name Katrina, the eleventh named storm of the 2005 hurricane season.[15] The Federal Emergency Management Agency (FEMA) activated its Hurricane Liaison Team (HLT), consisting of FEMA, NWS, and State and local officials. The HLT deploys to the National Hurricane Center to assist in the coordination of advisories with Federal, State, and local emergency management agencies, providing forecast updates and technical advice.[16] FEMA Region IX was notified to prepare for possible back-up should Mississippi or Georgia be affected. USNORTHCOM also issued a Warning Order for supporting commands to prepare for requests for Department of Defense (DOD) assets should the need arise.[17]

August 25, 2005

Katrina continued to gain strength throughout the day on Thursday, as it approached the southeastern coast of Florida.[18] At 3:30 PM EDT, Katrina was upgraded to a Category 1 hurricane and forecast to make landfall in Florida.

Meanwhile, advisories issued by the NWS Tropical Prediction Center (TPC) and the NHC predicted Katrina would turn toward the Alabama-Florida panhandle area after it crossed Florida and entered the Gulf of Mexico.[19] At 6:30

PM EDT, Hurricane Katrina made landfall in south Florida near the Miami-Dade and Broward County line, with sustained winds of up to 80 miles per hour and dropping as much as 14-16 inches of rain in some regions.[20] The Florida landfall resulted in more than a dozen deaths,[21] over 1.4 million power outages,[22] and pockets of severe flooding. Damage costs in south Florida amounted to just under $2 billion,[23] with an estimated $400 million in agricultural losses.[24]

Gulf Coast States and localities began hurricane preparations on Thursday, August 25, even as the storm approached its first landfall in Florida, by activating their emergency response elements, issuing emergency declarations, pre-positioning response assets, and planning for evacuations and sheltering. Because NWS advisories predicted Katrina would enter the Gulf and make landfall on the Northern Gulf Coast area, Alabama and Mississippi activated their Emergency Operations Centers (EOCs) to coordinate information and their State's resources for emergency response operations.[25]

In preparation for Florida landfall, FEMA delivered 100 truckloads of ice to staging areas in Georgia, and thirty-five truckloads of food and seventy trucks of water to Palmetto, Georgia. Also, anticipating a potential second Gulf Coast landfall, FEMA pre-staged over 400 truckloads of ice, more than 500 truckloads of water, and nearly 200 truckloads of food at logistics centers in Alabama, Louisiana, Georgia, Texas, and South Carolina.[26] This was the beginning of the pre-staging efforts that increased to the largest pre-positioning of Federal assets in history by the time Hurricane Katrina made its second landfall on August 29, 2005.[27] At this time, FEMA placed Rapid Needs Assessment and Emergency Response Teams – Advance Elements (ERT-As) on alert. An ERT-A is "the portion of the Emergency Response Team (ERT) that is the first group deployed to the field to respond to a disaster incident."[28] FEMA also conducted their first video teleconference, a call held each day at noon from August 25 until well after landfall. These video teleconferences helped synchronize Federal, State, and local responders and were a means of defining and coordinating assistance and support needs.[29]

Numerous private sector entities took action as well. Norfolk Southern Railroad, for example, recognized the potential impact of the loss of certain key bridges and pre-staged repair barges in order to be able to move in quickly to make repairs after the hurricane made landfall. The Cargill Corporation, an agricultural products and services company, also pre-positioned freighters offshore so that it could continue shipping grain internationally immediately after landfall.

KATRINA ENTERS THE GULF OF MEXICO

August 26, 2005

Katrina briefly weakened to a Tropical Storm as it passed over Florida in the early hours of Friday, August 26, but by 5:00 AM EDT, the NHC reported that the storm had once again strengthened to a Category 1 hurricane.[30] The hurricane continued moving further west, intensifying over the warm waters of the Gulf, rather than north toward the Alabama-Florida panhandle area as NWS had originally predicted.[31] This westward direction enabled the storm to strengthen first to a Category 1 and then intensify to a Category 2 hurricane over the course of the day.

In the afternoon of August 26, the NHC released a track forecasting the eye of Hurricane Katrina would pass just east of New Orleans on Monday, August

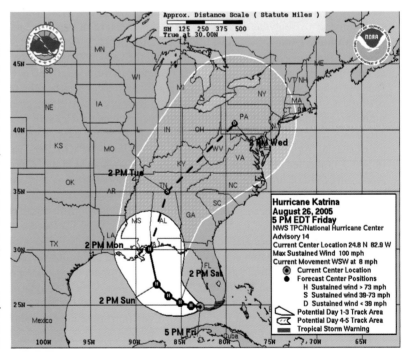

29.[32] This forecast and all subsequent NHC forecasts projected Hurricane Katrina would make its second landfall as a Category 4 or 5 storm along the Gulf Coast, in the Mississippi-Louisiana region.[33] The Center also forecasted that the accompanying coastal storm surge would cause flooding fifteen to twenty feet above normal tide levels where the eye of the hurricane would make landfall.[34] National Weather Service Director Johnson later testified before Congress that "forecasts of where Katrina would go were more accurate than usual, with all of the forecast tracks during the last forty-eight hours lining up almost directly on top of the actual track."[35] The last NHC Hurricane Katrina forecast on Friday, August 26, as the storm intensified in the Gulf of Mexico, gave Federal, State, local, and private sector officials, in hindsight, approximately fifty-six hours advance notice that the hurricane would make landfall near the City of New Orleans.[36]

Preparations took on a greater urgency on Friday, August 26, due to Hurricane Katrina's continuing intensification and west-southwest track from Florida into the Gulf of Mexico. Louisiana Governor Kathleen Blanco and Mississippi Governor Haley Barbour declared states of emergency for their respective States.[37] Gulf Coast States and localities expanded their EOC staffing and operations schedules in anticipation of Hurricane Katrina.[38] The Alabama, Louisiana, and Mississippi State EOCs soon were activated to their highest levels.[39]

State agencies began putting their response plans into action. The Louisiana State Police notified personnel assigned to the Traffic Control Center that they should report to the State EOC the following day, at 6:00 AM CDT, to prepare for emergency response operations.[40] The Louisiana National Guard began mobilizing 2,000 personnel while the Joint Forces headquarters-Louisiana National Guard activated its Joint Operations Center (JOC) at Jackson Barracks in New Orleans to coordinate their emergency response operations.[41] Governor Barbour issued an Executive Order that directed Major General Harold Cross, Adjutant General of the Mississippi National Guard, to prepare to use the Mississippi National Guard for disaster relief operations.[42] The Mississippi National Guard alerted military police and engineers, activated 750 personnel, and activated its EOC in Jackson.[43]

Worst Case Scenario

A catastrophic hurricane striking Southeast Louisiana has been considered a worst-case scenario that the region and many experts had known and feared for years. Much of Southeast Louisiana is at or below sea level, and experience had shown Gulf Coast hurricanes to be deadly. At the turn of the 20th Century, an unnamed Category 4 hurricane made landfall on September 8, 1900, in Galveston, Texas. With storm surges higher than fifteen feet and winds stronger than 130 mph, over 8,000 people perished—making it the deadliest disaster in American history.[44] Sixty-five years later, on September 9, 1965, Hurricane Betsy made its second landfall near Grand Isle, Louisiana, as a strong Category 3 storm. As an omen of things to come, Hurricane Betsy's storm surge and high winds hit Lake Pontchartrain just north of New Orleans, overtopping levees and flooding the city. Breaching the Florida Avenue levee, flood waters consumed the Lower 9th Ward of New Orleans, drowning many in their attics as they tried to escape. In total, seventy-five people were killed and over 160,000 homes were flooded.[45] Only four years later, Hurricane Camille, a Category 5 hurricane, struck the mouth of the Mississippi River on the night of August 17, 1969. Storm surges measuring over twenty-five feet, combined with winds estimated close to 200 mph, caused an estimated 335 deaths, destroyed or damaged 22,008 homes, and injured thousands in Louisiana, Mississippi, and Virginia.[46] In the decades that followed, experts attempted to model the likely impact of future hurricanes to improve protection in the Gulf Coast region.[47] In 2000, the U.S. Army Corps of Engineers' (USACE) modeled the effects of a slow moving Category 4 or any Category 5 hurricane on the region.[48] According to the Corps, New Orleans would be inundated by over twenty feet of water if such a hurricane took a "critical path" towards the city.[49] A weaker, slow moving hurricane can be as dangerous as a more powerful, faster moving storm because it can generate as much or more flooding by dropping more rainfall.[50] Vice Admiral Conrad C. Lautenbacher, Jr., Undersecretary of Commerce for Oceans and Atmosphere, stated in 2002 that the overtopping of the levees and subsequent flooding of the city could occur during slow moving Category 3, 4 or 5 storms.[51] Recognizing that current Federal, State, and local disaster response capabilities overall needed to be enhanced to better address possible effects of catastrophic disasters, FEMA provided funding for a ***Southeast Louisiana Catastrophic Hurricane Planning Project***, which brought together responders and decision makers from all levels of government and the American Red Cross to identify, analyze, and address the overwhelming operational complexities that would be involved in responding to a catastrophic hurricane striking southeast Louisiana.[52] *(continued next page)*

(*continued from previous page*) Planning workshops using a hypothetical catastrophic hurricane scenario (Hurricane Pam) to frame the discussions were used to identify and qualify the scale of requirements needed to build a plan for responding to a catastrophic hurricane. The initial planning group meeting was held between July 16 and July 23 in 2004 and included as many as 300 Federal, State, and local emergency response officials.[53] The results of this exercise revealed to the Louisiana Office of Homeland Security and Emergency Preparedness (LOHSEP) and FEMA the shortfalls in existing plans and were to be used to inform future development of State and Federal plans to address this potential catastrophe. At the first session, LOHSEP and Federal representatives identified a list of planning topics as the most urgent or complex topics needing discussion, including pre-landfall issues, search and rescue, and medical care, as well as mass sheltering and housing. Subsequent after-action review workshops did not reconvene until late July 2005, mere weeks before Hurricane Katrina made landfall. Although they failed to generate a comprehensive, integrated, and actionable plan in time for Hurricane Katrina, these workshops did have some positive impact. To quote one official: "the workshops and planning process—knowledge of inter-jurisdictional relationships and capabilities, identification of issues, and rudimentary concepts for handling the consequences—have been beneficial to all involved in the hurricane response."[54]

FEMA headquarters in Washington, DC, conducted the daily video teleconference from their National Response Coordination Center (NRCC) to exchange information and reconcile response activities among the FEMA Regions, the NHC, liaisons from various Federal agencies and departments responsible for disaster support, representatives from the States projected to be affected by the storm, and States monitoring and providing mutual aid to support their neighbors.[55]

August 27, 2005

Hurricane Katrina strengthened to a Category 3 storm before dawn on Saturday, August 27, and nearly doubled in size over the course of the day; tropical storm-force winds extended 85 miles from the storm's center at 2:00 AM EDT and 160 miles from the storm's center at 9:00 PM CDT.[56] National Hurricane Center forecasts warned the storm could continue to intensify and was expected to become a Category 4 storm,[57] pushing a powerful storm surge ahead of its path.[58] The Center issued updated hurricane watches and warnings throughout Saturday, with a hurricane watch eventually extending across the North Central Gulf Coast from Intra-coastal City, Louisiana, to the Florida-Alabama border.[59]

Despite hurricane watches and warnings throughout the day, it appeared many people along the Gulf Coast either remained unaware or unconcerned about the storm that would soon ravage their communities. For instance, according to Governor Blanco, State Representative Cedric Richmond called the Louisiana Governor on Saturday after visiting a ballpark where "approximately 700 people were present, and [he] learned that some people had not paid attention to the weekend news and did not realize the severity of the hurricane aiming at New Orleans." She recalled that he worried "many may have thought the hurricane was still targeting the Florida panhandle, as reported by the National Hurricane Center up until late Friday afternoon."[60]

As the storm strengthened, Louisiana and Mississippi State officials took steps to begin the evacuation of areas threatened by Hurricane Katrina throughout Friday evening and into Saturday morning. Early Saturday morning, Louisiana State Police Superintendent Colonel Henry Whitehorn and Louisiana Department of Transportation and Development Secretary Johnny Bradberry recommended to Governor Blanco that she implement the State's contra-flow plan. Governor Blanco and her staff had determined that a major evacuation of coastal Louisiana and New Orleans would be required. She and Governor Barbour discussed implementing their respective contra-flow plans on Saturday for interstate highways and other major roadways; the plans would reverse the flow of traffic on inbound lanes to facilitate the evacuation of the New Orleans metropolitan area.[61] Shortly thereafter, Louisiana Department of Transportation and Development officials informed Mississippi Department of Transportation officials that contra-flow in Louisiana would begin later that afternoon.[62] Louisiana State agencies also began implementing Phase I of the Louisiana Emergency Evacuation Plan, which included public communications, staging of assets, and other activities.[63] Louisiana and Mississippi implemented contra-flow plans on major highways at 4:00 PM CDT.[64] State law enforcement officers were deployed along the routes and in communities to assist evacuation operations. Louisiana established a Traffic Control Center (TCC) within the State EOC and began monitoring traffic volume and rate of flow.[65] Traffic increased throughout the day. By 7:00 PM CDT, traffic had begun to back up at the Louisiana-Texas border.[66] Louisiana and Mississippi had jointly revised their respective evacuation plans after encountering problems during Hurricane Ivan in 2004.[67]

Still, State and local officials knew that tens of thousands of Gulf Coast residents either could not or would not evacuate. A large number of residents who did not own a vehicle depended on relatives, neighbors, charitable organizations, or public transportation to evacuate; New Orleans hurricane plans estimated that over 100,000 residents did not own an automobile.[68] Evacuation also presented particular risks to the special needs population, which includes older adults and individuals with a disability. Individual and institutional caregivers faced the difficult choice between the dangers of evacuation and attempting to ride out the hurricane.[69]

In an effort to reach as many citizens as possible, Governor Blanco and her staff contacted clergy throughout Saturday night and early Sunday morning to ask them to urge their parishioners to evacuate immediately.[70] In addition, Louisiana churches had implemented "Operation Brother's Keeper," a program developed to help evacuate those who lacked transportation, but only four congregations were participating in the pilot program when Hurricane Katrina made landfall.[71]

Local governments across the northern Gulf Coast issued evacuation orders throughout Saturday. Voluntary evacuations for areas in Louisiana outside the levee protection district began in the morning. Lafourche, Plaquemines, St. Charles, and parts of St. Tammany Parishes ordered mandatory evacuations for their citizens during the day.[72] Mandatory evacuation orders were also issued for parts of Jefferson Parish. In New Orleans, Mayor Ray Nagin hosted a press conference that afternoon, during which he recommended evacuations of Algiers, the Lower Ninth Ward, and low-lying areas of the City.[73] Later, at 5:00 PM CDT, he formally called for voluntary evacuations of the City.[74] He also declared a state of emergency for New Orleans, which advised residents to undertake several precautionary measures such as stocking up on bottled water, batteries, and non-perishable food.[75] In a joint press conference with Governor Blanco, Nagin warned residents, saying "this is not a test. This is the real deal." By late afternoon, Mississippi's three vulnerable coastal counties—Hancock, Harrison, and Jackson—had also begun urging residents to evacuate, especially those living in low-lying areas and mobile homes.[76]

Many Gulf Coast residents had become so accustomed to hurricanes and tropical storms that they refused to evacuate despite the warnings.[77] As Hurricane Katrina approached Louisiana, Governor Blanco was concerned "that many people would play a familiar game of 'hurricane roulette'—tempting fate and staying home in a gamble that this storm would be no worse than the last one they weathered in their home." [78]

Hurricane Katrina's impending landfall required massive shelter operations in order to temporarily house thousands of people fleeing the Gulf Coast. On Saturday, August 27, shelters began opening throughout the region. In Mississippi, the American Red Cross opened shelters in schools and churches.[79] It also established an information center to direct evacuees to shelters in the Jackson area.[80] By 4:00 PM CDT, Louisiana's Office of Emergency Preparedness reported that four special needs shelters were open in Alexandria, Baton Rouge, Bossier City and Monroe, with four more scheduled to open at 8:00 PM CDT that evening.[81] Mayor Nagin also announced that the New Orleans Superdome would be open to City residents with special needs.[82] A special needs shelter "is intended for individuals who have no other resources and who need assistance that cannot be guaranteed in a regular shelter, i.e. medication that requires refrigeration, oxygen equipment, etc." However, it is not intended for patients who need substantial or constant medical care. [83] Texas officials also opened shelters on Saturday, including a 1,000 person capacity shelter at the Ford Center in Jefferson County.[84]

Louisiana and Mississippi State agencies deployed personnel and pre-positioned resources in the final two days before Hurricane Katrina's second landfall. The Mississippi Emergency Management Agency also deployed six area coordinators to six Gulf Coast counties to serve as liaisons with their EOCs.[85] Mississippi's State Emergency Response Team (ERT) deployed to Camp Shelby while National Guard emergency rescue assets were deployed to three coastal counties.[86] The Louisiana National Guard deployed liaison officers to the thirteen southernmost parishes projected to suffer the greatest impact from the storm.[87] Alabama officials began pre-positioning supplies at staging areas and other locations throughout the State.[88] Alabama National Guard troops were positioned in Mobile and Baldwin Counties in preparation for landfall, and Governor Bob Riley of Alabama, after being informed that Louisiana and Mississippi would suffer the brunt of the storm, offered Governors Blanco and Barbour whatever assistance his State could provide.[89] The Texas Governor's Division of Emergency Management deployed one

Regional Liaison Officer to Baton Rouge "to assist, coordinate, and monitor any requests for assistance that may develop as evacuations begin."[90]

As State and local governments were preparing their response and initiating evacuations, the Federal government was continuing preparations to support State and local responders. On the morning of August 27, forty-eight hours before Hurricane Katrina's second landfall, FEMA headquarters commenced Level 1 operations, requiring full staffing on a round-the-clock, seven-days-a-week basis.[91] FEMA was now at its highest alert. FEMA's regional headquarters for Regions IV (Atlanta, Georgia) and VI (Denton, Texas) went to Level 1 activation at Noon EDT and 11:00 AM CDT respectively.[92] At this point, all fifteen National Response Plan (NRP) Emergency Support Functions (ESFs) had been activated as well.[93]

With the regional and national headquarters at full alert, FEMA held another daily video teleconference at 12:00 PM EDT. "FEMA Region VI announced that its Mobile Emergency Response Support (MERS) detachment was en route to Camp Beauregard, Louisiana, to provide communications and operational and logistical support. It also announced that it had requested the deployment of the Denver MERS unit to Region VI headquarters in Denton to serve as a backup."[94] In addition, Region VI had staged at Camp Beauregard 270,000 liters of water, 680,000 pounds of ice, 15,120 tarps, and 328,320 Meals Ready to Eat (MRE).[95] By 5:00 PM EDT, the quantity of water stored at Camp Beauregard had doubled to 540,000 liters.[96] More commodities were pre-staged elsewhere in Region VI. The FEMA Logistics Representative reported that 102 trailers were "uploaded with water and MREs" at the FEMA Logistics Center in Ft. Worth, Texas.[97] Also at Noon that day, the ERT-N Blue Team was activated and deployed to Baton Rouge.[98] The ERT-A Blue Team is one of the Nation's three standing ERT-N teams. One of three teams— code-named Red, White, and Blue—is on call every month.[99] The ERT-N teams are the scalable principal inter- agency units that staff the JFO "for large-scale, high-impact events."

FEMA was working to pre-stage supplies in Region IV, too. At 1:15 PM EDT, FEMA issued its first Mission Assignment to USNORTHCOM "to provide NAS Meridian [Mississippi] as a FEMA operational Staging Base for pre-staging of FEMA supplies prior to landfall."[100] USNORTHCOM granted this request later that afternoon, releasing an Execute Order making Naval Air Station Meridian available to FEMA.[101]

Additionally, FEMA began activating the National Disaster Medical System (NDMS), Disaster Medical Assistance Teams (DMATs), and Urban Search and Rescue (US&R) teams[102] The DMATs are mobile self-contained medical teams with equipment and medical professionals trained and certified to provide emergency medical care to disaster victims. These teams are comprised of professionals from around the country organized and deployed by FEMA to support disaster response activities. The Urban Search and Rescue teams are similarly structured, but comprised of emergency responders, firefighters, and law enforcement personnel from around the country.

That evening, President Bush signed a Federal emergency declaration for the State of Louisiana, following a request from Governor Blanco earlier that day. President Bush issued additional emergency declarations for Mississippi and Alabama the following day, after requests from the governors of those States.[103] These declarations authorized Federal expenditures to assist State and local governments by providing resources and making other preparations to save lives and property from Hurricane Katrina's imminent impact.[104] These decisions were particularly important as they allowed delivery of pre-deployed Federal assistance. The issuance of a Presidential emergency declaration before landfall is extremely rare, and indicative of the recognition that Katrina had the potential to be particularly devastating. Since 1990, only one such incident, Hurricane Floyd in 1999, resulted in declarations before landfall.[105] By declaring emergencies in these three States, the President directed the Federal government to provide its full assistance to the area to save lives and property from Hurricane Katrina's imminent impact.[106]

On the evening of August 27, William Lokey, the ERT-N team leader, arrived in Baton Rouge, Louisiana, and was appointed Federal Coordinating Officer (FCO). As the senior Federal official in charge of supporting the State of Louisiana, he immediately began coordinating efforts with the Louisiana Office of Homeland Security and Emergency Preparedness.[107]

Hurricane Katrina's growing intensity on Saturday led NHC Director Mayfield to make personal calls to State and local officials in the region that evening to emphasize the threat posed by the storm. He warned Jefferson Parish officials that this could be the "big one." That evening, Director Mayfield briefed Governor Blanco, Governor

Barbour, Mayor Nagin, and Alabama Emergency Management Agency Chief of Operations Bill Filter about Hurricane Katrina's magnitude and the potential storm impacts.[108] Director Mayfield testified before Congress that he had only made such a call to warn a governor once before in his thirty-six year career.[109] Mayfield stated that "I just wanted to be able to go to sleep that night knowing that I did all I could do."[110]

At FEMA headquarters, the FEMA Director shared Mayfield's concern. Closing the noon video teleconference with his FEMA regional staff and the State EOCs, Michael Brown urged them to be vigilant, saying, "I know I'm preaching to the choir on this one, but I've learned over the past four and a half, five years, to go with my gut on a lot of things, and I've got to tell you my gut hurts with this one. It hurts. . . . So we need to take this one very, very seriously. . . . I want you guys to lean forward as far as possible. . . . Why is this important? Because I worry about the people in New Orleans, Louisiana, and Mississippi right now, and they're going to need our help . . ."[111]

August 28, 2005

Hurricane Katrina developed from a Category 4 to a Category 5 storm over a six-hour period on Sunday, August 28.[112] The storm had become "not only extremely intense but also exceptionally large."[113] The National Weather Service office in Slidell, Louisiana, issued a detailed, urgent warning of Hurricane Katrina's impending devastating impact on the Gulf Coast. The warning stated, "The majority of industrial buildings will become non-functional . . . High-rise office and apartment buildings will sway dangerously—a few to the point of total collapse. All windows will blow out. Airborne debris will be widespread—and may include heavy items such as household appliances and even light vehicles . . . Persons—pets—and livestock exposed to the winds will face certain death if struck."[114] The NHC issued advisories that warned the levees in New Orleans could be overtopped by Lake Pontchartrain and that significant destruction would likely be experienced far away from the hurricane's center.[115] The warning continued, "[m]ost of the area will be uninhabitable for weeks . . . Perhaps longer . . . Power outages will last for weeks . . . Water shortages will make human suffering incredible by modern standards."[116]

Prior to Hurricane Katrina's landfall, State and local officials did not use the Emergency Alert System (EAS) in Louisiana, Mississippi, or Alabama. However, the National Hurricane Center (NHC) disseminated warnings and forecasts via NOAA Radio and the internet, operating in conjunction with the EAS.[117] Initially, these reports were issued every six hours; however, as the storm neared landfall they were updated with increasing frequency.[118] In accordance with NOAA policy, local weather offices took over responsibility for these broadcasts shortly after Hurricane Katrina made landfall. At this time, Weather Service offices like the one in Slidell, Louisiana, began to transmit real-time hazard information using both NOAA Radio and the EAS. These reports were distributed to all area media outlets as well as local emergency management personnel. When the severity of the storm finally forced the Slidell weather office offline, operations were successfully transferred to weather centers in Mobile and Baton Rouge.

Taking heed of the continual warnings, most citizens evacuated, others showed up at a "shelter of last resort" and some hunkered down in their homes and would soon be struggling to survive the destructive forces of Katrina. For the region and its residents, Hurricane Katrina would bring devastation and the incredible human suffering that the NHC had predicted.

By early morning on Sunday, three State Liaison Officers (SLOs) had been deployed to Alabama, Florida, and Mississippi.[119] The U.S. Coast Guard, in preparation for anticipated operations, placed Disaster Assistance Response Teams (DARTs) on standby for deployment to Southeast Louisiana and evacuated its District 8 New Orleans Command Center to Integrated Support Command, Saint Louis, Missouri.[120]

Also early that morning, President Bush called Governor Blanco to urge that mandatory evacuation orders be issued for New Orleans.[121] After receiving a call from President Bush, Governor Blanco and Mayor Nagin held a joint press conference during which the Mayor ordered a mandatory evacuation of New Orleans.[122] Later that day, the President also participated in FEMA's daily video teleconference with DHS headquarters, FEMA headquarters, FEMA's regional offices, the National Hurricane Center, and representatives from Alabama, Florida, Georgia, Louisiana, Mississippi, Tennessee, Texas, and West Virginia. The President personally encouraged State and local officials to take all precautions and get word out to their citizens; he offered the full support and resources of the Federal government.[123] The President "received regular briefings, had countless conversations with Federal, State, and local officials, and took extraordinary steps prior to landfall."[124] The Louisiana EOC reported that evacuations were going well, that it had no unmet needs, and that FEMA was "leaning forward" as far as possible. The Mississippi EOC similarly reported that "FEMA has been great" and that, after a slow start, evacuations were going well.[125] Despite State assurances, the FEMA Director told all those on the call to be prepared for the impending requests for emergency aid from the States, expressed concern about the evacuation progress and the Superdome as a shelter of last resort, and echoed his previous day's comments about the need to remain vigilant.[126] Secretary Chertoff inquired into DOD's level of engagement with FEMA, to ensure coordination of DOD support should it become necessary, and was assured by Director Brown that DOD was fully engaged.[127] Following the video teleconference on Sunday, FEMA Director Michael Brown deployed from Washington to Baton Rouge.[128]

After the video teleconference, Homeland Security Secretary Michael Chertoff spoke with the participating State governors to ensure that their needs were being met. He later explained, "[m]y concern then was to talk off-line to the governors, to make sure the governors weren't going to tell me something privately that maybe they didn't want to share publicly, and they seemed satisfied at that point with the help they were getting."[129]

The President also issued a public statement, saying "[w]e cannot stress enough the danger this hurricane poses to Gulf Coast communities. I urge all citizens to put their own safety and the safety of their families first by moving to safe ground. Please listen carefully to instructions provided by State and local officials."[130]

By afternoon on August 28, States and localities across the Gulf Coast had just hours before tropical storm-force winds would curtail their contra-flow and other pre-landfall preparations. State and local officials in Alabama and Mississippi issued evacuation orders for low-lying areas vulnerable to Hurricane Katrina's storm surge and encouraged people in other areas to evacuate as well.[131]

The Gulf Coast States' planning and the contra-flow operations facilitated the safe evacuation of hundreds of thousands of people on Sunday, August 28.[132] However, by the late afternoon, Hurricane Katrina began to affect evacuations even though landfall remained over twelve hours away. Increasing winds around New Orleans' Louis Armstrong International Airport caused air carriers to begin reevaluating their plans and canceling flights. The last passenger flight departed at 4:30 PM CDT and the airport was officially closed at 6:43 PM CDT.[133] Contra-flow operations throughout the region ceased at 5:00 PM CDT due to high winds from Hurricane Katrina. Louisiana and Mississippi State officials continued to encourage people to evacuate even after contra-flow operations ceased. Governor Blanco later estimated that 1.2 million people, 92 percent of the affected population, evacuated prior to Hurricane Katrina's second landfall.[134] Still, tens of thousands, many of them the region's most vulnerable, remained in areas most threatened by the approaching hurricane.

By Sunday evening, shelter operations that had begun the previous day were in full force. Thousands of people displaced by Katrina were in shelters across the region. Federal, State, and local governments worked with the American Red Cross and other non-profit organizations to establish at least 114 shelters for over 28,000 people.[135] Texas had opened or placed on standby thirty-one shelters with room for 7,275 evacuees and established "shelter welcome centers" along I-20 and I-10 "to provide shelter information to evacuees."[136] The City of New Orleans, which had previously provided the Superdome as a shelter only for the special needs population, now opened it as a "shelter of last resort" for the general population.[137] Additional supplies were brought in to support the growing Superdome population despite increasingly worsening conditions.[138] It was estimated that there were 10,000 – 12,000 people at the Superdome by midnight, including 300-500 special needs evacuees.[139]

As Hurricane Katrina drew nearer, the requests for Federal assistance increased. The day before landfall, FEMA received numerous requests for resources from Alabama, Louisiana, and Mississippi.[140] Some last minute Louisiana requests were not met due to deteriorating weather conditions. For example, at noon on August 28, Louisiana requested 180,000 liters of water and 109,440 MREs for the Superdome. However, FEMA was only able to supply 90,000 liters of water and 43,776 MREs before the storm struck or high winds forced other trucks to turn back before they could reach the stadium.[141] Officials at all levels were unsure of who and how many people would come to the Dome and were modifying their special needs and commodities requests throughout the day. The American Red Cross determined the Superdome did not meet their safety criteria and refused to put their staff in harm's way, choosing rather to deliver any necessary aid to the Dome as soon as the storm had passed.[142]

During a press conference, in response to a question about the Superdome, the Mayor asserted that "the Superdome can probably accommodate 50,000, 60,000, 70,000 people." He advised that anyone seeking shelter there should "come with enough food, [non] perishable items to last for three to five days. Come with blankets, with pillows. No weapons, no alcohol, no drugs."[143]

The Louisiana National Guard also pre-positioned some supplies at the Superdome. Approximately 10,000 MREs and over 13,000 bottles of water were brought in on Saturday, when the stadium was opened as a special needs shelter for evacuees with heightened care requirements.[144] In addition to stocking the Superdome with food and water, the Louisiana National Guard sent additional personnel to the Superdome throughout the day on Sunday, August 28. The National Guard's Special Reaction Team, a unit "highly trained in Law Enforcement missions," arrived at 7:00 AM CDT with forty-six members.[145] The team "began conducting Law and Order/Area Security missions."[146] More National Guard forces got to the Dome in the early afternoon. By 3:00 PM CDT, the 527th Ready Reaction Forces had arrived in the Superdome with 220 personnel, and had as their principal mission crowd control.[147] The 225th Engineer Group joined that evening with 220 soldiers "to assist with security operations." Another 100 personnel from the 159th Fighter Wing came to help out with security.[148] Medical personnel arrived at the Superdome from the Louisiana National Guard contingent as well. "Five physicians, four nurses, six NCOs and twenty medics" deployed to the Superdome on August 28.[149] In all, "the total medical complement at the Superdome totaled 71 medical personnel."[150]

In addition to the mandatory evacuation order, Mayor Nagin announced Sunday that he had authorized New Orleans Police Department members and other City officials to commandeer private property for evacuation and shelter purposes, if necessary. Mayor Nagin said, "[t]he storm surge most likely will topple our levee system. So we are preparing to deal with that also."[151] The Louisiana State Police reported that one of its 800 MHz communications towers had been rendered inoperable and some troopers had been forced to seek shelter at hospitals.[152] Additionally, by August 28, fifteen of Louisiana's sixty-four parishes had issued mandatory, recommended, or precautionary evacuation orders.[153]

Hurricane Katrina: Federal Commodities on Hand Pre-Landfall (as of August 29, 2005)

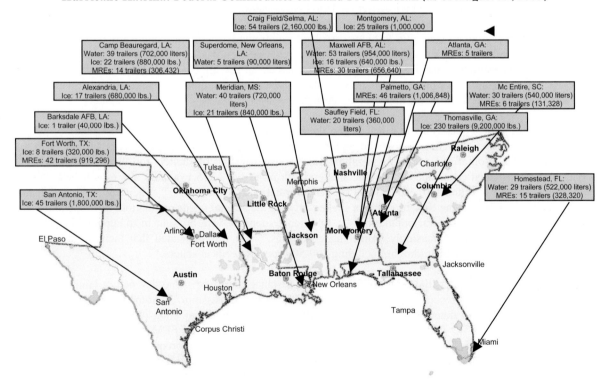

Pre-deployed assets were placed throughout the region to encircle the forecasted impact area. The amount of space required to house the large volumes of commodities and people required large industrial and military staging areas—often filling entire runways with hundreds of trailers—accessible to heavy equipment and aircraft. The staging areas were dispersed outside the projected path of the storm to avoid destruction of critical commodities and to maximize the ability to deploy to affected areas in the wake of the hurricane. On Sunday, FEMA opened a Federal logistics mobilization center at Barksdale Air Force Base in Louisiana,[154] quickly placing a MERS team there with a mobile communication command vehicle.[155] MERS assets were also deployed on-site into Mississippi, Florida, Georgia, and Texas, and other parts of Louisiana to support response operations."[156] Other Federally deployed teams in the region included seven Urban Search and Rescue Task Forces and thirty-three National Disaster Medical System teams, including Disaster Medical Assistance Teams, medical Strike Teams, a National Medical Response Team, Disaster Mortuary Operational Response Teams, and Veterinary Medical Assistance Teams. As of pre-landfall on the next day, a total of 43,776 MREs and 90,000 liters of water had been staged at the Superdome. Throughout the region there were pre-staged over 3.7 million liters of water, 4.6 million pounds of ice—with 13 million additional pounds of ice in cold storage ready to be deployed— and over 1.86 million MREs. Another 2.1 million MREs were positioned in Logistics Centers outside the region ready to be distributed (see Federal Commodities Map).[157]

THE STORM APPROACHES

As the sun set on Sunday, August 28, rain began to fall and the Gulf Coast had already started to feel Hurricane Katrina's effects.[158] The storm's high winds and hail forced public safety agencies across the Gulf Coast to curtail their operations. Traffic remained heavy on some highways as people tried to escape the storm in the final hours before second landfall. In shelters, hospitals, nursing homes, and residences across the Gulf Coast, people held their breath, hoping that Hurricane Katrina's impact would not be catastrophic. Federal, State, and local governments were poised to continue emergency activities as soon as Hurricane Katrina had passed. State and local governments, supported by the Federal government and FEMA, had carried out unprecedented preparations in comparison to those made for previous, "average" hurricanes. But Hurricane Katrina was not average, as would soon become vividly clear—it was a fierce hurricane with high wind speeds and a near-record storm surge that was heading directly toward a densely-populated urban area, much of which lay below sea level—six feet below on average across the city.[159] In less than twenty-four hours, Hurricane Katrina would change the region, its people, and the Nation.

CHAPTER FOUR: A WEEK OF CRISIS — AUGUST 29 – SEPTEMBER 5

Eastward from Lake Pontchartrain, across the Mississippi coast, to Alabama into Florida, millions of lives were changed in a day by a cruel and wasteful storm.

—President George W. Bush, September 15, 2005[1]

This chapter examines the response to Hurricane Katrina during the first week after landfall. The storm overwhelmed and, in some cases, incapacitated State and local emergency capabilities across the Gulf Coast, requiring an unprecedented Federal response to help evacuate, rescue, shelter, care for, and safeguard Hurricane Katrina's victims. The chapter discusses some of the extraordinary efforts taken by Federal departments and agencies in concert with our partners from the State and local governments, non-governmental organizations, and the private sector to respond to the storm's devastating impact. It also identifies deficiencies in actions taken and highlights actions we must take to improve our collective efforts in the future.

LANDFALL

Hurricane Katrina made landfall as a powerful Category 3 storm at 6:10 AM CDT on Monday, August 29 in Plaquemines Parish, Louisiana. The massive storm continued to move north, rolling over portions of the Louisiana coast before its eye came ashore near the mouth of the Pearl River in Mississippi. At the time, Hurricane Katrina had sustained winds over 115 mph and reported gusts as high as 130 mph.[2] The storm rapidly lost strength as it pushed inland through southern and central Mississippi; by 1:00 PM CDT, it had weakened to a Category 1 hurricane.[3] Six hours later, as it passed northwest of Meridian, Mississippi, Hurricane Katrina was further downgraded to a tropical storm.[4]

Hurricane Katrina generated violent waves and a massive storm surge before colliding with the Gulf Coast.[5] According to the National Oceanic and Atmospheric Administration (NOAA), Hurricane Katrina produced a storm surge as high as twenty-seven feet in Louisiana and Mississippi. Surge waters flooded over six miles inland in many parts of coastal Mississippi and up to twelve miles inland along rivers and bays. Hurricane Katrina also produced "very significant" storm surges approximately ten feet high as far east as Mobile, Alabama, where it caused flooding several miles inland along Mobile Bay.[6]

Disaster in the Gulf Coast

Hurricane Katrina's powerful winds, storm surge, and subsequent flooding destroyed communities and infrastructure along the Gulf Coast. The storm inflicted a terrible toll of human suffering, killing at least 1,330 and injuring thousands.[7] The Nation empathized with the harrowing stories of survival, loss, and family separation. President George W. Bush described this hurricane as "one of the worst natural disasters in our Nation's history."[8]

The nightmare scenario that some had predicted prior to Hurricane Katrina's landfall became a reality as those on the ground saw the devastation for the first time. According to NOAA, "entire coastal communities were obliterated, some left with little more than the foundations upon which homes, businesses, government facilities, and other historical buildings once stood."[9] Destroyed homes, beached vessels, collapsed bridges, uprooted trees, and other debris littered the ground and blocked waterways. After surveying the region from the air on August 30, Mississippi Governor Haley Barbour likened the scene to that of a nuclear detonation, stating, "I can only imagine that this is what Hiroshima looked like sixty years ago."[10]

Mississippi suffered extensive damage in all counties south of Interstate 20 and east of Interstate 55.[11] The city of Biloxi was "decimated," according to municipal government spokesman Vincent Creel. "It looks like a bomb hit it."[12] Major east-west highways in southern Mississippi became impassable due to storm debris: US-90 closed across the entire state and I-10 east-bound closed to the public, with only one west-bound lane open for emergency responders.[13] Hurricane Katrina left the downtown streets of Gulfport, Mississippi, under ten feet of water[14] and structures flooded for miles inland.[15] A Department of Homeland Security (DHS) report described the communications infrastructure in Biloxi and Gulfport as "non-existent."[16] In the words of Transportation Secretary Norman Mineta: "The Port of Gulfport, Mississippi was left with virtually nothing and must rebuild almost from scratch."[17] The storm devastated Waveland, Mississippi, wiping out all the local resources, including those that municipal officials had staged ten miles north of town.[18] Ninety-five percent of Waveland's residential and commercial structures were severely damaged.[19] Testifying before Congress a week after landfall, Governor Barbour lamented: "The 80 miles across the Mississippi Gulf Coast is largely destroyed. A town like Waveland Mississippi has no inhabitable structures—none."[20] Alabama suffered significant damage as well. For example, large amounts of debris necessitated the closure of Mobile's port.[21]

Hurricane Katrina inflicted devastating damage upon the region's energy and communications infrastructures. The Department of Energy (DOE) reported "unprecedented damage" to the U.S. energy sector[22] and noted that 2.5 million customers in Alabama, Louisiana, and Mississippi reported power outages.[23] Hurricane Katrina devastated communications infrastructure across the Gulf Coast, incapacitating telephone service, police and fire dispatch centers, and emergency radio systems. Almost three million customer phone lines were knocked out, telephone switching centers were seriously damaged, and 1,477 cell towers were incapacitated.[24] Most of the radio stations and many television stations in the New Orleans area were knocked off the air.[25] Paul McHale, the Assistant Secretary of Defense for Homeland Defense, summarized the damage by stating, "The magnitude of the storm was such that the local communications system wasn't simply degraded; it was, at least for a period of time, destroyed."[26]

The Gulf Coast region's health care infrastructure sustained extraordinary damage.[27] Such damage was particularly evident in New Orleans, where Hurricane Katrina destroyed several large hospitals, rendered many others inoperable, and forced the closure of nearly all other health care facilities. The region's most vulnerable residents and those individuals with special needs suffered terribly from Hurricane Katrina's impact and inadequate or nonexistent evacuation operations.[28] In addition, the storm stranded hundreds of hospital patients inside dark and flooded facilities that lacked basic supplies.[29] Some patients succumbed to the horrible conditions before they could be evacuated.[30] At St. Rita's Nursing Home in St. Bernard Parish, Louisiana, thirty-four nursing home residents drowned in the floods resulting from Hurricane Katrina.[31]

New Orleans

New Orleans sustained extensive damage as Hurricane Katrina passed to its east on the morning of August 29. Many high-rise buildings suffered blown out windows, while roof sections of the Louisiana Superdome—where over ten thousand people were sheltered—were stripped away. Mayor Ray Nagin later reported that in New Orleans, "primary and secondary power sources, sewerage and draining systems and communication and power lines were incapacitated."[32]

The storm surge, extreme amounts of rain, and high winds stressed the city's complex 350 mile levee system to its breaking point.[33] Several of the levees and floodwalls were overtopped, and some were breached throughout the day of landfall. It was these overtoppings and breaches of the levee system that led to the catastrophic flooding of New Orleans. In addition to the levee and floodwall breaches, many of the pumping stations—which would have otherwise removed water from the city and prevented some of the flooding—stopped working due to power outages and flooded pumping equipment.

On the day of landfall, authoritative reporting from the field was extremely difficult to obtain because of the widespread destruction of communications infrastructure, the incapacitation of many State and local responders, and the lack of Federal representatives in the city. As a result, local, State, and Federal officials were forced to depend on a variety of conflicting reports from a combination of media, government and private sources, many of which continued to provide inaccurate or incomplete information throughout the day, further clouding the understanding of what was occurring in New Orleans. In fact, some uncertainty about the specific causes and times of the breaches and overtoppings persists to this day.

> **The New Orleans Flood and Hurricane Protection System**
>
> Much of New Orleans is located below sea level; with the Mississippi River to the south, Lake Pontchartrain to the north, and Lake Borgne to the east, the area is prone to flooding from the river, the lakes, and the Gulf of Mexico. Development of a system to protect the city from flooding began when the city was founded in the early 1700s and has grown with the increase in population and expanded into additional flood prone areas. The New Orleans Flood and Hurricane Protection System is complex and massive, consisting of 350 miles of levees, which are embankments, usually earthen, that serve as flood barriers. The System also includes floodwalls, hundreds of bridges, closable gates, culverts and canals that facilitate transportation in and out of the system. It is comprised of a series of four main compartmented basins designed to limit the flooding impacts on the entire system resulting from individual failures of levees and floodwalls. In addition, large pump stations are used to pump out and redirect water from the city. These pumps are designed to mitigate flooding that results from significant rainfall and can, over time, remove water from moderate overtoppings.
>
> Currently, the levees offer protection ranging from eleven up to approximately seventeen and a half feet above sea level. The current system was designed to withstand a Mississippi River flood the size of the Flood of 1927 and a hurricane with wind conditions similar to a very strong Category 2 hurricane.
>
> **Breaching and Overtopping**
>
> Overtopping is a term used to describe the situation where the water level rises above the height of the levee or floodwall and consequently overtops, or flows over the structure. A breach is a break in the levee or floodwall. A prolonged overtopping can actually cause a levee or floodwall breach. In general, a breach can lead to more significant flooding than an overtopping since breaches take time to repair and until repaired continue to allow water to flow until the water level has receded below the height of the breach. Overtopping, on the other hand, will stop as soon as the water level recedes below the top of the levee or floodwall. Although the consequences are significantly different, from outward appearances, it is often difficult to differentiate a breach from an overtopping.

In addition to the dearth of reliable reporting regarding the situation in New Orleans, there was widespread confusion and misuse of the terms 'breach' and 'overtopping' by observers and reporters who did not fully understand the distinction between the two terms, or whose observations were not sufficient to enable differentiation of one from the other. Some overtopping of the levees was expected due to the intensity of the storm, which would result in localized flooding.[34] However, such overtopping would not have led to the catastrophic effects that occurred due to the levee and floodwall breaches. Further, the New Orleans Flood and Hurricane Protection System is designed so that individual breaches will not lead to catastrophic flooding. The compartmented design, with four main basins, is intended to minimize the threat of flood to the entire system.[35] Thus, had only one basin experienced serious overtopping or a breach, it would have been possible to avoid the catastrophic flooding New Orleans experienced.

Since some flooding was expected and severe flooding feared, the most important priority of local, State, and Federal officials was search and rescue. In anticipation of the storm on Sunday night and Monday morning, emergency responders were standing by to begin search and rescue as soon as it was safe to proceed.[36] This emphasis on search and rescue continued throughout Monday evening, with officials encouraging those who had evacuated prior to landfall to stay away so they did not impede emergency responders' efforts.[37] By Tuesday morning when the breaches of the levees had been confirmed, Federal, State, and local officials were already fully engaged in search and rescue efforts.[38] Regardless of the cause of the flooding, search and rescue had been and continued to be the first response priority.

As early as 9:12 AM EDT on August 29, the National Weather Service (NWS) received a report of a levee breach and shortly thereafter issued a flash flood warning, stating, "A levee breech [sic] occurred along the Industrial Canal at Tennessee Street. Three to eight feet of water is expected due to the breach."[39] However, as late as 6:00 PM EDT that day, the DHS Homeland Security Operations Center (HSOC) reported to senior DHS and White House officials that, "Preliminary reports indicate the levees in New Orleans have not been breached, however an assessment is still pending."[40]

A sampling of additional reporting follows.

The first DHS HSOC report that referenced potential levee issues was distributed at 10:50 AM EDT on August 29, and stated, "Some levees in the greater New Orleans area could be overtopped."[41] At 11:32 AM EDT, a DHS HSOC report stated that, after a call with State and Parish officials, "Major General Landreneau [Adjutant General for Louisiana] said that emergency personnel stationed at Jackson Barracks have confirmed that the waters are rising, although he could not say whether the cause was a levee breach or overtopping."[42] At a Noon FEMA teleconference, local officials gave spotty reporting to participating State and Federal officials. As DHS summarized the reports, "Some of the LA Parishes have 8 to 10 feet of water. . . . Some levee leakage, but no reported failures to date . . . levee in New Orleans is overflowing."[43]

Mid-afternoon on August 29, the U.S. Army Corps of Engineers (USACE) notified DHS of a reported levee overtopping in St. Bernard's Parish, a reported levee breach in the West Bank, and a small breach in Orleans Parish reported by local firefighters.[44]

At 6 PM EDT aboard a U.S. Coast Guard helicopter, Marty Bahamonde, a FEMA Public Affairs Official, observed the extent of the flooding and was "struck by how accurate" the earlier local reporting was of the levee breaches.[45] He then called FEMA Director Michael Brown and other FEMA officials with his eyewitness account at approximately 8 PM EDT that day.[46] Director Brown has testified that he subsequently called the White House to report the flooding information he received from Bahamonde.[47] Following the calls, Mr. Bahamonde arranged a conference call with State, regional, and FEMA officials to recount what he had seen.[48] An HSOC report marked 10:30 PM EDT, but not received at the White House until 12:02 AM EDT the next day, summarized the conference call and reported Mr. Bahamonde's observations on the extent of flooding throughout New Orleans.[49]

By morning light and with the passage of the storm, the extent of the flooding was apparent. At 6 AM EDT on August 30, the HSOC issued a report describing levee breaches at the Industrial Canal, 17th Street, and at Lake Ponchatrain.[50]

Throughout the morning and early afternoon on August 30, the USACE continued to determine the extent of the damage and assess whether the levees could be repaired.[51] At Governor Blanco's 3 PM EDT press conference on August 30, FEMA Director Michael Brown stated that no resources in fixing the levees would be spared, and that the USACE was diligently working on a repair plan.[52] The USACE worked throughout the remainder of Tuesday but despite best efforts, by Wednesday morning, it was becoming clear that the repairs could take weeks or months.

LESSON LEARNED RECOMMENDATION 15: Establish a National Operations Center to coordinate the National response and provide situational awareness and a common operating picture for the entire Federal government.

New Orleans flooded as the levees and floodwalls gave way and the pumping stations stopped operating; at its height, approximately 80 percent of New Orleans was filled with water up to twenty feet deep.[53] This unprecedented flooding transformed Hurricane Katrina into a "catastrophe within a catastrophe"[54] as the storm shattered the lives of countless residents and presented State and local officials with challenges far exceeding their capabilities.

Hurricane Katrina's Impact on State and Local Response

Many State and local public safety agencies suffered extensive damage to their facilities and equipment. The Grand Isle (Louisiana) Fire Department suffered "total destruction."[55] Fire departments in the Mississippi cities of Biloxi and Gulfport experienced similar fates, while Slidell, Louisiana, had to close over half its stations.[56] The Pascagoula (Mississippi) Police Department lost one-third of its vehicles. Some emergency personnel did not report to work. Warren J. Riley, Superintendent of the New Orleans Police Department, testified before Congress that, "Much has been said about officers abandoning their position during the storm, and it is true that about 147 officers abandoned their positions. However, they are no longer a part of the New Orleans Police Department."[57] Flooding in New Orleans on August 30 forced the closure of the Orleans Parish Emergency Operations Center (EOC).[58] In fact, the New Orleans Mayor's Office operated out of a Hyatt Hotel for several days after Hurricane Katrina's landfall, unable to establish reliable communications with anyone outside the hotel for nearly forty-eight hours.[59] This meant that the Mayor was neither able to effectively command the local efforts, nor was he able to guide the State and Federal support for two days following the storm.

The complete devastation of the communications infrastructure left responders without a reliable network to use for coordinating emergency response operations. Flooding blocked access to the police and fire dispatch centers in New Orleans; neither 911 service nor public safety radio communications functioned sufficiently.[60] In addition, the State of Louisiana's 800 MHz radio system, designed to be the backbone of mutual aid communications, ceased functioning, and repairs were delayed for several days.[61] Louisiana State Senator Robert Barham, chairman of the State Senate's homeland security committee, summed up the situation in Louisiana by stating, "People could not communicate. It got to the point that people were literally writing messages on paper, putting them in bottles and dropping them from helicopters to other people on the ground."[62]

Local emergency response officials found it difficult or impossible to establish functioning incident command structures in these conditions. Such structures would have better enabled local response officials to direct operations, manage assets, obtain situational awareness, and generate requests for assistance to State authorities. Without an incident command structure, it was difficult for local leaders to guide the local response efforts, much less command them. Members of the Hammond (Louisiana) Fire Department reported receiving "a lot of 'I don't knows' from [local] government officials"; another Louisiana firefighter stated, "the command structure broke down—we were literally left to our own devices."[63]

> **LESSON LEARNED:** The Department of Homeland Security, in coordination with the Environmental Protection Agency, should oversee efforts to improve the Federal government's capability to quickly gather environmental data and to provide the public and emergency responders the most accurate information available, to determine whether it is safe to operate in a disaster environment or to return after evacuation. In addition, the Department of Homeland Security should work with its State and local homeland security partners to plan and to coordinate an integrated approach to debris removal during and after a disaster.

State and local emergency responders throughout the affected region struggled to perform urgent response missions, including emergency medical services, firefighting, law enforcement, search and rescue, and support to shelters. Emergency responders operated in an environment involving extreme heat, chemicals, contaminated mud, downed power lines, and standing water.[64] The storm's surge flooded three Superfund[65] toxic waste sites in the New Orleans area, and destroyed or compromised at least 170 drinking water facilities and forty-seven wastewater treatment works along the Gulf Coast.[66] Emergency responders repeatedly exposed themselves to floodwater, chemicals, bacteria, and debris to perform life-saving missions.[67] Their willingness to work in these hazardous conditions is a powerful testament to their bravery and professionalism.

Governors Barbour and Blanco requested additional National Guard assets from other states through the Emergency Management Assistance Compact (EMAC) to assist State and local emergency responders.[68] National Guard forces continued to deploy to the region as States responded in the days following landfall.[69]

Search and Rescue

Hurricane Katrina's storm surge and subsequent flooding necessitated one of the largest search and rescue operations in the Nation's history. Thousands of firefighters, police officers, and medical personnel across all levels of government, together with citizen volunteers, braved life-threatening conditions to rescue people and animals from flooded buildings. Search and rescue missions were most urgent in New Orleans, where thousands needed to be plucked from rooftops and attics after the levee system failed. As Mayor Ray Nagin stated: "Thousands of people were stranded on their rooftops, or in attics, needing to be rescued. . . . Our first responders were jumping into the water to rescue people as 911 operators were consumed with traumatic calls for rescue. They received thousand upon thousands of frantic and desperate calls."[70]

Federal search and rescue assets from the Coast Guard, FEMA Urban Search and Rescue (US&R) Task Forces,[71] the Department of Defense (DOD),[72] and other Federal agencies worked in concert with State and local responders to rescue tens of thousands of people. Coast Guard teams alone ultimately rescued and evacuated over 33,000 people—over six times the number in an average year—[73]earning themselves the name the "New Orleans Saints."[74] Immediately following Hurricane Katrina's second landfall, Coast Guard assets began conducting rescue operations throughout the Gulf Region. Governor Barbour later testified that, "The night Katrina struck, Coast Guard helicopter crews from Mobile conducted search and rescue operations on the Coast. These fearless young men, who hung from helicopters on ropes, dangling through the air in the dark that first night, pulled people off of roofs and out of trees."[75] FEMA US&R teams also performed exceptionally well, ultimately rescuing over 6,500 people.[76] Within four hours of landfall, Army National Guard helicopters were airborne and actively performing rescue missions, with other National Guard personnel joining the effort on the ground.[77]

Despite these successes, search and rescue efforts revealed the need for greater coordination between the two constituent components of search and rescue: Urban Search and Rescue (US&R) and civil search and rescue (SAR). US&R refers to the specialized mission of rescuing victims trapped in collapsed structures.[78] In contrast, SAR constitutes all other missions, such as maritime, aeronautical, and land rescues.[79] However, there is no overarching plan that incorporates both aspects of search and rescue. The absence of such a plan led to coordination problems between US&R teams and SAR teams. Some teams displayed their own initiative to fill the gap in unified command, determining their own rescue priorities, areas to be searched, and locations to drop off the people they rescued.[80] Unfortunately, in some cases, rescuers were forced to leave people on highways where they were exposed to the elements and in continuing need of transportation, food, and water.[81]

Under the NRP, FEMA is authorized as the primary agency to coordinate US&R through Emergency Support Function-9 (ESF-9).[82] However, because the NRP focuses only on urban search and rescue, combined with the fact that US&R teams are neither adequately nor

> **LESSON LEARNED:** The Department of Homeland Security should lead an interagency review of current policies and procedures to ensure effective integration of all Federal search and rescue

consistently trained or equipped to perform rescues in a water environment, the NRP failed to anticipate, plan for, and ultimately integrate all of the Federal government's search and rescue assets during Katrina. For example, the Department of Interior (DOI) has valuable expertise in operating watercraft and conducting civil search and rescue operations. Unfortunately, because DOI is not formally considered a part of ESF-9, DOI's offers to deploy shallow-water rescue boats during the response apparently never reached the operational level. Had DOI been considered a supporting agency under ESF-9, its water assets would likely have been effectively integrated into response operations.

Post-Landfall Evacuations in New Orleans

As conditions in New Orleans worsened on August 30, due to the massive flooding, State and local officials began organizing a mass evacuation of the city. Since neither the Louisiana nor the New Orleans evacuation plans addressed evacuation protocols for post-landfall,[83] State and local officials worked with FEMA, DOD, and the Department of Transportation (DOT) to conduct the post-landfall evacuation.[84]

The Superdome presented the most immediate concern to officials. The population at the stadium continued to grow as thousands of people migrated there from their flooded homes.[85] The high floodwaters cut off access to the

Superdome, which made re-supply, evacuations, and other operations extremely difficult.[86] The facility had lost power during the storm, leaving only dim lighting from emergency generators. Louisiana National Guard personnel worked to protect the stadium's emergency generators from rising floodwaters.[87] The Louisiana National Guard later reported that, "The vast majority of the sheltered evacuees were good people who were trapped in a bad situation."[88] Conditions at the stadium became increasingly difficult due to the large numbers and the lack of air conditioning or running water.[89] On the morning of August 30, the U.S. Department of Health and Human Services (HHS) assessed the Superdome as "uninhabitable."[90]

Governor Blanco visited the Superdome on August 30 and concluded the stadium needed to be evacuated "as soon as possible."[91] Louisiana State and local officials could not manage a post-landfall evacuation operation of this magnitude without additional support. Shortly thereafter, FEMA personnel at the Superdome requested that FEMA headquarters provide buses to transport evacuees from the stadium. Within an hour of receiving the call, FEMA tasked the Department of Transportation—as coordinator of ESF-1, Transportation—to support the evacuation operations. DOT began assembling a bus fleet of over 1,100 vehicles, equal in size to some of the largest transit agencies in the Nation to evacuate thousands of persons from the Superdome and other parts of New Orleans.

Louisiana and Federal officials began contacting other States to relocate evacuees to their cities.[92] They worked together to develop plans to transport the people in the Superdome to out-of-state shelters. By the morning of August 31, Governor Blanco reached an agreement with Texas Governor Rick Perry to evacuate the thousands at the Superdome to the Houston Astrodome.[93] Significant numbers of federally-contracted buses began to arrive at the Superdome the evening of August 31.[94] Initially, evacuees were loaded onto buses and driven all the way to Houston. As the Houston Astrodome began to fill, however, Federal and State officials identified alternative destinations in multiple States and the District of Columbia.[95]

Both DOD and DOT worked with State and local officials to deliver food and water as well as develop plans to evacuate people from three other locations in the city: Algiers Point, the Convention Center, and the Interstate-10 (I-10) cloverleaf.[96] The Governor's office received reports of the crowds at the Ernest N. Morial Memorial Convention Center and the I-10 cloverleaf on August 31.[97] Reports began to arrive that large crowds had gathered at the Convention Center even though city officials had never intended it to be a shelter.[98] Without strong public messaging to inform them otherwise, many of these people had simply assumed that the Convention Center—as a large public building on high ground—would be a safe gathering place.[99] No food or water was pre-staged there because the facility was neither a shelter nor a designated evacuation point.[100]

In addition, large numbers of people gathered or were deposited by search and rescue teams—who were conducting boat and helicopter rescue operations with neither a coordinated plan nor a unified command structure—atop raised surfaces, such as the I-10 cloverleaf downtown. People brought to the raised surfaces as they transitioned to safety had little shelter from the sun and were in ninety-eight degree heat.[101] Faced with this increasingly dire situation, Governor Blanco used her executive authority to commandeer private school buses as evacuation assets, since many of the city's buses had been parked in lots that had flooded.[102] The Governor directed school buses to ferry the people atop the I-10 cloverleaf to safety outside of the city.[103]

By the morning of September 2, approximately fifteen thousand people had been evacuated from the Superdome, leaving approximately 5,500 remaining. Reports on exact numbers vary because the Superdome and Convention Center populations swelled after landfall, as additional evacuees continued to arrive while the evacuation was underway. "The last 300 [people] in the Superdome climbed aboard buses Saturday... Evacuations of the last remaining [people] at the arena were halted before dawn Saturday as authorities diverted buses to help some 25,000 refugees at the New Orleans Convention Center... The Texas Air National Guard estimated that between 2,000 and 5,000 people remained at the Superdome early on Saturday..." On Saturday, September 3, a representative of the State "Office of Emergency Preparedness put the figure at 2,000, and said [people] had recently begun flocking there not for shelter, but to escape New Orleans after they heard buses were arriving."[104]

Except for the ill or injured, no one was evacuated from the overcrowded Convention Center until Saturday, September 3.[105] By that point, however, over 35,000 people had been evacuated from New Orleans, including all the ill or injured at the Superdome.[106] As the evacuation progressed, the situation at the Convention Center and the Superdome stabilized, with food, water, and medical supplies available at both locations.[107] By September 4, DHS reported that the "Superdome and Convention Center have been evacuated; however, displaced persons continue to migrate to these sites and [will be] evacuated as required."[108]

In addition to ground operations, a joint DHS, DOT, and DOD airlift successfully evacuated over 24,000 people, constituting the largest domestic civilian airlift on U.S. soil in history.[109] Federal departments and agencies worked with State, local, and private sector officials to coordinate the operation. After the Federal Aviation Administration restored traffic control and runway operations at New Orleans's Louis Armstrong International Airport, DOT coordinated with private air carriers and the Department of Defense's Transportation Command (USTRANSCOM) to begin the massive airlift. DOT invited the Air Transport Association, the trade organization of principal U.S. airlines, to come to the NRCC to help coordinate with air carriers volunteering their services. In addition to these civilian flights, the Department of Defense simultaneously conducted a major medical airlift from the airport.[110] The DHS Transportation Security Administration (TSA) provided screeners and Federal Air Marshals to maintain security. Search and rescue helicopters brought people directly to the airport, while Federal Protective Service personnel escorted busloads of evacuees from the Superdome.[111] The TSA and other security personnel confiscated hundreds of weapons from evacuees at the airport, including ninety in the first three days of the airlift.[112]

Federal transportation coordinators had little situational awareness regarding the movement of evacuees due to the complete breakdown of the region's communications infrastructure. Specifically, Federal and State officials often had difficulty coordinating the departures and destinations of the large number of buses, trains, and aircraft involved in the evacuations. In one case, a fully provisioned train with room for six hundred evacuees left the city with fewer than one hundred passengers.[113] Buses and flights of evacuees were sometimes diverted, while en route, to new destinations without the knowledge of officials at either the original or new destinations. Without prior notice of the evacuees' arrival times, States sometimes had difficulty accommodating the enormous influx of people. In addition, some passengers reported that they had not been informed of their destinations when they boarded the evacuating flights and had no idea where they were when their flights landed. Speaking about the evacuees, Arkansas Governor Mike Huckabee relayed, "They have been treated like boxes, in many cases, warehoused."[114]

> **LESSON LEARNED**: The Department of Transportation, in coordination with other appropriate departments of the Executive Branch, must also be prepared to conduct mass evacuation operations when disasters overwhelm or incapacitate State and local governments.

Public Safety and Security

Law enforcement agencies across the Gulf Coast region faced countless challenges in the aftermath of Hurricane Katrina. People began looting in some areas as soon as the storm relented.[115] Violent crimes were committed against law enforcement officers and other emergency response personnel.[116] The storm's damage to equipment, facilities, communications, and jails limited the ability of authorities to respond to calls for help and to combat lawlessness.[117] It is clear that violent crime was less prevalent than initially reported, although reliable crime statistics are unavailable. Exaggerated, unconfirmed claims of violent crimes and lawlessness took on a life of their own in the absence of effective public information to counter them.[118]

Security problems in the Gulf Coast, both actual and perceived, obstructed the speed and efficiency of the Federal response and in some cases temporarily halted relief efforts.[119] Security concerns suspended search and rescue missions,[120] delayed the restoration of communications infrastructure,[121] and impeded medical support missions.[122] On August 31, most of the New Orleans police force was redirected from search and rescue missions to respond to the looting, detracting from the priority mission of saving lives. The lawlessness also delayed restoration of essential private sector services such as power, water, and telecommunications.[123] Federal officials attempted to have law enforcement officers protect emergency responders against security threats.[124] However, due to a lack of planning, arranging this support took several days, during which the situation grew worse.

A limited number of Federal law enforcement personnel were already assigned to local offices in New Orleans following the storm and immediately began organizing efforts to restore law and order, but additional Federal assistance was clearly needed. The Secretary of Homeland Security and the U.S. Attorney General directed their respective departments to send Federal law enforcement officers to assist the beleaguered city.[125] By September 3,

---

over 1,600 Federal law enforcement officers were in New Orleans.[126] The Louisiana Governor submitted a request to the Attorney General on September 4, formally seeking assistance from the Department of Justice (DOJ) pursuant to the Emergency Federal Law Enforcement Assistance Act. After coordinating with the Secretary of Homeland Security, the Attorney General granted the request the same day. Two days later, Governor Blanco sent a similar request to the Secretary, requesting DHS law enforcement support. The Secretary granted the request and sent additional DHS law enforcement officers to Louisiana.[127]

By September 5, the Department of Homeland Security had provided 1,444 officers and the Department of Justice had deployed 566 officers.[128] The numbers of Federal law enforcement officers continued to grow as the Department of Agriculture (USDA), Department of Interior, the Department of Treasury, the Department of Veterans' Affairs, the Environmental Protection Agency (EPA), and the U.S. Postal Inspection Service deployed personnel to the Gulf Coast.[129] Federal law enforcement officers performed such missions as protecting Federal property, conducting search and rescue missions, and assisting local law enforcement, particularly in New Orleans. However, several departments and agencies noted that they were impeded in their ability to provide immediate assistance due to the need for deputization to enforce State or Federal laws.[130] Federal planning should have anticipated the need for such deputization procedures.

Hurricane Katrina also crippled the region's criminal justice system. The exodus of the Gulf Coast population resulted in a significant loss of accountability of many persons under law enforcement supervision (*e.g.*, registered sex offenders, probationers).[131] The court systems in the disaster area ceased to function, causing a backlog of criminal prosecutions.[132] Prisoners were often hastily evacuated which created significant challenges for recordkeeping associated with prisoner movement. There was some initial confusion in the process of identifying and relocating prisoners; however, each eventually was accounted for.[133] The strain on the criminal justice system is largely attributable to the absence of contingency plans for these problems at all levels of government. While these issues remain foreseeable consequences of any major disaster, disaster plans did not adequately address the response necessary to prevent the problems encountered during the aftermath of Katrina.

> **LESSON LEARNED**: The Department of Justice, in coordination with the Department of Homeland Security, should examine Federal responsibilities for support to State and local law enforcement and criminal justice systems during emergencies and then build operational plans, procedures, and policies to ensure an effective Federal law enforcement response.

Federal Incident Management

The magnitude of the storm's destruction presented three immediate challenges for the Federal government. First, the sheer amount of destruction over such a large area created an enormous demand for emergency assistance such as fuel, medical supplies, food, shelter, and water. This demand, coupled with the austere conditions throughout the Gulf Coast following Katrina's landfall, exceeded FEMA's standard disaster delivery capabilities and processes. Mr. Scott Wells, who served as Deputy Federal Coordinating Officer (FCO) in Louisiana, later testified to Congress that "the response was not robust; it was not enough for the catastrophe at hand."[134] Second, localities needed assistance to perform emergency response operations and re-establish incident command. However, Hurricane Katrina's impact across the Gulf Coast region limited the use of normal mutual aid agreements, which rely on neighboring cities and counties for assistance. In this case, the neighboring jurisdictions were overwhelmed themselves and unable to provide assistance elsewhere. Assistance had to come from States outside the region and from the Federal government. This requirement for an active Federal role in emergency response operations was most pronounced in New Orleans. Finally, the communications problems had a debilitating effect on response efforts in the region and the overall national effort. Officials from national leaders to emergency responders on the ground lacked the level of situational awareness necessary for a prompt and effective response to the catastrophe. This was a recipe for an inefficient and ineffective Federal response.

On August 30, Secretary Chertoff declared Hurricane Katrina to be an Incident of National Significance (INS), the first ever formal declaration of this designation.[135] On the same day, he also appointed FEMA Director Michael Brown as the Principal Federal Official (PFO) for the Hurricane Katrina response.[136] A PFO is designated to facilitate Federal support to the unified command structure and coordinate overall Federal incident management. The PFO also provides a primary point of contact and situational awareness locally for the Secretary of Homeland

Security. However, according to the NRP, "The PFO does not direct or replace the incident command structure established at the incident, nor does the PFO have directive authority over the [Senior Federal Law Enforcement Official], FCO, or other Federal and State officials." [137] The FCO retains his authorities to coordinate Federal response activities under the Stafford Act. [138] As PFO, Brown had no authority over the FCOs. However, as the Director of FEMA, Brown was vested with the authority to directly oversee the FCOs, [139] thereby mitigating the PFO limitations. His subsequent PFO replacement had no such authority to work around this impediment, and as a result, was eventually made FCO as well. The multiple Federal coordinators with varying authorities frustrated State and local officials in the region. [140]

Also on August 30, DHS initiated a virtual National Joint Information Center (JIC) [141] and conducted the first of what would become daily National Incident Communications Conference Line (NICCL) calls with other Federal departments and agencies.

An important limiting factor of the Federal response, as discussed in the *Primer* chapter, is that the Federal response is predicated on an incident being handled at the lowest jurisdictional level possible. A base assumption to this approach is that, even in cases where State and local governments are overwhelmed, they would maintain the necessary incident command structure to direct Federal assets to where they are most needed. In the case of Katrina, the local government had been destroyed and the State government was incapacitated, and thus the Federal government had to take on the additional roles of performing incident command and other functions it would normally rely upon the State and local governments to provide.

> **LESSON LEARNED:** The Federal government should work with its homeland security partners in revising existing plans, ensuring a functional operational structure—including within regions— and establishing a clear, accountable process for all National preparedness efforts.

The Joint Field Office (JFO), which builds upon the State and local incident command structure, provides a single location for all Federal departments and agencies to acquire situational awareness, direction, mission assignments, and a forum to interface with other agencies. [142] It is essential for ensuring that all Federal response elements possess a common operating picture and synchronize their response operations and resources. However, in the case of Hurricane Katrina, the JFO was not established at the outset, and did not function as envisioned when it was established. Key PFO staff positions had not been identified prior to landfall, which forced Director Brown to assemble his staff in the midst of the disaster. [143] Brown was still working on a PFO organizational chart on the evening of August 31, almost sixty hours after landfall. Key components of the Baton Rouge JFO were still being assembled in the two weeks that followed. [144]

The JFO was located in Baton Rouge, Louisiana, near the State of Louisiana Emergency Operations Center (EOC). A Federal coordination center was not immediately established in New Orleans. The NRP does not contemplate subordinate structures to the JFO to coordinate Federal response actions in the event of multiple or geographically widespread catastrophes (i.e., multiple "ground zeros"). [145] In the absence of a command center near the major incident sites and a fully functioning JFO, agencies independently deployed resources, operated autonomously, and generated disparate reporting streams back to Federal authorities locally and in Washington. [146] This resulted in an often inconsistent and inaccurate operating picture of the disaster area for senior decision makers, duplication of efforts, gaps in addressing requests for assistance, and the inefficient allocation of resources.

Military Assistance

Active duty military and National Guard personnel provided critical emergency response and security support to the Gulf Coast during the height of the crisis. State active duty and Title 32 National Guard forces that deployed to Louisiana and Mississippi operated under the command of their respective Governors. [147] Title 10 active duty forces, on the other hand, fell under the command of the President and had more limited civil response authority. [148] On August 30, Deputy Secretary of Defense Gordon England authorized U.S. Northern Command (USNORTHCOM) and the Joint Chiefs of Staff to take all appropriate measures to plan and conduct disaster relief operations in support of FEMA. [149] USNORTHCOM established Joint Task Force Katrina (JTF-Katrina) at Camp Shelby to coordinate the growing military response to the disaster. [150]

By September 1, JTF-Katrina, commanded by LTG Honoré, included approximately 3,000 active duty personnel in the disaster area; within four days, that number climbed to 14,232 active duty personnel. LTG Honoré's leadership, combined with the Department of Defense's resources, manpower, and advanced planning, contributed to the military's success in the Federal response, especially in areas such as search and rescue, security, and logistical support. Two C-130 firefighting aircraft and seven helicopters supported firefighting operations in New Orleans.[151] By September 5, military helicopters had performed 963 search and rescue, evacuation, and supply delivery missions.[152] Military personnel also assisted Federal, State and local agencies with other needs as well. For example, DOD aircraft flew mosquito abatement aerial spraying missions over 2 million acres to prevent the spread of mosquito- and water-borne diseases.[153] Military personnel also performed such missions as salvage, sewage restoration, relief worker billeting, air traffic control, and fuel distribution.

The standard National Guard deployment coordination between State Adjutants General (TAGs) was effective during the initial response but was insufficient for such a large-scale and sustained operation.[154] To address this shortfall, LTG Blum, Chief of the National Guard Bureau, held a conference call on August 31 with all fifty-four TAGs to distribute requests for forces and equipment to all TAGs.[155]

> **LESSON LEARNED:** The Departments of Homeland Security and Defense should jointly plan for the Department of Defense's support of Federal response activities as well as those extraordinary circumstances when it is appropriate for the Department of Defense to lead the Federal response. In addition, the Department of Defense should ensure the transformation of the National Guard is focused on increased integration with active duty forces for homeland security plans and activities.

Guardsmen performed a range of missions, including search and rescue, security, evacuations, and distribution of food and water. In Mississippi, National Guard forces prepared Camp Shelby as a staging point for incoming forces and also engaged in law enforcement support, debris removal, shelter support and other vital operations.[156] Guardsmen from Texas and Pennsylvania supplied satellite phone communications to the response.[157] When a group of Pennsylvania Guardsmen arrived to fix a Louisiana woman's roof, she told the group: "That's a long way to come to help us. We're really grateful … you boys are going to heaven, I tell you."[158] By August 29, sixty-five National Guard helicopters were positioned throughout the Gulf Coast.[159] By September 2, nearly 22,000 National Guard soldiers and airmen had deployed to the region —including 6,500 in New Orleans alone[160]—breaking the National Guard's previous record for the largest response to a domestic emergency.[161] Eventually, over 50,000 National Guard members from fifty-four States, Territories, and the District of Columbia deployed to the Gulf Coast, providing critical response assistance during this week of crisis.[162] The robust active duty and National Guard response played a crucial role in the effort to bring stability to the areas ravaged by Hurricane Katrina.

A fragmented deployment system and lack of an integrated command structure for both active duty and National Guard forces exacerbated communications and coordination issues during the initial response. Deployments for Title 32 (National Guard) forces were coordinated State-to-State through EMAC agreements and also by the National Guard Bureau. Title 10 (active duty) force deployments were coordinated through USNORTHCOM. Once forces arrived in the Joint Operations Area, they fell under separate command structures, rather than one single command. The separate commands divided the area of operations geographically and supported response efforts separately, with the exception of the evacuations of the Superdome and the Convention Center in New Orleans.[163] Equipment interoperability problems further hindered an integrated response. Similar issues of bifurcated operations and interoperability challenges were also present between the military and civilian leadership.[164] This lack of interoperable communications was apparent at the tactical level, resulting from the fact that emergency responders, National Guard, and active duty military use different equipment.[165]

Federal Communications Assistance

Although the Federal government pushed assets into the Gulf Coast region to fill communication gaps created by Hurricane Katrina we could have and should have done more. FEMA had pre-positioned two of their five Mobile Emergency Response Support (MERS) detachments in the Gulf and quickly moved them to the affected areas in Louisiana and Mississippi soon after landfall.[166] MERS detachments consist of an array of vehicles and trained personnel and provide mobile communications, operational support, and logistical power generation assets—

including satellite communications, dozens of phone and data lines, heating and air conditioning, power generation, fuel, potable water, and office functionality— to support the operations of Federal, State, and local authorities.[167] Because MERS is a system of divisible assets and not a rigid unit, a single MERS detachment can provide limited support to multiple field operating sites within the disaster area simultaneously.[168]

> **LESSON LEARNED**: The Department of Homeland Security should review our current laws, policies, plans, and strategies relevant to communications. Upon the conclusion of this review, the Homeland Security Council, with support from the Office of Science and Technology Policy, should develop a National Emergency Communications Strategy that supports communications operability and interoperability.

The Federal government must keep some MERS detachments at locations outside the incident area in case there is another catastrophe or event, but additional MERS support should have been deployed to the Gulf when it became apparent that those pre-positioned were insufficient for an incident of Katrina's magnitude. At the time, some key Federal officials both on the ground and back in Washington did not know that there were additional MERS available.

To augment FEMA's efforts, DOD deployed available communications assets to the affected areas, such as its Deployable Joint Command and Control System.[169] On August 31, National Guard Bureau Chief LTG Blum reported that DOD was "pushing every communications asset that we have."[170] Further, the National Interagency Fire Center provided 3,200 radios, thirty-eight satellite systems, and several other communication modules in order to supplement the Gulf region's damaged communication networks.

The DHS National Communications System (NCS) also contributed to communications recovery efforts following Hurricane Katrina. NCS linked the telecommunications industry with the relevant government agencies through the National Coordinating Center (NCC).[171] The NCC coordinated with MCI and AT&T, as well as USNORTHCOM to identify and deploy mobile communication assets to the Gulf region both prior to, and following, landfall.[172] Further, due to the destruction of the communications infrastructure, the NCS was required to perform new functions, such as providing interim Land Mobile Radio systems, used to connect two-way radio users to a central dispatcher, to first responders in devastated Louisiana parishes.[173] By September 1, mobile communications systems were beginning to provide much needed telephone and two-way radio communications in Louisiana and Mississippi with additional systems en route to support the entire affected area.[174]

Federal Resource Challenges

The aftermath of Hurricane Katrina left the Gulf Coast in desperate need of resources and assistance. Nearly a quarter of a million people in shelters relied on shipments of ice, food, and water to meet their basic needs.[175] Hospitals, shelters, and other critical facilities required diesel fuel to run their back-up generators. Many evacuees lacked access to medical providers and supplies. Emergency responders conducting life-saving operations demanded additional supplies and fuel. FEMA's pre-positioned supplies proved inadequate to meet these demands throughout the region after landfall.[176] To fill this gap, the Federal government sent more resources to Louisiana in the first two weeks after Hurricane Katrina than it had sent to Florida for all of the previous year's hurricanes combined.[177]

As Hurricane Katrina made landfall, Director Brown provided public assurances that FEMA was prepared to act to meet the logistical challenge.[178] FEMA personnel soon discovered, however, that the quantity of material requested post-landfall outstripped their logistical capabilities. FEMA simply could not procure enough resources to match the rate at which commodities were being consumed. The agency's contracts with private companies, though sufficient for smaller disasters, were incapable of supplying

> **LESSON LEARNED:** The Department of Homeland Security, in coordination with State and local governments and the private sector, should develop a modern, flexible, and transparent logistics system. This system should be based on established contracts for stockpiling commodities at the local level for emergencies and the provision of goods and services during emergencies. The Federal government must develop the capacity to conduct large-scale logistical operations that supplement and, if necessary, replace State and local logistical systems by leveraging resources within both the public sector and the private sector.

---

the enormous quantities of resources needed.[179]   As a result, shortages plagued the affected area. In Mississippi, FEMA personnel were unable to meet requirements submitted by staging areas.[180] William Carwile, the FCO for Mississippi, recalled that there was a huge gap "between what we required on the ground and what they were sending us."[181] In some areas, local officials who requested high-demand resources, such as generators, received no shipments of those supplies from FEMA until weeks after landfall.[182]

Ineffective communications between FEMA and other Federal departments and agencies prevented available Federal resources from being effectively used for response operations. The USDA observed that its personnel "had difficulty in getting FEMA to take advantage of the resources available to them because of the unfamiliarity of some FEMA employees with USDA programs. Likewise, many USDA employees were unfamiliar with FEMA programs and procedures." The Department of Interior also offered valuable assistance. In the aftermath of the hurricane, DOI delivered a comprehensive list of its deployable assets that were immediately available for humanitarian and emergency assistance, including such items as 300 dump trucks and other vehicles, 119 pieces of heavy equipment, 300 boats, eleven aircraft, fifty to seventy-five maintenance crews. Although DOI repeatedly attempted to provide these assets through the process established by the NRP, there was no effective mechanism for efficiently integrating and deploying these resources. DOI offered 500 rooms and other sites for shelters or housing. The Departments of Veterans Affairs (VA), Housing and Urban Development (HUD), and Agriculture (USDA) also offered thousands of housing units nationwide to FEMA for temporary assignment to evacuees. FEMA officials said that the need to negotiate conditional requirements in some cases prevented them from accepting some Federal agencies' offers of housing resources. Most of the thousands of housing units made available by other Federal agencies were not offered to evacuees and were never used.

The private sector too met roadblocks in its efforts to coordinate with the Federal government during the response. For example, the American Bus Association spent an entire day trying to find a point of contact at FEMA to coordinate bus deployment without success.[183] Federal procurement officers also neglected to draw upon retailers' supply lines to get the resources that victims needed. To this end, despite an acute shortage of blue tarps to cover damaged roofs, Federal officials were slow to draw upon the corporate supply chains that deliver tarps to the stores that sell them. For example, one private sector company had 600,000 tarps available.

> **_LESSON LEARNED:_** The Department of Homeland Security, working collaboratively with the private sector, should revise the National Response Plan and finalize the Interim National Infrastructure Protection Plan to be able to rapidly assess the impact of a disaster on critical infrastructure. We must use this knowledge to inform Federal response and prioritization decisions and to support infrastructure restoration in order to save lives and mitigate the impact of the disaster on the Nation.

Throughout the weeks following Hurricane Katrina, the Department of Commerce worked to close the gap between the private and the public sector. The Department set up an informational website and hotline to provide businesses with a one-stop source of information on contracting opportunities.[184] The Department also granted certain companies prioritized access to the raw materials needed to restore the region's crippled infrastructure, even when the resources had previously been contracted to other parties.[185]

As logistics problems were now obvious to all, FEMA turned to DOD for major support in this area.[186] On September 3, Secretary Rumsfeld directed USNORTHCOM to execute greater logistical support operations in both Louisiana and Mississippi.[187]

Offers of Charitable Assistance

FEMA could neither efficiently accept nor manage the deluge of charitable donations.[188] Private sector companies also encountered problems when attempting to donate their goods and services to FEMA for Hurricane Katrina response efforts.

Other countries made generous offers of assistance that the Federal government had difficulty integrating into the ongoing response operations. Absent an implementation plan for the management of foreign material assistance, valuable resources often went unused, which frustrated many donor countries. Inadequate planning delayed the overall process of accepting and receiving disaster aid from abroad. For example, after Switzerland had loaded relief supplies onto an aircraft, FEMA requested that the country send only the portion FEMA required to meet response needs. As the generous contribution of supplies could not be unloaded quickly and repackaged into the smaller quantities in a timely manner, the U.S. Embassy in Bern and the Government of Switzerland cancelled the entire flight.[189] A German company offered the use of a $3 million integrated satellite and cellular telephone system capable of handling 5,000 calls at once, only to wait five days for a written deployment order from USNORTHCOM.

The same was true of foreign financial assistance. There was no means of accepting, allocating and disbursing funds that would also ensure transparency and acknowledgement of donors. The Federal government eventually developed a process to accept financial gifts from foreign countries,[190] but because there was no pre-established plan, implementation

> **LESSON LEARNED:** The Department of State, in coordination with the Department of Homeland Security, should review and revise policies, plans, and procedures for the management of foreign disaster assistance. In addition, this review should clarify responsibilities and procedures for handling inquiries

was a slow and often frustrating process. The U.S. Agency for International Development (USAID) sent liaisons to FEMA field locations on September 2 to coordinate the delivery of foreign disaster relief.[191] However, it took several days for the international aid staging area at Little Rock Air Force Base, Arkansas, to become operational.[192] Before this staging area was established, foreign aid could not be efficiently unloaded and distributed. The Federal government's inability to utilize its own resources, or those offered to it, caused great concern for the American public.

Federal Health and Medical Support

The public health and medical situation throughout the Gulf Coast required substantial Federal resources to prevent even further loss of life. On August 31, HHS Secretary Leavitt declared a Federal Public Health Emergency for the Gulf Coast region. This emergency declaration allowed HHS to waive certain requirements for such programs as Medicare, Medicaid, and the State Children's Health Insurance Program. It also allowed HHS to make grants and enter into contracts more expeditiously.[193] Immediate public health and medical support challenges included the identification, triage, and treatment of acutely sick and injured patients; the management of chronic medical conditions in large numbers of evacuees with special health care needs; the assessment, communication, and mitigation of public health risks; mortuary support; and the provision of assistance to State and local health officials to quickly reestablish health care delivery systems and public health infrastructures.[194]

Federal departments and agencies worked together to attempt to meet these challenges, beginning before Hurricane Katrina's landfall and continuing long after. HHS and DOD health officials collaborated with State and local health officials, maintained situational awareness for their respective agencies, and hastened the direction of medical and public health assets. National Disaster Medical System (NDMS) teams also formed an integral component of the medical response to Hurricane Katrina, collectively treating over 100,000 patients.[195] Several agencies assigned responsibilities in the NRP under ESF-8, Public Health and Medical Services, sent liaisons to the HHS Operations Center in Washington, D.C., and the HHS Secretary's Emergency Response Teams (SERTs) in the affected States. The Department of Veterans Affairs (VA) used its extensive resources to deliver care to evacuees and veterans from the affected region.

HHS deployed medical supplies and personnel to bolster State and local public health capacity in the region. It provided pharmaceuticals and other medical supplies from the Strategic National Stockpile (SNS) beginning with pre-landfall deliveries to the Superdome. By September 3, HHS had delivered 100 tons of medical supplies from the SNS to Louisiana. HHS also deployed twenty-four public health teams that included epidemiology, food safety, sanitation, and toxicology experts.

Medical and public health assets provided excellent care to thousands of displaced patients with both acute injuries and with chronic medical conditions, many of whom had multiple complex medical requirements. According to the Governors from the Gulf Region, medical and public health professionals were true heroes of the Hurricane Katrina response. They often had to improvise and use their own initiative because the system was slow to deploy them from staging areas or failed to adequately supply them. A member of an American Red Cross inspection team, Dr. Hilarie H. Cranmer, wrote, "[i]n a little over four days, our multidisciplinary and interagency teams assessed more than 200 shelters housing nearly 30,000 people. Amazingly, in a majority of cases, the basic public health needs were being met."[196] Federal, State, local, private sector, and volunteer health care providers across the Gulf Coast took the initiative to overcome the inefficiencies of the medical support system and meet their patients' needs.[197] Louisiana State University worked with the State Office of Emergency Preparedness, Federal personnel, and responders from outside the region to turn its Pete Maravich Assembly Center into an acute care medical facility. Within a week, the facility processed approximately 6,000 patients and more than a thousand prescriptions.[198]

HHS struggled in its NRP role as coordinating agency for ESF-8. HHS lacked control over vital medical assets, over-relied on departmental routines, and did not have adequate disaster plans. FEMA compounded HHS coordination difficulties. FEMA deployed NDMS teams without HHS's oversight or knowledge. FEMA administrative delays in issuing mission assignments exacerbated the lack of coordination within ESF-8 and created additional inefficiencies. In order to respond swiftly, HHS felt compelled to take emergency response actions without mission assignments, bypassing FEMA. While this may have pushed additional assets to the region, it also had a deleterious effect on the Federal government's situational awareness of its deployed assets.

> **LESSON LEARNED:** In coordination with the Department of Homeland Security and other homeland security partners, the Department of Health and Human Services should strengthen the Federal government's capability to provide public health and medical support during a crisis. This will require the improvement of command and control of public health resources, the development of deliberate plans, an additional investment in deployable operational resources, and an acceleration of the initiative to foster the widespread use of interoperable electronic health records systems.

FROM RESPONSE TO RECOVERY

Federal Coordination

After a week of crisis, Federal, State, and local officials began transitioning to a more organized and sustained response. As requirements eased and material flowed into the region, Federal departments addressed those problems that had afflicted their response during its first week. The establishment of JFOs in several States across the Gulf Coast in the following weeks enhanced the Federal response by providing the coordination and management that had been largely absent.[199] On September 5, Secretary Chertoff appointed Vice Admiral (VADM) Thad Allen to the position of Deputy PFO. At that time, the Louisiana JFO was still a temporary office near the Louisiana Emergency Operations Center in Baton Rouge, almost eighty miles from New Orleans. However, to gain greater visibility of the disaster area, VADM Allen stood up a "PFO-Forward Headquarters" in New Orleans on the USS Iwo Jima on September 7.[200] The PFO-Forward rapidly increased the effectiveness of the Federal response by providing a Federal unified command close to the disaster scene. On September 9, Secretary Chertoff appointed VADM Allen to replace Michael Brown as PFO for Hurricane Katrina.[201] Director Brown returned to Washington to assume his duties as FEMA Director, rather than managing the field operations for Katrina.[202] On September 21, VADM Allen was given additional authorities when he was appointed FCO, in addition to PFO.[203] VADM Allen's appointments ultimately proved critical for energizing the JFO and the entire Federal response to Hurricane Katrina.[204]

The formation of Federal coordination entities also improved law enforcement operations. On September 6, the two Senior Federal Law Enforcement Officials (SFLEOs) [205] each representing the DOJ and DHS, respectively, established a Law Enforcement Coordination Center (LECC)[206] in New Orleans to help coordinate law enforcement personnel operating in the city and surrounding parishes. For the first time during the hurricane response, New Orleans now had a unified command for law enforcement comprised of the New Orleans Police Department, the Louisiana State Police, the National Guard, and all Federal law enforcement personnel.[207] Improved coordination, combined with increased Federal law enforcement assistance, strengthened public safety and security in New Orleans. On September 12, the DOD stated that there was "[v]ery little criminal activity" in New Orleans, and that the "military presence deters criminals before damage can be done."[208] By September 13, the City of New Orleans reported law enforcement and military personnel had successfully reestablished security in the City.[209]

Improved security and the deployment of additional Federal personnel also facilitated search and rescue operations, particularly in New Orleans. By this point, most of the people stranded on rooftops had been rescued, so operations focused more on door-to-door searches. Rescue teams completed primary ground searches in New Orleans on

September 12, and spent the next two weeks entering buildings to locate trapped survivors and deceased victims.[210] FEMA Urban Search and Rescue teams completed all Mississippi assignments on September 10 and ended all operations in Louisiana twenty days later.[211]

The DHS Public Affairs Office established a Joint Information Center (JIC) in Baton Rouge on Wednesday, September 6, to provide accurate and timely information on the Federal response and relief efforts as well as to counter misinformation.[212] The formation of a second facility in New Orleans three days later improved the flow of accurate information back to the Baton Rouge JIC. These JICs helped to stem the spread of rumors and unsubstantiated reports that had plagued public information efforts during the first week after landfall.

> **LESSON LEARNED:** The Department of Homeland Security should develop an integrated public communications plan to better inform, guide, and reassure the American public before, during, and after a catastrophe. The Department of Homeland Security should enable this plan with operational capabilities to deploy coordinated public affairs teams during a crisis.

Federal and State officials struggled to locate, recover, and identify the hundreds of deceased victims. While mortuary affairs is generally a State and local responsibility, the NRP is unclear about the appropriate Federal role, leading to substantial confusion.[213] FEMA established body collection points at Gulfport, Mississippi, and St. Gabriel, Louisiana, in the days following Hurricane Katrina's landfall.[214] From August 31 to September 4, FEMA also deployed ten Disaster Mortuary Operational Response Teams (DMORTs) and both of its Disaster Portable Morgue Units (DPMU) to help State and local personnel identify and process bodies at those collection points.[215] On September 1, FEMA reached a verbal agreement with Kenyon International Emergency Services, a disaster management contractor, to retrieve and transport bodies.[216] However, difficulties finalizing the agreement with Kenyon hindered body recovery efforts on the ground.[217] Frustrated Kenyon executives withdrew from their agreement with FEMA; this led FEMA to request that DOD take over the body recovery effort until another contractor could be found.[218]

Disagreement between Federal and State officials over body recovery responsibilities continued for weeks after landfall. Federal officials maintained that body recovery was ultimately a State responsibility with the Federal government providing support only.[219] In a September 13 press conference, Governor Blanco expressed her dismay and blamed FEMA for failing to "break through the bureaucracy" to finalize a contact with Kenyon International. On September 13, Governor Blanco directed the Louisiana Department of Health and Hospitals to sign its own written contract with Kenyon, even though the Governor believed that "recovery of bodies is a FEMA responsibility."[220] The deployed DMORTs performed well in extraordinarily difficult circumstances. Though they found themselves in the midst of a catastrophic disaster and caught in a public political dispute, they carried out their mission with great professionalism and compassion.

Meeting Victims' Needs

The national effort to meet the needs of Hurricane Katrina victims expanded in the weeks after landfall. Government, private sector, faith-based, non-profit, and other volunteer personnel collaborated in innovative ways to provide medical, financial, and housing assistance. For example, former Presidents George H.W. Bush and Bill Clinton are distributing over $90 million they raised following Hurricane Katrina to Gulf Coast higher education institutions, local and regional faith-based organizations, and the States of Louisiana, Mississippi and Alabama.[221] At the National Book Festival in September attendees collected donated books to help Gulf Coast schools and libraries replace the books that were destroyed by the hurricane.[222]

Federal responders overcame many of the initial public health challenges as increasing numbers of medical personnel and supplies flowed into the region. The continuing efforts of medical personnel to vaccinate Hurricane Katrina evacuees prevented most communicable diseases from spreading in the densely populated shelters.[223] By mid-September, the HHS's public health response transitioned focus from acute public health issues to include less imminent concerns, such as child care support, mental health services, and treatment services for substance abuse.[224]

On September 7, FEMA announced that it had instituted the Expedited Assistance Program to speed the delivery of assistance to Hurricane Katrina victims.[225] This enabled registrations to grow from 261,946 on September 5 to over one million ten days later.[226] FEMA delivered over $1 billion in assistance to evacuees in all fifty States and the District of Columbia by September 17—less than three weeks after landfall.[227] However, this extraordinary and unprecedented effort was frequently overshadowed by problems encountered by evacuees in their attempts to register for or receive assistance. For example, FEMA established Disaster Recovery Centers (DRCs) in the Gulf Coast region that were not structured to process disaster assistance registrations.[228] The DRCs also were not set up to assist victims in obtaining the other Federal assistance that they were already receiving before Katrina, such as Social Security and Veteran's Benefits. Staff at the DRCs directed victims to register by telephone or via the Internet.[229] Since many households in Hurricane Katrina-affected areas were without power or telephone service, such instructions left many without the means to file their registrations.[230] In addition, FEMA had not determined the capacity of existing Federal agency call centers and telephone banks to handle increased call volumes. Consequently, victims registering for assistance via telephone repeatedly encountered long delays and disconnected calls.[231]

> **LESSON LEARNED:** The Department of Health and Human Services should coordinate with other departments of the Executive Branch, as well as State governments and non-governmental organizations, to develop a robust, comprehensive, and integrated system to deliver human services during disasters so that victims are able to receive Federal and State assistance in a simple and seamless manner. In particular, this system should be designed to provide victims a consumer oriented, simple, effective and single encounter from which they can receive assistance.

At times, FEMA public statements regarding the provision of assistance were confusing or incomplete. For example, FEMA announced that it was making $2,000 cash payments to qualified/registered disaster victims and that these funds would be provided through various means, including by debit card.[232] However, it made this announcement before the debit cards were widely available and did not provide detailed guidance on distribution procedures.[233] This led to widespread confusion and frustration. Security personnel had to lock down the Houston Astrodome during the distribution of debit cards due to unrest among evacuees.[234]

Faith-based, non-profit, and other non-government and volunteer organizations continued to provide essential support to Hurricane Katrina victims. For example, in Harris County, Texas, the Citizen Corps Council—a volunteer organization under the auspices of DHS—coordinated private sector contributions and the mobilization of 60,000 volunteers.[235] The Citizen Corps volunteers created an evacuee "city," which at its peak sheltered more than 27,000 people at the Reliant Center, Reliant Arena, and the Astrodome.[236] The Southern Baptist Convention of the North American Mission Board and other faith-based organizations provided food and shelter to many evacuees and helped them find temporary and permanent housing.[237]

However, faith-based and non-governmental groups were not adequately integrated into the response effort.[238] These groups often encountered difficulties coordinating their efforts with Federal, State and local governments, due to a failure to adequately address their role in the NRP.[239] Major Todd Hawks of the Salvation Army testified to Congress that the Salvation Army, "wasn't permitted to have a liaison officer in the State's Emergency Operations Center (EOC). As a result,

> **LESSON LEARNED:** The Federal response should better integrate the contributions of volunteers and non-governmental organizations into the broader national effort. This integration would be best achieved at the State and local levels, prior to future incidents. In particular, State and local governments must engage NGOs in the planning process, credential their personnel, and provide them the necessary resource support for their involvement in a joint response.

we had to obtain critical information second-hand through Voluntary Organizations Active in a Disaster (VOAD)— if we received the information at all." Hawks stated this situation further complicated the Salvation Army's relief effort.[240] Reverend Larry Snyder, President of Catholic Charities USA, remarked, "In spite of Catholic Charities having available FEMA trained and certified disaster response staff, we were not always allowed admittance to FEMA operations and the local EOCs. This significantly impaired a more coordinated response by all of us." These groups succeeded in their missions, mitigated suffering and helped victims survive mostly in spite of, not because of, the government. These groups deserve better next time. Jim Towey, Director of the White House Office of Faith-Based and Community Initiatives, said these folks were the foot soldiers and armies of compassion that victims of Katrina so desperately needed.

> **LESSON LEARNED:** Using established Federal core competencies and all available resources, the Department of Housing and Urban Development, in coordination with other departments of the Executive Branch with housing stock, should develop integrated plans and bolstered capabilities for the temporary and long-term housing of evacuees. The American Red Cross and the Department of Homeland Security should retain responsibility and improve the process of mass care and sheltering during disasters.

Locating temporary or long-term housing for Hurricane Katrina evacuees presented significant challenges for Federal officials. The supply of temporary housing in the disaster area, such as hotels and apartments, was quickly depleted, while FEMA's effort to provide trailers to evacuees foundered due to inadequate planning and poor coordination.[241] Moving evacuees into trailers was delayed because of FEMA's failure to plan for the provision of delivery transportation and infrastructure support such as water and electrical hook-up.[242] The shelter population plummeted from nearly 273,000 on September 5 to about 135,000 on September 10 as evacuees found temporary or other housing opportunities.[243] Although FEMA had planned to place all evacuees into temporary housing by October 1,[244] nearly 16,000 victims of Hurricane Katrina and Hurricane Rita, which made landfall near the Texas-Louisiana border on September 24, still remained in shelters in mid-October.[245] FEMA also did not provide expedited direct rental assistance to individuals until late September.[246] Those out of shelters were mostly placed in hotels, which only delayed the permanent housing problem. Further, the uncertainty of relocation fostered constant anxiety in the already traumatized victims of Katrina.

Housing and other assistance issues persisted even as response operations gave way to recovery and rebuilding efforts. They are critical for determining whether the region will retain its people and their unique culture. These remain central issues for Donald Powell, appointed by President Bush on November 1, 2005, to serve as the Coordinator of Federal Support for the Gulf Coast's Recovery and Rebuilding.[247]

CONCLUSION

Hurricane Katrina necessitated a national response that Federal, State, and local officials were unprepared to provide. The methods that had been employed successfully for the 243 previous major disaster declarations since January 2001 proved inadequate for Hurricane Katrina's magnitude.[248] The Federal response suffered from significant organization and coordination problems during this week of crisis. The lack of communications and situational awareness had a debilitating effect on the Federal response. Even after coordinating elements were in place, Federal departments and agencies continued to have difficulty adapting their standard procedures to this catastrophic incident. The Federal government's problems responding to Hurricane Katrina illustrate greater systemic weaknesses inherent in our current national preparedness system: the lack of expertise in the areas of response, recovery, and reconstruction. Insufficient planning, training, and interagency coordination are not problems that began and ended with Hurricane Katrina. The storm demonstrated the need for greater integration and synchronization of preparedness efforts, not only throughout the Federal government, but also with the State and local governments and the private and non-profit sectors as well.

CHAPTER FIVE: LESSONS LEARNED

This government will learn the lessons of Hurricane Katrina. We are going to review every action and make necessary changes so that we are better prepared for any challenge of nature, or act of evil men, that could threaten our people.

—President George W. Bush, September 15, 2005[1]

The preceding chapters described the dynamics of the response to Hurricane Katrina. While there were numerous stories of great professionalism, courage, and compassion by Americans from all walks of life, our task here is to identify the critical challenges that undermined and prevented a more efficient and effective Federal response. In short, what were the key failures during the Federal response to Hurricane Katrina?

We ask this question not to affix blame. Rather, we endeavor to find the answers in order to identify systemic gaps and improve our preparedness for the next disaster – natural or man-made. We must move promptly to understand precisely what went wrong and determine how we are going to fix it.

After reviewing and analyzing the response to Hurricane Katrina, we identified seventeen specific lessons the Federal government has learned. These lessons, which flow from the critical challenges we encountered, are depicted in the accompanying text box. Fourteen of these critical challenges were highlighted in the preceding Week of Crisis section and range from high-level policy and planning issues (e.g., the Integrated Use of Military Capabilities) to operational matters (e.g., Search and Rescue).[2] Three other challenges – Training, Exercises, and Lessons Learned; Homeland Security Professional Development and Education; and Citizen and Community Preparedness –

Hurricane Katrina Critical Challenges
1. National Preparedness
2. Integrated Use of Military Capabilities
3. Communications
4. Logistics and Evacuations
5. Search and Rescue
6. Public Safety and Security
7. Public Health and Medical Support
8. Human Services
9. Mass Care and Housing
10. Public Communications
11. Critical Infrastructure and Impact Assessment
12. Environmental Hazards and Debris Removal
13. Foreign Assistance
14. Non-Governmental Aid
15. Training, Exercises, and Lessons Learned
16. Homeland Security Professional Development and Education
17. Citizen and Community Preparedness

are interconnected to the others but reflect measures and institutions that improve our preparedness more broadly. These three will be discussed in the Report's last chapter, *Transforming National Preparedness*.

Some of these seventeen critical challenges affected all aspects of the Federal response. Others had an impact on a specific, discrete operational capability. Yet each, particularly when taken in aggregate, directly affected the overall efficiency and effectiveness of our efforts. This chapter summarizes the challenges that ultimately led to the lessons we have learned. Over one hundred recommendations for corrective action flow from these lessons and are outlined in detail in Appendix A of the Report.

Critical Challenge: National Preparedness

Our current system for homeland security does not provide the necessary framework to manage the challenges posed by 21st Century catastrophic threats. But to be clear, it is unrealistic to think that even the strongest framework can perfectly anticipate and overcome all challenges in a crisis. While we have built a response system that ably handles the demands of a typical hurricane season, wildfires, and other limited natural and man-made disasters, the system clearly has structural flaws for addressing catastrophic events. During the Federal response to Katrina[3], four critical flaws in our national preparedness became evident: Our processes for unified management of the national response; command and control structures within the Federal government; knowledge of our preparedness plans; and regional planning and coordination. A discussion of each follows below.

Unified Management of the National Response

Effective incident management of catastrophic events requires coordination of a wide range of organizations and activities, public and private. Under the current response framework, the Federal government merely "coordinates" resources to meet the needs of local and State governments based upon their requests for assistance. Pursuant to the National Incident Management System (NIMS) and the National Response Plan (NRP), Federal and State agencies build their command and coordination structures to support the local command and coordination structures during an emergency. Yet this framework does not address the conditions of a catastrophic event with large scale competing needs, insufficient resources, and the absence of functioning local governments. These limitations proved to be major inhibitors to the effective marshalling of Federal, State, and local resources to respond to Katrina.

Soon after Katrina made landfall, State and local authorities understood the devastation was serious but, due to the destruction of infrastructure and response capabilities, lacked the ability to communicate with each other and coordinate a response. Federal officials struggled to perform responsibilities generally conducted by State and local authorities, such as the rescue of citizens stranded by the rising floodwaters, provision of law enforcement, and evacuation of the remaining population of New Orleans, all without the benefit of prior planning or a functioning State/local incident command structure to guide their efforts.

The Federal government cannot and should not be the Nation's first responder. State and local governments are best positioned to address incidents in their jurisdictions and will always play a large role in disaster response. But Americans have the right to expect that the Federal government will effectively respond to a catastrophic incident. When local and State governments are overwhelmed or incapacitated by an event that has reached catastrophic proportions, only the Federal government has the resources and capabilities to respond. The Federal government must therefore plan, train, and equip to meet the requirements for responding to a catastrophic event.

Command and Control Within the Federal Government

In terms of the management of the Federal response, our architecture of command and control mechanisms as well as our existing structure of plans did not serve us well. Command centers in the Department of Homeland Security (DHS) and elsewhere in the Federal government had unclear, and often overlapping, roles and responsibilities that were exposed as flawed during this disaster. The Secretary of Homeland Security, is the President's principal Federal official for domestic incident management, but he had difficulty coordinating the disparate activities of Federal departments and agencies. The Secretary lacked real-time, accurate situational awareness of both the facts from the disaster area as well as the on-going response activities of the Federal, State, and local players.

The National Response Plan's Mission Assignment process proved to be far too bureaucratic to support the response to a catastrophe. Melvin Holden, Mayor-President of Baton Rouge, Louisiana, noted that, "requirements for paper work and form completions hindered immediate action and deployment of people and materials to assist in rescue and recovery efforts."[4] Far too often, the process required numerous time consuming approval signatures and data processing steps prior to any action, delaying the response. As a result, many agencies took action under their own independent authorities while also responding to mission assignments from the Federal Emergency Management Agency (FEMA), creating further process confusion and potential duplication of efforts.

This lack of coordination at the Federal headquarters-level reflected confusing organizational structures in the field. As noted in the *Week of Crisis* chapter, because the Principal Federal Official (PFO) has coordination authority but lacks statutory authority over the Federal Coordinating Officer (FCO), inefficiencies resulted when the second PFO was appointed. The first PFO appointed for Katrina did not have this problem because, as the Director of FEMA, he was able to directly oversee the FCOs because they fell under his supervisory authority.[5] Future plans should ensure that the PFO has the authority required to execute these responsibilities.

Moreover, DHS did not establish its NRP-specified disaster site multi-agency coordination center—the Joint Field Office (JFO)—until after the height of the crisis.[6] Further, without subordinate JFO structures to coordinate Federal response actions near the major incident sites, Federal response efforts in New Orleans were not initially well-coordinated.[7]

Lastly, the Emergency Support Functions (ESFs) did not function as envisioned in the NRP. First, since the ESFs do not easily integrate into the NIMS Incident Command System (ICS) structure, competing systems were implemented in the field – one based on the ESF structure and a second based on the ICS. Compounding the coordination problem, the agencies assigned ESF responsibilities did not respect the role of the PFO. As VADM Thad Allen stated, "The ESF structure currently prevents us from coordinating effectively because if agencies responsible for their respective ESFs do not like the instructions they are receiving from the PFO at the field level, they go to their headquarters in Washington to get decisions reversed. This is convoluted, inefficient, and inappropriate during emergency conditions. Time equals lives saved."

Knowledge and Practice in the Plans

At the most fundamental level, part of the explanation for why the response to Katrina did not go as planned is that key decision-makers at all levels simply were not familiar with the plans. The NRP was relatively new to many at the Federal, State, and local levels before the events of Hurricane Katrina.[8] This lack of understanding of the "National" plan not surprisingly resulted in ineffective coordination of the Federal, State, and local response. Additionally, the NRP itself provides only the 'base plan' outlining the overall elements of a response: Federal departments and agencies were required to develop supporting operational plans and standard operating procedures (SOPs) to integrate their activities into the national response.[9] In almost all cases, the integrating SOPs were either non-existent or still under development when Hurricane Katrina hit. Consequently, some of the specific procedures and processes of the NRP were not properly implemented, and Federal partners had to operate without any prescribed guidelines or chains of command.

Furthermore, the JFO staff and other deployed Federal personnel often lacked a working knowledge of NIMS or even a basic understanding of ICS principles. As a result, valuable time and resources were diverted to provide on-the-job ICS training to Federal personnel assigned to the JFO. This inability to place trained personnel in the JFO had a detrimental effect on operations, as there were not enough qualified persons to staff all of the required positions. We must require all incident management personnel to have a working knowledge of NIMS and ICS principles.

Insufficient Regional Planning and Coordination

The final structural flaw in our current system for national preparedness is the weakness of our regional planning and coordination structures. Guidance to governments at all levels is essential to ensure adequate preparedness for major disasters across the Nation. To this end, the Interim National Preparedness Goal (NPG) and Target Capabilities List (TCL) can assist Federal, State, and local governments to: identify and define required capabilities and what levels of those capabilities are needed; establish priorities within a resource-constrained environment; clarify and understand roles and responsibilities in the national network of homeland security capabilities; and develop mutual aid agreements.

Since incorporating FEMA in March 2003, DHS has spread FEMA's planning and coordination capabilities and responsibilities among DHS's other offices and bureaus. DHS also did not maintain the personnel and resources of FEMA's regional offices.[10] FEMA's ten regional offices are responsible for assisting multiple States and planning for disasters, developing mitigation programs, and meeting their needs when major disasters occur. During Katrina, eight out of the ten FEMA Regional Directors were serving in an acting capacity and four of the six FEMA headquarters operational division directors were serving in an acting capacity. While qualified acting directors filled in, it placed extra burdens on a staff that was already stretched to meet the needs left by the vacancies.

Additionally, many FEMA programs that were operated out of the FEMA regions, such as the State and local liaison program and all grant programs, have moved to DHS headquarters in Washington. When programs operate out of regional offices, closer relationships are developed among all levels of government, providing for stronger relationships at all levels. By the same token, regional personnel must remember that they represent the interests of the Federal government and must be cautioned against losing objectivity or becoming mere advocates of State and local interests. However, these relationships are critical when a crisis situation develops, because individuals who have worked and trained together daily will work together more effectively during a crisis.

> **LESSON LEARNED:** The Federal government should work with its homeland security partners in revising existing plans, ensuring a functional operational structure—including within regions—and establishing a clear, accountable process for all National preparedness efforts. In doing so, the Federal government must:
> - Ensure that Executive Branch agencies are organized, trained, and equipped to perform their response roles.
> - Finalize and implement the National Preparedness Goal.

Critical Challenge: Integrated Use of Military Capabilities

The Federal response to Hurricane Katrina demonstrates that the Department of Defense (DOD) has the capability to play a critical role in the Nation's response to catastrophic events. During the Katrina response, DOD – both National Guard and active duty forces – demonstrated that along with the Coast Guard it was one of the only Federal departments that possessed real operational capabilities to translate Presidential decisions into prompt, effective action on the ground. In addition to possessing operational personnel in large numbers that have been trained and equipped for their missions, DOD brought robust communications infrastructure, logistics, and planning capabilities. Since DOD, first and foremost, has its critical overseas mission, the solution to improving the Federal response to future catastrophes cannot simply be *"let the Department of Defense do it."* Yet DOD capabilities must be better identified and integrated into the Nation's response plans.

The Federal response to Hurricane Katrina highlighted various challenges in the use of military capabilities during domestic incidents. For instance, limitations under Federal law and DOD policy caused the active duty military to be dependent on requests for assistance. These limitations resulted in a slowed application of DOD resources during the initial response. Further, active duty military and National Guard operations were not coordinated and served two different bosses, one the President and the other the Governor.

Limitations to Department of Defense Response Authority

For Federal domestic disaster relief operations, DOD currently uses a "pull" system that provides support to civil authorities based upon specific requests from local, State, or Federal authorities.[11] This process can be slow and bureaucratic. Assigning active duty military forces or capabilities to support disaster relief efforts usually requires a request from FEMA,[12] an assessment by DOD on whether the request can be supported, approval by the Secretary of Defense or his designated representative, and a mission assignment for the military forces or capabilities to provide the requested support. From the time a request is initiated until the military force or capability is delivered to the disaster site requires a 21-step process.[13] While this overly bureaucratic approach has been adequate for most disasters, in a catastrophic event like Hurricane Katrina the delays inherent in this "pull" system of responding to requests resulted in critical needs not being met.[14] One could imagine a situation in which a catastrophic event is of such a magnitude that it would require an even greater role for the Department of Defense. For these reasons, we should both expedite the mission assignment request and the approval process, but also define the circumstances under which we will push resources to State and local governments absent a request.

Unity of Effort among Active Duty Forces and the National Guard

In the overall response to Hurricane Katrina, separate command structures for active duty military and the National Guard hindered their unity of effort. U.S. Northern Command (USNORTHCOM) commanded active duty forces, while each State government commanded its National Guard forces. For the first two days of Katrina response operations, USNORTHCOM did not have situational awareness of what forces the National Guard had on the ground. Joint Task Force Katrina (JTF-Katrina) simply could not operate at full efficiency when it lacked visibility of over half the military forces in the disaster area.[15] Neither the Louisiana National Guard nor JTF-Katrina had a good sense for where each other's forces were located or what they were doing. For example, the JTF-Katrina Engineering Directorate had not been able to coordinate with National Guard forces in the New Orleans area. As a result, some units were not immediately assigned missions matched to on-the-ground requirements. Further, FEMA requested assistance from DOD without knowing what State National Guard forces had already deployed to fill the same needs.[16]

Also, the Commanding General of JTF-Katrina and the Adjutant Generals (TAGs) of Louisiana and Mississippi had only a coordinating relationship, with no formal command relationship established. This resulted in confusion over roles and responsibilities between National Guard and Federal forces and highlights the need for a more unified command structure.[17]

Structure and Resources of the National Guard

As demonstrated during the Hurricane Katrina response, the National Guard Bureau (NGB) is a significant joint force provider for homeland security missions. Throughout the response, the NGB provided continuous and integrated reporting of all National Guard assets deployed in both a Federal and non-Federal status to USNORTHCOM, Joint Forces Command, Pacific Command, and the Assistant Secretary of Defense for Homeland Defense. This is an important step toward achieving unity of effort. However, NGB's role in homeland security is not yet clearly defined. The Chief of the NGB has made a recommendation to the Secretary of Defense that NGB be chartered as a joint activity of the DOD.[18] Achieving these efforts will serve as the foundation for National Guard transformation and provide a total joint force capability for homeland security missions.[19]

> ***LESSON LEARNED:*** The Departments of Homeland Security and Defense should jointly plan for the Department of Defense's support of Federal response activities as well as those extraordinary circumstances when it is appropriate for the Department of Defense to lead the Federal response. In addition, the Department of Defense should ensure the transformation of the National Guard is focused on increased integration with active duty forces for homeland security plans and activities.

Critical Challenge: Communications

Hurricane Katrina destroyed an unprecedented portion of the core communications infrastructure throughout the Gulf Coast region. As described earlier in the Report, the storm debilitated 911 emergency call centers, disrupting local emergency services.[20] Nearly three million customers lost telephone service. Broadcast communications, including 50 percent of area radio stations and 44 percent of area television stations, similarly were affected.[21] More than 50,000 utility poles were toppled in Mississippi alone, meaning that even if telephone call centers and electricity generation capabilities were functioning, the connections to the customers were broken.[22] Accordingly, the communications challenges across the Gulf Coast region in Hurricane Katrina's wake were more a problem of basic *operability*,[23] than one of equipment or system *interoperability*.[24] The complete devastation of the communications infrastructure left emergency responders and citizens without a reliable network across which they could coordinate.[25]

Although Federal, State, and local agencies had communications plans and assets in place, these plans and assets were neither sufficient nor adequately integrated to respond effectively to the disaster.[26] Many available communications assets were not utilized fully because there was no national, State-wide, or regional communications plan to incorporate them. For example, despite their contributions to the response effort, the U.S. Department of Agriculture (USDA) Forest Service's radio cache—the largest civilian cache of radios in the United States—had additional radios available that were not utilized.[27]

Federal, State, and local governments have not yet completed a comprehensive strategy to improve operability and interoperability to meet the needs of emergency responders.[28] This inability to connect multiple communications plans and architectures clearly impeded coordination and communication at the Federal, State, and local levels. A comprehensive, national emergency communications strategy is needed to confront the challenges of incorporating existing equipment and practices into a constantly changing technological and cultural environment.[29]

> **LESSON LEARNED:** The Department of Homeland Security should review our current laws, policies, plans, and strategies relevant to communications. Upon the conclusion of this review, the Homeland Security Council, with support from the Office of Science and Technology Policy, should develop a National Emergency Communications Strategy that supports communications operability and interoperability.

Critical Challenge: Logistics and Evacuation

The scope of Hurricane Katrina's devastation, the effects on critical infrastructure in the region, and the debilitation of State and local response capabilities combined to produce a massive requirement for Federal resources. The existing planning and operational structure for delivering critical resources and humanitarian aid clearly proved to be inadequate to the task. The highly bureaucratic supply processes of the Federal government were not sufficiently flexible and efficient, and failed to leverage the private sector and 21st Century advances in supply chain management.

Throughout the response, Federal resource managers had great difficulty determining what resources were needed, what resources were available, and where those resources were at any given point in time. Even when Federal resource managers had a clear understanding of what was needed, they often could not readily determine whether the Federal government had that asset, or what alternative sources might be able to provide it. As discussed in the *Week of Crisis* chapter, even when an agency came directly to FEMA with a list of available resources that would be useful during the response, there was no effective mechanism for efficiently integrating and deploying these resources. Nor was there an easy way to find out whether an alternative source, such as the private sector or a charity, might be able to better fill the need. Finally, FEMA's lack of a real-time asset-tracking system – a necessity for successful 21st Century businesses – left Federal managers in the dark regarding the status of resources once they were shipped.[30]

Our logistics system for the 21st Century should be a fully transparent, four-tiered system. First, we must encourage and ultimately require State and local governments to pre-contract for resources and commodities that will be critical for responding to all hazards. Second, if these arrangements fail, affected State governments should ask for additional resources from other States through the Emergency Management Assistance Compact (EMAC) process. Third, if such interstate mutual aid proves insufficient, the Federal government, having the benefit of full transparency, must be able to assist State and local governments to move commodities regionally. But in the end, FEMA must be able to supplement and, in catastrophic incidents, supplant State and local systems with a fully modern approach to commodity management.

> **LESSON LEARNED:** The Department of Homeland Security, in coordination with State and local governments and the private sector, should develop a modern, flexible, and transparent logistics system. This system should be based on established contracts for stockpiling commodities at the local level for emergencies and the provision of goods and services during emergencies. The Federal government must develop the capacity to conduct large-scale logistical operations that supplement and, if necessary, replace State and local logistical systems by leveraging resources within both the public sector and the private sector.

With respect to evacuation—fundamentally a State and local responsibility—the Hurricane Katrina experience demonstrates that the Federal government must be prepared to fulfill the mission if State and local efforts fail. Unfortunately, a lack of prior planning combined with poor operational coordination generated a weak Federal performance in supporting the evacuation of those most vulnerable in New Orleans and throughout the Gulf Coast following Katrina's landfall. The Federal effort lacked critical elements of prior planning, such as evacuation routes, communications, transportation assets, evacuee processing, and coordination with State, local, and non-governmental officials receiving and sheltering the evacuees. Because of poor situational awareness and communications throughout the evacuation operation, FEMA had difficulty providing buses through ESF-1, Transportation, (with the Department of Transportation as the coordinating agency).[31] FEMA also had difficulty delivering food, water, and other critical commodities to people waiting to be evacuated, most significantly at the Superdome.[32]

> **LESSON LEARNED:** The Department of Transportation, in coordination with other appropriate departments of the Executive Branch, must also be prepared to conduct mass evacuation operations when disasters overwhelm or incapacitate State and local governments.

Critical Challenge: Search and Rescue

After Hurricane Katrina made landfall, rising floodwaters stranded thousands in New Orleans on rooftops, requiring a massive civil search and rescue operation. The Coast Guard, FEMA Urban Search and Rescue (US&R) Task Forces,33 and DOD forces,[34] in concert with State and local emergency responders from across the country, courageously combined to rescue tens of thousands of people. With extraordinary ingenuity and tenacity, Federal, State, and local emergency responders plucked people from rooftops while avoiding urban hazards not normally encountered during waterborne rescue.[35]

Yet many of these courageous lifesavers were put at unnecessary risk by a structure that failed to support them effectively. The overall search and rescue effort demonstrated the need for greater coordination between US&R, the Coast Guard, and military responders who, because of their very different missions, train and operate in very different ways. For example, Urban Search and Rescue (US&R) teams had a particularly challenging situation since they are neither trained nor equipped to perform water rescue. Thus they could not immediately rescue people trapped by the flood waters.[36]

Furthermore, lacking an integrated search and rescue incident command, the various agencies were unable to effectively coordinate their operations.[37] This meant that multiple rescue teams were sent to the same areas, while leaving others uncovered.[38] When successful rescues were made, there was no formal direction on where to take those rescued.[39] Too often rescuers had to leave victims at drop-off points and landing zones that had insufficient logistics, medical, and communications resources, such as atop the I-10 cloverleaf near the Superdome.[40]

> **LESSON LEARNED:** The Department of Homeland Security should lead an interagency review of current policies and procedures to ensure effective integration of all Federal search and rescue assets during disaster response.

Critical Challenge: Public Safety and Security

State and local governments have a fundamental responsibility to provide for the public safety and security of their residents. During disasters, the Federal government provides law enforcement assistance only when those resources are overwhelmed or depleted.[41] Almost immediately following Hurricane Katrina's landfall, law and order began to deteriorate in New Orleans. The city's overwhelmed police force–70 percent of which were themselves victims of the disaster—did not have the capacity to arrest every person witnessed committing a crime, and many more crimes were undoubtedly neither observed by police nor reported. The resulting lawlessness in New Orleans significantly impeded—and in some cases temporarily halted—relief efforts and delayed restoration of essential private sector services such as power, water, and telecommunications.[42]

The Federal law enforcement response to Hurricane Katrina was a crucial enabler to the reconstitution of the New Orleans Police Department's command structure as well as the larger criminal justice system. Joint leadership from the Department of Justice and the Department of Homeland Security integrated the available Federal assets into the remaining local police structure and divided the Federal law enforcement agencies into corresponding New Orleans Police Department districts.

While the deployment of Federal law enforcement capability to New Orleans in a dangerous and chaotic environment significantly contributed to the restoration of law and order, pre-event collaborative planning between

Federal, State, and local officials would have improved the response. Indeed, Federal, State, and local law enforcement officials performed admirably in spite of a system that should have better supported them. Local, State, and Federal law enforcement were ill-prepared and ill-positioned to respond efficiently and effectively to the crisis.

In the end, it was clear that Federal law enforcement support to State and local officials required greater coordination, unity of command, collaborative planning and training with State and local law enforcement, as well as detailed implementation guidance. For example, the Federal law enforcement response effort did not take advantage of all law enforcement assets embedded across Federal departments and agencies. Several departments promptly offered their assistance, but their law enforcement assets were incorporated only after weeks had passed, or not at all.[43]

Coordination challenges arose even after Federal law enforcement personnel arrived in New Orleans. For example, several departments and agencies reported that the procedures for becoming deputized to enforce State law were cumbersome and inefficient. In Louisiana, a State Police attorney had to physically be present to swear in Federal agents. Many Federal law enforcement agencies also had to complete a cumbersome Federal deputization process.[44] New Orleans was then confronted with a rapid influx of law enforcement officers from a multitude of States and jurisdictions—each with their own policies and procedures, uniforms, and rules on the use of force—which created the need for a command structure to coordinate their efforts.[45]

Hurricane Katrina also crippled the region's criminal justice system. Problems such as a significant loss of accountability of many persons under law enforcement supervision,[46] closure of the court systems in the disaster,[47] and hasty evacuation of prisoners[48] were largely attributable to the absence of contingency plans at all levels of government.

> **LESSON LEARNED:** The Department of Justice, in coordination with the Department of Homeland Security, should examine Federal responsibilities for support to State and local law enforcement and criminal justice systems during emergencies and then build operational plans, procedures, and policies to ensure an effective Federal law enforcement response.

Critical Challenge: Public Health and Medical Support

Hurricane Katrina created enormous public health and medical challenges, especially in Louisiana and Mississippi—States with public health infrastructures that ranked 49th and 50th in the Nation, respectively.[49] But it was the subsequent flooding of New Orleans that imposed catastrophic public health conditions on the people of southern Louisiana and forced an unprecedented mobilization of Federal public health and medical assets. Tens of thousands of people required medical care. Over 200,000 people with chronic medical conditions, displaced by the storm and isolated by the flooding, found themselves without access to their usual medications and sources of medical care. Several large hospitals were totally destroyed and many others were rendered inoperable. Nearly all smaller health care facilities were shut down. Although public health and medical support efforts restored the capabilities of many of these facilities, the region's health care infrastructure sustained extraordinary damage.[50]

Most local and State public health and medical assets were overwhelmed by these conditions, placing even greater responsibility on federally deployed personnel. Immediate challenges included the identification, triage and treatment of acutely sick and injured patients; the management of chronic medical conditions in large numbers of evacuees with special health care needs; the assessment, communication and mitigation of public health risk; and the provision of assistance to State and local health officials to quickly reestablish health care delivery systems and public health infrastructures.[51]

Despite the success of Federal, State, and local personnel in meeting this enormous challenge, obstacles at all levels reduced the reach and efficiency of public health and medical support efforts. In addition, the coordination of Federal assets within and across agencies was poor. The cumbersome process for the authorization of reimbursement for medical and public health services provided by Federal agencies created substantial delays and frustration among health care providers, patients and the general public.[52] In some cases, significant delays slowed the arrival of Federal assets to critical locations.[53] In other cases, large numbers of Federal assets were deployed, only to be grossly underutilized.[54] Thousands of medical volunteers were sought by the Department of Health and

Human Services (HHS), and though they were informed that they would likely not be needed unless notified otherwise, many volunteers reported that they received no message to that effect.[55] These inefficiencies were the products of a fragmented command structure for medical response; inadequate evacuation of patients; weak State and local public health infrastructures;[56] insufficient pre-storm risk communication to the public;[57] and the absence of a uniform electronic health record system.

> **LESSON LEARNED:** In coordination with the Department of Homeland Security and other homeland security partners, the Department of Health and Human Services should strengthen the Federal government's capability to provide public health and medical support during a crisis. This will require the improvement of command and control of public health resources, the development of deliberate plans, an additional investment in deployable operational resources, and an acceleration of the initiative to foster the widespread use of interoperable electronic health records systems.

Critical Challenge: Human Services

Disasters—especially those of catastrophic proportions—produce many victims whose needs exceed the capacity of State and local resources. These victims who depend on the Federal government for assistance fit into one of two categories: (1) those who need Federal disaster-related assistance, and (2) those who need continuation of government assistance they were receiving before the disaster, plus additional disaster-related assistance. Hurricane Katrina produced many thousands of both categories of victims.[58]

The Federal government maintains a wide array of human service programs to provide assistance to special-needs populations, including disaster victims.[59] Collectively, these programs provide a safety net to particularly vulnerable populations.

The Emergency Support Function 6 (ESF-6) Annex to the NRP assigns responsibility for the emergency delivery of human services to FEMA. While FEMA is the coordinator of ESF-6, it shares primary agency responsibility with the American Red Cross.[60] The Red Cross focuses on mass care (*e.g.* care for people in shelters), and FEMA continues the human services components for ESF-6 as the mass care effort transitions from the response to the recovery phase.[61] The human services provided under ESF-6 include: counseling; special-needs population support; immediate and short-term assistance for individuals, households, and groups dealing with the aftermath of a disaster; and expedited processing of applications for Federal benefits.[62] The NRP calls for "reducing duplication of effort and benefits, to the extent possible," to include "streamlining assistance as appropriate."[63]

Prior to Katrina's landfall along the Gulf Coast and during the subsequent several weeks, Federal preparation for distributing individual assistance proved frustrating and inadequate. Because the NRP did not mandate a single Federal point of contact for all assistance and required FEMA to merely coordinate assistance delivery, disaster victims confronted an enormously bureaucratic, inefficient, and frustrating process that failed to effectively meet their needs. The Federal government's system for distribution of human services was not sufficiently responsive to the circumstances of a large number of victims—many of whom were particularly vulnerable—who were forced to navigate a series of complex processes to obtain critical services in a time of extreme duress. As mentioned in the preceding chapter, the Disaster Recovery Centers (DRCs) did not provide victims single-point access to apply for the wide array of Federal assistance programs.

> **LESSON LEARNED:** The Department of Health and Human Services should coordinate with other departments of the Executive Branch, as well as State governments and non-governmental organizations, to develop a robust, comprehensive, and integrated system to deliver human services during disasters so that victims are able to receive Federal and State assistance in a simple and seamless manner. In particular, this system should be designed to provide victims a consumer oriented, simple, effective, and single encounter from which they can receive assistance.

Critical Challenge: Mass Care and Housing

Hurricane Katrina resulted in the largest national housing crisis since the Dust Bowl of the 1930s. The impact of this massive displacement was felt throughout the country, with Gulf residents relocating to all fifty States and the

District of Columbia.[64] Prior to the storm's landfall, an exodus of people fled its projected path, creating an urgent need for suitable shelters. Those with the willingness and ability to evacuate generally found temporary shelter or housing. However, the thousands of people in New Orleans who were either unable to move due to health reasons or lack of transportation, or who simply did not choose to comply with the mandatory evacuation order, had significant difficulty finding suitable shelter after the hurricane had devastated the city.[65]

Overall, Federal, State, and local plans were inadequate for a catastrophe that had been anticipated for years. Despite the vast shortcomings of the Superdome and other shelters, State and local officials had no choice but to direct thousands of individuals to such sites immediately after the hurricane struck. Furthermore, the Federal government's capability to provide housing solutions to the displaced Gulf Coast population has proved to be far too slow, bureaucratic, and inefficient.

The Federal shortfall resulted from a lack of interagency coordination to relocate and house people. FEMA's actions often were inconsistent with evacuees' needs and preferences. Despite offers from the Departments of Veterans Affairs (VA), Housing and Urban Development (HUD) and Agriculture (USDA) as well as the private sector to provide thousands of housing units nationwide, FEMA focused its housing efforts on cruise ships and trailers, which were expensive and perceived by some to be a means to force evacuees to return to New Orleans.[66] HUD, with extensive expertise and perspective on large-scale housing challenges and its nation-wide relationships with State public housing authorities, was not substantially engaged by FEMA in the housing process until late in the effort.[67] FEMA's temporary and long-term housing efforts also suffered from the failure to pre-identify workable sites and available land and the inability to take advantage of housing units available with other Federal agencies.

> **LESSON LEARNED:** Using established Federal core competencies and all available resources, the Department of Housing and Urban Development, in coordination with other departments of the Executive Branch with housing stock, should develop integrated plans and bolstered capabilities for the temporary and long-term housing of evacuees. The American Red Cross and the Department of Homeland Security should retain responsibility and improve the process of mass care and sheltering during disasters.

Critical Challenge: Public Communications

The Federal government's dissemination of essential public information prior to Hurricane Katrina's Gulf landfall is one of the positive lessons learned. The many professionals at the National Oceanic and Atmospheric Administration (NOAA) and the National Hurricane Center worked with diligence and determination in disseminating weather reports and hurricane track predictions as described in the *Pre-landfall* chapter. This includes disseminating warnings and forecasts via NOAA Radio and the internet, which operates in conjunction with the Emergency Alert System (EAS).[68] We can be certain that their efforts saved lives.

However, more could have been done by officials at all levels of government. For example, the EAS—a mechanism for Federal, State and local officials to communicate disaster information and instructions—was not utilized by State and local officials in Louisiana, Mississippi or Alabama prior to Katrina's landfall.[69]

Further, without timely, accurate information or the ability to communicate, public affairs officers at all levels could not provide updates to the media and to the public. It took several weeks before public affairs structures, such as the Joint Information Centers, were adequately resourced and operating at full capacity. In the meantime, Federal, State, and local officials gave contradictory messages to the public, creating confusion and feeding the perception that government sources lacked credibility. On September 1, conflicting views of New Orleans emerged with positive statements by some Federal officials that contradicted a more desperate picture painted by reporters in the streets.[70] The media, operating 24/7, gathered and aired uncorroborated information which interfered with ongoing emergency response efforts.[71] The Federal public communications and public affairs response proved inadequate and ineffective.

> **LESSON LEARNED:** The Department of Homeland Security should develop an integrated public communications plan to better inform, guide, and reassure the American public before, during, and after a catastrophe. The Department of Homeland Security should enable this plan with operational capabilities to deploy coordinated public affairs teams during a crisis.

Critical Challenge: Critical Infrastructure and Impact Assessment

Hurricane Katrina had a significant impact on many sectors of the region's "critical infrastructure," especially the energy sector.[72] The Hurricane temporarily caused the shutdown of most crude oil and natural gas production in the Gulf of Mexico as well as much of the refining capacity in Louisiana, Mississippi, and Alabama. "[M]ore than ten percent of the Nation's imported crude oil enters through the Louisiana Offshore Oil Port"[73] adding to the impact on the energy sector. Additionally, eleven petroleum refineries, or one-sixth of the Nation's refining capacity, were shut down.[74] Across the region more than 2.5 million customers suffered power outages across Louisiana, Mississippi, and Alabama.[75]

While there were successes, the Federal government's ability to protect and restore the operation of priority national critical infrastructure was hindered by four interconnected problems. First, the NRP-guided response did not account for the need to coordinate critical infrastructure protection and restoration efforts across the Emergency Support Functions (ESFs). The NRP designates the protection and restoration of critical infrastructure as essential objectives of five ESFs: Transportation; Communications; Public Works and Engineering; Agriculture; and Energy.[76] Although these critical infrastructures are necessary to assist in all other response and restoration efforts, there are seventeen critical infrastructure and key resource sectors whose needs must be coordinated across virtually every ESF during response and recovery.[77] Second, the Federal government did not adequately coordinate its actions with State and local protection and restoration efforts. In fact, the Federal government created confusion by responding to individualized requests in an inconsistent manner.[78] Third, Federal, State, and local officials responded to Hurricane Katrina without a comprehensive understanding of the interdependencies of the critical infrastructure sectors in each geographic area and the potential national impact of their decisions. For example, an energy company arranged to have generators shipped to facilities where they were needed to restore the flow of oil to the entire mid-Atlantic United States. However, FEMA regional representatives diverted these generators to hospitals. While lifesaving efforts are always the first priority, there was no overall awareness of the competing important needs of the two requests. Fourth, the Federal government lacked the timely, accurate, and relevant ground-truth information necessary to evaluate which critical infrastructures were damaged, inoperative, or both. The FEMA teams that were deployed to assess damage to the regions did not focus on critical infrastructure and did not have the expertise necessary to evaluate protection and restoration needs.[79]

The Interim National Infrastructure Protection Plan (NIPP) provides strategic-level guidance for all Federal, State, and local entities to use in prioritizing infrastructure for protection.[80] However, there is no supporting implementation plan to execute these actions during a natural disaster. Federal, State, and local officials need an implementation plan for critical infrastructure protection and restoration that can be shared across the Federal government, State and local governments, and with the private sector, to provide them with the necessary background to make informed preparedness decisions with limited resources.

> **LESSON LEARNED:** The Department of Homeland Security, working collaboratively with the private sector, should revise the National Response Plan and finalize the Interim National Infrastructure Protection Plan to be able to rapidly assess the impact of a disaster on critical infrastructure. We must use this knowledge to inform Federal response and prioritization decisions and to support infrastructure restoration in order to save lives and mitigate the impact of the disaster on the Nation.

Critical Challenge: Environmental Hazards and Debris Removal

The Federal clean-up effort for Hurricane Katrina was an immense undertaking. The storm impact caused the spill of over seven million gallons of oil into Gulf Coast waterways. Additionally, it flooded three Superfund[81] sites in the New Orleans area, and destroyed or compromised numerous drinking water facilities and wastewater treatment plants along the Gulf Coast.[82] The storm's collective environmental damage, while not creating the "toxic soup" portrayed in the media, nonetheless did create a potentially hazardous environment for emergency responders and the general public.[83] In response, the Environmental Protection Agency (EPA) and the Coast Guard jointly led an interagency environmental assessment and recovery effort, cleaning up the seven million gallons of oil and resolving over 2,300 reported cases of pollution.[84]

While this response effort was commendable, Federal officials could have improved the identification of environmental hazards and communication of appropriate warnings to emergency responders and the public. For example, the relatively small number of personnel available during the critical week after landfall were unable to conduct a rapid and comprehensive environmental assessment of the approximately 80 square miles flooded in New Orleans, let alone the nearly 93,000 square miles affected by the hurricane.[85]

Competing priorities hampered efforts to assess the environment. Moreover, although the process used to identify environmental hazards provides accurate results, these results are not prompt enough to provide meaningful information to responders. Furthermore, there must be a comprehensive plan to accurately and quickly communicate this critical information to the emergency responders and area residents who need it. [86] Had such a plan existed, the mixed messages from Federal, State, and local officials on the reentry into New Orleans could have been avoided.

Debris Removal

State and local governments are normally responsible for debris removal. However, in the event of a disaster in which State and local governments are overwhelmed and request assistance, the Federal government can provide two forms of assistance: debris removal by the U.S. Army Corps of Engineers (USACE) or other Federal agencies, or reimbursement for locally contracted debris removal.[87]

Hurricane Katrina created an estimated 118 million cubic yards of debris. In just five months, 71 million cubic yards of debris have been removed from Louisiana, Mississippi, and Alabama. In comparison, it took six months to remove the estimated 20 million cubic yards of debris created by Hurricane Andrew.[88]

However, the unnecessarily complicated rules for removing debris from private property hampered the response.[89] In addition, greater collaboration among Federal, State, and local officials as well as an enhanced public communication program could have improved the effectiveness of the Federal response.

> **LESSON LEARNED:** The Department of Homeland Security, in coordination with the Environmental Protection Agency, should oversee efforts to improve the Federal government's capability to quickly gather environmental data and to provide the public and emergency responders the most accurate information available, to determine whether it is safe to operate in a disaster environment or to return after evacuation. In addition, the Department of Homeland Security should work with its State and local homeland security partners to plan and to coordinate an integrated approach to debris removal during and after a disaster.

Critical Challenge: Managing Offers of Foreign Assistance and Inquiries Regarding Affected Foreign Nationals

Our experience with the tragedies of September 11th and Hurricane Katrina underscored that our domestic crises have international implications. Soon after the extent of Hurricane Katrina's damage became known, the United States became the beneficiary of an incredible international outpouring of assistance. One hundred fifty-one (151) nations and international organizations offered financial or material assistance to support relief efforts.[90] Also, we found that among the victims were foreign nationals who were in the country on business, vacation, or as residents. Not surprisingly, foreign governments sought information regarding the safety of their citizens.

We were not prepared to make the best use of foreign support. Some foreign governments sought to contribute aid that the United States could not accept or did not require. In other cases, needed resources were tied up by bureaucratic red tape.[91] But more broadly, we lacked the capability to prioritize and integrate such a large quantity of foreign assistance into the ongoing response. Absent an implementation plan for the prioritization and integration of foreign material assistance, valuable resources went unused, and many donor countries became frustrated.[92] While we ultimately overcame these obstacles amidst the crisis, our experience underscores the need for pre-crisis planning.

Nor did we have the mechanisms in place to provide foreign governments with whatever knowledge we had regarding the status of their nationals. Despite the fact that many victims of the September 11, 2001, tragedy were foreign nationals, the NRP does not take into account foreign populations (*e.g.* long-term residents, students, businessmen, tourists, and foreign government officials) affected by a domestic catastrophe. In addition, Federal, State, and local emergency response officials have not included assistance to foreign nationals in their response planning.

Many foreign governments, as well as the family and friends of foreign nationals, looked to the Department of State for information regarding the safety and location of their citizens after Hurricane Katrina. The absence of a central system to manage and promptly respond to inquires about affected foreign nationals led to confusion.[93]

> ***LESSON LEARNED:*** The Department of State, in coordination with the Department of Homeland Security, should review and revise policies, plans, and procedures for the management of foreign disaster assistance. In addition, this review should clarify responsibilities and procedures for handling inquiries regarding affected foreign nationals.

Critical Challenge: Non-governmental Aid

Over the course of the Hurricane Katrina response, a significant capability for response resided in organizations outside of the government. Non-governmental and faith-based organizations, as well as the private sector all made substantial contributions. Unfortunately, the Nation did not always make effective use of these contributions because we had not effectively planned for integrating them into the overall response effort.

Even in the best of circumstances, government alone cannot deliver all disaster relief. Often, non-governmental organizations (NGOs) are the quickest means of providing local relief, but perhaps most importantly, they provide a compassionate, human face to relief efforts. We must recognize that NGOs play a fundamental role in response and recovery efforts and will contribute in ways that are, in many cases, more efficient and effective than the Federal government's response. We must plan for their participation and treat them as valued and necessary partners.

The number of volunteer, non-profit, faith-based, and private sector entities that aided in the Hurricane Katrina relief effort was truly extraordinary. Nearly every national, regional, and local charitable organization in the United States, and many from abroad, contributed aid to the victims of the storm. Trained volunteers from member organizations of the National Volunteer Organizations Active in Disaster (NVOAD), the American Red Cross, Medical Reserve Corps (MRC), Citizen Emergency Response Team (CERT), as well as untrained volunteers from across the United States, deployed to Louisiana, Mississippi, and Alabama.

Government sponsored volunteer organizations also played a critical role in providing relief and assistance. For example, the USA Freedom Corps persuaded numerous non-profit organizations and the Governor's State Service Commissions to list their hurricane relief volunteer opportunities in the USA Freedom Corps volunteer search engine. The USA Freedom Corps also worked with the Corporation for National and Community Service, which helped to create a new, people-driven "Katrina Resource Center" to help volunteers connect their resources with needs on the ground.[94] In addition, 14,000 Citizen Corps volunteers supported response and recovery efforts around the country.[95] This achievement demonstrates that seamless coordination among government agencies and volunteer organizations is possible when they build cooperative relationships and conduct joint planning and exercises before an incident occurs.[96]

Faith-based organizations also provided extraordinary services. For example, more than 9,000 Southern Baptist Convention of the North American Mission Board volunteers from forty-one states served in Texas, Louisiana, Mississippi, Alabama, and Georgia. These volunteers ran mobile kitchens and recovery sites.[97] Many smaller, faith-based organizations, such as the Set Free Indeed Ministry in Baton Rouge, Louisiana, brought comfort and offered shelter to the survivors. They used their facilities and volunteers to distribute donated supplies to displaced persons and to meet their immediate needs.[98] Local churches independently established hundreds of "pop-up" shelters to house storm victims.[99]

More often than not, NGOs successfully contributed to the relief effort in spite of government obstacles and with almost no government support or direction. Time and again, government agencies did not effectively coordinate relief operations with NGOs. Often, government agencies failed to match relief needs with NGO and private sector capabilities. Even when agencies matched non-governmental aid with an identified need, there were problems moving goods, equipment, and people into the disaster area. For example, the government relief effort was unprepared to meet the fundamental food, housing, and operational needs of the surge volunteer force.

> **_LESSON LEARNED:_** The Federal response should better integrate the contributions of volunteers and non-governmental organizations into the broader national effort. This integration would be best achieved at the State and local levels, prior to future incidents. In particular, State and local governments must engage NGOs in the planning process, credential their personnel, and provide them the necessary resource support for their involvement in a joint response.

CHAPTER SIX: TRANSFORMING NATIONAL PREPAREDNESS

Hurricane Katrina was an extraordinary storm that caused destruction on a scale never before seen from a natural disaster in the United States. The continuing Federal response—the largest disaster relief and recovery effort in our Nation's history—likewise has been unprecedented and extraordinary. But what we owe the people of the Gulf Coast, and all Americans, is the best possible response.

We must expect more catastrophes like Hurricane Katrina—and possibly even worse. In fact, we will have compounded the tragedy if we fail to learn the lessons—good and bad—it has taught us and strengthen our system of preparedness and response. We cannot undo the mistakes of the past, but there is much we can do to learn from them and to be better prepared for the future. This is our duty.

The preceding chapter outlined in detail fourteen of the seventeen specific lessons the Federal government has learned from our response to Hurricane Katrina; the remaining three will be discussed more fully here. These seventeen lessons, and the 125 recommendations that flow from them, represent specific challenges for corrective action. But we also recognize that to overcome these challenges and fully accomplish the intent of the attendant recommendations, we require a *transformation* of our homeland security architecture.

In the aftermath of another American catastrophe—the terrorist attacks of September 11—we transformed our government architecture, policies, and strategies in a comprehensive effort to defeat terrorism and better protect and defend the homeland. With the creation of the Department of Homeland Security, the post of Director of National Intelligence, the passage of the USA PATRIOT Act, and the codification of both the National Counterterrorism Center and the National Counterproliferation Center, we have undertaken the most extensive reorganization of the Federal government since 1947.[1] We have created top-level policy guidance through the *National Security Strategy*, the *National Strategy for Homeland Security* and the *National Strategy for Combating Terrorism*, all of which identify strategic objectives to secure the United States, its citizens and interests from terrorist attacks.[2] Most important, we have pursued our policies and objectives through concrete action. In concert with our coalition partners, we have been on the offense, waging an unremitting campaign of direct and continuous action against our terrorist enemies and the deadly scourge of terror and intimidation more broadly. These actions, combined with an array of defensive measures at home and abroad, have enhanced the safety and security of the American people.

Preparedness is inextricably intertwined with our national security, counterterrorism, and homeland security strategies. As discussed throughout this report, we have taken essential steps over the past five years—through plans, policies, and guidelines such as the *National Response Plan*, the *National Incident Management System*, the *Interim National Infrastructure Protection Plan*, and the *Interim National Preparedness Goal*—to strengthen our ability to prepare for, protect against, respond to, and recover from the natural and man-made disasters that will occur.[3]

But we must go further. We must continue to build upon the foundation of national and homeland security we have established since 9/11 to improve our preparedness capabilities. Our response to Hurricane Katrina demonstrated the imperative to integrate and synchronize our policies, strategies, and plans—among all Federal, State, local, private sector, and community efforts and across all partners in the professions of prevention, protection, response, and recovery—into a unified system for homeland security. This unifying system will ensure *National Preparedness*.

> **National Preparedness** involves a continuous cycle of activity to develop the elements (e.g., plans, procedures, policies, training, and equipment) necessary to maximize the capability to prevent, protect against, respond to, and recover from domestic incidents, especially major events that require coordination among an appropriate combination of Federal, State, local, tribal, private sector, and non-governmental entities, in order to minimize the impact on lives, property, and the economy.
>
> —*Interim National Preparedness Goal*, March 2005[4]

Today there is a national consensus that we must be better prepared to respond to events like Hurricane Katrina. While we have constructed a system that effectively handles the demands of routine, limited natural and man-made disasters, our system clearly has structural flaws for addressing catastrophic incidents. But we as a Nation—Federal, State, and local governments; the private sector; as well as communities and individual citizens—have not developed a shared vision of or commitment to *preparedness*: what we must do to prevent (when possible), protect against, respond to, and recover from the next catastrophe. Without a shared vision that is acted upon by all levels of our Nation and encompasses the full range of our preparedness and response capabilities, we will not achieve a truly transformational *national* state of preparedness.

There are two immediate priorities for this transformation:

1. Define and implement a comprehensive National Preparedness System; and

2. Foster a new, robust Culture of Preparedness.

A NATIONAL PREPAREDNESS SYSTEM

Shortfalls in the Federal response to Hurricane Katrina highlight that our current homeland security architecture—to include policies, authorities, plans, doctrine, operational concepts, and resources at the Federal, State, local, private sector, and community levels—must be strengthened and transformed. At the most fundamental level, the current system fails to define Federal responsibility for national preparedness in catastrophic events. Nor does it establish clear, comprehensive goals along with an integrated means to measure their progress and achievement. Instead, the United States currently has guidelines and individual plans, across multiple agencies and levels of government that do not yet constitute an *integrated* national system that ensures unity of effort.[5]

In addition, as described in the narrative section of this report, the response to Hurricane Katrina demonstrated that our current system is too reactive in orientation. Our decades-old system, built on the precepts of federalism, has been based on a model whereby local and State governments wait to reach their limits and exhaust their resources before requesting Federal assistance. Federal agencies could and did take steps to prepare to extend support and assistance, but tended to provide little without a prior and specific request. In other words, the system was biased toward requests and the concept of "pull" rather than toward anticipatory actions and the proactive "push" of Federal resources.

While this approach has worked well in the majority of disasters and emergencies, catastrophic events like Hurricane Katrina are a different matter. The current homeland security environment—with the continuing threat of mass casualty terrorism and the constant risk of natural disasters—now demands that the Federal government actively prepare and encourage the Nation as a whole to plan, equip, train, and cooperate for all types of future emergencies, including the most catastrophic.

A useful model for our approach to homeland security is the Nation's approach to *national security*. Over the past six decades, we have created a highly successful national security system. This system is built on deliberate planning that assesses threats and risks, develops policies and strategies to manage them, identifies specific missions and supporting tasks, and matches the forces or capabilities to execute them. Operationally organized, it stresses the importance of unity of command from the President down to the commander in the field.

Perhaps most important, the national security system emphasizes feedback and periodic reassessment. Programs and forces are assessed for readiness and the degree to which they support their assigned missions and strategies on a continuing basis. Top level decision-makers periodically revisit their assessments of threats and risks, review their strategies and guidance, and revise their missions, plans, and budgets accordingly.[6]

This national security system was not created overnight. It has taken almost sixty years to build and refine. Beginning with the National Security Act of 1947-mandated creation of the Department of Defense, the Central Intelligence Agency, and the National Security Council (NSC), this system has evolved substantially through the years.[7] It has taken time to create a strong NSC that has integrated interagency policies and efforts. Similarly, it took decades to build first the Office of the Secretary of Defense and then the Joint Staff as the central management elements for the Department of Defense. We did not accomplish the complete intent of the 1947 reforms for national security system until Congress passed the *Goldwater-Nichols* defense reorganization legislation in 1986, and the Federal government put those reforms in place in following years.[8]

The lessons of the national security system's evolution will help us to transform our five-year old homeland security system. Of course, homeland security demands are complex. While responsibility for national security rests with the Federal government working with its international partners, the precepts of federalism make every level of government and region of the country both a contributor to, and responsible for, homeland security.

There are significant institutional and intergovernmental challenges to information and resource sharing as well as operational cooperation. These barriers stem from a multitude of factors—different cultures, lack of communication between departments and agencies, and varying procedures and working patterns among departments and agencies. Equally problematic, there is uneven coordination in pre-incident planning among State and local governments. For example, our States and territories developed fifty-six unique homeland security strategies, as have fifty high-threat, high-density urban areas.[9] Although each State and territory certainly confronts unique challenges, without coordination this planning approach makes the identification of common or national solutions difficult. Furthermore, our current approach to response planning does not sufficiently acknowledge how adjoining communities and regions can and do support each other. For example, there is wide disparity in emergency response capabilities across the country's many local jurisdictions. Yet we currently lack the means to assess and track what these disparities are and, consequently, how we must plan to account for them in a crisis.

The remainder of this section describes the key elements of the National Preparedness System. These include the guiding vision for preparedness as well as clarification of the Federal government's central role in organizing the national efforts of our homeland security partners. The section also explains the essential importance of building operational capabilities in the Federal government by: a) Strengthening the operational management capacity of the Department of Homeland Security and strengthening its field elements; b) Reinforcing the DHS role as incident manager for the Federal response; and c) Strengthening the response capabilities of other departments and agencies in the Federal government. This section also highlights the essential roles for training, education, and exercises as well as the importance of feedback—through readiness assessment and lessons learned—and processes for undertaking corrective actions. The section concludes with a discussion of the essential role of Congress in supporting the National Preparedness System and related transformation.

A Preparedness Vision

A National Preparedness System must begin with a common vision for preparedness—what end-state are we seeking to achieve and how do we plan to get there? In Homeland Security Presidential Directive 8 (HSPD-8), the President called for the creation of a comprehensive national preparedness system, starting with a "national domestic all-hazards preparedness goal." [10] This Goal was to outline key preparedness priorities, objectives, targets, and desired outcomes. In response to HSPD-8, DHS has developed an *Interim National Preparedness Goal* that reflects the Department's progress to date to develop each of those elements in coordination with other entities.[11] It will remain in effect until superseded by the final National Preparedness Goal, which awaits completion.

We must now translate this Goal into a robust preparedness system that includes integrated plans, procedures, policies, training, and capabilities at all levels of government. The System must also incorporate the private sector, non-governmental organizations, faith-based groups, and communities, including individual citizens. The desired end-state of our National Preparedness System must be to achieve and sustain risk-based target levels of capability to prevent, protect against, respond to, and recover from major events in order to minimize the impact on lives, property, and the economy.

The *Homeland Security Strategy* and HSPD-8 provide the framework for the National Preparedness System. From this guidance comes the requirement for risk-based capabilities at the Federal, State and local levels that must enable the Nation to respond to a range of disasters—both man-made and natural. The required capabilities determine readiness targets for organizations at all levels. A unified effort from all homeland security stakeholders to commit the requisite resources, training, and exercising must support these targets and asset requirements.

Our National Preparedness System must also have appropriate feedback and assessment mechanisms to ensure that progress is made and that our goals are being realized. As called for in the *Interim National Preparedness Goal*, we must establish a readiness baseline for capabilities at the Federal, State, and local levels. This baseline should include an inventory of our preparedness assets as well as a metrics-based assessment of current capabilities. Thereafter, we must assess the gap between our present and target levels of capability. Over time, we must track our progress in closing these gaps.

Finally, the National Preparedness System must emphasize preparedness for *all hazards*. Most of the capabilities necessary for responding to natural disasters are also vital for responding to terrorist incidents. Yet for a variety of reasons, much of the Federal government, Congress, and the Nation at large have continued to think about terrorism and natural disasters as if they are competing priorities rather than two elements of the larger homeland security challenge. The lessons of 9/11 and Hurricane Katrina are that we cannot choose one or the other type of disaster. We must be prepared for all hazards.

The Federal Government's Role in the "National" System

Building upon the President's *Homeland Security Strategy*, Homeland Security Presidential Directives, and the *Interim National Preparedness Goal*, the Federal government must clearly articulate national preparedness goals and objectives; it must create the infrastructure—through the definition of common strategies and interoperable capabilities—for ensuring unity of effort; and it must manage the system for measuring effectiveness and assessing preparedness at all levels of government. Put another way, the Federal government must develop common doctrine and ensure alignment of preparedness plans, budgets, grants, training, exercises, and equipment.

While each State will have its own strategy and a multitude of local capabilities to meet the needs of its citizens, the Federal government—through the Department of Homeland Security—must work with State, local, and regional entities to develop strategies and plans that define how each State manages disasters within their borders as well as regionally, beginning at the local level. DHS must also identify how State, local, regional, and private-sector preparedness activities support the national strategy.

Transformation Within the Federal Government: Building Operational Capability

The creation of an effective National Preparedness System will require the Federal government to transform the way it does business. The most important objective of this Federal transformation must be to build and integrate *operational capability*. Each Federal department or agency with homeland security responsibilities needs operational capability—or the capacity to get things done—to translate executive management direction promptly into results on the ground. It includes the personnel to make and communicate decisions; organizational structures that are assigned, trained, and exercised for their missions; sufficient physical resources; and the command, control, and communication channels to make, monitor, and communicate decisions.

As described in the preceding narrative, the response to Hurricane Katrina required that the Federal government both support State and local efforts while conducting response operations in the field, in addition to making policy or implementing programs. With the exceptions of the Department of Defense and the Coast Guard—two organizations with considerable operational capabilities—the Federal government was at times slow and ineffective in responding to the massive operational demands of the catastrophe.

These shortfalls were not due to the absence of top level plans such as the *National Response Plan* and the *National Incident Management System*. Rather, the problem is that these plans lack clarity on key aspects and have operational gaps, as discussed in previous chapters, and have not been effectively integrated and translated into action. Prior training, exercising, and equipping proved inadequate to the task of effectively responding to Hurricane Katrina. There is a difference between a plan (saying "this is what we need to do") and a trained, resourced set of defined missions (saying "this is what we are going to do, and this is how we are going to organize, train, exercise, and equip to do it"). For any plan to work, it must first be broken down into its component parts. Next, the plan's requirements should be matched to the human and physical assets of each responsible department, agency, or organization.

The imperative, therefore, is to organize coherent, proactive management of responses to catastrophic events. Virtually all elements of the Federal government must be operational—to respond to catastrophic events with unified effort. There are three principal requirements to achieve this transformational goal:

1. Strengthening DHS institutions to manage the Federal response as well as enhancing DHS regional and field elements.

2. Reinforcing the Secretary of Homeland Security's position as the President's manager of the Federal response; and

3. Strengthening the response capabilities—management and field resources—of other Federal departments and agencies.

The Department of Homeland Security

Since the Department was created in January 2003, the management and personnel of the Department of Homeland Security have undertaken their responsibilities with energy and professionalism. Their courage and commitment to their mission have improved the security of all Americans.

But the Federal response to Hurricane Katrina demonstrated that the energy and professionalism of DHS personnel was not enough to support the Department's role as the manager of the Federal response. In particular, DHS lacked both the requisite headquarters management institutions and sufficient field capabilities to organize a fully successful Federal response effort. Within the Department, therefore, it is essential to strengthen the DHS headquarters elements to *direct* the Federal response while also providing appropriate resources to DHS field elements so that they can make an impact on the ground.

In order to strengthen DHS's operational management capabilities, we must structure the Department's headquarters elements to support the Secretary's incident management responsibilities. First and most important, Federal government response organizations must be co-located and strengthened to manage catastrophes in a new *National Operations Center (NOC)*. The mission of the NOC must be to coordinate and integrate the national response and provide a common operating picture for the entire Federal government. This interagency center should ensure National-level coordination of Federal, State, and local response to major domestic incidents. It must combine and co-locate the situational awareness mission of the Homeland Security Operations Center (HSOC), the operational mission of the National Response Coordination Center (NRCC), and the strategic role currently assigned to the Interagency Incident Management Group (IIMG). During an incident, all department and agency command centers, as well as the Joint Field Office (JFO) at the disaster site, must provide information to the NOC, which develops a National common operating picture capable of being exported in real time to other Federal operations centers.

The NOC must be staffed by an experienced, well-trained, and resourced cadre of personnel who are prepared to provide expert strategic and operational management of Federal responses to catastrophic incidents. For example, these personnel must include logistical experts with the management tools to track moving resources anywhere across the Nation and ensure timely delivery of aid to affected areas. This staff must also include operations experts who understand how to combine existing resources into effective response packages for any scenario. In addition to a robust permanent staff, the NOC must include a "battle roster" of personnel who will surge to expand and sustain the NOC's capacity during a crisis.

The DHS headquarters must also possess a robust capability for deliberate operational planning. Rather than waiting for the next disaster, DHS planners must apply lessons learned as well as develop detailed operational plans that anticipate the requirements of future responses and what capabilities can be matched to them in what timeframe. Using these operational plans and capability inventories as baseline data, the Headquarters planning staff can conduct national readiness assessments, highlighting priorities for subsequent preparedness investments, training, and exercising.

Below the headquarters level within DHS, we must build up the Department's regional structures. As noted above, the integration of State and local strategies and capabilities on a regional basis is a homeland security priority. Homeland security regional offices should be the means to foster State, local and private sector integration. Furthermore, DHS regional structures are ideally positioned to pre-identify, organize, train, and exercise future Principal Federal Officials and Joint Field Office staffs. Each DHS regional organization should possess the capacity to establish a self-sufficient, initial JFO on short notice anywhere in its region.

More broadly, the Department of Homeland Security must possess field personnel with the necessary resources, training, and national support. As a start, we must improve and emphasize plans that stress a proactive DHS role—in particular, the *Catastrophic Incident Annex* and *Catastrophic Incident Supplement* of the *NRP*. But DHS must also have available operational funds so that it can "lean forward" in future crises, to take anticipatory actions without budgetary concern or risk of subsequent criticism for a false alarm. In the event of a surprise contingency, battlefield commanders should not have to wait for the release of funds to execute their pre-assigned missions. The same flexibility should be afforded to our Federal homeland security responders.[12]

Managing the Interagency Process in Homeland Security Response

In order to create robust homeland security response capabilities, we must also transform our Federal interagency processes. Most important, we must eliminate the extraordinary red tape and resulting delays in the process of requests for assistance in response efforts. Too often during the Hurricane Katrina response we found that the Federal government did not effectively use assets at the ready because the necessary requests were being "coordinated" somewhere in the bureaucracy. The solution is to enshrine in the Federal government one of the central tenets of the *National Incident Management System*—Unified Command. We must transform our approach for catastrophic incidents from one of bureaucratic *coordination* to proactive unified command that creates true unity of effort. As set forth in *NIMS*, "In a [Unified Command] structure, the individuals designated by their jurisdictional authorities . . . must jointly determine objectives, strategies, plans, and priorities and work together to execute integrated incident operations and maximize the use of assigned resources."[13]

At the Federal level, the most urgent step in creating unity of effort will be to reinforce the Secretary of Homeland Security as the Federal government's preparedness and incident manager. In order to create unity of effort at the Federal level, the Department should manage and orchestrate the specialized efforts of other Federal departments and agencies within their core competencies. Although DHS by Presidential directive has this mission,[14] its internal structures and relationships across the

Advantages of Using Unified Command[13]
▪ A single set of objectives is developed for the entire incident.
▪ A collective approach is used to develop strategies to achieve incident objectives.
▪ Information flow and coordination is improved between all jurisdictions and agencies involved in the incident
▪ All agencies with responsibility for the incident have an understanding of joint priorities and restrictions.
▪ No agency's legal authorities will be compromised or neglected.
▪ The combined efforts of all agencies are optimized as they perform their respective assignments under a single Incident Action Plan.

Federal government do not position it to fully succeed. The current arrangements are an awkward mix of the traditional, FEMA-led, approach to interagency coordination and the Homeland Security Act's creation of a powerful Department of Homeland Security.

One model for the command and control structure for the Federal response in the new National Preparedness System is our successful defense and national security statutory framework. In that framework, there is a clear line of authority that stretches from the President, through the Secretary of Defense, to the Combatant Commander in the field. When a contingency arises, the Combatant Commander in that region executes the missions assigned by the Secretary of Defense and the President. Although the Combatant Commander might not "own" or control forces on a day-to-day basis, during a military operation he controls all military forces in his theater: he exercises the command authority and has access to resources needed to affect outcomes on the ground.

Figure 6.1 portrays the structure for command and control of defense operations. Unity of command is established in a chain of command from the President through the Secretary of Defense to the Combatant Commander. The Combatant Commander possesses operational control over forces and resources provided by the armed services. The Intelligence Community additionally provides essential information—warning and situational awareness—to the commander in the field. The system makes a clear distinction between operations—in which the Combatant Commander is the center of activity—and the provision of operational resources. In the latter case, the Armed Services are responsible for the training and equipping of forces.

Figure 6.1: Command and Control of Defense Operations

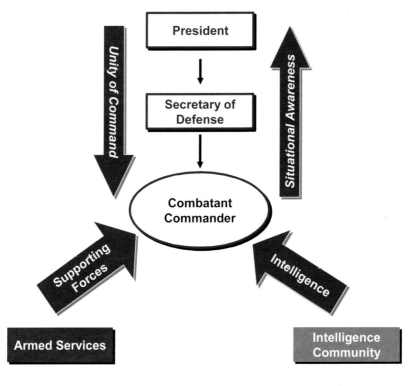

The model somewhat parallels the original conception of the Federal homeland security response. In particular, the President directs the Secretary of Homeland Security, who coordinates interagency actions at the senior level while supervising the field commander for the Federal response—the Principal Federal Official (PFO). The PFO, in turn, is supported with resources provided by DHS and other interagency departments and agencies.

As described in HSPD-5, Cabinet members are to support the Secretary of Homeland Security as the President's incident manager directing and coordinating the Federal response.[15] At the PFO level, this can be accomplished by ensuring that the Federal Coordinating Officer (FCO)—who possesses authority over resources—works for the PFO.[16]

However, the comparison between the homeland security and defense operations models breaks down in two significant ways. First, the Federal commander only manages *Federal* resources in homeland security. In almost every circumstance, State and local governments maintain operational control over their own resources. Second, the Secretary of Homeland Security and the PFO must request Federal assets from other departments and agencies; they do not command the resources of other departments and agencies. HSPD-5 makes clear that one Cabinet member cannot alter or impede the ability to carry out the authorities of Federal departments and agencies to perform their responsibilities under law.[17] Rather, HSPD-5 anticipates that future events will necessarily involve a joint approach given that several departments and agencies have distinct statutory authorities (e.g., the Attorney General for criminal investigation of terrorist acts, the Secretary of Defense for command over our military forces, and so forth).

In this vein, we must similarly transform the existing system of Emergency Support Functions (ESFs). A vestige of the 1992 *Federal Response Plan*,[18] the precursor to the *NRP*, these capability-specific coordination mechanisms, at a minimum, must be reconciled to the *NIMS* as well as responsive to the orders of the Principal Federal Official. More fundamentally, we must examine whether we should reorganize and, in some cases, redefine the ESF structures, while building DHS command and control mechanisms.[19]

These interagency management changes recognize that Federal response to catastrophic events—potential or actual—must be both efficient and effective in meeting the needs of the victims. Without infringing upon the statutory responsibilities of the Cabinet departments and agencies, we must ensure that the President's incident manager is able to call upon the full range of the Federal government's response assets, and to aggressively orchestrate, lead, and coordinate their use in response operations.

Operational Capabilities in Other Federal Departments/Agencies

Beyond changes to DHS and the structure of Federal response, there is still a compelling need to strengthen operational capabilities across the Federal government. Those departments and agencies that have a responsibility to participate in a catastrophic response must build up their crisis deployable capabilities as well as their effective operational management.

To start, all Federal departments and agencies should have operational command and control structures that comply with the *National Incident Management System*. Secretaries and directors throughout the government must operate jointly, using the same systems, doctrine, and terminology. Similarly, in support of crisis operational capability, each department and agency must develop a deliberate planning capability. Planning should include not only the response plans themselves but also, both personnel and funding to train professional planners.

With these new operational planning functions, Federal departments and agencies must build the detailed supporting plans, concepts, and staffing to execute their *NRP* and emergency response missions. During Hurricane Katrina, it became clear that most Federal departments and agencies had not developed—much less exercised—standard operating procedures for their response.

An additional imperative is for all Federal departments and agencies to develop "battle rosters" of trained personnel who should deploy when their organization is called upon to support a Federal response to a catastrophic event. The development of these rosters must coincide with the implementation of training certification programs that ensure that personnel are trained and skilled to a high, uniform standard.

Homeland Security Training, Education, and Exercising

An effective National Preparedness System requires that management and response personnel, especially those in the field, are well versed in their missions. At all levels of government, we must build a leadership corps that is fully educated, trained, and exercised in our plans and doctrine. Training is not nearly as costly as the mistakes made in a crisis. Equally important, this corps must be populated by *leaders* who are prepared to exhibit innovation and take the initiative during extremely trying circumstances.

As discussed in the narrative, the response to Hurricane Katrina revealed a lack of familiarity with incident management, the planning discipline, legal authorities, capabilities, and field-level crisis leadership. Many Federal, State, and local officials lacked a fundamental understanding of the *National Response Plan*, the *NIMS*, and State and local response plans. The first priority for training is to ensure that our emergency managers fully understand our preparedness and response plans and doctrine. To that end, we must train all emergency managers with responsibility for the Federal response in the *National Response Plan* and the *National Incident Management System*. At the same time, the Department of Homeland Security must continue to condition its State assistance grants on all relevant State and local emergency response personnel being *NIMS* and *NRP* trained and capable.[20] DHS and its Federal partners should develop and deploy mobile training teams to support this effort.

Beyond current plans and doctrine, we require a more systematic and institutional program for homeland security professional development and education. While such a program will center on the Department of Homeland Security, it should extend to personnel throughout all levels of government having responsibility for preventing, preparing for, responding to, and recovering from natural and man-made disasters. For example, DHS should establish a National Homeland Security University (NHSU)—analogous to the National Defense University—for senior homeland security personnel as the capstone for homeland security training and education opportunities. [21] The NHSU, in turn, should integrate homeland security personnel from State and local jurisdictions as well as other Federal departments and agencies.

Over the long term, our professional development and education programs must break down interagency barriers to build a unified team across the Federal government. Just as the Department of Defense succeeded in building a joint leadership cadre, so the rest of the Federal government must make familiarity with other departments and agencies a requirement for career advancement.[22]

> **LESSON LEARNED:** The Department of Homeland Security should develop a comprehensive program for the professional development and education of the Nation's homeland security personnel, including Federal, State and local employees as well as emergency management persons within the private sector, non-governmental organizations, as well as faith-based and community groups. This program should foster a "joint" Federal Interagency, State, local, and civilian team.

Where practicable, interagency and intergovernmental assignments for Federal personnel must build trust and familiarity among diverse homeland security professionals. These assignments will break down organizational stovepipes, advancing the exchange of ideas and practices. At a minimum, we should build joint training and educational institutions for our senior managers in homeland security-related departments and agencies.

These Federal professional development and education programs must integrate participants from other homeland security partners—namely, State and local governments as well as the private sector, non-governmental organizations, and faith-based organizations. As in every homeland crisis, it is inevitable that Federal, State, and local homeland security officials will come together to respond, and so it is important that we recognize the value in the old military adage that we must "train as you fight; fight as you train."

Pursuant to HSPD-8, the National Preparedness System should include a robust program of homeland security exercises at all levels of government and across all disciplines.[23] The Department of Homeland Security should serve as the President's executive agent in developing and managing a National Exercise and Evaluation Program (NEEP). The NEEP should consolidate all existing interagency homeland security-related exercise programs at the Federal level with existing DHS National Exercise Program and Homeland Security Exercise and Evaluation Program (HSEEP) through common doctrine, objectives, and management.[24] The NEEP should sponsor an aggressive program of joint exercises that involve all levels of government, as well as problem-specific exercises at particular levels of government. NEEP planning, moreover, must be integrated with a robust national homeland security training program. Moreover, the Program must emphasize intelligence-driven, threat-based scenarios that stress the system. In particular, we should not shy away from exercising worst case scenarios that "break" our homeland security system. Arguably, those scenarios will provide us the most meaningful, if sobering, lessons.

Assessments, Lessons Learned, and Corrective Actions

The success of the National Preparedness System over time will depend upon the quality of its metrics-based assessment and feedback mechanisms. In particular, the System must possess the means to measure progress towards strategic goals and capability objectives. It must systematically identify best practices and lessons learned in order to share them with our homeland security partners throughout the Nation. It must also have an effective process for conducting corrective or remedial actions when a system challenge is identified.

With common goals and performance metrics, the new National Preparedness System must first provide us with the capacity to create a national preparedness baseline that, at a minimum, serves as an inventory of our capabilities. More importantly, the baseline will tell us how prepared we are *today* in each of our jurisdictions and nationally. Reviewed at the Federal level and compared against the National Preparedness Goal, the System must also identify gaps in our national capabilities. These gaps can then serve as the priority targets for the homeland security grant process. In turn, the grant process must be tied to performance metrics that assess progress toward meeting national objectives. The President's Management Agenda has proven an effective tool applied to Federal department and agency performance that has recently, as a result of this review, been extended to include State and local homeland security programs that are federally funded.[25]

> **LESSON LEARNED:** The Department of Homeland Security should establish specific requirements for training, exercise, and lessons learned programs linked through a comprehensive system and common supporting methodology throughout the Federal, State and local governments. Furthermore, assessments of training and exercises should be based on clear and consistent performance measures. DHS should require all Federal and State entities with operational homeland security responsibilities to have a lessons learned capability, and DHS should ensure all entities are accountable for the timely implementation of remedial actions in response to lessons learned.

Furthermore, this National Preparedness System must be dynamic. Like the national security system described above, we must routinely revisit our plans and reassess our capabilities in order to account for evolving risks, improvements in technological capabilities, and preparedness innovations.

An integrated National Preparedness System must identify and share lessons learned and best practices both within departments and agencies and across jurisdictions. We understand that for many aspects of homeland security there is no single, best way of doing business. Our National Preparedness organization should systematically investigate and seek out innovative approaches being applied in the various localities, States, departments, agencies, and the private sector. The system should circulate the most promising of these practices, as well as any lessons—positive *and* negative—on a continuous basis, so that we never stop improving our security.

Finally, we must ensure that problems identified in our training, exercises, and lessons learned programs are corrected. Too often, after-action reports for exercises and real-world incidents highlight the same problems that do not get fixed—the need for interoperable communications, for example. Thus, the circle of the National Preparedness System must be closed by a Remedial Action Management Program (RAMP) that is led by DHS and coordinated by the Homeland Security Council but is resident in and executed by individual departments and agencies. Department and agency RAMPs must translate findings of homeland security gaps and vulnerabilities into concrete programs for corrective action. Then the RAMPs must track that the appropriate corrective actions are fully implemented in a timely fashion.

The Role of Congress

The challenges of transformation are not limited to the Executive Branch of government. Despite previous calls for transformation from national commissions, the U.S. Congress has not fully transformed itself for homeland security.[26] The numerous congressional committees in both houses that authorize and appropriate funds for homeland security inevitably produce competing initiatives and requirements. For example, the Secretary of Homeland Security and his leadership team were required to testify at 166 hearings before 61 full committees and subcommittees in the Senate and House of Representatives and provided over 2,000 briefings during 2005 as of October 14, 2005.[27] At best, the many priorities distract us from the true, *top priorities*. At worst, the many priorities and requirements can contradict each other.

Moreover, Congress has not yet embraced a purely risk-based funding approach to homeland security priorities. Although the U.S. House of Representatives and U.S. Senate have passed several forms of grant reform legislation that would permit DHS to increase the prioritization of homeland security spending on the basis of risk, the two bodies have failed to reconcile their differences.[28] Until we as a Nation agree to a solely risk-based approach, we are in danger of allocating our limited resources in ways that do not prioritize funding to meet national homeland security goals and objectives.

Finally, our experience in building an effective national security system demonstrates that Congress will be an essential partner as we continue to transform our homeland security system. Implementing the Goldwater-Nichols defense reform, for example, required legislation, and the durability of our homeland security reforms and the new National Preparedness System will require comparable support and participation from our Congressional partners.

How Much is Enough?

An age-old question for national security and, now, homeland security planning is *how much is enough?* In particular, at what level of preparedness do we feel confident that we have adequately accounted for the threats we face, our vulnerabilities, and the means we have to manage them? Recognizing that the future is uncertain and that we cannot anticipate every threat, we as a Nation must rely on a capabilities-based planning approach[29] to answering these questions: we must set levels of capabilities—at Federal, State, and local levels as among our other homeland security partners—that we conclude are appropriate to meet the range of risks that we may confront in the future.

In order to help identify the range of future plausible risks, the Department of Homeland Security has produced a set of fifteen *National Planning Scenarios* (see Figure 6.2). The Scenarios were designed to illustrate a myriad of tasks and capabilities that are required to prepare for and respond to a range of potential terrorist attacks and natural disasters that our Nation may confront. They identify the potential scale, scope, and complexity of fifteen incidents that would severely harm our Nation's citizens, infrastructure, economy, and threaten our way of life. Examples include an outbreak of pandemic influenza on U.S. soil, a major earthquake in a U.S. city, and the detonation of a ten-kiloton nuclear device in a large U.S. metropolitan area. The Scenarios also include a Category 5 hurricane hitting a major metropolitan area.[30]

**Figure 6.2. U.S. Natural Disasters that Caused the Most Death and Damage to Property
in Each Decade, 1900-2005, with 2004 Major Hurricanes,
September 11ᵗʰ Terrorist Attacks, and Selected National Planning Scenarios[31]
Damage in Third Quarter 2005 dollars**

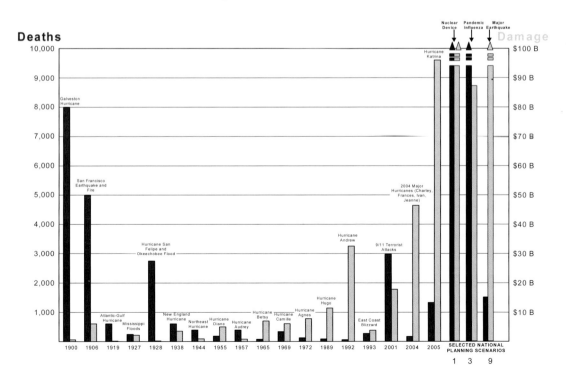

The Scenarios, which were meant to be illustrative of a wide variety of hazards, generally do not specify a geographic location, and the impacts are meant to be scalable for a variety of population considerations. Ultimately, they give homeland security planners a tool that allows for the flexible and adaptive development of capabilities as well as the identification of needed capability levels to meet the National Preparedness Goal.

While the National Planning Scenarios have been effective tools for generating dialogue on response capabilities, they do not fully anticipate some of the worst disaster scenarios. Scenario 10, for example, depicts the effects of a Category 5 hurricane hitting a major metropolitan area in the United States. However, in the Scenario, the Category 5 hurricane actually causes fewer deaths and less destruction than did Hurricane Katrina, a Category 3, because the Scenario only characterizes the destruction caused to a metropolitan area, while a storm like Hurricane Katrina may span three or more States. Further, although the Scenario acknowledges potential delays and difficulties in evacuation, realistic circumstances such as Katrina may be worse, where more than 100,000 residents did not evacuate.[32]

Scenario 1, the detonation of a ten-kiloton nuclear device in an American city by a terrorist group, suffers from similar limitations and fails to fully challenge our plans and preparation skills. Although devastating in terms of both death and destruction, a ten-kiloton bomb is a relatively small nuclear device. Moreover, the Scenario does not anticipate one of the most demanding characteristics of past al-Qaida operations: multiple, simultaneous attacks. How much more taxing would it be to respond to multiple and simultaneous nuclear, chemical, or biological incidents? If the purpose of the National Planning Scenarios is to provide a foundation for identifying the capabilities required to meet all hazards, the Scenarios must press us to confront the most destructive challenges.

Hurricane Katrina severely stressed our current national response capabilities. However, as depicted in Figure 6.2, three other National Planning Scenarios—an act of nuclear terrorism (Scenario 1), an outbreak of pandemic influenza (Scenario 3), and a 7.5 magnitude earthquake striking a major city (Scenario 9)—are more daunting still. Compared with the deaths and economic chaos a nuclear detonation or influenza outbreak could unleash, Hurricane Katrina was small. But even these scenarios do not go far enough to challenge us to improve our level of preparedness. Until we can meet the standard set by the most demanding scenarios, we should not consider ourselves adequately prepared.

The most recent Top Officials ("TOPOFF") exercise in April 2005 revealed the Federal government's lack of progress in addressing a number of preparedness deficiencies, many of which had been identified in previous exercises. This lack of progress reflects, in part, the absence of a remedial action program to systematically address lessons learned from exercises. To ensure appropriate priority and accountability are being applied to address these continuing deficiencies, the Assistant to the President for Homeland Security and Counterterrorism now annually conducts four Cabinet-level exercises with catastrophic scenarios. To date, a catastrophic exercise with a pandemic scenario was conducted in December 2005; the next exercise is scheduled for this March.

While the National Planning Scenarios represent a good start for our national process of capabilities-based planning for homeland security, we must orient the National Preparedness System towards still greater challenges. We must not shy away from creating planning scenarios that stress the current system of response to the breaking point and challenge our Nation in ways that we wish we did not have to imagine. To that end, we must revise the planning scenarios to make them more challenging. Among other characteristics, they must reflect both what we know and what we can imagine about the ways our enemies think—that they will not hit us hard just once, but that they will seek to cause us damage on significant scale in multiple locations simultaneously. We must not again find ourselves vulnerable to the charge that we suffered a "'failure of imagination' and a mind-set that dismissed possibilities."[33]

Envisioning a National Preparedness System

Figure 6.3 provides an illustration of how our existing homeland security strategy, doctrine, and capabilities can be unified into a single National Preparedness System. The graphic ties together the priorities described throughout this section into a new transformational construct. The strengths of this System include first and foremost *integration* of strategy, doctrine, capabilities, response activities, and exercises, as well as assessment and evaluation. The graphic also highlights the feedback mechanisms that must be built into the System. In particular, as described above, the System must include routine reporting and assessment of program performance metrics, the readiness of particular capabilities, as well as best practices and lessons learned from exercises and activities. These assessments and findings must be reported back, as appropriate, to inform key components throughout the System.

The National Preparedness System graphic additionally highlights the constituent elements of operational capabilities: deliberate planning, resources, logistics, training, and education. Moreover, the graphic notes the importance of unity of effort in exercises and the conduct of response activities in incidents.

As described above, the National Preparedness System must be dynamic, flexible, and responsive to new developments. Like our national security system, the strategy, doctrine, and capabilities of the System should be reviewed periodically to determine their continued relevance to current challenges. Similarly, periodic reviews must assess the continued internal consistency of the System—e.g., do the doctrine and capabilities support the strategy?

Key inputs to the System include the current national vision for preparedness, laws, and policies and the use of capability-based planning that prioritizes investments to fill gaps identified by needs assessments. An equally important input is the current assessment of risks—what threats does the Nation currently confront, what are our current vulnerabilities, and what are the consequences? Against the current assessment of risks, we must continually evaluate our capability to respond effectively.

Finally, our planning and operational documents should define the critical roles played by all of our homeland security partners in the Preparedness System. Federal, State, and local governments play prominent roles throughout the System—from strategy development to assessment and lessons learned. Additionally, the private sector, NGOs, faith-based groups, communities, and individuals play important roles in operational capabilities as well as response activities.

Figure 6.3: A Shared Vision of Preparedness

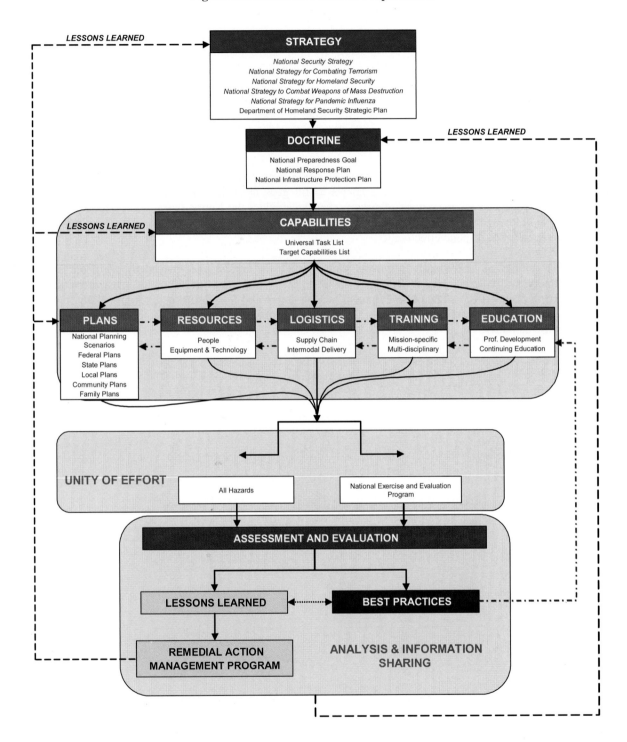

CREATING A CULTURE OF PREPAREDNESS

The second element of our continuing transformation for homeland security perhaps will be the most profound and enduring—the creation of a Culture of Preparedness. A new preparedness culture must emphasize that the entire Nation—Federal, State, and local governments; the private sector; communities; and individual citizens—shares common goals and responsibilities for homeland security. In other words, our homeland security is built upon a foundation of partnerships. And these partnerships must include shared understanding of at least four concepts:

- The certainty of future catastrophes;

- The importance of initiative;

- The roles of citizens and other homeland security stakeholders in preparedness; and

- The roles of each level of government and the private sector in creating a prepared Nation.

Future Challenges

The first principle for a Culture of Preparedness must be a shared acknowledgement that creating a prepared Nation will be a continuing challenge. Optimism is fundamental to the American character. While it always energizes us, it also grounds us in times of tragedy and loss. We must guard against our optimism leading us to a dangerous sense of complacency. Complacency of our citizens presents a great challenge. We are fortunate that, because of the courage and self-sacrifice of public servants across all levels of government, we have not suffered another terrorist attack on our homeland since 2001. But we are a Nation at war, and we have a responsibility to be prepared. We must temper our optimism with sober recognition of the certainty of future catastrophes. We cannot prevent natural disasters. And though we work tirelessly against them, we cannot anticipate nor prevent every type of terrorist attack against the homeland. As the Irish Republican Army once warned British Prime Minister Margaret Thatcher after narrowly missing her in an assassination attempt: terrorists only need to be successful once; but we, their targets, must be successful everyday.[34] We know that our enemies plot further attacks against us. We must continue to prevent them and, if necessary, respond. Regrettably, lives will be lost, citizens displaced, and property destroyed.

The certainty of future challenges should inform our national expectations. As a Nation, we will prepare ourselves in the most effective ways we know. Our Culture of Preparedness, therefore, must emphasize the importance of flexibility and readiness to cope with an uncertain future. While we cannot predict the future to our satisfaction, we can build capabilities that prepare us for a broad range of challenges. Perhaps equally important, we can ensure that our preparedness plans, thinking, and "imagination" do not become so rigid that we cannot rapidly adapt to unforeseen challenges.[35]

Initiative

Despite reforms that encourage a proactive, anticipatory approach to the management of incidents, the culture of our response community has a fundamental bias towards *reaction* rather than *initiative*. As a result, our national efforts too often emphasize response and clean-up efforts at the expense of potentially more cost-effective anticipatory actions that might prevent or mitigate damage.

The need for anticipatory response is a pillar of the National Response Plan. A list of Key Concepts in the *National Response Plan* places it second only to "systematic and coordinated incident management." Specifically, the *NRP* calls for:

> Proactive notification and deployment of Federal resources in anticipation of or in response to catastrophic events in coordination and collaboration with State, local, and tribal governments and private entities when possible.[36]

Similarly, our Culture of Preparedness must stress initiative at all levels. Fundamentally, our Preparedness System and Culture must encourage and reward innovation. To do so, we must build a system and approach that better aligns authority and responsibility—those who are responsible for a mission or task must have the authority to *act*. In the same vein, an alignment of authority and responsibility provides us the ability to assess our performance—collectively and individually. Performance assessment and accountability, however, must not be *blame*.[37] Our current culture of blame threatens both individual and institutional initiative, resourcefulness, and enterprise across the homeland security, law enforcement, and intelligence fields. It is time that Congress, the Executive Branch, and all of our homeland security partners develop a consensus regarding a reasonable balance of accountability, responsibility, and authority at all levels. Otherwise, the culture of blame and its related acrimony will debilitate us.

Citizen Preparedness

Our preparedness culture must also emphasize the importance of citizen and community preparedness. Citizen and community preparedness are among the most effective means of preventing terrorist attacks as well as protecting against, mitigating, responding to, and recovering from all hazards.[38] For example, the Citizen Corps in Harris County, Texas, brought together over 50,000 volunteers to support American Red Cross efforts and staff evacuation centers throughout Houston. As a joint team, they created an actual working city (with its own zip code) for Hurricane Katrina victims sheltering in the Astrodome.[39]

Thus, citizens and communities can help themselves by becoming more prepared. If every family maintained the resources to live in their homes without electricity and running water for three days, we could allocate more Federal, State, and local response resources to saving lives. Similarly, if every family developed their own emergency preparedness plan, they almost certainly would reduce the demand for outside emergency resources. As the 9/11 Commission Report states, "One clear lesson of September 11 is that individual civilians need to take responsibility for maximizing the probability that they will survive, should disaster strike."[40]

LESSON LEARNED: The Federal government, working with State, local, NGO, and private sector partners, should combine the various disparate citizen preparedness programs into a single national campaign to promote and strengthen citizen and community preparedness. This campaign should be developed in a manner that appeals to the American people, incorporates the endorsement and support of prominent national figures, focuses on the importance of individual and community responsibility for all-hazard disaster preparedness, provides meaningful and comprehensive education, training and exercise opportunities applicable to all facets of the American population, and establishes specialized preparedness programs for those less able to provide for themselves during disasters such as children, the ill, the disabled, and the elderly.

Leadership at all levels will be essential in helping to transform citizen preparedness. First, responsible public officials at the Federal, State, and local levels as well as prominent national figures should begin a public dialogue that emphasizes common themes regarding the importance of citizen preparedness. DHS should continue to build upon those programs and institutions that already work, such as Department of Education elementary and secondary school programs; Citizen Corps; State and local government training programs; and Federal cooperation with the National Governors Association. Nongovernmental organizations can also play a key role in this area. DHS has made some important progress in this area with its *Ready.gov* initiative and its public service announcements program with the Ad Council.[41] But more needs to be done. Encouraging preparedness awareness and activity is a shared responsibility across all levels of government that we must make a priority. Preparedness today will save lives tomorrow.

In addition, DHS and other Federal agencies should identify both the individual skills and capabilities that would help citizens in a disaster as well as the types of messages from trusted leaders that would encourage citizens to be better prepared. Public awareness messaging must shift to include more substantive information, as opposed to just telling our citizens that they need to "do something." For example, the "Stop, Drop, and Roll" campaign used so successfully in fire safety as part of the "Learn Not to Burn"[42] program provided citizens with specific steps to take. Other successful campaigns include the National Highway Traffic Safety Administration's "Buckle Up America" campaign,[43] which prescribes proper use of seat belt and child safety seats. As with so many of these successful campaigns, the Nation's children can help lead the way.[44]

Other Homeland Security Stakeholders and Preparedness

We must build upon our initial successful efforts to partner with other homeland security stakeholders—namely the private sector, non-governmental organizations, and faith-based groups.[45] Each of these groups plays a critical role in preparedness. To the extent that we can incorporate them into the National effort, we will be reducing the burden on other response resources so that Federal, State, and local responders can concentrate our energies on those with the greatest need.

Private sector companies own and operate 85 percent of our Nation's critical infrastructure.[46] Transportation, electricity, banking, telecommunications, food supply, and clean water are examples of services relying on infrastructure that have become basic aspects of our daily lives. Yet, these services are often only noticed when they are disrupted and when the American public expects speedy restoration. In fact, the Nation relies on "critical infrastructure" to maintain its defense, continuity of government, economic prosperity, and quality of life. The services provided by these interconnected systems are so vital that their disruption will have a debilitating impact on national security, the economy, or public health and safety.

Companies are responsible for protecting their systems, which comprise the majority of critical infrastructure. Because of this, private sector preparation and response is vital to mitigating the national impact of disasters. Government actions in response to a disaster can help or hamper private sector efforts. However, governments cannot plan to adequately respond unless the private sector helps them understand what infrastructure truly is critical. Likewise, businesses cannot develop contingency plans without understanding how governments will respond. To maximize the Nation's preparedness, Federal, State, and local governments must join with the private sector to collaboratively develop plans to respond to major disasters. There are important initiatives in this area already underway by the Business Round Table (BRT) and Business Executives for National Security (BENS) project.[47] We must encourage and build upon these efforts. The private sector must be an explicit partner in and fully integrated across all levels of response—Federal, State, and local.

Non-governmental organizations play essential roles in preparedness by complementing and supporting preparedness efforts. In times of crisis, NGOs—especially community groups, faith-based organizations, places of worship, and relief organizations—provide essential human faces, helping hands, compassion, and comfort to all American people, whether or not they are victims of an incident. As such, they fill an essential need in the response system in ways far beyond the capacity of the Government. Thus, their contributions must be fully integrated at all levels—Federal, State, and local.

The Role of Each Level of Government in a Culture of Preparedness

Today, we operate under two guiding principles: a) that incident management should begin at the lowest jurisdictional level possible, and b) that, for most incidents, the Federal government will generally play a supporting role to State and local efforts.[48] While these principles suffice for the vast majority of incidents, they impede the Federal response to severe catastrophes. In a catastrophic scenario that overwhelms or incapacitates local and State incident command structures, the Federal government must be prepared to assume incident command and get assistance directly to those in need until State and local authorities are reconstituted.

The National Preparedness System must also recognize the role of the Federal government for monitoring and guiding national preparedness efforts. In particular, the system must ensure that the Federal government assesses the preparedness of localities across the country with an eye towards identifying the Federal response requirement for each. In addition, Federal, State, local, and private sector partners must agree on a system in which the Federal government responds more actively and effectively while respecting the role of State and local governments.

The new culture of preparedness must stress *partnership* among all levels of government. Local governments will continue to have responsibility for providing the immediate response capabilities for the vast majority of incidents while State governors will continue to have sovereign responsibilities to protect their residents. Yet preparedness must emphasize the shared nature of these responsibilities in a catastrophic event. State governments must work with their local jurisdictions to ensure that they have developed plans and capabilities that are appropriate for the homeland security challenges confronting them. Both State and local governments must also reach out to their citizens, private sector, and community groups to promote their preparedness efforts.

Furthermore, in the new culture of preparedness, State and local governments must continually seek to work with their neighboring jurisdictions. Building upon the successes of interstate cooperation programs such as the Emergency Management Assistance Compact (EMAC),[49] the Federal government must take an active role in encouraging and facilitating these partnerships. Regional collaboration at the State and local levels will help the Nation to reduce overlapping or redundant capabilities as well as to minimize capability gaps. Moreover, active regional collaboration will likewise be a means for identifying and sharing homeland security lessons learned and best practices.

Finally, in our new Culture of Preparedness, all required response assets and resources of the Federal government must integrate and synchronize to ensure an effective national response to a crisis. In practical terms, this entails stepping away from the bureaucratic view of a particular department or agency's institutional interests. Instead, we must continually build preparedness partnerships across the Federal government as well as with State and local governments.

FOSTERING TRANSFORMATION

Our continuing transformation is not a choice but an absolute necessity. We must begin a national dialogue on shared responsibilities and expectations for preparedness. As highlighted throughout this report, the American concept of federalism requires that any transformation must involve and accommodate all levels of government and communities across the Nation.

The objectives of this dialogue must be first to establish reasonable expectations of what government can and cannot do in response to catastrophes. Our citizens need to know what to expect from their government, in order to make sure they do everything possible at their level to protect themselves and their loved ones.

Second, this dialogue must develop a shared understanding of the need for active Federal management of the National Preparedness System, to include:

- Setting metrics for State, local, community, and individual preparedness;

- Developing and implementing a system to assess that preparedness as well as to establish clear responsibilities and accountability; and

- Identifying the circumstances under which the Federal government will push capabilities independent of request.

Finally, this dialogue must result in a shared understanding of roles and responsibilities in preparedness for catastrophic events, to include those of:

- The Federal government;

- State governments;

- Local governments;

- The private sector (including non-governmental organizations and faith-based organizations); and

- Communities and individual citizens.

CHAPTER SEVEN: EPILOGUE

Each morning as the sun rises over the Gulf Coast, determined residents of Louisiana, Mississippi, and Alabama begin another day in the long trial of reviving their communities and rebuilding their lives. They continue to grieve for those who were lost. For all of them, Katrina and its aftermath remain a painful, challenging, and ever-present reality.

These human dimensions and their indelible images of despair and destruction must remain sharply in focus as we address the lessons we have learned from our Federal response to Hurricane Katrina. The seventeen specific lessons we have identified resulted in 125 recommendations, which have been reviewed by all relevant Federal departments and agencies. They soon will enter a review process, which will help to refine the recommendations, as necessary, as well as develop implementation plans and attendant timelines.

These recommendations for corrective action are substantial, and the task to implement them will be a weighty one. Arriving at sound policy decisions is difficult enough, but the path to effectuating significant, transformational change within bureaucracies can be a lengthy process. But if the lessons of Katrina really are to be learned, this change is imperative.

The 2006 hurricane season is just over three months away. Even while the homeland security policy community undertakes the deliberative process to implement the lessons we have learned from Katrina, there are specific actions we can and should undertake now – in parallel with the policy process – to be better prepared for future emergencies. We propose to undertake the following activities before June 1:

- Ensure that, in the event of another disaster, we are able to co-locate relevant Federal, State, and local decision-makers, including leaders of State National Guards, to enhance unity of effort

- For events preceded by warning, ensure we are prepared to pre-position a fully resourced and integrated interagency Federal Joint Field Office (JFO) to coordinate and, if necessary, direct Federal support to the disaster

- Ensure situational awareness by establishing rapid deployable communications as well as instituting a structure for consolidated Federal operational reporting to the Department of Homeland Security

- In order to enhance coordination of military resources supporting the response, co-locate a single Department of Defense point of contact at the JFO and current FEMA regional offices

- To ensure the most effective employment of Federal disaster relief personnel and assets, designate locations throughout the country for receiving, staging, moving, and integrating them

- Identify and develop rosters of Federal, State, and local government personnel who are prepared to assist in disaster relief

- Employ all available 21st Century technologies both to update and utilize the national Emergency Alert System in order to provide the general public with advanced notification of and instruction for disasters and emergencies

- Encourage States to pre-contract with service providers for key disaster relief efforts, such as debris removal and the provision of critical commodities

- Enhance the mechanism for providing Federal funds to States for preparations upon warning of an imminent emergency

- Improve delivery of assistance to disaster victims by streamlining registration, expediting eligibility decisions, tracking movements of displaced victims, and incorporating safeguards against fraud

- Enhance on-going review of State evacuation plans and incorporate planning for Continuity of Government to ensure continuation of essential and emergency services

We have already begun collaborating with the Department of Homeland Security to implement many of these steps. The completion of the tasks above will better position the Federal government to respond to natural and man-made disasters more effectively and efficiently in the near-term. And as the Federal government works to implement these steps and the full 125 recommendations contained in this Report, we encourage State and local governments, all facets of the private sector as well as the media to undertake a review of their own respective roles and responsibilities in both preparing for and responding to catastrophic events. In the end, what we require for a fully successful national response to all 21st Century hazards is to build upon the national and homeland security foundations we have established since 9/11 and implement a unified system of National Preparedness.

We are confident that the lessons we have learned from Hurricane Katrina and the accompanying recommendations we propose will yield preparedness dividends that transcend Federal, State, and local boundaries. Their full implementation will help the Nation – all levels of government, the private sector, and communities and individual citizens – achieve a shared commitment to preparedness. Together, we will strengthen our ability to prepare for, protect against, respond to, and recover from a wide range of catastrophic possibilities that are as varied as the mind of a terrorist and as random as the weather. There is no greater mission, and no greater tribute to the victims of Hurricane Katrina.

APPENDICES

Appendix A – Recommendations

Appendix B – What Went Right

Appendix C – List of Acronyms

Appendix D – Staff Page

Appendix E – Endnotes

APPENDIX A – RECOMMENDATIONS

1. **National Preparedness**	(Recommendations 1 – 21)
2. **Integrated Use of Military Capabilities**	(Recommendations 22 – 32)
3. **Communications**	(Recommendations 33 – 37)
4. **Logistics and Evacuation**	(Recommendations 38 – 43)
5. **Search and Rescue**	(Recommendations 44 – 48)
6. **Public Safety and Security**	(Recommendations 49 – 56)
7. **Public Health and Medical Support**	(Recommendations 57 – 62)
8. **Human Services**	(Recommendations 63 – 67)
9. **Mass Care and Housing**	(Recommendations 68 – 72)
10. **Public Communications**	(Recommendations 73 – 77)
11. **Critical Infrastructure and Impact Assessment**	(Recommendations 78 – 85)
12. **Environmental Hazards and Debris Removal**	(Recommendations 86 – 88)
13. **Foreign Assistance**	(Recommendations 89 – 97)
14. **Non-Governmental Aid**	(Recommendations 98 – 103)
15. **Training, Exercises, and Lessons Learned**	(Recommendations 104 – 111)
16. **Homeland Security Professional Development and Education**	(Recommendations 112 – 118)
17. **Citizen and Community Preparedness**	(Recommendations 119 – 125)

Critical Challenge: National Preparedness

Lesson Learned: The Federal government should work with its homeland security partners in revising existing plans, ensuring a functional operational structure—including within regions—and establishing a clear, accountable process for all National preparedness efforts. In doing so, the Federal government must:
- Ensure that Executive Branch agencies are organized, trained, and equipped to perform their response roles.
- Finalize and implement the National Preparedness Goal.

Recommendations:

National Response Plan and the National Incident Management System

1. **DHS should establish an interagency team of senior planners with appropriate emergency management experience to conduct a comprehensive, 90-day review of the NRP and the NIMS.** One of the main goals of this review will be to provide a cross-walk between the NIMS and the NRP to ensure that the two plans are properly integrated and clearly explained. Using feedback and lessons learned from the Hurricane Katrina response, including addressing relevant recommendations from the Katrina Lessons Learned Review Group, the interagency group led by DHS and overseen by HSC will develop findings and recommendations for changes to the NRP and request detailed comments and feedback from all agencies. Before changes are finalized, the group will test the recommended changes through tabletop exercises to ensure the suggested changes are clear and improve the NRP. Revisions should include the development and promulgation of guidance on the purpose and procedures for declaring Incidents of National Significance and the development of a streamlined, standardized mission assignment process and clearly delineate the consequences of an INS declaration. A second, independent group of subject-matter experts from across the State and local emergency response and homeland security community and the private sector should then review and validate the group's recommendations. Following the completion of the 90 day review, the recommended modifications to the NRP will be expeditiously reviewed through the HSC interagency policy process.

    a. **Revise the NRP to address situations that render State and local governments incapable of an effective response.** The NRP does not adequately anticipate that the Federal government may need to temporarily assume some inherently State and local responsibilities and augment State and local incident command staff during a catastrophic incident.   The Federal government should develop plans to build and temporarily command the ICS until the local or State authorities are able to recover from the initial impact of the catastrophic incident and perform their roles under ICS. These plans should utilize any available State or local assets that may remain operational and necessarily require collaborative planning between Federal, State, and local authorities. These revisions should also be incorporated into the NRP-CIA and CIS. This effort should be part of the 90 day interagency review effort.

    b. **Realign ESFs to NIMS structure.** Although the NRP base plan was predicated on the NIMS incident command system, the Emergency Support Functions (ESFs) were taken from the old Federal Response Plan and were not adequately realigned to fit within the NIMS structure. The ESFs should be realigned to fit within the NIMS structure to ensure coordination and efficiency. Rather than having each ESF function independently undertaking common functions (i.e., operations, planning, logistics, finance/administration), the ESF structure should be realigned to separate operational elements from common support requirements.

    c. **Require agencies to develop integrated operational plans, procedures and capabilities for their support to the base NRP and all ESFs and Support Annexes.** The NRP required each ESF primary agency to "develop standard operating procedures (SOPs) and notification protocols." Each primary department or agency for each ESF and support annex should develop a detailed operations plan on how they will become operational and coordinate with other annexes and ESFs during a major incident. These operational plans should conform to NIMS and be consistent with the recommended reconfiguration of the ESF structure. These plans should be exercised yearly through either National, departmental, or agency exercises. It should be recognized that these plans will take time to create and will need to be developed in collaboration with State and local officials.

    d.   All Federal departments and agencies should align their response structures to NIMS. In accordance with this alignment, the entire Federal response structure should be NIMS based, reporting through one unified command using the same terminology and basic organizational structure. Although ICS is a field command structure, developing an understanding of the ICS at all levels will eliminate confusion, standardize operations throughout the government, and limit unnecessary interference with field command. DHS should lead a review of all Federal department and agency response operations plans to guarantee conformance with NIMS and the NRP, from response teams to command post operations.

        1)   DHS should establish performance measures and metrics to allow an objective assessment of NRP and NIMS implementation status for all departments and agencies, and state and local governments.

        2)   After the establishment of the performance metrics, all departments and agencies will report to the President through the Homeland Security Council (HSC) within 60 days on all NRP/NIMS implementation efforts to date and on whether they have met the guidance goals established in HSPD-5. The HSC will assess the progress of NIMS implementation for each department and agency.

        3)   To ensure that State and local governments fully implement NIMS requirements to be eligible for Homeland Security Grant Program funding in fiscal year 2007 and thereafter, DHS should formally review all NIMS compliance certifications through a peer review process, in addition to a self-certification process. The peer review process should: (1) verify the satisfaction of training, planning, exercising, and other NIMS metrics; and (2) promote the sharing of lessons learned and best practices for institutionalizing the NIMS.

2.   DHS should institute a formal training program on the NIMS and NRP for all department and agency personnel with incident management responsibilities. The key to the implementation of ICS is training. All departments and agencies should undertake an aggressive ICS training program for all personnel who may deploy during a disaster. It is essential that personnel have a working knowledge of ICS before a disaster occurs. Adequate training will be a component of the NRP/NIMS assessment. In order to effectively implement the NRP and NIMS, senior officials at departments and agencies must also be familiar with the requirements for their ESF roles, increased participation for specific scenarios, how to request and assign assets, how to work within a JFO structure, and the level of representation and participation coordinating entities require. DHS should therefore develop and deliver detailed briefings and instructions on the NIMS and NRP to all relevant Federal decision-makers including each Cabinet Secretary and their emergency response staff. Additionally, DHS should develop and deliver similar briefings and instructions tailored to relevant state and local decision makers, the private sector and Non-Governmental Organizations.

3.   DHS should lead an interagency effort to develop and resource a deliberative, integrated and Federal planning and execution system to meet the requirements of the revised NRP. Departments and agencies should have both personnel and funds to be able to train, exercise, plan and detail staff to disaster response activities to enable better execution of their roles and responsibilities. Specific contingency plans must be integrated so that capabilities and gaps are identified and addressed.

Departments and agencies should develop and resource "Force Packages" of rapidly deployable operational capabilities that meet the re-organized ESF requirements within 90 days of completing the revised NRP.

The Department of Homeland Security: A Regional Structure for Preparedness

4.   DHS should develop and implement Homeland Security Regions that are fully staffed, trained, and equipped to manage and coordinate all preparedness activities and any emergency that may require a substantial Federal response. Homeland Security Regions should be created and each region should be

---

staffed with a preparedness group populated by subject matter experts from across the Federal government. Special consideration should be given to developing a separate National Capital Region due to the unique requirements associated with enduring constitutional government. The group's goal within each region should be to prepare for disasters, conduct training, coordinate and integrate planning, measure capability and preparedness, and respond to a disaster if one occurs. The group should also help to ensure that Federal spending in the region is spent to bolster capabilities as outlined in the National Preparedness Goal. The size of the preparedness group should be determined by the size of the region, propensity of the region to experience a natural disaster or terrorist attack, risks within the region and general State and local preparedness measured against the National Preparedness Goal.

5. **Each Regional Director should have significant expertise and experience, core competency in emergency preparedness and incident management, and demonstrated leadership ability.** The Regional Director should have full situational awareness of all events, risks, and response capabilities within the region. When an event occurs in the region, the Regional Director should be ready to become the PFO and should coordinate or direct as appropriate the Federal response assets deployed within the operational area. The Regional Director as PFO should establish and direct the Regional Response Coordination Center (RRCC). These Regional Directors will comprise the professional PFO cadre and receive initial and on-going PFO training.

6. **The PFO should have the authority to execute responsibilities and coordinate Federal response assets.** The PFO should have the same authority as an FCO to manage and coordinate the Federal response to a disaster. The PFO should have the authority to make any operational decisions necessary, within the law, without having to obtain approval from headquarters. Giving the PFO this authority could be accomplished without a change to the Stafford Act by simply designating the PFO as an FCO. Alternatively, the Secretary of Homeland Security or the FEMA Director could delegate their authority to oversee FCO to the PFO. This action does not require demoting FCO's within a particular region to Deputy FCOs. The FCO will retain all current authorities under the Stafford Act and will report through the PFO. An incident covering multiple states will require multiple FCOs operating concurrently under the command of the PFO.

7. **Each Homeland Security Region must be able to establish a self-sufficient, initial JFO anywhere within the region.** The rapid establishment of a JFO is the keystone to effective Federal emergency response. It is critical that each Region have the resources, equipment, and personnel to establish a JFO after a major disaster. This JFO should be built using available State, local, and/or National Guard infrastructure. It should also be built in such a way that Federal officials can collaborate with their State and local counterparts and thereby better complement their response operations. The JFO must also be completely self-sufficient, with food, water, power, communications equipment, and housing for personnel, to enable deployment to areas where critical infrastructure are damaged or destroyed. To the extent possible for an anticipated event, the organization of the JFO should begin before the event. For a no-notice event, each region should have the ability to establish an initial JFO within 12 hours. To assist in this effort, each region should pre-identify JFO locations in areas with large populations. The ability to establish a JFO after a major disaster directly enhances the Federal government's ability to maintain continuity of operations (COOP). Each regional JFO should also identify and conduct exercises at their respective COOP sites.

8. **Each region must be able to establish and resource rapidly deployable, self-sustaining incident management teams (IMT) to execute the functions of the JFO and subordinate area commands that are specified in the NRP and NIMS.** The regional headquarters should create IMT's that can rapidly respond to a disaster with robust, deployable communication packages and assist in establishing the command and control structures required in NIMS and the NRP. IMTs should be composed of experts in ICS who can establish a command for the Federal response to connect with State and local response structures during disasters and large scale events. IMTs should maintain certification in all levels of ICS for each ICS command element.

9. **DHS should establish several strategic-level, standby, rapidly deployable interagency task forces capable of managing the national response for catastrophic incidents that span more than one Homeland Security Region.** These Joint Interagency Headquarters should be led by a senior official from a

pre-designated pool of individuals with significant emergency management experience and assessed as capable of serving as the PFO for a catastrophic incident. Standard operating procedures, requisite billet structure, and training requirements for the coordination of Federal support to multiple Joint Field Offices should be developed. When stood up to support the National response to a catastrophic incident, the Joint Interagency Headquarters should be manned by an experienced incident management staff drawn from a pool of pre-designated and trained interagency personnel, and supported with dedicated communications and transportation assets capable of self-deploying in any environment.

Incident Management Organization and Capabilities at the Federal Level

10. **Integrate and synchronize the preparedness functions within the Department of Homeland Security.** The recently established DHS Preparedness Directorate resulting from Secretary Chertoff's review of the Department's core policies, operations and structure should be fully implemented. To expand upon this initiative, DHS should integrate and synchronize the preparedness functions with the response, recovery and operational support activities currently located elsewhere in the department. Specifically, DHS should consider adding an Assistant Secretary for Preparedness Programs and an Assistant Secretary for Operational Plans, Training and Exercises, and an Executive Director for Public and Citizen Preparedness to the Undersecretary of Preparedness' senior staff, which currently includes Assistant Secretaries for Grants and Training, Infrastructure Protection and Cyber & Telecommunications, plus the Chief Medical Officer, Fire Administrator, the Office of State and Local Coordination and the National Capital Region Director. This adjustment to the DHS headquarters will integrate all the preparedness functions of the Department and preserves FEMA as an independent operating agency to perform their response and recovery mission. There should be no artificial, functional, or geographic divide between the components of the Preparedness Directorate. The Undersecretary for Preparedness along with the FEMA Director should serve as the senior advisers to the Secretary on all matters related to the Federal response during an incident.

11. **DHS should establish a permanent standing planning/operations staff housed within the National Operations Center** (see recommendation #15). This body would evaluate the integration of Federal department and agency plans to ensure they align with resource availability. This group would replace the IIMG and be charged with coordinating national-level support to a region or multiple regions during a catastrophe, and staff interagency operational and policy decisions raised to the Disaster Response Group (see recommendation #19). The permanent group would be staffed by the interagency at the GS-15/0-6 level and comprise individuals with significant planning, preparedness, and response experience.

12. **All departments and agencies should develop emergency response plans and a response capability.** Many departments and agencies that traditionally do not have emergency response missions or roles assisted in the Hurricane Katrina response. To perform more effectively in future disasters, all Federal departments and agencies should develop emergency plans and possess the ability to operate in an emergency situation. Departments and agencies should coordinate and integrate their response planning efforts with those of other Federal agencies. DHS should be responsible for providing logistical support to these agency response teams in the field to avoid unnecessary duplication and expense of every Federal agency purchasing emergency response equipment for catastrophic incidents. Many Federal agencies will not have to respond to an emergency unless it is a catastrophic event.

13. **A unified departmental external affairs office should be created within DHS that combines legislative affairs, intergovernmental affairs, and public affairs as a critical component of the preparedness and response cycle.** DHS should create an Under Secretary for External Affairs fully staffed and capable of performing the roles of legislative, intergovernmental, and public affairs. DHS already has an Assistant Secretary for Public Affairs and an Assistant Secretary for Legislative Affairs. Therefore, an Assistant Secretary for Intergovernmental Affairs should be created. The DHS Regions should mirror this organizational structure and staff an external affairs function including intergovernmental affairs staff to better communicate with State and local officials before, during, and after disaster response. DHS should revise the NRP to include a deployable intergovernmental affairs surge capacity under ESF-15. The ESF-15 should be lead by the DHS Assistant Secretary of External Affairs.

14. **HSC should lead an interagency review to update or modify as necessary Executive Order 12656, dealing with updated national security emergency preparedness policies and strategies to ensure that continuity planning is expanded to include all hazards.** This order directs the head of each Federal department and agency to "assist State, local, and private sector entities in developing plans for mitigating the effects of National security emergencies and for providing services that are essential to a National response" (*Sec. 201 (9))*. DHS should implement the order through an aggressive program designed to assist State and local governments in developing continuity of operations (COOP) plans. The order states that the Secretary of Homeland Security is responsible to "guide and assist State and local governments and private sector organizations in achieving preparedness for National security emergencies, including development of plans and procedures for assuring continuity of government, and support planning for prompt and coordinated Federal assistance to States and localities in responding to National security emergencies." Investments in planning may be funded through Federal homeland security grants in conformance with the National Preparedness Goal. All Federal Agencies must have COOP plans at the headquarters, regional, and local level and should follow the guidance set forth in Federal Preparedness Circular 65 (FPC65) *Federal Executive Branch Continuity of Operations (COOP)*, June 15, 2004.

15. **Establish a National Operations Center to coordinate the National response and provide situational awareness and a common operating picture for the entire Federal government.** This interagency center will allow for National-level coordination of Federal/State/local response to major domestic incidents. This center will combine, co-locate, and replace the situational awareness mission of the Homeland Security Operations Center (HSOC), the operational mission of the National Response Coordination Center (NRCC) and the role of the IIMG, and be staffed with full time detailed employees assigned to a planning cell from relevant departments and agencies. Staffed and managed by interagency officials, it will also provide situational awareness and a common operating picture on a real-time basis during a domestic emergency for the White House and all agencies. All department and agency command centers will provide information to the National Operations Center (NOC), which will develop a National common operating picture capable of being exported to the White House Situation Room and other Federal operations centers as necessary. The National Operations Center should be located and designed to meet the requirements of Enduring Constitutional Government. DHS will serve as the Executive Agent for the NOC and it will function as a true interagency command center.

16. **Establish a National Information and Knowledge Management System.** Departments and agencies, working with the NOC and the Program Manager for Information Sharing, should develop a national system of information management to provide a common operating picture which allows for the processing and timely provisioning of interagency information sources (*e.g.* DOD National Military Command System, National Counterterrorism Center, FBI Strategic Information Operations Center). These information sources should be viewable at all Federal operation centers utilizing compatible geo-spatial information systems, and should operate on both classified (SIPRNET) and unclassified systems to allow State and local emergency management interface and integration.

17. **Establish a National Reporting System.** Departments and agencies, through the NOC, should establish a single reporting system to establish a uniform information flow to senior decision makers. A single reporting system should be used to provision relevant information for the right decision maker, at the right time, and in a usable format. This reporting system should incorporate the existing uniform reports utilized in the ICS.

18. **Establish National Information Requirements and a National Information Reporting Chain.** Departments and agencies, through the NOC, should develop information requirements at each level of the incident command structure to ensure that valuable, accurate information is reported in a timely manner. A national reporting chain should be established to ensure a standard information flow through all levels of the incident command structure.

19. **Establish the Disaster Response Group (DRG).** The HSC should establish the DRG to create a forum where strategic policy and interagency coordination and deconfliction can take place. These decisions would then be implemented through the NOC. This HSC-chaired group would address issues that cannot be resolved at lower levels, and either resolve them or develop decision recommendations for Deputies and Principals.

The group would function in a manner analogous to the Counterterrorism Security Group (CSG). As such it would meet on a regular basis on preparedness and response policy and implementation issues and then more frequently as required during a crisis.

National Preparedness System

20. **Future preparedness of the Federal, State, and local authorities should be based on the risk, capabilities and needs structure of the National Preparedness Goal (NPG).** Before an effective response plan can be created and an effective response implemented, gaps or shortfalls in required capability must be identified. Pursuant to HSPD-8, DHS should develop a system to assess the level of national preparedness by assessing the levels of capability identified in the NPG through performance metrics outlined in the Target Capabilities List (TCL). DHS should assess the Nation's preparedness yearly and should, in conjunction with the interagency, recommend appropriate adjustments to the NPG, TCL and yearly priorities for Homeland Security Grants. This will enable organizations across the Nation to identify capabilities that need improvement and develop and maintain capabilities at levels needed to manage major events using the NRP and NIMS. The deficiencies in Federal, State, and local response to Hurricane Katrina highlight the need for a more efficient National preparedness system. For example, States should utilize their licensing authorities to require providers of essential services and commodities, such as gas stations, pharmacies, and cell tower operators to equip their facilities with generators to enable them to operate in an emergency where central power is lost. Federal, State and local departments and agencies all share the responsibility for protecting and responding to their citizens and should use the NPG and TCL as a planning tool to:

   a. Define required capabilities and what levels of those capabilities are needed. DHS should also lead a process to determine what capabilities articulated in the NPG are within the purview of the Federal government, what levels of those capabilities are required, and finally which Departments and Agencies should develop and maintain those levels of capability. The information should be included in the NPG;

   b. Revise the NPG as appropriate to define appropriate support roles for Federal and State employees to perform as emergency staff when an emergency prevents them from performing their regular duties.

   c. Strategies for meeting the NPG required levels of capability should be developed that prioritize investments on the basis of risk, need and National priorities in HSPD-8;

   d. Establish priorities within a resource-constrained environment;

   e. Clarify and understand roles and responsibilities in the National network of homeland security capabilities and revise the NPG as appropriate;

   f. Develop mutual aid agreements and Emergency Management Assistance Compacts that are informed by the requirements in the NPG and are synchronized in a manner to deliver the right capability at the right time to the right place to meet the right need; and

   g. Establish a program to measure and assess the effectiveness of preparedness capabilities across the Nation using the President's Management Agenda Score Card tool, and tie performance results to Homeland Security Grant Program funding.

21. **DHS should develop and maintain a National inventory of Federal capabilities.** Effective response plans cannot be developed absent a consideration of resources and capabilities. The Federal capabilities and corresponding assets and resources should be inventoried and placed into a database, per HSPD-8, by DHS. Key to this real-time inventory will be awareness of which assets are available during a disaster and of their deployment timeline from notification. Furthermore, DHS was required to establish a National inventory of Federal assets by Section 7406 of the Intelligence Reform and Terrorism Prevention Act of 2004.

a. DHS should coordinate with other Federal agencies and States to identify physical locations around the country that could be used as crisis support centers or bases for receiving, staging and integrating emergency management resources during disasters.

Critical Challenge: Integrated Use of Military Capabilities

Lesson Learned: The Departments of Homeland Security and Defense should jointly plan for the Department of Defense's support of Federal response activities as well as those extraordinary circumstances when it is appropriate for the Department of Defense to lead the Federal response. In addition, the Department of Defense should ensure the transformation of the National Guard is focused on increased integration with active duty forces for homeland security plans and activities.

Recommendations:

22. **DOD and DHS should develop recommendations for revision of the NRP to delineate the circumstances, objectives, and limitations of when DOD might temporarily assume the lead for the Federal response to a catastrophic incident.** Katrina demonstrated the importance of prior planning for rapid and complex response efforts. DOD should develop plans to lead the Federal response for events of extraordinary scope and nature (*e.g.,* nuclear incident or multiple simultaneous terrorist attacks causing a breakdown in civil society).

23. **DOD should revise its Immediate Response Authority (IRA) policy to allow commanders, in appropriate circumstances, to exercise IRA even without a request from local authorities.** DOD should work with DHS and State officials to improve integration of military response capabilities.

24. **DOD and DHS should plan and prepare for a significant DOD supporting role during a catastrophic event.** DOD's joint operational response doctrine is an integral part of the national effort and must be fully integrated into the national response at all levels of government. DOD should have a contingency role and a requirement to assist DHS with expertise in logistics, planning, and total asset visibility. DOD should coordinate with DHS and DOT to identify DOD's contingency role in airport operations and evacuations, and the planning and use of Ready Reserve Fleet vessels for housing, evacuation, communications, command, control, and logistics. The NRP and Catastrophic Incident Supplement (CIS) should specify the specific requirements for DOD resources based on the magnitude and type of a catastrophic event.

25. **DOD should provide support from the National Geospatial Intelligence Agency (NGA) and the National Security Agency (NSA) as part of overall DOD support to DHS under the NRP to provide technical skills, situational awareness, imagery support, analysis and assessment for responding to catastrophic events. Requests for situational awareness capabilities should follow DOD processes for asset allocation. DOD will ensure requests for assistance are identified and satisfied for access to NGA, NSA and other Combat Support Agency's capabilities.** NGA and NSA have significant technical capabilities that should be integrated into the Nation's preparation and response efforts. NGA and NSA have the capability to rapidly provide situational awareness and analysis. The response to Hurricane Katrina highlighted that NGA and NSA possess unique capabilities that can be utilized in homeland missions, to include severe weather events. The NSA was instrumental in matching up missing family members, and the NGA provided valuable overhead imagery of the disaster site. Defined roles in homeland security missions will allow for these capabilities to be better budgeted, developed, and ultimately leveraged. In support of missions in the homeland where DHS is the Primary Federal Agency, DHS should levy tasking requirements. These agencies have established relationships with governmental and private/commercial entities, which can be integrated as part of a larger national response effort. NGA and NSA roles and support to the homeland security mission should be added into the agencies' core mission statements. NGA and NSA support should be coordinated with civil agencies providing geospatial support and analysis, including the U.S. Geological Survey. These agencies need resources to perform homeland security functions. In order to meet these new mission requirements these agencies need to expand from a legacy focus of being a producer to a broader role as a service provider.

26. **Set standards for "pushing" the pre-positioning of Federal assets to States and locals, in the case of an imminent catastrophe.** DHS should create a civil operational planning capability to push assets that is robust, agile, and deployable; otherwise, the response will rely heavily on DOD capabilities. Factors slowing delivery of commodities require review and solutions adapted prior to future disasters. DHS should include much better planning efforts between State and Federal emergency management logisticians and operations personnel, the assistance and advice of DOD strategic logistics planners, and more robust private sector partnerships. DHS should mandate the use of pre-competed private sector contracts for capabilities ranging from airlift to advanced communications and life support and have available a rapid response capability similar to DOD. Federal funding should be predicated on States entering into their own contractual agreements, pre-crisis, with the private sector for procurement and delivery of commodities.

27. **In addition to the National Guard, the other Reserve Components of the military services should modify their organization and training to include a priority mission to prepare and deploy in support of homeland security missions.** Reserve components historically have focused on military and war fighting missions, which will continue; however, we should recognize that the Reserve components are too valuable a skilled and available resource at home not to be ready to incorporate them in any Federal response planning and effort. Additionally, efforts should be made to leverage Reserve civilian skills in disaster relief efforts.

28. **DOD should consider fully resourcing the JTF State Headquarters to address capabilities gaps and to enhance readiness.** Enhance National Guard capabilities by resourcing and fully implementing Joint Force Headquarters (JFHQ) State. JFHQ-State transformation is key to rapid deployment of National Guard forces in response to a catastrophe.

    The transformation of JFHQ-State and other National Guard capabilities for homeland security missions will ensure response forces are available in each DHS region. These capabilities should support NRP requirements including: security, maintenance, aviation, engineer, medical, communications, transportation, and logistics. The National Guard should develop rapid reaction forces capable of responding to an incident within 24 hours. This is vital to future rapid deployment of National Guard forces in response to a catastrophe. This transformation, as it nears completion, must continue to take root within DOD.

    JFHQ State will provide the command structure in which to lead and direct arriving Federal response capabilities, forming the backbone of State Incident Command System (ICS) and, as a result, the Federal Joint Field Office (JFO). It will facilitate unity of effort and provide the situational awareness needed for an effective response. To that end, the Command, Control, Communications, and Information (C3I) structure must be interoperable and satisfy a common set of mission essential tasks.

29. **Develop the capability to rapidly activate a JTF-State for contingencies.** JTF-State is a forward deployed command group that can stage assets (by conducting reception, staging, onward movement, and integration); provide situational awareness and initial command and control for both State governors (for National Guard troops) and USNORTHCOM (for Federal active duty troops); and provide State level components to a Federal active duty JTF, should one be required. JTF-State coordinates with USNORTHCOM and State authorities to ensure the application of the full capability of the Joint Force for domestic response missions. A key component of the JTF-State should be the State's WMD CSTs. The option to expanding the role of the CSTs to an all-hazards response team should be explored. This may require additional resources, but would improve situational awareness and command and control capabilities at the State level.

    A JTF-State model streamlines the command structure exercising command and control over all assigned forces supporting civil authorities. The JTF command and control architecture should provide a wide network to build a single common operating picture that increases situational awareness and redundancy. The JTF should assume command and control of Federal active duty forces and National Guard forces from other States. As part of the JFHQ State, the JTF maintains and provides trained and equipped forces and capabilities. If and when necessary, this JTF model enables a National Guard Commander familiar with State and local area of operations to serve both in a Federal and State status providing both unity of effort and unity of command for Federal and State forces.

30.   **DOD should consider assigning additional personnel (to include General officers) from the National Guard and the reserves of the military services to USNORTHCOM to achieve enhanced integration of Active and reserve component forces for homeland security missions.**

31.   **DOD should support DHS development of an analysis and operational planning capability to enable DHS to predict detailed requirements and plan for specific actions needed to respond to future disasters.** This DOD/DHS element should assess past catastrophic disasters and the successes and failures of the overall responses to those events. This information should inform detailed planning for future disaster response, and allow determination of specific decision points to aid rapid decision making. Ultimately a fully mature DHS planning capability should have additional utility by deploying during future catastrophic events and translating initial damage assessments into accurate needs assessments for local, State and Federal authorities.

32.   **DOD should consider chartering the NGB as a joint activity of the DOD. Responsibilities should include:**

   a.   Serve as the focal point in developing, managing, and integrating employment of joint National Guard capabilities for the Joint Staff and the Departments of the Army and Air Force in support of the Combatant Commands.

   b.   Act as the DOD channel of communication to and from the National Guard of the States and Territories.

   c.   Support all Combatant Commanders in developing joint operational requirements for contingency and response plans. Specifically support U.S. Joint Forces Command (USJFCOM), USNORTHCOM, U.S. Pacific Command (USPACOM), U.S. Southern Command (USSOUTHCOM), U.S. Strategic Command (USSTRATCOM) and the States and Territories in developing strategy and contingency plans for homeland defense missions.

   d.   Administer Army and Air Force programs; acquire, distribute, and manage resources; plan, coordinate, and provide situational awareness and other support to the Combatant Commanders.

Critical Challenge: Communications

Lesson Learned: The Department of Homeland Security should review our current laws, policies, plans, and strategies relevant to communications. Upon the conclusion of this review, the Homeland Security Council, with support from the Office of Science and Technology Policy, should develop a National Emergency Communications Strategy that supports communications operability and interoperability.

Recommendations:

33.   **DHS should complete the review of National Security and Emergency Preparedness (NS/EP) communications policy by April 30, 2006.** As requested by the Homeland Security Council and the National Security Council, DHS should conduct this review to provide a preliminary strategic "plan for integrating communications for all levels of crisis in light of evolving threats and new and converging technologies, and for organizational and policy changes." This review and resulting strategic plan will advance communications capability planning for the Nation's response posture.

34.   **HSC and OSTP should lead an interagency review of all current policies, laws, plans, and strategies that address communications and integrate them into a National Emergency Communications Strategy.** The review should include:

   a.   The development of an overarching National Emergency Communications Strategy should address a full range of hazards;

b.   A national emergency communications strategy should consider the direction of the telecommunications industry and supporting recommendations of the President's National Security Telecommunications Advisory Council;

c.   State and local emergency prevention, preparedness, and response personnel must maximize the resources provided by, and implement the procedures contained in, the Homeland Security Grant Program;

d.   Federal, State, and local entities should use the Target Capabilities List (TCL) as a reference to develop emergency communications strategies. The resulting strategies will enhance operability and support future interoperable emergency communications capabilities. State and local standards and performance measures for achieving for interoperability should be tied to Homeland Security Grant Program funding criteria;

e.   By March 1, 2006, HSC and OSTP should organize an interagency group to begin the development of a national emergency communications strategy. An interim strategy, to be completed May 31, 2006, should provide sufficient guidance and direction to address the deficiencies identified in the Hurricane Katrina response.

35.   **DHS should revise the NRP to conform to the new National Emergency Communications Strategy.** The NRP should include sufficient guidance on communications operations when responding to a disaster. This guidance should address the full spectrum of possible effects to the Nation's communications system from disasters and detail the required responses. It should also ensure that response operations employ all available communications assets to support operability and interoperability. The following areas should be addressed as part of the revision of the NRP:

a.   Communications procedures and guidelines need to be defined, implemented, and practiced through simulations and exercises. Measurement of progress to increase overall crisis communications capability will be graded against the President's Management Agenda criteria;

b.   Updated communications guidance must also emphasize the ability of emergency responders and private security officials to share information and use available communication systems to connect with authorities at all levels of government. Planning needs to cover not only system connectivity, but also operating practices, business processes, and initial data sets to make the system work;

c.   The NRP's ESF-2 must direct the integration of all available Federal, State, local, and private communications assets. The full integration of communications capability requires an assessment of Federal assets and an inventory of available capability. During emergencies, ESF-2 must have the authority to implement, resource, and restore communications;

d.   State and local first responders must satisfy the requirements of the Target Capabilities List, in order to receive Federal funding.

36.   **DHS should develop and maintain a national crisis communication system to support information exchange from the President, across the Federal government, and down to the State level.**

37.   **DHS should establish and maintain a deployable communications capability, to quickly gain and retain situational awareness when responding to catastrophic incidents.** To restore operability and achieve interoperability, there is a strong need for rapidly deployable, interoperable, commercial, off-the-shelf equipment that can provide a framework for connectivity among Federal, State, and local authorities. A deployable capability to "reach-back" to "large headquarters units capable of providing superior support to deployed elements from their home stations where they have better facilities, resources and access to information," can achieve initial operability. This transformational capability should ensure decision makers at all levels of government have accurate and complete data to assess courses of action. Inadequate situational awareness during the response to Hurricane Katrina resulted in decision makers relying on

incorrect and incomplete information. DHS progress in this regard is essential to ensure adequate situational awareness. It must therefore set measurable goals and use the President's Management Agenda initiatives to encourage progress and accountability toward achieving them. Available technologies can provide short-term operability and support long-term interoperability for emergency responders. However, to keep pace with technology changes, DHS should consider commercial, off-the-shelf solutions.

Critical Challenge: Logistics and Evacuation

Lesson Learned: The Department of Homeland Security, in coordination with State and local governments and the private sector, should develop a modern, flexible and transparent logistics system. This system should be based on established contracts for stockpiling commodities at the local level for emergencies and the provision of goods and services during emergencies. The Federal government must develop the capacity to conduct large-scale logistical operations that supplement and, if necessary, replace State and local logistical systems by leveraging resources within both the public sector and the private sector. The Department of Transportation, in coordination with other appropriate departments of the Executive Branch, must also be prepared to conduct mass evacuation operations when disasters overwhelm or incapacitate State and local governments.

Recommendations:

38. **DHS should partner with State and local governments, other Federal agencies and the private sector to develop an efficient, transparent and flexible logistics system for the procurement and delivery of goods and services during emergencies. DHS should develop a logistics system, utilizing an integrated supply chain management approach, capable of supporting large-scale disaster operations by leveraging resources within both the public sector and the private sector.**

    a. **DHS should identify private sector resources that can be leveraged to supplement and provide surge capacity to the Federal support to disaster operations, execute direct vendor delivery contingency contracts with these sources prior to disasters, and encourage State and local governments to do the same.** Such contracting practices would eliminate time-consuming and inefficient negotiations during emergencies. By utilizing direct vendor delivery contracts, shipments are sent directly to the customer from the supplier, bypassing unnecessary storage points. Participating State governments would identify their anticipated requirements and coordinate with DHS to ensure that contingency contracts are executed to meet those needs.

    b. **DHS should require that local and State governments establish contracts with private sector vendors for disaster relief supplies in advance of an emergency with the assurance of reimbursement should these contracts be activated in a post disaster declaration environment.**

    c. **Federal government should allocate strategic goods and services or conduct re-supply operations during a catastrophic disaster when shortfalls occur in local and State resources.** The new logistics system developed in concert with State and local governments, and the private sector should be transparent to all managers within the system (Federal, State and local governments and the private sector). The system should be comprehensive so that the full range of logistical requirements and the flow of goods and services can be tracked from provider to receiver. The system should take into account all the sources of logistical provisions such as mutual aid agreements within States, EMAC agreements between States, contracts between the private sector and Federal and State governments, and agreements between non-governmental, community, faith-based and volunteer organizations and Federal and State governments. The system should be designed to allow all Federal, State and local logistics managers to monitor the execution of mutual aid agreements between Federal homeland security regions, and to allow Federal prioritization of strategic logistics resources in circumstances where State and/or regional resources are depleted.

    d. DHS should improve planning and coordination with State and local partners, non-governmental organizations, and the private sector. DHS should ensure that its logistics system leverages the capabilities within local and State governments and all other potential reliable and credible resources. DHS should work with the National Emergency Management Association to ensure the full coordination of Federal logistical support, provided under the Stafford Act, with State logistical support provided under EMAC. The use of commercial logistics best practices in supply chain management should be used to minimize the need for the Federal government to stockpile materials. Charities and faith based organizations should be fully integrated into resource planning and be incorporated into the supply chain in their local areas. Federal, State, and local logistical planners should use the best practices from successful large private sector companies as well as from DOD as the standard to develop improved operational capabilities and coordination procedures in the new logistics system.

    e. DHS, in cooperation with other departments and agencies, should develop the capability to identify sources of assets within the Federal government, and to track the movement of supplies during a disaster. This information would be extremely useful to resource managers at all levels of government during disasters.

    f. DHS should establish a Chief Logistics Officer to oversee all logistics operations across multiple support functions. The Chief Logistics Officer (CLO) would be responsible for developing and maintaining an integrated supply chain management system. This system should be structured in ways that are compatible with the structure of the National Incident Management System. The CLO would guide and assist those Federal, State and local organizations that manage emergency response assets and commodities, enabling them to procure and deliver supplies for emergency operations. The CLO would be responsible for logistics technology and software solutions that allow emergency managers to have visibility of all assets in the supply chain and to be able to access those supplies. A CLO should also be established in each homeland security regional office.

    g. DOD should detail logistics planners to DHS to assist in developing this logistics system. DOD and DHS should review and consider supply chain management best practices in developing the DHS logistics system. DOD should assist DHS in developing its logistics system; train DHS personnel in logistics management; exercise the DHS logistics system; and assist operating DHS' logistics management system until a fully mature capability exists.

39. **DHS should streamline its procedures for issuing mission assignments to other departments and agencies. These mission assignments will be identified in advance of an emergency so that logisticians can operationalize assets and provide resource support rapidly. In addition, other departments and agencies should establish procedures for promptly executing mission assignments.** The goal of these efforts is to minimize the delays observed during Hurricane Katrina when departments or agencies were slow to act because they either had not received a FEMA mission assignment, or did not have an effective system for executing the mission assignment once received.

40. **The Office of Management and Budget (OMB) should consider the efficacy of the Executive Branch and departments and agencies having the flexibility to transfer funds across accounts in advance of supplemental funding for immediate use during catastrophes in order to execute the departments' and agencies' respective missions under the National Response Plan.** Transferred funds would not supplant the Disaster Relief Fund that is controlled and dispersed by DHS through the mission assignment process. Rather, it would provide the flexibility to use all sources of funds to fund emergency response actions in the aftermath of a catastrophic event in circumstances where the DHS mission assignment process is insufficient or inappropriate to handle the requirements of responding to the disaster.

41. **Designate DOT as the primary federal agency responsible for developing the Federal government's capability to conduct mass evacuations when disasters overwhelm State and local governments. DOT should, in coordination with HHS, DOD, VA, DHS and the American Red Cross (ARC) plan, train and conduct exercises for the timely evacuation of patients and transportation of medical supplies and personnel.** DOT, which is the primary agency for ESF-1, is best positioned to develop the capability to

conduct and coordinate mass evacuation and associated critical tasks. DOT should identify, prioritize, and approve plans to: transport patients to and from all Federal medical treatment facilities, and; assemble and pre-deploy caches of medical supplies to strategic locations. Such proactive efforts should improve the ability of Federal agencies to conduct patient evacuations when State and local agencies are unable to do so in a timely or effective manner. DOT should coordinate directly with HHS, DOD, VA, USDA, DHS and ARC, as well as State and local agencies, to plan, train and exercise for mass evacuations. In addition to assisting States in planning and preparing for mass evacuations, ESF-1 would conduct evacuation operations when State and local governments are unable to do so. ESF-8 would retain primary responsibility for coordinating the evacuation of seriously ill or injured persons. In addition, USDA (one of the primary agencies for ESF-11: Agriculture and Natural Resources) would plan and manage the evacuation of animals. It should be understood that the development of these capabilities will take time and in most cases will be grown to full capacity incrementally.

42. **DHS should require State and local governments, as a condition for receiving Homeland Security grants, to develop, implement, and exercise emergency evacuation plans and to cooperate fully with all Federal evacuation activities.** DHS has commendably incorporated a similar requirement in its FY 2006 Homeland Security Grant Program. State and local governments should use the National Preparedness Goal's Target Capabilities List (TCL) as a standard for the development of these evacuation plans. In addition to those TCL capabilities, State and local evacuation plans should specify procedures to address the pre-positioning of food, medical and fuel supplies. These plans should address establishing first-aid stations, tracking and coordinating movements of evacuees, evacuating pets, unaccompanied minors, the elderly, and evacuating people who lack the means to leave voluntarily. Each State, starting in FY 07, should receive an annual evacuation readiness status report. This report will be in the form of an evacuation readiness "report card" that will grade the ability of the State to conduct evacuation operations. The report card will be based on exercises, training, effective use of Federal grant monies, and other relevant criteria as a condition of further grant funding. Much like the President's Management Agenda, States will be given the expected results which they need to accomplish with their grant funding. This assessment would not only classify each State on its level of evacuation readiness, but also track how well homeland security grant funds are spent for evacuation planning. States that do not use their grant funds effectively would have their grant funds reduced or terminated.

43. **DHS should, in coordination with DOT, evaluate all State evacuation plans as well as the evacuation plans of the 75 largest urban areas.** As the President declared when he addressed the Nation from Jackson Square in New Orleans, "Our cities must have clear and up-to-date plans for . . . evacuating large numbers of people in an emergency." DHS reviewed State catastrophic planning, including evacuation planning, and submitted a Congressionally mandated report to Congress on February 10, 2006. In addition, DHS and DOT are jointly reviewing evacuation plans for the Gulf Region, their findings due to Congress on June 1, 2006. These two departments should report their findings to the President through the Assistant to the President for Homeland Security and Counterterrorism concurrently with their submission to Congress. These reviews should specifically address special needs populations, people who lack the means to evacuate voluntarily, and the evacuation of animals, as well as other aspects of evacuation planning mentioned in Recommendation 5 above.

    a. **Consideration should be given to revising the Stafford Act to restrict reimbursement eligibility to only those States that have met basic performance requirements for critical functions such as mass evacuation.**

Critical Challenge: Search and Rescue

Lesson Learned: The Department of Homeland Security should lead an interagency review of current policies and procedures to ensure effective integration of all Federal search and rescue assets during disaster response.

Recommendations:

44. **DHS should lead an interagency team to review and revise the NRP to ensure the integration of all Federal search and rescue assets. This review should:**

    a. **Expand ESF-9 to ensure the coordination of all Federal search and rescue operations, not just urban search and rescue.** Under this new construct, both the urban and civil search and rescue coordinators would report to the Operations Section Chief under the Incident Commander. This structure is consistent with the National Search and Rescue Plan (NSP) requirement for the civil search and rescue coordinator to serve as the search and rescue representative to the Incident Commander, as well as with NIMS and ICS principles that place both urban search and rescue and civil search and rescue under the Operations Section. It would allow both coordinators to support each other and share resources, depending on the nature of the incident. Ideally, the ESF-9 coordinator in the Joint Field Office (JFO) should have extensive training and education in both urban search and rescue and civil search and rescue.

    b. **Require coordination throughout Incident Command to ensure continuity of care for those rescued.** The ESF-9 coordinator should work with the logistics section under ESF-5: Emergency Management and the other ESF's grouped under the Emergency Services Branch (including ESF-8: Public Health and Medical Services) to ensure victims receive medical care and are transported to an adequate housing shelter.

    c. **ESF-9 must include the United States Forest Service's (USFS), DOI and EPA capabilities to perform search and rescue operations.** USFS is given the role as primary agency under ESF-4: Firefighting and as supporting agency under ESF-9. DOI is a principal partner with USFS in carrying out ESF-4 functions. As firefighters make up a large percentage of FEMA Urban Search and Rescue teams, their expertise and capabilities should also contribute to search and rescue operations. Under ESF-9, the mission statements of USFS and DOI should include the availability of firefighting personnel, not just equipment and supplies, for use in search and rescue operations. ESF-9 must include the capabilities of all participants in the National Search and Rescue Committee.

45. **The National Search and Rescue Committee should revise the National Search and Rescue Plan (NSP) to include disaster response operations.** The NRP references the NSP as a supporting operational document. However, the NSP is confusing because it specifically states that it does not cover overall response to disaster operations, as called for in the NRP. The NSP should therefore be revised to clarify its role in disaster response operations. The revision should specifically address air traffic control and coordination.

46. **Each State and major city should incorporate Search and Rescue and US&R annexes into their overall disaster response plans.** Federal grant assistance should require each State, under the State Homeland Security Grant Program, and urban area under the Urban Areas Security Initiative, develop a search and rescue annex within its specific disaster response plan, as part of its concept of operations. This search and rescue annex should be scalable, modular, organized along ICS principles, and be all-hazards in scope. It should also specifically delineate which agencies have primary responsibility for each aspect of search and rescue. The plan should specify in what order Federal assistance assets or State-to-State mutual aid assets (through the Emergency Management Assistance Compact) will be requested and detail how search and rescue coordination will be integrated into incident command. These search and rescue annexes should identify where victims are to be taken in the event Federal, State, and local logistical support to the victims is required. Representatives of National Search and Rescue committee organizations should assist the development of State and local search and rescue plans.

47. **DHS should expand the National Preparedness Goal's Target Capabilities List (TCL) Capability: Urban Search and Rescue to require Federal Urban Search and Rescue teams and State and local entities to train, equip, and exercise for civil search and rescue missions.** Currently, this capability only focuses on urban search and rescue and does not include any of the types of civil search and rescue, such as maritime rescue. An expanded capability should use the NSP as the guide for including civil search and rescue performance standards. State and local entities not currently in the national civil search and rescue community could then use the expanded search and rescue capability as a reference to plan, train, and exercise for both urban search and rescue and civil search and rescue missions. Funding for urban search and rescue teams should reserve a portion of their funding allocated to train and equip FEMA Urban Search and Rescue Task Force members for civil search and rescue operations.

48. **DHS should create a national search and rescue volunteer certification program.** This national certification should be used to verify the identity and the level of skills and training of search and rescue volunteers. Volunteers could report to "reception centers," which should be established along the perimeter of any impacted area to receive spontaneous volunteers. A national certification program would speed the incorporation of these individuals into the unified search and rescue command structure and greatly increase the effectiveness of the response. Voluntary organizations such as the National Association of Search and Rescue (NASAR) should be requested to assist with such a certification program.

Critical Challenge: Public Safety and Security

Lesson Learned: The Department of Justice, in coordination with the Department of Homeland Security, should examine Federal responsibilities for support to State and local law enforcement and criminal justice systems during emergencies and then build operational plans, procedures, and policies to ensure an effective Federal law enforcement response.

Recommendations:

Law Enforcement

49. **DHS should, in coordination with DOJ, revise the National Response Plan to provide more effective coordination of the law enforcement response to a disaster by clarifying and expanding the role and mission of the Public Safety and Security support function and the Senior Federal Law Enforcement Officer. The revised NRP should:**

    a. **Designate DOJ as the primary agency responsible for the ESF-13 Public Safety and Security function.** The NRP designates DHS and DOJ to serve jointly as primary agencies for the ESF-13 function. This diffusion of responsibility creates unnecessary confusion at the scene of the crisis and violates the principle of unity of command. We recognize that DHS has significant law enforcement assets, both in Washington DC and in field offices throughout the country. However, the Attorney General is, by law, the President's primary law enforcement officer. DOJ's long experience and recognized public law enforcement responsibility for prosecuting Federal crimes, in addition to its existing ties with the State and local law enforcement communities, make it best positioned to assume the lead role, though it still must continue to work in partnership with DHS. Through its United States Attorneys Offices in all 50 states and through the FBI's 100 Joint Terrorism Task Forces, DOJ has the capability to leverage these important relationships with State and local law enforcement. We also consider DOJ to have greater traditional law enforcement experience, whereas DHS's law enforcement programs are more specialized, focusing on areas such as border control, aviation security, and protective services. In addition, giving DOJ responsibility for leading the Public Safety and Security support function will let DHS focus on its overall coordination of emergency response mission.

    b. **Finalize the drafting of Public Safety and Security policies and procedures.** The Public Safety and Security (ESF-13) Annex of the NRP required primary and support agencies to define their functions and develop policies and procedures by April 2005, four months after the NRP was issued. While drafts exist, this effort needs immediate completion to provide clarity to the organization and functions of the Public Safety and Security support function.

c. **Specify that the Attorney General will, in consultation with the Secretary of Homeland Security, designate the SFLEO.** When the Secretary of Homeland Security declares an Incident of National Significance (INS), the Attorney General should promptly designate the SFLEO; during a non-INS event, the Attorney General may appoint an SFLEO if needed. Also, the NRP should give the Attorney General the authority to designate a Deputy SFLEO from a department other than that of the SFLEO. In recognition of the Secretary of Homeland Security's role in coordinating the Federal response under HSPD-5, the Attorney General should consult with the Secretary prior to designating the SFLEO.

d. **Include a new position designated as the "Senior Civilian Representative of the Attorney General" (SCRAG).** As with the SFLEO, the Attorney General should immediately appoint the SCRAG to serve as the Attorney General's representative for issues requiring senior-level involvement of a DOJ official. Whereas the SFLEO is responsible for managing the operational aspects of the Federal law enforcement response, the SCRAG will assist as needed in resolving any significant law enforcement policy issues that might arise with State or local officials, or between Federal official.

e. **Require the establishment of a law enforcement coordination center within the Joint Field Office (JFO) to coordinate the Federal, State, and local law enforcement response during all types of emergencies.** While the NRP includes such an entity for a terrorist-related incident or a National Special Security Event, it does not clearly set forth how Federal law enforcement coordinates with its State and local counterparts during other incidents.

50. **DOJ should lead the development of the capability to surge Federal law enforcement resources in the immediate aftermath of a disaster.** As outlined by the NRP, law enforcement personnel should be drawn from the following sources, in this order: 1) Civilian law enforcement and National Guard from affected State; 2) Civilian law enforcement and National Guard from other States; and 3) Civilian law enforcement from Federal agencies. To maximize the availability of law enforcement assets from each of these categories, the following should be done:

a. **DOJ should establish a program to review State and local plans for continuity of operations for law enforcement and the criminal justice system during a crisis.**

b. **DOJ should develop a program to increase States' awareness of the procedures for requesting Federal law enforcement assistance under the Emergency Federal Law Enforcement Assistance Act.**

c. **DOJ should lead an interagency effort to catalogue the Federal law enforcement assets within the Executive Branch.** This effort will serve as the basis for developing a database of assets available for use during an INS, in order to ensure appropriate use of all available Federal law enforcement assets.

d. **DOJ and DHS should each develop, in coordination with the other, the capability to rapidly deploy a contingent of Federal law enforcement officers to prevent and respond to civil disorder.** Consistent with the principle that law enforcement is the responsibility of local and State governments, this force should deploy only in the event that State authorities request Federal assistance pursuant to the Emergency Federal Law Enforcement Assistance Act, or as otherwise directed by the President. However, the NRP should make clear that where, as in this case, the need for additional law enforcement resources is manifest and obvious, it should be the Attorney General's responsibility, after notifying the Secretary of Homeland Security, to make an offer of Federal law enforcement support to the affected Governor.

51. **DOJ should develop procedures for streamlined deputization of qualified Federal law enforcement officers.** This effort should address circumstances where Federal law enforcement personnel require *Federal* deputization to enforce Federal laws outside their jurisdiction, or *State* deputization to enforce State laws.

DOJ should work together with the States' Attorneys General to develop agreements whereby a State requesting Federal law enforcement assistance agrees in advance to grant limited State law enforcement authority to Federal agents for the duration of the emergency.

52. **DOJ should, in coordination with DHS, further incorporate force protection into Federal response planning, to prevent disruption of Federal agencies' operations and to protect Federal personnel and property.** While the Public Safety and Security annex of the NRP designates force protection as an ESF-13 responsibility, further response planning is required on this issue in light of the problems encountered during Hurricane Katrina.

Criminal Justice

53. **DOJ should, in coordination with the Administrative Office of the U.S. Courts, develop a program to ensure the continuity of the Federal criminal justice system and to provide assistance to States in developing complementary plans.** While the operation and continuity of the court system falls under the purview of the Judicial Branch, the Department of Justice should ensure that adequate plans exist to ensure the continuity of its critical prosecutorial functions. Components of DOJ such as the U.S. Marshals Service and the Bureau of Prisons are critical to the operations of the Federal court system and must be incorporated into the contingency planning.

54. **DOJ should develop plans to improve the accountability for persons under supervision by the Federal criminal justice system, and to provide assistance to States in developing complementary plans.**

55. **DOJ, in coordination with DHS, should establish a program to provide oversight and technical assistance for States' emergency plans for evacuating prisoners in the event of a disaster.** Although evacuation of State and local prisoners is primarily a State and local responsibility, prisoners are protected by Federal civil rights laws and thus the Federal government has an interest in ensuring that such evacuations are appropriately planned and implemented.

56. **DHS and DOJ should coordinate their respective grant and assistance funding programs to States and local governments to establish uniform standards and conditions of awards in furtherance of the above recommendations.** If both departments should determine a need for legislation to remedy the disparate standards or criteria for different grant sources, OMB should consult with the departments to draft proposed legislation.

Critical Challenge: Public Health and Medical Support

Lesson Learned: In coordination with the Department of Homeland Security and other homeland security partners, the Department of Health and Human Services should strengthen the Federal government's capability to provide public health and medical support during a crisis. This will require the improvement of command and control of public health resources, the development of deliberate plans, an additional investment in deployable operational resources, and an acceleration of the initiative to foster the widespread use of interoperable electronic health records systems.

Recommendations:

57. **HHS should lead a unified and strengthened public health and medical command for Federal disaster response.**

   a. **HHS should develop a comprehensive plan to identify, deploy and track Federal public health and medical assets (human, fixed and materiel) for use during a catastrophic event.** HHS should assume primary control of the public health and medical support effort, coordinating the activities of supporting agencies from a central location. The Secretary of HHS should be aware of, and in charge of coordinating, all Federal medical and public health assets available for use. All Federal departments must support and facilitate HHS in the execution of its responsibilities to coordinate all Federal public health and medical assets. Medical operations are highly dependent on efficient inter-agency cooperation and the successful completion of tasks is dependent on a fully integrated Federal effort.

b. **HHS in coordination with OMB and DHS should draft proposed legislation for submission to Congress, to transfer NDMS from DHS to HHS.** As the agency charged in HSPD-5 with the overall coordination of disaster response in America, DHS should clearly articulate the operational requirements for disaster medical assistance. HHS should then be responsible for building and maintaining the appropriate operational capability: it should guide, direct, and develop the NDMS and integrate it into other HHS operational elements. NDMS is a critical component to the success of any Federal disaster response requiring medical support. As such, public health professionals and emergency medical responses should be managed and overseen by HHS which has the greatest health experience and expertise. Thus, NDMS should be returned to the direct command of HHS. It should be understood that the development of these capabilities will take time and in most cases will be grown to full capacity incrementally.

c. **HHS should organize, train, equip, and roster medical and public health professionals in pre-configured and deployable teams**. These personnel should be comprised of officers of the Commissioned Corps of the U.S. Public Health Service, the Medical Reserve Corps (MRC), the NDMS, health care providers within DOD and the VA, and volunteer health professionals from the private sector. This is consistent with the HHS efforts to enhance the medical and public health response to meet future challenges by transforming the United States Public Health Service Commissioned Corps. This will enable a critical emergency response resource to address public health challenges more quickly and efficiently. The Commissioned Corps will increase its ranks, streamline its assignment and deployment process, and increase its ability to recruit the best and the brightest to defend the Nation's public health. HHS announced administrative steps toward this end. HHS has also drafted legislation in this area and forwarded it to OMB for Administration review and clearance. HHS should be given appropriate authorities to carry out this responsibility and should establish and test a system to quickly and efficiently identify, credential and assign personnel to missions.

58. **HHS should ensure coordination and oversight of emergency, bioterrorism, and ongoing public health preparedness needs**. In a public health emergency, the Secretary of HHS should have the integrated support of the public health and public health emergency preparedness programs. Within HHS, two Staff Division and seven Operating Division Assistant Secretary level positions oversee some aspect of public health programs, many of which have overlapping functions in an emergency response. The Secretary of HHS should review this issue and determine how best to ensure the integration of all relevant HHS information and functions during a public health emergency.

59. **The Surgeon General should routinely communicate public health, as well as individual and community preparedness guidance to the general population.** While there are other prominent and capable Federal health officials, the Surgeon General's stature and credibility should be used to repeatedly and proactively deliver a consistent public health preparedness message to the public. This will not only help to increase personal, community and national disaster preparedness, it will also make the Surgeon General a more effective and credible source of guidance during public health emergencies.

60. **Create and maintain a dedicated, full time, and equipped response team composed of Commissioned Corps officers of the U.S. Public Health Service.** The size of this team would be determined by the Corps' senior leadership, and be sufficient to meet the response needs as set forth by the Secretary. This team, overseen by the Surgeon General, could rapidly and effectively deploy to any event requiring medical and public health expertise and remain on station as long as needed. Other Corps officers, NDMS, the MRC, and the private sector could augment the team under the Surgeon General's command as required.

61. **DHS and HHS should look for the means to increase the capacities and capabilities of local and State health infrastructures.** Local and State health departments are the foundation upon which the National public health preparedness rests. HHS and DHS provide Federal grants to local and State health departments,

but additional funding is needed in view of the threats to the Nation from: weapons of mass destruction; biological agents; pandemic influenza and natural disasters. Grant funds from HHS and DHS should be synchronized to maximize the benefit to local and State health departments. Furthermore, all grant funding must be targeted toward increasing needed capabilities and then be reviewed to grade State and local performance according to the Presidential Management Agenda.

62. **Accelerate the HHS initiative to foster widespread use of interoperable electronic health (EHR) records systems, to achieve development and certification of systems for emergency responders within the next 12 months**. The adoption of interoperable EHR systems will support first responders and health providers and dramatically improve the quality and efficacy of care to displaced patients across a population. The President signed an Executive Order, *Incentives for the Use of Health Information Technology and Establishing the Position of the National Health Information Technology Coordinator,* on April 27, 2004, that provides guidance for the development of a nationwide interoperable health information technology.

Critical Challenge: Human Services

Lesson Learned: The Department of Health and Human Services should coordinate with other departments of the Executive Branch, as well as State governments and non-governmental organizations, to develop a robust, comprehensive, and integrated system to deliver human services during disasters so that victims are able to receive Federal and State assistance in a simple and seamless manner. In particular, this system should be designed to provide victims a consumer oriented, simple, effective, and single encounter from which they can receive assistance.

Recommendations:

63. **Assign HHS the responsibility for coordinating the provision of human services during disasters.** HHS should serve as the single Federal coordinating agency, with full situational awareness across agencies, and manage the delivery of services by other Federal departments. HHS working with DHS should review and, as appropriate, amend the NRP to ensure a single point of contact for victims to access all applicable Federal human services in an emergency and a capable deployment plan to enable this effort.

   a. **Federal agencies with an ongoing role in delivering human services should be prepared to do so in a disaster environment.** In addition to HHS, other Federal agencies have responsibility for providing human services. All Federal agencies responsible for the administration of human service programs should plan and prepare for the delivery of services in a disaster environment, with HHS coordinating and authorizing reimbursement for their respective disaster-related expenditures. Federal agencies that routinely deliver human services should build on established relationships with State and local agencies and private sector organizations, but also create contingency plans to assure the independent delivery of Federal assistance when necessary.

64. **HHS should inventory all Federal human services. As part of this effort HHS should:**

   a. **Inventory the range of human services programs of the Federal government.** There are thousands of human service programs across the interagency, many of which are jointly administered by State and local agencies. A catalogue of available programs will facilitate the prioritization and delivery of services, especially during emergency situations.

   b. **Identify current statutory authorities that permit the waiver of impediments to the delivery of services during an emergency.** Knowing which regulations can be waived will help responding agencies to more efficiently deliver services in emergency settings when speed is a high priority. Agencies should identify current waiver authority and impediments to service delivery and should provide HHS with suggested threshold criteria for triggering waiver authority. Agencies should also identify current authority for reimbursing disaster-related administrative costs and related impediments to reimbursing service providers for legitimate costs.

65. **HHS should develop a simple, comprehensive, and efficient means for disaster victims to enroll for all available human services at a single encounter.** Many important human service programs have wide variation in eligibility requirements. HHS' coordination and integration role is vital in helping to simplify access to complex and varied human service programs. Upon completion of the inventory of programs and available Federal facilities, HHS should prioritize the delivery of human service programs and develop plans to establish "one-stop" centers where disaster victims would enroll in Federal, State, local, and non-governmental human assistance programs. These "one stop" centers should complement the continued and expanded use of simplified telephone and internet-based registration modalities. The goal should be for the victim to go to one physical location, encounter one person who gathers all the necessary data and inputs it into a database that is shared and transparent among all human service providers at the Federal, State and local level as required. This will likely increase efficiency, reduce frustration of evacuees and expedite the delivery of services for eligible recipients.

a. **Task the appropriate Federal agencies to develop processes to assess disaster victims' needs and process their applications for assistance within consolidated "one-stop" centers.** These processes should avoid duplication of effort, employ streamlined in-take and case management strategies and foster the interagency administration of human services in a disaster area.

b. **HHS working with DHS should work to include faith-based, community, and non-profit organizations in the emergency planning, preparedness, and delivery of human services.** These private sector organizations contributed greatly to the Hurricane Katrina response. They should actively participate in all phases of a Federal disaster response and HHS should specifically facilitate access to their services in all "one-stop" centers.

c. **HHS in coordination with DHS should oversee the development of deployable interagency teams to assess human service needs and deliver assistance.** Created before the disaster, these teams can be deployed immediately to the disaster area to begin coordinating access to human services. These teams should be composed of knowledgeable and experienced Federal employees as well as personnel from State and local agencies and the private sector, as appropriate. They should serve in the "one stop" centers and also visit shelters and other locations necessary to facilitate the deliver of human services.

d. **HHS working with DHS and the Department of Labor should inventory existing Federal infrastructure and resources which could be utilized for provisions of consolidated services to affected areas.** Contingency plans should be developed for the utilization of Federal facilities, equipment such as phones, computers, and personnel on short-notice to provide consolidated services in response to a crisis. These plans should be exercised and evaluated on a routine basis.

66. **HHS and DHS should jointly work with the private sector to encourage the development of a capacity to voluntarily store and retrieve personal identifying information.** Encourage the private sector development of a capability for individuals to voluntarily submit their personal identifying information for virtual storage that citizens and their families could access during emergencies. The capability is best thought of as a 21st century version of a bank vault, with virtual safe deposit boxes for information. Disaster victims could access the virtually stored data to apply for Federal assistance, medical treatment, or insurance benefits. Because of the sensitivity of the personal data stored, strict privacy limitations and protections would be required. HHS should consider how their experience with Electronic Health Records (EHR) might inform such an effort.

67. **Existing Federal sources of information should be identified which might assist Federal authorities upon an emergency or disaster declaration by the President.** While numerous current Federal information sources exist (such as those maintained by SSA, DHS, VA, Treasury and the Department of Defense), they are not designed to identify or track individuals. Limited emergency access to existing Federal information sources should be considered and evaluated for their potential value in improving the Federal response. The development and deployment process must account for privacy, security, scalability, and compatibility

Critical Challenge: Mass Care and Housing

Lesson Learned: Using established Federal core competencies and all available resources, the Department of Housing and Urban Development, in coordination with other departments of the Executive Branch with housing stock, should develop integrated plans and bolstered capabilities for the temporary and long-term housing of evacuees. The American Red Cross and the Department of Homeland Security should retain responsibility and improve the process of mass care and sheltering during disasters.

Recommendations:

68. **ARC and DHS should retain the mass care and sheltering responsibility during disasters.** With long-standing experience providing mass care and shelters during disasters, ARC is a highly valued national asset: it must be a primary agency, along with DHS. ARC has extensive experience with mass care and sheltering during disasters, however, their status as a non-government organization limits their access to Federal planning meetings. DHS and ARC should strengthen their planning and operational relationships with HUD. HUD's expertise lies in the provision of mid- and long-term housing. To assure the appropriate expertise is brought to bear in all phases of a disaster (preparation, response, recovery and rebuilding) and a seamless integration of care for disaster victims, HUD, DHS and ARC must develop a close working relationship, not just during crises. During non-emergency times, they must jointly plan for mass care and housing during disasters. In conjunction with other Federal agencies, they must train for disasters and conduct exercises to evaluate the response readiness of the Federal government.

69. **Designate HUD as the lead Federal agency for the provision of temporary housing.** HUD, with extensive experience providing housing resources for those in need, must use its extensive network of regional offices and State and local housing agencies, to prepare for potential relocation emergencies. While there will always be a need for some victims to remain on their property while rebuilding their homes, the provision of trailers should not be the default means of temporary housing offered to all evacuees leaving shelters. HUD, rather than DHS, should be the lead Federal agency for housing and HUD should devote resources to gain this competency with support from ARC, and other Federal agencies. HUD must create a professional staff to augment its current housing capacity in order to create the ability to arrange housing for disaster victims and adequately train, exercise and resource this capability. But, DHS should retain its vital coordinating function for the entire disaster response. It should be understood that the development of these capabilities will take time and in most cases will be grown to full capacity incrementally.

70. **Assist States and municipalities in developing mass relocation plans for each major metropolitan area and inventories of existing shelters and shelter sites.** Such plans must match mass evacuation plans developed for metropolitan areas and should include the pre-identification of sites suitable for the establishment of shelters. Plans should also include appropriate guidelines regarding suitable shelters and thorough inventories of shelters already in existence. HUD should receive the lead role in relocation planning and inventorying shelters, with DOT, DOI and USDA assuming supporting roles. HUD can combine data from Federal, State, and local sources to compile inventories and establish the frequency of inventory updates. Federal grant money should be predicated on States and municipalities periodically updating their relocation plans and shelter inventories.

71. **DHS should develop a system to maintain awareness of the movement of shelter and temporary housing residents.** Local, State, and Federal officials in charge of sheltering evacuees must know the number and type (*e.g.,* number of disabled, number of minors) of evacuees in addition to their names and personal identifying data as they move between shelters and from shelters to temporary housing. This will improve allocation of resources to shelters (such as food and water), as well as the reunion of separated family members. Such a system must complement other systems to register evacuees for available social services.

72. **DHS should review and revise the Federal regulations under the Stafford Act to emphasize "location-independent" housing assistance.** Current regulations allow payment of rental subsidies to disaster victims, but not the routine payment of security deposits or utility fees. Reimbursement for repairs to existing

available housing units are also not authorized, effectively precluding the use of a large supply of federally controlled units that may only need minor repairs in order to be occupied. These restrictions effectively push many people to trailers and other manufactured housing units, while leaving other available housing vacant. Revising these housing regulations would allow greater flexibility in meeting urgent housing needs in the aftermath of a disaster.

Critical Challenge: Public Communications

Lesson Learned: The Department of Homeland Security should develop an integrated public communications plan to better inform, guide, and reassure the American public before, during, and after a catastrophe. The Department of Homeland Security should enable this plan with operational capabilities to deploy coordinated public affairs teams during a crisis.

Recommendations:

73. **DHS should revise the NRP to improve the Public Affairs Support and External Affairs annexes to ensure a better coordinated, more effective response.**

    a. DHS should revise standing operating procedures, command relationships, training, organizational structure, and communications between Federal Public Affairs Offices (PAOs) and their State and local counterparts.

    b. DHS should revise the NRP to delineate clearly when National and Incident JICs should be required to activate and deactivate. This guidance should also determine the proper location and number of JICs to be established in response to catastrophes.

    c. DHS should revise the NRP to delineate a clear structure for a fully coordinated, integrated, and synchronized public communications strategy, across the Federal government and with State and locals.

74. **DHS should establish rapidly deployable Public Affairs teams, able to operate self-sufficiently, in austere conditions. These deployable Public Affairs teams should be established across all Federal departments and agencies with key Homeland Security responsibilities.** These teams should be capable of providing Public Affairs assistance within hours to incident locations. These teams could be used to form the Incident JIC. All Federal departments and agencies with domestic operational responsibilities should establish programs to use embedded media where appropriate.

75. **DHS should expand Federal partnership programs with State and local Public Affairs Officials (PAO).**

    a. DHS should strengthen its relationship with groups such as the National Governors Association to provide joint incident communications training programs for State governments.

    b. DHS should also strengthen relationships with the Defense Information School, Navy Post Graduate School, National Defense University, and other academic institutions. These Federal partners can assist in providing training and certification to State and local emergency management and the PAOs of key DHS organizations (*e.g.,* DHS, FEMA, U.S. Coast Guard) and personnel such as PFO and Federal Coordinating Officer candidates. Such training would help to improve incident communications efforts.

76. **Develop a Public Communications Coordination capability for crisis communications at the White House.** Designate a senior White House Communications official to be responsible for the Homeland Security Council and crisis communications portfolio. In close collaboration with DHS' Office of Public Affairs, this official would be responsible for:

a. Coordination of public communications and public affairs within the homeland across all relevant Federal departments and agencies;

b. Establishing a permanent strategic communications capability, to facilitate messages to the public, the media, and all departments and agencies;

c. Developing a national public communications and public affairs strategic plan;

d. Develop "Risk Communications" to communicate pre-incident expectations to private citizens. This may be carried out by identifying credible spokespersons who can frequently update the public on preparedness, current threats and crisis communications.

77. DHS should establish an integrated public alert and warning system in coordination with all relevant departments and agencies.

a. The system, building on the Emergency Alert System (EAS), must leverage advanced communication technologies and existing Federal, State, and local systems.

b. Federal, State and local levels of government must have the means to communicate essential and accurate emergency information to the public prior to, during and after a catastrophe.

c. Use the National Preparedness Goal's Target Capabilities List as a reference to build and sustain the system.

Critical Challenge: Critical Infrastructure and Impact Assessment

Lesson Learned: The Department of Homeland Security, working collaboratively with the private sector, should revise the National Response Plan and finalize the Interim National Infrastructure Protection Plan to be able to rapidly assess the impact of a disaster on critical infrastructure. We must use this knowledge to inform Federal response and prioritization decisions and to support infrastructure restoration in order to save lives and mitigate the impact of the disaster on the Nation.

Recommendations:

78. DHS should revise the National Response Plan to:

a. **Provide for a stronger Infrastructure Support Branch in the National Operations Center.** The Infrastructure Support Branch will coordinate among the appropriate ESF's to ensure that the guidance developed by the Critical Infrastructure Policy Coordinating Committee is followed for infrastructure protection and restoration after an event. In addition, this branch will coordinate with critical infrastructure sectors, provide senior leaders with a summary of reports and modeling, and develop recommended preemptive and responsive actions to remediate or mitigate the impact of the loss of critical infrastructure. These optional actions will be based on reports from the Impact Assessment Working Group, the National Infrastructure Simulation and Analysis Center (NISAC), Sector Coordinating Councils, and consultation with DHS/IP.

b. **Strengthen the role and responsibility of the Infrastructure Liaison.** Currently, the Infrastructure Liaison is designated by DHS/IP, to serve as the principal advisor to the JFO Coordination Group regarding all national and regional level critical infrastructure and key resource incident-related issues. This role should be more clearly defined, and have greater responsibility which should include a designated group of trained critical infrastructure staff from Federal departments and agencies including DHS staff versed in infrastructure protection that are available for immediate deployment to the JFO to fill the role of the expanded Infrastructure Liaison group. The liaison should: (1) Gather and fuse relevant data about private infrastructure operational status; (2) Coordinate overall Federal response efforts for infrastructure restoration and recovery; and (3) Strengthen direct communications with private infrastructure owners and operators. This expanded Infrastructure Liaison will incorporate the Private Sector Liaisons to ensure unity of effort.

Policy and Planning

79. **DHS should revise the National Preparedness Goal to require the collaborative development of regional disaster plans (such as those required by the DHS Urban Area Security Initiative) with the private sector.** This activity will not only prepare the Federal government to respond, but will set private sector expectations of specific actions the government will take in response to a disaster.

80. **Set basic criteria for private sector preparedness against which these regional plans can be measured.** There is a lack of a clear and agreed upon prioritized implementation plan to address the coordinated restoration and protection of critical infrastructure during times of limited resources and competing demands. Basic levels of private sector preparation similar to those outlined in the National Preparedness Goal should be set and used to measure progress in restoration planning.

81. **DHS should review, revise, and finalize the Interim NIPP within 90 days to:**

    a. **Standardize Federal government policy to link the prioritization of both protection and restoration.** Linking prioritization for protection to prioritization for restoration will motivate private sector participation in the effort to prioritize critical infrastructure and to develop disaster response plans.

    b. **Require the use of a systems and resiliency approach to determine the global consequence of the loss of each asset.** Using a systems approach will clearly identify the assets in each region whose loss has the greatest potential to cause a national impact.

    c. **Address cross sector dependencies in the systems approach.** As outlined in the National Strategy for the Physical Protection of Critical Infrastructures and Key Assets, critical infrastructure restoration and protection efforts should take into account the five cross-sector security priorities.

    d. **Add an annex to the interim NIPP to describe how those policy considerations that are learned in the prioritization for protection will be used to develop restoration priorities.** The Federal government can develop priorities for restoring critical infrastructure using much of the same information used to prioritize protecting it. Having restoration priorities will allow the Federal government to make crisis decisions informed by clearly established restoration priorities.

Information

82. **DHS should expand the National Infrastructure Simulation and Analysis Center's (NISAC) Modeling and Analysis capability to allow more robust and accurate systems modeling.** Sector specific agencies should provide the NISAC with any modeling available to their department for their assigned sector, and all NISAC analyses should in turn be shared with sector specific agencies. In addition, as directed in HSPD-7 the Department of Homeland Security will work with other appropriate Federal departments and agencies to geospatially map, image and analyze critical infrastructure.

83. **The National Economic Council should form an Impact Assessment Working Group to provide an overall economic impact assessment of major disasters, including the Departments of Homeland Security, Treasury, Commerce, Energy (Energy Information Administration) and Labor as well as the President's Council of Economic Advisers.** Since Hurricane Katrina, NISAC has significantly improved their capability to provide reports detailing the cascading impact of major disasters on the Nation's infrastructure but it does not include a robust assessment of the economic impacts. The various economic modeling expertise of the members of the Impact Assessment Working Group should be incorporated into the NISAC models.

84. **The Department of Commerce should lead, in cooperation with the Department of Treasury, Homeland Security, and other sector specific agencies as appropriate, the development of a proposal to the Department of Homeland Security for incentives and other mechanisms to motivate private sector cooperation and participation in efforts to prioritize infrastructure protection.** This group should review the Defense Production Act, the Protected Critical Infrastructure Information Act, as well as financial incentives. These incentives should then be incorporated into the articulation of a business case for private sector participation in infrastructure protection. This business case should discuss protection and prioritized restoration as well as encourage private sector infrastructure resiliency and redundancy. In addition, States are encouraged to share best practices regarding financial incentives to motivate private sector cooperation and participation in infrastructure protection and restoration efforts.

85. **DHS should share the plans and policy for Federal response and delineated roles and responsibilities with the private sector.** The National Response Plan urges businesses to develop disaster contingency plans. Businesses have been unable to develop completely effective contingency plans without understanding the actions Federal, State, and local governments will take in response to a disaster. Furthermore, the Federal government has been unable to develop agreed upon response plans for prioritized restoration. The first step to establishing a collaborative planning and exercise program with the private sector is to, with appropriate protections, share relevant sections of the NRP with key private sector partners.

<u>Critical Challenge</u>: **Environmental Hazards and Debris Removal**

<u>Lesson Learned</u>: **The Department of Homeland Security, in coordination with the Environmental Protection Agency, should oversee efforts to improve the Federal government's capability to quickly gather environmental data and to provide the public and emergency responders the most accurate information available, to determine whether it is safe to operate in a disaster environment or to return after evacuation. In addition, the Department of Homeland Security should work with its State and local homeland security partners to plan and to coordinate an integrated approach to debris removal during and after a disaster.**

<u>Recommendations</u>:

86. **DHS, in coordination with EPA, DOL/OSHA, HHS, DOC/NOAA, and DOD/USACE, should:**

    a. **DHS should enhance the Emergency Response Team (ERT) capability to conduct initial environmental assessments and communicate warnings to the general public and emergency responders by adding HHS and DOL/OSHA members. DHS should lead the collaborative development of detailed plans to guide initial environmental assessment operations under the NRP.**

    b. **DOL/OSHA should lead the development of operational procedures for Worker Health and Safety.** Planning must include pre-disaster identification of potential hazards to inform out-of-area responders.

87. **DHS, in coordination with EPA, HHS, OSHA, and DOE should develop an integrated plan to quickly gather environmental data and provide the public and emergency responders the most accurate information available to decide whether it is safe to operate in a disaster environment or return after evacuation.** This plan should address how to best communicate risk, as well as determine who is accountable for making the determination that an area is safe. It should also address the need for adequate laboratory capacity to support response to all hazards. The plan should be completed in 180 days.

88. **DHS should jointly lead DOD/USACE, DOI, USDA, and EPA to address and coordinate debris removal issues as part of ESF operational procedures. The procedures should include an integrated public communication approach for debris removal, especially as it applies to private property.**

Critical Challenge: **Managing Offers of Foreign Assistance and Inquiries Regarding Affected Foreign Nationals**

Lesson Learned: **The Department of State, in coordination with the Department of Homeland Security, should review and revise policies, plans, and procedures for the management of foreign disaster assistance. In addition, this review should clarify responsibilities and procedures for handling inquiries regarding affected foreign nationals.**

Recommendations:

89. **DOS should lead the revision of the International Coordination Support Annex to the NRP, clarifying responsibilities of DOS, the Department of Homeland Security (DHS), DOD, and other supporting agencies in response to domestic incidents.** This revision should begin immediately.

90. **Prior to June 1, 2006, DOS and DHS should lead an interagency effort that will quickly develop procedures to review, accept or reject any offers of international assistance for a domestic catastrophic incident. This should include an appropriate mechanism, led by DHS and supported by DOS and Treasury, to receive, disburse, and audit any cash assistance received in support of victim needs. These operating procedures should include**:

   a. A coordination process among Federal agencies and non-governmental partners to solicit, accept, receive, integrate and distribute foreign assistance;

   b. An expedited review process for international aid that addresses both critical needs and legitimate foreign policy objectives;

   c. The inclusion of a USAID representative to the Joint Field Office (JFO);

   d. The inclusion of a representative from USAID/OFDA on the State Department Task Force and a DOS representative on USAID/OFDA's Response Management Team to improve interagency coordination; also the addition of a DHS representative to both task forces to provide more efficient information sharing about assistance needs on the ground.

91. **DHS should lead an interagency effort to create and routinely update a prioritized list of anticipated disaster needs for foreign assistance and a list of items that cannot be accepted. These lists should be completed before June 1, 2006.** These lists would be based upon notional planning scenarios, State/local emergency managers' anticipated requirements, and current legal impediments on prohibited forms of aid. Once complete, DHS should distribute these lists to all appropriate agencies, to include regulatory agencies, in order to address regulatory barriers in advance.

92. **DOS should establish, before June 1, 2006, an interagency process to: determine appropriate uses of international cash donations; to ensure timely use of these funds in a transparent and accountable manner; to meet internal Federal government accounting requirements; and to communicate to donors how their funds were used.**

93. **Public and Diplomatic Communications during domestic emergencies should both encourage cash donations -- preferably to recognized nonprofit voluntary organizations with relevant experience -- and emphasize that donations of equipment or personnel should address disaster needs.** Financial contributions provide emergency managers maximum flexibility to meet requirements in crises and avoid regulatory challenges. In a catastrophe, rapid, proactive communication of requirements reduces the potential for the refusal of assistance. The Department of State should have domestic crisis communications procedures in place before June 1, 2006.

94. **The Department of State and the Department of Homeland Security should, before June 1, 2006, jointly develop procedures to ensure that the needs of foreign missions are included in domestic plans for tracking inquires regarding persons who are unaccounted for in a disaster zone.**

   a. During a crisis, DOS and USAID should provide DHS with personnel who have technical expertise in humanitarian and disaster management issues, to include population displacement.

   b. In improving their strategies for providing faster information and assistance to American citizens, Federal, State, and local emergency management officials should include provisions covering the needs of affected foreign nationals. To ensure these provisions meet U.S. legal obligations under the Vienna Convention on Consular Relations, these officials should work with DOS. DOS in turn should inform foreign missions about these provisions. This should be accomplished through changes to the NRP, and through refinement of agencies' NRP implementation plans.

95. **DHS and DOS should revise the NRP to include DOD and USDA-Food Safety Inspection Service as cooperating agencies to the International Coordination Support Annex.** Including DOD more directly in foreign assistance management would leverage existing relationships with partner military establishments and help to ensure that staging areas for the acceptance of foreign aid are preplanned and quickly available.

96. **DHS should include DOS and foreign assistance management in domestic interagency training and exercise events. Inclusion in the new National Exercise Program (NEP) should occur before the end of FY06.**

97. **DHS should provide daily disaster response situational updates through the Secretary of State to all Chiefs of Mission or Chargés d'Affaires.** These updates should improve situational awareness and provide information to address host government concerns or questions.

Critical Challenge: Non-governmental Aid

Lesson Learned: The Federal response should better integrate the contributions of volunteers and non-governmental organizations into the broader national effort. This integration would be best achieved at the State and local levels, prior to future incidents. In particular, State and local governments must engage NGOs in the planning process, credential their personnel, and provide them the necessary resource support for their involvement in a joint response.

Recommendations:

98. **DHS should revise the NRP to designate responsibility for coordinating non-governmental assistance, including faith-based organizations, during emergencies.** These responsibilities should fully address the following:

   a. Improve communication of requirements from the incident site;

   b. Pre-identify and catalogue non-governmental goods and build a process to deploy these goods to specific regions for catastrophic events;

   c. Develop a statewide support function for volunteers (both pre-trained and spontaneous) in each State to assist local emergency managers and NGOs to prepare for, respond to, and recover from disasters;

   d. Recruit, train and identify National Incident Management System (NIMS) trained volunteers;

   e. Incorporate NGOs into the planning, training, and exercising process; and

   f. Ensure there is a mechanism to coordinate spontaneous, unaffiliated volunteers.

99. **DHS should establish an office with responsibility for integrating non-governmental and other volunteer resources into Federal, State, and local emergency response plans and mutual aid agreements. Further, DHS should establish a distinct organizational element to assist faith-based organizations.** There is no single office within DHS that is responsible for integrating non-governmental and faith-based assistance into emergency response planning. By establishing such an office, DHS can foster an integrated planning process through which government at all levels can identify and communicate their requirements to NGOs during response and recovery operations. This office should also study and recommend improvements to the process to deploy resources and personnel to specific regions for catastrophic events, through emergency assistance compacts or other mechanisms.

The responsibilities of the office should include, but not be limited to the following:

    a. Increasing relationship-building to include conducting a national conference for NGOs and the private sector on emergency preparedness and response where they can share best practices;

    b. Identifying potential donation sources; and

    c. Identifying and eliminating difficulties pre-incident that NGOs encounter with the Federal government when delivering services.

    d. Inventory, develop partnerships with and promote the best practices of successful Faith-Based disaster relief programs such as the United States Emergency Chaplains Corps.

100. **DHS should condition State and local grants, under the Homeland Security Grant program, on incorporating NGOs and the private sector into their emergency planning, training, exercises, and disaster relief efforts.** These revised plans should include the following:

    a. Participation of NGOs, including small regional and local groups, in planning for disaster response and recovery efforts; and

    b. Pre-determined roles and responsibilities for volunteer organizations, which identify their mission, capabilities, training, and certification.

An improved plan to incorporate and connect volunteers and private sector assets with emergency management officials would have enabled the better use of NGO contributions. Some states have improved how NGOs respond to incidents by creating a volunteer and social service infrastructure. In Florida and North Carolina, NGOs and emergency managers have formalized their relationships at the State and local level by including a volunteer coordinator in the State EOC. As a result, their State and local emergency managers better understand what non-governmental assistance is available before, during, and after a disaster.

Federal, State, and local officials should use the National Preparedness Goal's *Target Capabilities List: Volunteer Management and Donations* as the standard to improve capabilities. The next version of the Target Capabilities List should expand the explanation of the roles and responsibilities of volunteer organizations and include establishing their role in staffing State emergency operations centers.

101. **DHS should improve access to, and awareness of, private sector and non-governmental resources available for use during emergency response operations.** This process should include the following:

    a. Pre-arranged and contingency contracting;

    b. Provision of requirements estimates to NGOs and private sector organizations that are willing to provide resources during catastrophic events;

    c. Consistent, accurate, and timely messaging of resource needs to NGOs;

d. Providing NGOs and private sector organizations with information on reimbursement and access to Federal aid;

e. Development of robust donations and volunteer management software system standards;

f. Completing the development of a credentialing system, already being created by FEMA's NIMS Integration Center, to allow authorized volunteers and workers restoring critical infrastructure access to relief sites; and

g. Identification of what Federal, State, or local support NGOs will need to sustain operations (sanitation, electricity, food, and water).

The Federal government cannot comprehensively plan and coordinate how NGOs and private sector entities will respond locally or regionally in a catastrophic disaster. State and local officials must take the lead in planning the best use of non-governmental resources at the local level. All States should consider existing models to coordinate and integrate non-governmental resources in disaster planning and response, recognizing that business-government partnerships require a level of trust and agility most easily built at the regional level. One such model which has proven successful is the Business Executives for National Security (BENS) Business Force project. Business Force partnerships of regional, State, and local officials, together with businesses and NGOs, have been successful in emergency response planning and using private sector resources and volunteers to fill gaps in preparedness and response capabilities. The BENS model also includes a web-based catalogue of private sector resources. The Federal government should recognize that the private/non-government sectors often perform certain functions more efficiently and effectively than government because of their expertise and experience in applying successful business models. These public-private partnerships should be facilitated, recognized, and funded.

Additionally, integrating regional partnerships and resource databases (like the ones created by BENS) with national databases and response capabilities gives incident commanders full visibility of supply and volunteer sources. The capability to draw on these resources should inform and be part of Federal, State, and local logistics systems and response plans.

102. Legal and liability impediments to the use and coordination of non-governmental and private sector resources during a catastrophic event should be removed. Measures that should be implemented include:

a. DHS should lead an interagency effort to remove Federal legal and liability impediments to the use and coordination of non-governmental and private sector resources during a catastrophic event. Encourage the passage and enactment of S.1747, currently pending in the 109th Congress, a Bill to limit liability for volunteers and those providing goods and services for disaster relief.

b. Recommending uniform provisions for State law similar to the Non-Liability of Federal Government provision in the Stafford Act, to ease State and local government fear of legal liability;

c. Recommending uniform State "good Samaritan" laws to protect organizations donating goods and services from legal liability;

d. Revision of the two-year maximum service rule for national service programs, such as AmeriCorps, to allow experienced volunteers to continue serving after two years; and

e. Simplification and clarification of Federal auditing and oversight procedures during a disaster. We should allow trusted organizations (those with established Federal relationships) to respond quickly during a disaster and wait to review their activities post-disaster.

103. **DHS should encourage NGOs and the private sector to plan their giving streams at the local level in order to provide comprehensive support to affected local areas during an emergency and prevent duplication of relief efforts.** By improving the integration of planning among voluntary organizations at the local level, these organizations will be better positioned to serve citizens during an emergency. FEMA should authorize local voluntary organizations to accept gifts and donations of cash, goods, and services pledged to FEMA at the local level.

Critical Challenge: Training, Exercises, and Lessons Learned

Lesson Learned: The Department of Homeland Security (DHS) should establish specific requirements for training, exercise, and lessons learned programs linked through a comprehensive system and common supporting methodology throughout the Federal, State and local governments. Furthermore, assessments of training and exercises should be based on clear and consistent performance measures. DHS should require all Federal and State entities with operational Homeland Security responsibilities to have a lessons learned capability, and DHS should ensure all entities are accountable for the timely implementation of remedial actions in response to lessons learned.

Recommendations:

104. **DHS should finalize the Target Capabilities List (TCL).** DHS should finalize the TCL by the end of Second Quarter, FY06 with input from Federal, State, local and professional entities in order to evaluate preparedness. The TCL should define performance-based standards and outcomes grounded in capabilities which can be used to assess a State's ability to properly execute a desired mission. Without the TCL, training and exercises have no goal against which to measure their performance. Consequently, lessons are not learned or incorporated into the capabilities-based planning process.

105. **Strengthen Homeland Security Council (HSC) coordination of Federal emergency training, exercises and lessons learned.** Homeland Security Council should designate a Senior Director of Education, Training, Exercises, and Lessons Learned. The most recent Top Officials ("TOPOFF") exercise in April 2005 revealed the Federal government's lack of progress in addressing a number of preparedness deficiencies, many of which had been identified in previous exercises. This lack of progress reflects, in part, the absence of a remedial action program to systematically address lessons learned from exercises. To ensure appropriate priority and accountability are being applied to address these continuing deficiencies, the Assistant to the President for Homeland Security and Counterterrorism now annually conducts four Cabinet-level exercises with catastrophic scenarios. The HSC, weighing a variety of factors, should:

    a. Establish the National goals of what should be trained and exercised for the coming year and make recommendations for follow-on goals;

    b. Ensure the establishment of a Remedial Action Management Program (RAMP) to ensure agencies are enacting lessons learned to improve response capabilities. The RAMP would provide the basis for systematically identifying, analyzing, and monitoring the implementation of initiatives aimed at resolving deficiencies uncovered in exercises, training events, real-world events, and policy discussions. Equally important, the RAMP would conduct remedial action tracking and long-term trend analysis, ensuring that remedial actions are completed and inform the cycle of preparedness activities. This program will provide the Federal Interagency with the means of overcoming the perennial problem of observing the same issues repeatedly characterized as "lessons learned" in reports compiled following major events;

    c. Review Senior Official exercise priorities to ensure more challenging scenarios based on the most catastrophic threats (natural and man-made) that exercise the National Goals and the use of Federal resources; and

d. Ensure all Cabinet Secretary, Deputy Secretary, Under Secretary and other appropriate personnel, especially those who are identified as primary or supporting agencies of Essential Support Functions, train and exercise on their respective roles for catastrophic events. This will help to meet the Interim National Preparedness Goal Overarching Priorities to "Implement the National Incident Management System and National Response Plan" through the use of Senior Official Exercises (SOEs).

106. **All agencies with operational components should establish and fund Remedial Action Management Programs (RAMPs).** All agencies with operational components should establish and fund RAMPs to identify and incorporate lessons learned by the end of FY06. This program will enable Federal agencies to overcome the perennial problem of observing recurring problems in AARs. To assist in this effort, DOD should work closely with DHS to establish the overall program, using the current DOD model as a basis.

107. **DHS should conduct State and local officials training and exercises.** Key State and local officials should participate in training and exercises to ensure Governors and their cabinets attend a training course on their roles and responsibilities during a disaster and be exercised annually. The same will hold true for mayors of UASI cities and their Urban Area Working Group. These steps will help the Nation meet the Interim National Preparedness Goal, Overarching Priorities to "Implement the National Incident Management System and National Response Plan" and "Expand Regional Collaboration." Lack of coordination should be taken into consideration for future grant funding.

108. **DHS should restructure the TOPOFF Exercise Series.** DHS should restructure the scope and scale of the TOPOFF exercise series to provide maximum effectiveness for its participants before execution of the FY07 Full-Scale Exercise. Though the intention of TOPOFF was to utilize terrorist based scenarios, further scenarios should encompass all-hazards and be HSC-vetted. Scenarios for future exercises should include recovery issues that explore the role of the private sector and non-governmental agencies, including faith based organizations.

These restructured TOPOFF exercises should use a variety of exercise types, as outlined in the NEEP. Rather than simply conducting full-scale exercises every two years, the TOPOFF structure should execute a series of exercises every year identify lessons learned from those exercises in a timelier manner and issue an AAR that identifies the remedial actions to be taken with a deadline for implementation.

109. **DHS should develop an Exercise Series to Evaluate Nationwide Preparedness Utilizing the Final TCL.** DHS should provide a series of exercises to all Urban Area Security Initiative cities and State capitals. The purpose of these exercises should be to evaluate and provide a baseline for the Nation's overall preparedness. These exercises should be provided through G&T's Direct Support program. Once a current baseline of preparedness measures at the State level has been identified, each State, starting in FY 07, should get an annual level of preparedness status report. This report will be in the form of a comprehensive preparedness "report card" that will grade capabilities, exercises, training, effective use of federal grant monies, and other relevant criteria as a condition of further grant funding. Much like the President's Management Agenda, States will be given the expected results which they need to accomplish with their grant funding. This "report card" would not only classify each State on their level of preparedness, but also track how well homeland security grant dollars are spent. States that do not use their grant dollars effectively would have their grant dollars reduced or terminated.

110. **DHS should consolidate the DHS Training and Exercise Structure.** DHS should consolidate homeland security related training and exercise assets in a new Office of Training, Exercises and Lessons Learned (TELL) during FY06. This office should reside under the Preparedness Directorate and reflect the continuing transformation within DHS. DHS should separate training and exercise components currently within the G&T and place those assets within the new TELL. Key components should include, but not be limited to: Noble Training Center, Center for Domestic Preparedness, National Emergency Training Center, National Exercise and Evaluation Program.

111. **DHS should establish a National Exercise and Evaluation Program (NEEP).** Building on the existing NEP, DHS should coordinate the establishment of a NEEP for homeland security related exercises by the end

of FY06. As currently constructed the NEP does not include and coordinate the full range of National homeland security exercise programs. DHS should provide a "National Exercise Strategy" as prescribed by HSPD-8. The NEEP should designate HSEEP as the common exercise methodology across all levels of government, so all exercises are using the same doctrine. The NEEP should also include domestic and international exercises that enable Federal, State and local governments to improve interagency coordination across all types of crises. DHS should provide, on a periodic basis, consolidated Federal homeland security training and exercise schedule and a status report on lessons learned and appropriate follow-up from completed exercises to the HSC's Director of Training, Exercises, and Lessons Learned. DOD's Chairman's Exercise Program and the joint Exercise Program) should not fall under DHS domain, but appropriate exercises should be coordinated with DHS and incorporated in the NEP/NEEP.

To assist Federal, State and local collaboration, DHS should develop and fund a National Exercise Simulation Center (SIMCEN), similar to the Department of Defense's Joint Warfighting Center. The SIMCEN would act as a tool to simulate the Federal role in emergency response and be capable of working with State and local exercises. This SIMCEN should be designed to mirror the National operations center and provide a learning environment for Federal agencies. Agencies should be appropriately resourced, so that they are able to provide personnel to attend training and operate at the SIMCEN. DHS should support the use of simulation and modeling to assist in the development of operational procedures and exercises (particularly those based on catastrophic incidents) and as a resource to assist in responding to catastrophic incidents. Simulations of this type should be run out of the SIMCEN.

Critical Challenge: Homeland Security Professional Development and Education

Lesson Learned: The Department of Homeland Security should develop a comprehensive program for the professional development and education of the Nation's homeland security personnel including Federal, State and local employees as well as emergency management persons within the private sector, non-governmental organizations, as well as faith-based and community groups. This program should foster a "joint" Federal Interagency, State, local, and civilian team.

Recommendations:

112. **Each Federal department and agency assigned specific homeland security roles should establish a homeland security professional development program that encompasses career assignments, education, exercises, and training.** All departments and agencies assigned specific homeland security roles should establish professional development programs to insure they have the skilled personnel necessary to execute these responsibilities. These personnel must have the requisite professional credentials and experiences, knowledge of their organization's emergency responsibilities, and understanding of other organizations' related emergency responsibilities. Homeland security professional development programs should include *interagency* and *intergovernmental* (*i.e.*, Federal, State, and local governments) perspectives. Further, the scope of homeland security requires that these programs focus on all hazards: terrorism, natural disasters, accidents, and other disasters. Departments and agencies must determine which offices are assigned homeland security roles and responsibilities, and should also determine the education, training, and technical expertise required for homeland security senior leaders and crisis managers. Each should establish education, exercise, and training requirements for personnel assigned to offices with homeland security responsibilities throughout all levels of government.

113. **OPM should establish, and Federal Departments and agencies should implement a career development process that mandates interagency and intergovernmental assignments as well as professional education.** These career development processes must require and reward interagency and intergovernmental homeland security assignments. Such assignments will enable homeland security professionals to understand the roles, responsibilities, and cultures of other organizations and disciplines. Interagency and intergovernmental assignments will build trust and familiarity among homeland security professionals from differing perspectives. These assignments will also break down barriers between organizations, thus

enhancing the exchange of ideas and practices. The need for intergovernmental assignments should be determined on a case-by-case basis.

    a.   **Each career development program should require that homeland security personnel complete interagency or intergovernmental assignments, and professional education, prior to assignment to senior managerial positions, including the Senior Executive Service (SES).** Interagency and intergovernmental assignments should be designed to build a cadre of homeland security professionals across all levels of government who possess common knowledge of operational roles and responsibilities. Career development programs must reward strong academic performance in professional education programs.

    b.   **Departments and agencies should establish fellowships that allow State and local homeland security professionals to serve in a related Federal department or agency for a limited period of time.** This can promote the development of a common planning culture and foster collaboration among Federal, State, and local governments. Further, these fellowships can enhance partnerships that result in more effective and efficient emergency responses.

    c.   **The White House should consider if legislative or regulatory changes are required to facilitate interagency and intergovernmental assignments.** The Goldwater-Nichols Act of 1986 transformed the Department of Defense (DOD) into a truly integrated department by requiring an assignment in another branch of the Armed Forces as a prerequisite for promotion to flag or general officer. Similar legislation should be considered for the Federal government to achieve the same sort of integration across Executive Branch departments and agencies.

114.   **The Department of Homeland Security should establish an interagency working group to establish specific goals with objective standards against which Department and Agency progress toward full implementation of effective professional development programs can be measured.** The interagency working group should ensure consistency and uniformity among Federal homeland security professional development programs. The interagency working group should provide quarterly reports to the Secretary of Homeland Security and the Assistant to the President for Homeland Security and Counterterrorism on the status of Federal homeland security professional development programs.

115.   **DHS should provide training, technical, and other assistance in support of other departments' and agencies' homeland security professional development programs.** DHS should expand its use of innovative techniques and technologies to enhance the quality and dissemination of homeland security education and training. This may include the use of distance learning programs and interactive computer methodologies. DHS must expand its efforts to promote awareness and implementation of the NIMS and the NRP throughout Federal, State, and local governments, and private sector.

116.   **DHS should establish a National Homeland Security University (NHSU) for senior officials that serves as a capstone to other educational and training opportunities.** An NHSU should be established to provide a strategic perspective of homeland security and counterterrorism that transcends organizations, levels of government, response disciplines, and the private sector. This requires that the NHSU faculty and student body include interagency, intergovernmental, and private sector representatives. NHSU programs should prepare officials for senior homeland security and counterterrorism assignments in Federal, State, and local governments. To achieve this, the NHSU curriculum should focus on all hazards and all phases of emergency preparedness and response. It should expand students' understanding of the strategic aspects of homeland security and counterterrorism planning, policy development, incident management, and support functions, among other topics. NHSU educational programs must be scalable and portable in order to reach the widest audiences. NHSU should offer traditional in-residence courses in Washington, DC. It should also offer regional and virtual educational programs, and utilize innovative educational methodologies, such as simulation centers, for use by faculty, students, and government officials. The NHSU should serve as a center of homeland security and counterterrorism strategic thought and expertise for the nation. DHS should consider leveraging the infrastructure and expertise at the National Defense University by partnering with

DOD to have the NHSU be a joint DHS/DOD initiative that focuses on both Homeland Security and Homeland Defense.

117. **Federal departments and agencies should strengthen their existing homeland security educational and training programs.** The Emergency Management Institute, the Naval Postgraduate School, the National Defense University, and other university programs are critical national resources for developing skilled and knowledgeable homeland security professionals. Departments and agencies should ensure that these and other similar homeland security educational programs have the greatest impact. This should include requiring State and local participation in such programs through Federal fellowships. This will provide the Nation with a cadre of trained homeland security professionals. DHS should support these educational and training programs by providing them with curricula and other technical assistance. DHS should pursue opportunities to replicate innovative educational programs, such as the joint New York City Fire Department-U.S. Military Academy's Counterterrorism Leadership Program.

118. **The White House should consider establishing a Presidential Board to review the national security, homeland security, and counterterrorism professional development programs of Federal departments and agencies to identify opportunities for further integration.** The Nation can no longer view national security, homeland security, and counterterrorism independently. Federal professional development programs must recognize the interdependencies among all three and adjust their respective career assignments, education, exercises, and training accordingly. The Board should provide a roadmap for uniting the efforts of DHS, DOD, and other departments and agencies in educating, training and preparing our leaders for their crucial roles in safeguarding the Nation. Further, this review should promote the establishment of a common security paradigm that integrates national security, homeland security, and counterterrorism. This review should also identify opportunities for greater collaboration and integration. Importantly, this vision is not to eliminate the departments' own professional development programs, each of which serves an important role and is tailored to meet the needs of their respective organizations.

Critical Challenge: Citizen and Community Preparedness

Lesson Learned: The Federal government, working with State, local, NGO, and private sector partners, should combine the various disparate citizen preparedness programs into a single national campaign to promote and strengthen citizen and community preparedness. This campaign should be developed in a manner that appeals to the American people, incorporates the endorsement and support of prominent national figures, focuses on the importance of individual and community responsibility for all-hazard disaster preparedness, provides meaningful and comprehensive education, training and exercise opportunities applicable to all facets of the American population, and establishes specialized preparedness programs for those less able to provide for themselves during disasters such as children, the ill, the disabled, and the elderly.

Recommendations:

119. **DHS should make citizen and community preparedness a National priority. To facilitate this initiative, Cabinet Secretaries and other prominent National public figures (*e.g.* the Surgeon General) should serve as spokespersons to promote citizen and community preparedness.** The Secretary of Homeland Security, Secretary of Education, United States Surgeon General, and other National public figures, should publicize the importance of the community and individual preparedness. The goal of this effort should be to have citizens better understand the role and limitations of government and to encourage individual preparedness.

  a. In addition, DHS should continue to research means to lower the barriers to personal preparedness and adapt outreach and instructional materials to address the findings. Public awareness messaging should shift to include more substantive information within the message, as opposed to telling citizens they need to "do" something. For example, the "Stop, Drop, and Roll" campaign used so successfully in fire safety as part of the "Learn Not to Burn" program embedded the message and provided citizens with an action.

Other successful campaigns include the National Highway Traffic Safety Administration's "Click It or Ticket" program which fines drivers for not wearing their seatbelt, and the "Buckle Up America" campaign which prescribes proper use of seat belt and child safety seats.

    b.   DHS should leverage the success of public education conducted by fire departments nationwide which has reduced the loss of lives and property by fire. The Citizen Corps public education effort should be integrated with the DHS's United States Fire Administration so that preparedness efforts of local fire departments can be expanded to include citizen and community preparedness. Additionally, DHS should leverage the success of the USAonwatch program to form a National Network of Community Watches comprised of citizen volunteers to develop best practices, a common doctrine and metrics for all-hazards community preparedness.

    c.   The newly created Office of Public and Community Preparedness should continue to assist with implementing National strategies for citizen preparedness and communities. However, this office should be removed from the Office of Grants and Training, so as to focus solely on homeland security policies, plans, strategies, and guidance at the Federal, State, and local levels which highlight citizen and community preparedness.

120. **DHS should consider increasing grant funding for citizen and community preparedness programs and where program metrics demonstrate effectiveness, DHS should consider allowing greater use of Federal funds for Citizen Corps Council staff positions at the State and local level within the FY07 grant program.** State and local governments generally do not have full time staff assigned to support this critical component of community preparedness. The availability of full-time positions at the State and local level for the Citizen Corps to coordinate the government and community planning is critical. Locations with full-time staff assigned to this tend to have developed robust plans. While Citizen Corps has existed since 2002, funding for the program has not been consistent.

121. **DHS should build baseline skills and capabilities needed by all citizens and communities.** DHS needs to establish a comprehensive list of skills and capabilities to assess how well citizens are prepared utilizing resources such as the Rand Corporations "Individual Preparedness and Response to Chemical, Radiological, Nuclear, and Biological Terrorist Attacks." These baseline skills include assembling preparedness kits, developing communications plans, training in basic first aid, and learning how to react to a variety of hazards and disasters. Additionally, the DHS should develop a process to evaluate national progress toward improved citizen preparedness capabilities through the use of the Target Capabilities List and established metrics, evaluated annually as a condition of receiving Homeland Security grant funding.

122. **DHS should develop tools for State and local governments to use in order to prepare, train, exercise, and engage citizens and communities in all areas of preparedness in FY06.** Special consideration should be given to persons with disabilities, health problems, language barriers, income barriers, and unaccompanied minors. Planning also needs to contemplate household pets and other animals. Developing these tools at the National level, in partnership with non-governmental organizations, private sector, emergency responders, and experts on vulnerable populations, will achieve economies of scale. Providing tools, such as instructor guides and participant handbooks for classroom based instruction, identified standardized skills and capabilities, and strategic planning guidance, will elevate National preparedness without depleting scarce resources at the local level.

Although DHS and other organizations already have established websites to assist with community preparedness (*e.g.*,www.ready.gov, www.prepare.org), there is no measure to evaluate if they have increased overall citizen preparedness.

123. **The Department of Education (DOEd), working with DHS, should include individual and community preparedness into current elementary and secondary educational programs.** The DOEd should recommend funding to better student preparedness initiatives and disseminate teaching materials. Schools should use materials and curricula developed by DHS and the American Red Cross to prepare students.

Students should be required to take courses in first aid, disaster preparedness or other related topics as a part of their curriculum starting in FY07.

School programs on littering, recycling, anti-smoking and seat belt safety have demonstrated their effectiveness at helping to achieve National community goals beyond just students. We should build on these successful initiatives to educate and prepare our children and their families for the threats of the 21st Century.

124. **DHS should immediately highlight preparedness best practices through the DHS Lessons Learned and Information Sharing website (*www.llis.gov*) and the Citizen Corps Council's National conference.** By identifying best practices during exercises and audits, Citizen Corps Councils will be able to keep abreast of the emerging trends in citizen preparedness.

125. **Working with the National Governors Association, DHS should encourage the establishment of State tax relief holidays throughout the year to allow citizens to purchase disaster preparedness supplies.** Providing periodic tax breaks throughout the year would encourage people to purchase emergency supplies. These tax holidays should consider the State of Florida's model in defining what types of supplies would qualify. The government should also work closely with the private sector to build "preparedness packs" in various sizes (individual through family size) for sale at low cost, much as the American Red Cross has done.

APPENDIX B – WHAT WENT RIGHT

But there are lessons learned that we don't need to change: the lesson of courage…the determination of our citizens…the compassion of our fellow citizens…the decency of men and women.

—President George W. Bush, January 12, 2006[1]

The devastation of Hurricane Katrina will forever be seared into our country's memory. Visions of our citizens stranded on highway overpasses, of debris-filled plots where grand houses once stood, and of babies being hoisted onto roofs to avoid the surging water, continue to haunt us to this day. But there are other stories from Katrina, stories that may only be known by a few, but that are appreciated deeply by those involved. These are the stories of the men and women of our military, our law enforcement and fire departments, our private citizens, non-government organizations and our faith based groups. These are the stories of the human side of Katrina. It is important that we do not let the horror of the storm overshadow the true courage, determination, compassion and decency of the American people. Although many efforts are described below, what follows is at best only a partial representation of the enormity of the American spirit.

Preparation and Response to Katrina

We have identified numerous areas in which the Federal, State and local governments could have better prepared for, responded to, and recovered from the storm, but it is also important to acknowledge that we pre-staged more assets and pre-deployed more personnel than we have for any other storm in American history. And we have tried to include throughout the review some examples of the many good lessons of courage, compassion, and initiative that saved lives and reduced suffering.

In 1992, Hurricane Andrew struck densely populated urban areas in southeastern Florida as a Category 5 storm and provides the closest comparison to Hurricane Katrina. They were two of the most destructive storms ever to strike the United States, but Katrina affected an area three times as large, caused two to six times the economic damage, and killed up to twenty times as many people—this was partially due to Katrina's large wind field and the high storm surge, which proved far more damaging than the more compact Andrew.

Prior to both hurricanes, the National Weather Service provided repeated and accurate warnings, but local populations did not fully evacuate—greatly magnifying human suffering in the wake of the storm. Andrew and Katrina both overwhelmed State and local responders, but the Federal response to Katrina was greatly improved due to better preparations prior to landfall.

Non-governmental Organizations

The number of volunteer and non-profit organizations providing support to the Hurricane Katrina relief effort was truly extraordinary. Virtually every national, regional and local charitable organization in the U.S., and many from abroad, contributed aid to the victims of Hurricane Katrina. To assist in the coordination of these offers of assistance, the ***USA Freedom Corps*** (Freedom Corps) and the ***Governor's State Service Commissions*** rallied non-profit organizations to list volunteer opportunities in the Freedom Corps volunteer search engine. The Freedom Corps also worked with the *Corporation for National and Community Service* to create a Katrina Resource Center that helped groups of volunteers connect their resources with needs on the ground.[2]

The *Citizen Corps* coordinated volunteer efforts throughout the country, with more than 14,000 Citizen Corps volunteers from all 50 states and the District of Columbia actively involved in response and recovery efforts across America. The Harris County, Texas, Citizen Corps Council brought together an enormous number of volunteers to support the American Red Cross and staffed evacuation centers throughout Houston. They processed over 8,000 volunteers in one day, and an average of 3,500 per day overall. These volunteers allowed for the creation of an actual city (with its own zip code) for nearly 25,000 Louisiana evacuees sheltering in the Houston Reliant Astrodome. They were successful because they had coordinated ahead of time with local businesses and volunteer groups, and because they were familiar with and implemented elements of the Incident Command System.[3]

Faith-based organizations supported the relief effort as well. For example, 6,000 *Southern Baptist Relief* volunteers from 36 state conventions served in Louisiana, Mississippi, Alabama, Georgia, and Texas following the hurricane and flood. These volunteers ran mobile kitchens, and recovery sites.[4] They also established hundreds of "pop-up" shelters created by churches or other agencies.[5] *Operation Blessing*, comprised of a network of faith-based partners and resources, provided food and shelter to help those in need and transported food and other supplies with their own fleet of trucks.[6] They also made over $4 million in Fast Cash Grants available to church and smaller relief groups throughout the affected region.[7] Members of the *Salvation Army* came from across the nation and served over one million meals, sheltered more than 31,000 people in seven states, and provided aid to displaced citizens in thirty states.[8] The Salvation Army not only strengthened the social service infrastructure in those states directly impacted by the hurricane and flood—they did so nationwide. The Salvation Army's network alone fielded more than 60,000 health and welfare inquiries and helped to locate 25,508 people to date.[9] These and many other faith-based organizations filled the gaps that other private and public sector organizations could not. *Christ in Action*, an inter-denominational non-profit organization from Manassas, Virginia deployed volunteers and mobile kitchens to Gulfport, MS and began feeding people on September 1. After 115 days of operations, Christ in Action served over 420,000 meals and repaired over 500 houses in time for families to reoccupy their homes by Christmas. Based upon lessons learned from this experience, Dr. Denny Nissley, the Director of Christ in Action, is organizing a Coalition of Faith-Based First Responders from around the Nation to be prepared for the next major disaster. This Coalition will perform disaster relief training for volunteers and will maintain a current roster of thousands of volunteers who can be quickly called upon to provide support during the next major disaster.

Private citizens also provided assistance and resources in the aftermath of the storm. Dr. Carrie Oliver from Texas, operating independently, arrived with three RVs pulling 16-foot trailers driven by herself, her husband and friends to Baton Rouge shortly after the storm hit. The RVs were full of medical supplies, food, and water. Back in Texas, Dr. Oliver runs a large clinic, and she had brought all available medical supplies and had purchased the vehicles, trailers, and other supplies with her own money.

Dr. Oliver initially planned on heading directly to New Orleans, but officials in Livingston Parish did not think it was safe. Instead Dr. Oliver was incorporated into responding to other parishes. The supplies and personnel were divided into three teams, and with the assistance of a helicopter procured from the Louisiana Office of Homeland Security and Emergency Preparedness, Dr. Oliver flew ahead to different parish localities, and had the three teams follow by ground. Besides initially helping in Livingston Parish shelters, the teams visited different areas in Washington, St. Tammany, Tangipahoa, and Jefferson Parishes, and set up walk-in clinics operating out of the RVs.

Later, the RVs were used to set up a mobile hospital unit and decontamination clinic at the Children's Hospital in the City of New Orleans 2nd Precinct to take care of injured soldiers, police, and other responders who could not otherwise get medical care.

After three days, Dr. Oliver returned to Texas, but left everything she had brought with her. She signed over the titles to the vehicles, trailers and supplies. Livingston Parish officials continued to use the RVs and supplies for relief missions to surrounding parishes and New Orleans, as well as for longer trips, such as one to distribute equipment to police officers in Mississippi.[10]

Other organizations worked tirelessly to assist emergency responders that, due to the storm, did not have the equipment and means to effectively carry out their duties. Amateur Radio Operators from both the ***Amateur Radio Emergency Service*** and the ***American Radio Relay League,*** monitored distress calls and rerouted emergency requests for assistance throughout the U.S. until messages were received by emergency response personnel. A distress call made from a cell phone on a rooftop in New Orleans to Baton Rouge was relayed, via ham radio, from Louisiana to Oregon, then Utah, and finally back to emergency personnel in Louisiana, who rescued the 15 stranded victims.[11] Ham radio operators voluntarily manned the amateur radio stations at sites such as the National Hurricane Center, Hurricane Watch Net, Waterway Net, Skywarn and the Salvation Army Team Emergency Radio Network.[12]

State Governments Support Other Critical Services

Other State Governments volunteered to provide non-response related critical services that the States of Louisiana and Mississippi could no longer provide. Multiple State Public Health Laboratories volunteered to assist the devastated Louisiana and Mississippi State Public Health Laboratories. Florida sent a mobile drinking water lab and personnel to Mississippi, helping to prevent people from getting sick from contaminated water. Iowa personnel performed 12,000 newborn screening tests, critical to the health of our youngest citizens, as they must be performed quickly in order to provide immediate treatment. The efforts to shoulder some of the burden were and continue to be coordinated through the non-profit organization representing these laboratories, the ***Association of Public Health Laboratories***, and the State laboratories themselves.[13]

Local Officials

Many of those called upon to do the toughest work were those that had lost the most. Members of local fire departments, police departments, and emergency service units worked tirelessly despite being victims themselves. Many lost their homes, cars, and possessions. Others lost their families and loved ones. Yet these very people returned to work to protect and serve the people to whom they had made a commitment. They often worked their shifts without knowledge of where there family was, or where they would sleep that night. Despite these obstacles, they continued to perform their duties.

Some members of the Waveland, MS Police Department stayed at their police station during the storm. There came a point when the flooding from the storm surge became so great that they clung desperately to a bush located in the front yard of the station for five hours. When the surge subsided, the men returned to their duties, rescuing and saving those that remained in the 7,000 person town.

When the officers of the Waveland Police Department wanted to return to their duty, a few problems arose. Cars, equipment, radios, they had lost it all. The State of Florida, which was leaning forward with their State Emergency Response Team (SERT), immediately responded following the storm. The State of Florida deployed personnel, equipment and commodities to Mississippi to aid response and recovery from the devastating impact of Hurricane Katrina. In the hours and days after the catastrophic storm, Governor Jeb Bush pledged the support of Florida to Mississippi Governor Haley Barbour. Resources from Florida were mobilized through the Emergency Management Assistance Compact. These efforts represent Florida's largest state-to-state assistance in history. Law Enforcement officers who are an integral part of the Florida SERT assisted the Waveland, MS Police Department by providing relief so police officers could return to their homes and account for their families.

Other cities and states sent their police and fire departments to help their fellow departments that were crippled by the storm. ***The Fire Department of New York City*** (FDNY) and the ***New York City Police Department (NYPD),*** two organizations that themselves suffered a devastating loss four years prior, deployed staff and equipment to assist in the recovery effort. FDNY sent over 660 fire department staff, including firefighters, fire officers, emergency medical technicians, paramedics, counselors, physicians, and communications personnel to assist the crippled New Orleans Fire Department.[14] NYPD sent more than 300 officers to support the effort to restore order. Additionally, the State of New York sent more than 100 officers and the Department of Corrections sent more than 250 officers. The City's Urban Search and Rescue Team (New York Task Force One - NYTF-1), which is made up of NYPD, FDNY, and Office of Emergency Management personnel, was deployed to Mississippi at FEMA's request to support rescue efforts along the Gulf Coast. Fire trucks, police cruisers, school buses, transit buses, and other equipment and goods, bearing the seal of the State or City of New York were abundant during the response.

In Louisiana, the ***Livingston Parish Office of Homeland Security and Emergency Preparedness*** conducted search and rescue missions in the City of New Orleans, for 16 days after the storm with the ***Arizona National Guard 855th Military Police***, at great personal expense and risk. To Livingston's credit, they augmented the New Orleans 2nd District Police Department (NO 2nd PD), at their request, to perform these missions. At one point the NO 2nd PD ammunition was down to "the rounds on their belts" and their uniforms were starting to rot off their bodies. Livingston Parish provided supplies and medical care, and provided means of communication to the NO 2nd PD via the Parishes radios and satellite phones as the NO 2nd PD had no communications devices that worked.

The Parish also provided a critically important security function, escorting medical assets to and from hospitals trying to care for injured and sick, and providing cover for New Orleans Police personnel during their operations. The primary resource that responded to this request was the Sheriff's Department Special Response Team (SRT) who ran missions and provided security escorts. The SRT was specifically requested because of their outstanding skill, having won several State SRT competitions.

The Parish exceeded its duty by responding into the State of Mississippi, surrounding Parishes, and the City of New Orleans. The Parish procured large amounts of supplies, out of their own operating budget, without knowing whether they would be reimbursed, and ultimately became a critical component in the flow of goods to help the devastated region. As this aid was not forthcoming from other sources, Livingston Parish personnel saved many lives during this disaster.

Private Sector Organizations

Private sector organizations provided commodities, services, expert advice, financial donations and volunteer groups to assist in the relief efforts. ***FedEx*** facilitated equipment and supply distribution, particularly for the American Red Cross.[15] ***Dell, Home Depot, IBM, Lenovo, Pfizer, Wal-Mart***, and other corporations gave millions of dollars in cash and in-kind donations to support immediate relief and recovery efforts as well as long-term rebuilding.[16]

Vanguard Technologies, Inc., "showed up the day after the storm and provided communications when we had none," said St. Bernard's Parish officials. Vanguard Technologies, a small Louisiana business, provided Saint Bernard and Plaquemines parishes with innovative internet protocol (IP) network solutions and utilized a Point of Presence (POP) internet connectivity, that remained fully operational during Katrina, when no other company, big or small, was able to restore crucial communications in this devastated area. Vanguard also deployed a fully operational, redundant, broadband, wireless IP network, covering more than 100 square miles, within five days of Katrina's Gulf Coast landfall. The networks supported: Voice-over-Internet Protocol (VoIP) telephony; Video surveillance over IP; mobile video surveillance; high speed World Wide Web internet access; email communications via simple mail transfer protocol (SMTP); and web mail services. Vanguard, to date, continues servicing the parishes with critical communications access linking key government services and facilities.

Private companies also worked hard to mitigate the economic damage that Hurricane Katrina was sure to bring. ***Norfolk Southern Railroad*** recognized the potential impact of the loss of certain key bridges, and pre-staged repair barges just outside the hurricane impact area. After the Hurricane passed, the barges moved in and quickly repaired the bridges to minimize the impact on the flow of commerce. By pre-positioning freighters offshore and swiftly returning their grain transport facilities to operational status, the ***Cargill Corporation*** started shipping grain internationally almost immediately after landfall. With over half of all U.S. grain exports flowing through ports affected by Hurricane Katrina from 17 different states[17] this single action had a significantly positive national economic impact.

Academic institutions across the country accepted students who had been displaced from their universities and provided them with financial assistance. For example, the Office of Student Aid and Scholarships at ***Louisiana State University*** (LSU) administered a Hurricane Katrina/Rita Student Relief Fund to assist students who had lost financial support or were displaced by the hurricane and flood. In addition, the LSU campus hosted one of the largest peacetime triage operations in the history of the United States.

While State and local governments, non-governmental organizations, private companies and even individual citizens were pulling together to provide services for the victims of the storm and assistance for the public services that were overwhelmed or incapacitated, the departments and agencies of the U.S. Federal government pulled its resources and personnel to mitigate the devastation that Katrina would bring.

The Department of Homeland Security

Almost 6,000 **U.S. Coast Guard** personnel (active duty, Reserve, Auxiliary, and civilian members) from throughout the country conducted one of the largest search and rescue missions in its history as part of an even larger multi-agency, multi-level search and rescue effort. They retrieved more than 33,000 people along the Gulf Coast, including more than 12,000 by air, and 11,000 by surface, plus 9,403 evacuated from hospitals. Almost one-third of the Coast Guard's entire fleet was dedicated to rescue efforts. Coast Guard personnel also worked tirelessly in multi-agency teams to reconstitute waterways and conduct environmental assessments. They restored hundreds of buoys and channel markers that were missing or destroyed in the hurricane. Their efforts to restore these and other navigational aids and waterways, allowed maritime industry in the area to return to normal faster.

> Having evacuated with boats on trailers prior to the storm, Petty Officer Jessica Guidroz, a coxswain at the Coast Guard Station New Orleans, could not return to the station by road after the hurricane passed. She and her crew launched their boat and headed toward the station. Finding the station occupied by rescued victims already, she established order at the station and then piloted a twenty-five foot boat through Metairie and Lakeview, banging on roofs and yelling, scanning for open attic windows, and convincing reluctant evacuees to leave. Learning of a large number of trapped residents, she proceeded to lead a squadron of eight boats and crews in the evacuation of approximately 2,000 people from the campus of the University of New Orleans. Like most of the station crew, she lived nearby and lost all her personal possessions to the storm, yet put her duty first. After several days piloting a boat into devastated neighborhoods, ferrying thousands of people to safety, and seeing destruction on a scale so vast that it seemed surreal, Guidroz was moved when she saw an image on television. She had been haunted by the memory of a young mother who had almost been trampled during the evacuation. She remembered how "the baby was wearing this diaper that you know hadn't been changed in days." That night, a news channel showed images from the Houston Astrodome, and there she was – the lady with the baby. "She was in Houston now, and she looked like she'd showered and her kid had on clean clothes. That moment is when it clicked," Guidroz said. "Here was someone we had actually helped, and it fell into place that we were doing something that really mattered, something really good."

> Petty Officer Moises Rivera-Carrion of the Coast Guard served as a rescue swimmer aboard Coast Guard HH-60J helicopters responding to the devastation caused by Hurricane Katrina. During almost three days of operations in an urban setting with hazards including unlit towers, downed power lines, and contaminated floodwaters, Petty Officer Rivera-Carrion tested the limits of his skill and endurance while rescuing 269 survivors trapped on rooftops and balconies throughout New Orleans and southwest Louisiana.

> With 50 plus knot winds blowing debris, Petty Officer Rodney L. Gordon landed in the first aircraft to return to New Orleans and immediately began a series of complex electrical and mechanical repairs vital to sustaining what quickly grew into the largest air rescue operation in Coast Guard history. Scrambling to locate and cannibalize broken and non-essential equipment until supply lines could be restored, he repaired failed and failing emergency generators, power lines, and dozens of destroyed components. He restored power to vital operations and communications facilities, including the Naval Air Station control tower, enabling the successful control and dispatch of thousands of military and Coast Guard aircraft sorties on rescue and evacuation missions. Most critically, the viability of the entire joint service air rescue operation was jeopardized by the electrical failure of the base's enormous aviation fuel distribution plant. He took charge and single-handedly performed a complex rewiring of its emergency generators, enabling hundreds of aircraft to continue lifesaving missions.

The heroics of Petty Officer Guidroz, Petty Officer Rivera-Carrion and Petty Officer Rodney L. Gordon are only a few of the multiple USCG stories from Katrina. However, their stories, and many more are the reason that the Coast Guard was soon given the moniker, in a New Orleans Newspaper, of the "New Orleans Saints."

Responsible for more than 180,000 employees, the Department of Homeland Security was duly praised for the efforts of the United States Coast Guard. However, additional DHS units brought many other life-saving and order-restoring employees and talents to the preparation, response and recovery operations.

DHS *Customs and Border Protection* and DHS *Immigration and Customs Enforcement* leaders sought to match their resources with the needs of the affected populations in Louisiana, Mississippi, and Alabama. They took clothing, toys, linens and other useful items seized and forfeited at U.S. ports of entry for violations of federal law—more than 100,000 pieces as of this writing—and delivered them directly to the victims of the hurricane and flood.[18] They filled the needs of people who had lost these basic items at minimal cost to the government, using goods that they had seized during the course of everyday operations. Their practical and innovative thinking and actions helped these victims directly, returning to them some possessions, as well as the sense of security such possessions convey.

> On September 5, 2005 Immigration and Customs Enforcement (ICE) / Federal Protection Service (FPS) Sergeant Matthew Pinardi was securing the FEMA morgue detail near Interstates 10 and 610 in New Orleans. He observed a young male riding a bike across the overpass and witnessed the man hit the retaining wall. The young man flipped over the railing and landed some fifty feet below in water over his head. Sergeant Pinardi called for additional assistance, traversed the embankment and at great personal peril entered flood waters to rescue the young man. The man was pulled to safety and transported by emergency medical services to a FEMA National Disaster Medical System medical clinic.

Staff within the *Federal Emergency Management Agency* (FEMA) worked hard to deliver aid and services to those affected by the hurricane and flood. Drawing upon their previous experiences with natural and manmade disasters, FEMA staff distributed more than $5 billion in federal aid to more than 1.7 million households in the affected region by February 1, 2006.[19] FEMA also mobilized elements of the National Disaster Medical System (NDMS), such as Disaster Medical Assistance Teams (DMATs), deploying them to the Gulf States to assist with emergency health care delivery. For example, a DMAT stationed in Florida was deployed to Mississippi, where it set up operations in an abandoned medical center that had been put out of service by the flood. Over a two week period, this DMAT treated more than 3,000 patients that were able to make it to the medical center, and treated another 2,000 by sending teams of their own personnel out into the surrounding area.[20]

Also part of the National Disaster Medical System, the Disaster Mortuary Operational Response Teams (DMORTs) created a large, temporary morgue in St. Gabriel, Louisiana, to support the entire state,[21] and supplemented and otherwise provided mortuary services in Louisiana and Mississippi. DMORT members deployed from throughout the Nation to assist. These specialists worked with local medical, mortuary, and forensic professionals, and provided needed mortuary services, equipment, and personnel. Especially important were the services that trained personnel provided in identifying the dead. They worked with x-rays and DNA samples and communicated information with compassion to families waiting to hear news of their loved ones. Despite some primitive conditions (e.g., with only a roof and intermittent power), team members helped to identify not only those killed by the hurricane and flood, but also those bodies that were unearthed from cemeteries and mausoleums. Their duties were made even more challenging by the destruction of medical, dental and other records, and the inability of many people to accurately determine whether those people they sought were dead or missing. They drew upon both technical expertise and personal empathy to address the needs of both the dead and the living. [22]

Department of Defense

Well before Hurricane Katrina struck the Gulf Coast, the Department of Defense (DOD) prepared for the 2005 hurricane season. Based on prior assistance for hurricane recovery operations, on August 19th the Secretary of Defense approved a standing order to prepare and organize for severe weather disaster operations. This order expedited the pre-positioning of senior military representatives known as Defense Coordinating Officers, to act as liaisons with other governmental organizations in the projected disaster area prior to an event. The order also authorized the use of DOD installations as logistical staging areas for FEMA. U.S. Northern Command directed a number of emergency deployment readiness exercises prior to FEMA requests, spending training funds to pre-position response capability. Once officially activated and deployed, DOD provided logistics support to FEMA, helping the Agency to track items in motion.[23]

The U.S. *Army Corps of Engineers* led the removal of 224 billion gallons of water from New Orleans in 43 days, enabling recovery and repair operations. By improving their pumping capacity and efficiency, adding pumps, creating intentional breaches, and developing other on-the-spot workarounds, they were able to reduce the estimated time to clear New Orleans of water by approximately 50 percent.[24]

U.S. Army soldiers provided a number of services in support of Local, State, Federal, and private-sector activities, including medical treatment (e.g., thousands of immunizations), debris clearing, evacuation, planning, and performance of search and rescue missions.[25] The *U.S. Marine Corps* helped local governments reinvigorate their infrastructures[26] and augmented search and rescue operations. In one particularly noteworthy case, two Marines using a borrowed boat rescued 150 people in 36 hours.[27] The Mississippi *National Guard*, supported with Guard members from many other States, performed superbly throughout the response, carrying out a number of duties, including clearing key roads, search and rescue, and getting supplies into the hands of victims as quickly as possible.[28] The *U.S. Navy* mobilized more than 10,000 naval personnel to the affected Gulf coast region, as well as 68 aircraft, and 16 ships,[29] including amphibious construction equipment and mobile diving salvage units, particularly useful in flood conditions.[30]

> Prior to Katrina's landfall, twenty-one Seabees from Naval Mobile Construction Battalion 133 and Naval Mobile Construction Battalion 7, led by a Navy Chief Warrant Officer answered the call to vigilantly support the staff and residents of the Armed Forces Retirement Home in Gulfport, Mississippi. Located about two hundred yards from the Gulf of Mexico, the home had evacuated all but fifty patients in anticipation of Hurricane Katrina. Seabees postured themselves on the ground floor of the building, and began bracing the structure against a thirty foot tidal surge and winds recorded in excess of 120 miles per hour. When the storm surge forced its way into the building, generator power was lost, and in the darkness, amidst rushing water, tidal pull and life-threatening debris, these Seabees as young as 18 years old and hailing from every area of the country, evacuated fifty bed-ridden and wheel-chair bound retirees and numerous staff members, as well as all medical oxygen tanks, to the upper floors of the building. Their actions saved lives and helped prevent the home from succumbing to total physical devastation.

The 53rd Weather Reconnaissance Squadron (also known as the Hurricane Hunters), of the 403rd Wing, is composed of *U.S. Air Force* Reservists. Flying out of Keesler Air Force Base in Biloxi, Mississippi, it is the only military unit flying into hurricanes and tropical storms.[31] The unit followed Hurricane Katrina from inception to landfall, and provided critical reconnaissance information to the National Hurricane Center throughout the event.[32] They maintained daily hurricane vigilance. Other Air Force personnel supported recovery and relief operations, including transportation of more than 13,000 people, air traffic control, and aerial lift, refueling, photography, search and rescue, and medical evacuation.[33]

The *National Geospatial-Intelligence Agency* (NGA) started collecting key infrastructure-related information (i.e. on airports, hospitals, police stations, emergency operations centers, highways, schools, etc.) well in advance of landfall and got this information into the hands of Federal, State, and local first responders in the affected region. As the storm was tracked, NGA pre-deployed analysts and mobile systems to the affected areas that provided expertise and information on the ground and facilitated the delivery of additional information from NGA offices elsewhere. Because they had assets in place and focused on the region, NGA provided the first comprehensive overview of the damage resulting from the hurricane and flood. NGA merged imagery with other information, creating hundreds of intelligence products per day that could be used and applied by response professionals to aid in decision-making. NGA assessments were multi-dimensional, timely, relevant, and continuous. They addressed many issues, including but not limited to: recovery planning and operations, transportation infrastructure, critical and catastrophic damage, dike stability and breaches, industry damage, and hazard spills. The NGA World Wide Navigational Warning Service also provided navigation information to the U.S. Navy, Merchant Marine, and Coast Guard, and relayed messages from the National Weather Service to people at sea. NGA also aided in the location and recovery of oil platforms. The imagery activities of NGA were essential to the restoration of critical infrastructure.[34]

Department of Justice

The **Bureau of Prisons** provided extensive support to the Hurricane Katrina relief efforts. Some of those accomplishments included transporting 4,000 Louisiana Department of Corrections inmates out of New Orleans jails. Busses staffed by Bureau personnel from both within and outside of the region were dispatched to assist with this operation. The agency also transported fifty-five inmates from the St. Charles Parish Jail to the Federal Detention Center in Houston, Texas at the request of the U.S. Marshals Service, as well as seventy inmates from Harrison and Pearl River Counties, Mississippi to the northern part of that state. In addition to moving inmates, Bureau of Prisons staff provided supplies to the storm ravaged region. Specifically, staff from the U.S. Penitentiary in Atlanta, Georgia and the Federal Prison Camp in Montgomery, Alabama delivered to New Orleans toothpaste, toothbrushes, soap, shampoo, mouthwash, disposable personal sanitation packs, 600 Meals Ready to Eat (MRE), 600 hot trays of potato dinners, 600 cans of orange juice, eighty cases of water bottles, sheets, linen and pillows.

The **Federal Bureau of Investigation** recognized that there was a lack of unified law enforcement leadership, and no central coordination for law enforcement in New Orleans, and created a Law Enforcement Coordination Center (LECC).[35] Once the LECC was established, all law enforcement personnel and agencies (including those provided by the National Guard) had a unified command structure. This allowed every law enforcement agency operating in the New Orleans area to coordinate with other agencies.[36] Additionally, senior federal law enforcement officials from the FBI and DHS not only coordinated the response of the Federal law enforcement agencies, they also brought the New Orleans Police Department command element together for the first time since the hurricane struck. Further, they integrated Federal law enforcement assets and personnel into the remaining local police structure.

> FBI Special Agent in Charge Michael Wolf and U.S. Immigration and Customs Enforcement (ICE) Assistant Director Michael Vanacore, were appointed to serve as the Co-Senior Federal Law Enforcement Officials (SFLEO) under the NRP. Within a day of their appointment and for the first time since Katrina made landfall, the SFLEOs brought together all the Federal law enforcement agencies operating in the New Orleans area with the State police to coordinate efforts. The SFLEOs established a Law Enforcement Coordination Center (LECC) first in Baton Rouge and subsequently in New Orleans modeled after the FBI's Joint Operations Center. The LECC coordinated all law enforcement activities in the New Orleans area, bringing together Federal, State, and local law enforcement to including National Guard and DOD military police to provide assistance and support to the New Orleans Police Department. The rapid establishment of the LECC led to the rapid coordination of law enforcement activities and the restoration of law and order in New Orleans.

The **United States Attorney's Office** for the Eastern District of Louisiana supported law enforcement operations during the first week following Hurricane Katrina's impact. They were required to quickly set up two completely new offices in Baton Rouge and Houma, Louisiana. A large portion of their employees worked hard to accomplish this. However, certain members of their staff particularly distinguished themselves during the initial period when their operations were being conducted out of the U.S. Attorney's Office for the Middle District of Louisiana. Despite being dislocated from their homes and having the option of administrative leave, many of these employees went to Baton Rouge on their own to become involved in operations. Other essential employees came in to perform necessary tasks without any assurance that they would have a place to stay.

> Assistant United States Attorney (AUSA) Michael Magner evacuated to Baton Rouge, Louisiana where he arranged for his own lodging. He was one of the first AUSAs to report for duty and coordinated the manning of the regional jail facility established at the New Orleans bus station, personally performing several twenty-four hour shifts. He also supervised the handling of complaints and judicial appearances in cases involving persons arrested on criminal charges during that initial period. AUSA Stephen Higginson moved in with a friend in Baton Rouge while his family evacuated to Boston, Massachusetts. He immediately began handling a number of thorny legal issues that had arisen while at the same time performing twenty-four hour shifts at the bus station. AUSA Brian Marcelle, while providing for his wife and two infant children, voluntarily performed twenty-four hour shifts at the bus station, handled complaints, and made judicial appearances in cases involving persons arrested on criminal charges during that initial period.

On September 4, 2005, the **Bureau of Alcohol, Tobacco, Firearms and Explosives** (ATF) received a tip from a resident regarding gunfire in a New Orleans neighborhood. ATF Special Response Team (SRT) members responded, equipped with night vision goggles, and witnessed two individuals shooting at a helicopter as it flew overhead. The two men fled to a residence, and the SRT personnel entered the location and seized two handguns. One of the subjects, a convicted felon, gave a statement regarding the incident and was the first person federally arrested by any agency in the aftermath of Hurricane Katrina.

ATF agents also provided critical supplies on numerous occasions (including food, water, clothing, protective equipment, and ammunition) to the New Orleans Police Department (NOPD). On September 1, an ATF agent responded to New Orleans to provide assistance and emergency provisions to an NOPD Task Force Officer conducting post-storm operations. On September 2, upon arriving in New Orleans and setting up camp at a post office in the Algiers neighborhood, ATF SRT agents offered assistance to the NOPD SWAT team and 4th district officers. The police officers advised they had not seen or heard from any federal agency and were glad to see the ATF personnel, as they were running low on ammunition, food and water. The ATF SRT provided the NOPD with these supplies and immediately began assisting with law enforcement missions.

On September 3, ATF New Orleans Field Division agents provided security at a Mandeville, Louisiana hospital to which a large number of evacuees were being airlifted. Due to aircraft coming under fire, the hospital requested that ATF provide armed support for a rescue mission into the city to evacuate patients and personnel from Tulane University Hospital. Two agents assisted on this mission resulting in the rescue/evacuation of fourteen people. Agents also provided an armed escort for a transport shipment of emergency medical supplies from the New Orleans Airport to the Mandeville hospital.

Beginning on September 8, ATF SRT responded on several occasions with NOPD to clear the Fisher Housing Development after receiving reports of sniper fire. Several firearms were recovered, but the reports of sniper fire continued. On September 10, ATF SRT, acting on a tip, deployed to the Fisher Housing Development and found an AK-47 assault weapon with a 100 round magazine. It is believed that this was the weapon used during the reported sniper shootings in the area. After seizing the weapon, no more sniper reports were made.

ATF SRT personnel also established a medical facility to provide medicine and prescription drugs (e.g., insulin) to individuals in need and living in the area of the SRT base at the Algiers post office. ATF SRT personnel went to residences and nursing homes to provide food, water, and much-needed medical attention to people who could not or would not leave their homes. On September 4, with the assistance of the Louisiana Department of Wildlife and Fisheries, ATF personnel rescued at least twenty-three people, including one ATF employee, who were trapped in their homes.

Throughout the response to Hurricane Katrina, ATF continued to reach out to the sick and elderly citizens in the New Orleans area. On September 13, as Hurricane Rita was headed toward the Gulf Coast, SRT personnel went to all of the sick and elderly people known to them in the New Orleans area and attempted to convince them to evacuate. The many people that chose to remain in their homes were provided with food and water. Additionally, ATF agents rescued scores of domesticated animals throughout the response to the hurricane.

In response to the housing shortage, New Orleans ATF Field Division agents opened their residences to provide lodging to coworkers who were displaced from their homes and to other ATF agents on detail from other parts of the country. Agents assisted in the cutting and clearing of fallen trees at the residences of a number of field division personnel, and assisted many division personnel in returning to their residences in severely damaged areas to conduct damage assessments and retrieve personal effects. New Orleans Field Division agents provided personal security for Assistant United States Attorneys for the Eastern District of Louisiana returning to their offices and residences to retrieve important case information.

Deputy United States Marshal (DUSM) Justin Vickers of the New Orleans **U.S. Marshals Service** office found out there was a stranded elderly lady (in her 80s) in an apartment complex. Although she was able to call out by telephone; she was confused and unable to provide her apartment number and street address. DUSM Vickers was able to locate the complex and find her. He not only rescued her from the abandoned complex but also found her suitable care in a family's home located in Baton Rouge.

Department of Health and Human Services

The *Agency for Healthcare Research and Quality* (AHRQ), part of the Department of Health and Human Services (HHS) quickly identified the need for specific guidance on how to get hospitals in the region affected by the hurricane and flood reopened and running again. The Agency developed easy to read information, and checklists regarding supplies, medications, staffing, patient transport, reopening evaluation, and management.[37] AHRQ developed this information and got it into the hands of the State and Local leaders responsible for making hospitals function again.

The *Centers for Disease Control and Prevention* (CDC) deployed approximately 200 personnel to the affected region, including the following specialties: public health nursing, occupational, laboratory, medical, epidemiology, sanitation, environmental health, disease surveillance, public information and health risk communication. CDC led and/or assisted with a variety of emergency public health programs.[38] CDC immunization experts helped to provide vaccines and vaccinate children displaced by Hurricane Katrina, especially those staying in evacuation centers. Most importantly, they determined which diseases would result from the hurricane and flood, and not only monitored the region for them, they also communicated information on these diseases and others the public might be worried about, helping to allay public fears.[39] They helped to fill gaps in the public health infrastructure, prevented disease from gaining a foothold in the already devastated region, and communicated health-related information to the public.

Many victims of the hurricane and flood took charge of their own medical care to the extent that they could. In response to their demands for more information, for two weeks immediately after the hurricane and flood, the *National Institutes of Health* (NIH) expanded their program for medical consultation to not only help health care providers throughout the Nation, but also specifically assist patients and the worried well in the affected region. Working with their partners in academic medical centers and professional medical societies, NIH opened and manned phone lines all day every day to answer questions about a variety of diseases and cases involving complicated medical treatment. NIH immediately recognized that they were in the best position to match medical experts with health care providers and patients in need of answers – providing both groups with the information they needed to better manage health care concerns in the midst of the crisis.[40]

The *U.S. Public Health Service* staff from the Bureau of Prisons Federal Medical Center in Carswell, Texas provided support in response to Hurricane Katrina in a number of ways. For example, Lieutenant Commander Christopher L. McGee, Social Worker, was deployed for two weeks serving in a special needs shelter for elderly, wounded, and cognitively-impaired persons. While on a mission to locate a missing shelter resident, he and two National Guards members found a man lying on the ground surrounded by several other men that were hitting and kicking him. Specialists Christopher L. Horne and Mark D. Miller from the 528th Engineering unit, and Lieutenant Commander McGee intervened and stopped the assault, and then provided emergency care to the victim. While awaiting emergency medical response, the victim became combative and had to be restrained until paramedics arrived. After treatment, the man was safely returned to his family in Arizona the next day. During his tour, Lieutenant Commander McGee and his team, were able to locate and reunite approximately 296 shelter residents with family or community support systems. Additionally, Commander William Resto-Rivera and his medical team provided treatment and services to more than 130 elderly nursing home residents who had been displaced, and then prepared them for immediate movement. Captain Barbara J. Jenkins, Nurse Manager of Carswell's Mental Health Inpatient Unit, also performed brief mental health assessments for over 250 soldiers and civilians, both responders and victims.

Department of Energy

Colonial and Plantation Pipelines, major suppliers of fuel for the eastern US, were not operating due to lack of power at their pumping stations in Mississippi and Louisiana due to effects of Hurricane Katrina. The Department of Energy (DOE) persuaded Entergy and Mississippi Power to elevate the electrical restoration of these pumping stations to near the top of the priority list. Mississippi Power elevated restoration of Collins, Mississippi to their number one priority. Unfortunately, the assessments of the electrical grid revealed damage to multiple transmission lines. Entergy also had responsibility for restoring power to several of the pump stations. Entergy raised the pump stations in their priority list and were able to restore power to some of the lesser damaged facilities quickly. As a result of the lengthy restoration time, Colonial contracted for some generators. After these initial contracts were superseded by FEMA for use on lifesaving activities, The Department of Transportation, as the lead for Emergency Support Function 1 (ESF-1) under the NRP, coordinated transport and delivery of large emergency generators to petroleum and natural gas industry sites that lacked power following the hurricanes. At FEMA's request, ESF-1 also obtained the needed waivers so that these generators could be moved by road and rail. Colonial worked with DOE to request that FEMA recognize Colonial Pipeline as critical infrastructure and part of the necessary emergency response, providing critical fuel to the recovery effort. DOE worked with FEMA to get emergency responder identification for Colonial contractors and staff to expedite their travel through the police barricades and into the disaster area. DOE worked with Mississippi Highway Patrol to provide the company the information they needed to get into the disaster areas and checked road availability at the pumping stations. As Colonial attempted to restore power and deliver generators to these sites, their crews reported criminal activity and gunshots. Colonial stated they needed protection or would have to cease work and depart. DOE arranged with the Mississippi Highway Patrol to provide police protection to three of the Colonial pumping stations.

DOE provided a situation brief and recommendations regarding getting electricity back on at the water pumps at Lake Livingston Pumping Station. This pumping station supplies Houston with water. After speaking to all parties, it was determined that four different groups were preparing four different solutions involving portable generation. DOE, as the lead for ESF-12, pulled CenterPoint Energy, Entergy, Army Corps of Engineers, City of Houston, and the Coastal Water Authority (who ran the pumping station) together on a conference call to discuss the situation (note there was not a lot of communication between CenterPoint Energy and Entergy up to this point). CenterPoint Energy suggested energizing an open link between CenterPoint Energy and Entergy and letting CenterPoint Energy repair three lines between Entergy substations and to serve the pump station load from CenterPoint. ESF-12 strongly recommended to the PFO that this become the number one solution since this would provide a more stable source of power for the pumping stations. Late night on Sunday September 25, CenterPoint Energy contacted the DOE Emergency Operations Center to ask for permission to make the connection. Within minutes of that call, ESF-12 at the Austin JFO gave the verbal go-ahead to CenterPoint to proceed with its work on getting the pump station up. The work was completed two days later and the pump station came back on line just as the water supply was down to about a one day supply.

ESF-12 in Alabama was asked to contact an Alabama pole-making company (Cahaba) and attempt to get them fuel so they could continue their pole-making/treating (they make 4000 poles per day). The Governor of Alabama was made aware of the plight of Cahaba which was producing poles for Entergy and Mississippi Power (ESF-12 at the Mississippi EOC confirmed with Entergy and Mississippi Power that this pole supply was critical) and ESF-12 was tasked with getting them fuel. ESF-12 spoke with all parties with involved (Hunt Oil, Stephens Oil Distributor, and Cahaba) and got Hunt Oil to release the needed fuel beginning the following day, the day that Cahaba was going to have to shutdown their pole-making due to lack of fuel. ESF-12 personnel drafted a letter to Hunt Oil that was signed by the FCO and sent out a half hour later. Six pole-making companies in MS had shut down and the utilities were using the poles as fast as they were produced. Cahaba made 4000 poles per day and is the largest pole making company in the world. Without these poles, restoration would have severely been affected.

The Louisiana Offshore Oil Port was also partially damaged and initially shut down by Hurricane Katrina. This facility is the only US facility capable of offloading ultra large tankers and pumps about 1 million barrels of oil a day. DOE facilitated their access to emergency communications; worked with the local utilities to prioritize their restoration of commercial power; assisted in getting delivery of food and water to the on-site crew; and facilitated their communication with the U.S. Coast Guard to get their shipping lanes surveyed, which resulted in a U.S. Navy minesweeper being deployed to the area.

Department of Transportation

The Department of Transportation (DOT) successfully coordinated one of the largest airlifts in its history to support the emergency evacuation of more than 66,000 citizens from New Orleans. This large and complex operation involved three federal Departments and a fleet of private sector and military aircraft.[41] Additionally, the DOT *Federal Aviation Administration* quickly restored air traffic control and runway operations at the Louis Armstrong International Airport in New Orleans. This not only facilitated the delivery of relief supplies into the area, but also enabled federal authorities to execute a massive airlift of New Orleans evacuees. The Air Transport Association also coordinated forty domestic flights with continual DOD and civilian flights to evacuate a total of 24,000 people.

As a member of the DOT Region Ten Emergency ESF-1 response cadre, John Calvin was deployed for a period of over five weeks to the Louisiana State EOC and to the JFO in Baton Rouge. Working more than eighteen hours each day as part of the FEMA Emergency Response Team-Advance (ERT-A) he played a crucial role in post-landfall evacuation operations. Using ESF-1 controlled helicopters, he personally coordinated and led the evacuation of over 200 patients and staff, many of whom were non-ambulatory, from the rooftop of the flooded Louisiana State University hospital in downtown New Orleans. This dangerous but urgent lifesaving mission was undertaken voluntarily on John Calvin's part and at considerable risk, despite the fact that helicopter evacuations are not part of the traditional ESF-1 function. Additionally, John Calvin worked almost constantly, often on less than three hours sleep, coordinating military and ESF-1 buses and aircraft during the early phases of the evacuation. His personal efforts were instrumental in moving 210,000 people from New Orleans to shelters

Department of Housing and Urban Development

Working with the U.S. Conference of Mayors and the National Association of Counties, the Department of Housing and Urban Development (HUD) coordinated the identification of housing opportunities for hurricane victims. As a result, numerous cities, counties, and Indian Tribes offered housing and transportation to displaced persons. For example, the cities of Detroit and Philadelphia offered housing for over 1,000 displaced individuals. Allegheny County, Pennsylvania also offered to house 1,000 persons. HUD then worked with FEMA to match displaced individuals with vacant housing. HUD also sent personnel to Disaster Recovery Centers in states that were directly affected by the hurricane and flood, as well as in Arkansas, Florida, North Carolina, Tennessee, and Texas to meet with people displaced from their homes, and personally help them find temporary and permanent housing in host cities.[42] HUD used key interpersonal skills and relationships it had developed over the years, successfully matching the newly homeless with homes.

Department of Agriculture

Prior to Katrina making landfall, the *Food and Nutrition Service* (FNS) had proactively pre-positioned food in warehouses in Louisiana and Texas, making the food readily available for disaster meal service programs. FNS continued its efforts to ensure adequate supplies of food were on hand or nearby by airlifting initial supplies of infant formula and baby food products to Louisiana, Texas, Alabama and Mississippi and then following up with additional baby food supplies for delivery via land transportation (this amounted to approximately two million pounds). Additional commodities (approximately twenty million pounds), that included fruits, juices, vegetables, meats and grains, were also procured and/or diverted from existing USDA and other state sources to assist with congregate meal service and provide families with food packages until the Disaster Food Stamp Program could provide food relief (certain locations in the hardest hit areas could not operate the Disaster Food Stamp Program because there were no retail outlets available). Additionally, schools outside the devastated areas were granted waivers which permitted the service of free meals to children who had fled the devastated areas and began attending school elsewhere. FNS also promptly implemented the Food Stamp Program's first National Evacuee Policies that enabled State agencies that were not affected by the hurricane or that were not administering a disaster program to immediately issue disaster benefits to individuals and families who evacuated to their States. FNS approved over seventy waivers to affected States to issue benefits under the disaster authority. FNS also expanded the range of foods that could be purchased with food stamps in Louisiana, Mississippi, Florida, Alabama, and Texas, and approved alternate procedures for use and replacement of food stamp benefit cards to improve a household's ability to purchase food.

About 3,000 members of the *Forest Service* also deployed to the region to support response efforts. Arriving in Mississippi, Louisiana, Florida, and Alabama, Forest Service personnel established support camps, provided aviation assistance, and transported desperately needed supplies to relief workers. The base camps they established were capable of supporting 1,000 emergency responders at each site. They bolstered the destroyed aircraft infrastructure in the region with their own fixed wing planes and helicopters. They also helped navigate the Federal procurement system and successfully obtained needed emergency response supplies. These activities allowed local and state emergency response personnel to focus on response rather than worrying about the supplies and other support they needed.[43]

> Many organizations and agencies that responded to Hurricane Katrina and the ensuing flood arrived in the region without much experience with or knowledge of the affected States and their geography. National Guard member Ronnie Davis – also of the USDA *National Resources Conservation Service* (NRCS) – utilized the organization's digital data (ordinarily used to produce conservation plans and generated in Texas) and its Digital Topographic Support System to create the much needed maps of the affected regions of Mississippi. Davis and his team set up the system on an airport runway, and using a National Guard generator, managed to produce over 800 maps to support sector operations. In addition to hand-delivering these maps to National Guard units, the team also delivered maps to local police, law enforcement officers arriving from other States, and FEMA. According to Davis, his "...work for NCRCS just transitioned into what was needed to help with Hurricane Katrina relief in Mississippi and to support the local governments."[44]

The *Animal and Plant Health Inspection Service* (APHIS) sent fifty veterinarians and wildlife experts to the region to rescue animals – pets, zoo animals, and livestock. They augmented and provided veterinary services in Louisiana and Mississippi, saving more than 10,000 animals from the flooding of New Orleans. They delivered fresh water and bales of hay to starving cattle. They also successfully rescued mice that were part of Tulane University's cancer research program. APHIS helped many animals survive until they could be reunited with their owners, reduce the economic impact of further agricultural losses, and maintain research continuity.[45]

Through its Emergency Conservation Program, the *Farm Service Agency* (FSA) provided funding to help farmers and ranchers rehabilitate farmland damaged by the hurricane and flood. Administered by FSA state and county committees, this program provided the additional resources needed to remove debris from farmland, and restore farm-related infrastructure (e.g., fencing). FSA also decided to change its policy for those affected by the disaster, allowing eligible producers to receive 100% cost-share assistance in implementing an approved practice (instead of the usual 75%).[46]

The USDA program for *Rural Development* did not wait to be asked and instead, reached out to those displaced by the hurricane and flood. It offered direct loan borrowers a "no-questions-asked" moratorium on their mortgage payments, while simultaneously working with guaranteed lenders to prevent any liquidation actions and offer payment forbearance. The program also actively looked to fill the housing gaps that could not be addressed by FEMA and the Small Business Administration by finding alternative lodging for those that had been displaced, and making these victims a higher priority for Rural Development housing. For example, the program arranged to let tenants use vacant seasonal labor housing units while repairs were being made to their own homes. Rural Development looked for ways to make its own activities bend to meet the housing needs generated by this catastrophe, while continuing to meet their ongoing commitments to rural communities throughout the Nation.[47]

Many scientific federal organizations worked with scientists in the affected region to continue their research. For example, the *Agricultural Research Service* (ARS), the in-house research arm of the U.S. Department of Agriculture (USDA), did not allow the hurricane to derail important ongoing agricultural research throughout the Nation. When the USDA Southern Regional Research Center in New Orleans was severely damaged by Hurricane Katrina, ARS quickly relocated some of the scientists, support staff, and their families to the U.S. Plant, Soil and Nutrition Laboratory in New York. ARS provided support to these families, facilitated the continuation of their research, and gave them the opportunity to collaborate with other scientists from the Cornell University Departments of Plant Pathology and Animal Science.[48] ARS and other federal agencies, such as the *Department of Commerce National Institute of Standards and Technology* and the *Department of Energy Office of Science* provided scientists with the resources and support they needed to continue their research in spite of the hurricane and flood.[49]

Department of Commerce

Clearly understanding the impact of the hurricane and flood on businesses in the region, the *Minority Business Development Agency* of the Department of Commerce (DOC) sent business development specialists to the region to provide on-the-ground assistance to the owners of the more than 59,000 minority firms in Louisiana, Mississippi, and Alabama, as well those that temporarily relocated to Texas. MBDA established a minority business development center in Houston to assist with loan applications, business plans, insurance claims, reconstruction of business records, and business administration. Instead of letting these businesses slide, MBDA helped get owners back on their feet quickly.[50]

Elements of the *National Oceanic and Atmospheric Administration* (NOAA) were proactive and vigilant. The National Hurricane Center (part of the NOAA National Weather Service) accurately predicted and tracked the size, scale, and path of Hurricane Katrina. Further, Max Mayfield, Director of the National Hurricane Center, personally made phone calls to local, State and Federal leaders to apprise them of the situation, aggressively contacting officials in the affected areas to warn them.[51] Members of the National Weather Service knew that the time would come to issue warnings, and they developed them ahead of time, evaluating data and basing the warning language on various scenarios, so that when certain criteria were met (as with Hurricane Katrina), they did not have to waste time creating statements—they could issue them immediately.

The National Weather Service also correctly realized that the levees were breaching and issued a flash flood warning at 8:14 AM Monday, August 29, saying, "A levee breach occurred along the industrial canal at Tennessee Street. Three to eight feet of water is expected due to the breach."[52] These organizations correctly characterized the situation, identified the danger, and got the word out clearly and promptly.

During the response to Hurricane Katrina, the DOC *National Telecommunications and Information Administration* (NTIA) correctly and immediately identified the need for additional communications bandwidth, and allocated more than 1,100 frequencies to nine Federal agencies which allowed them to operate their land mobile, aeronautical, maritime, and satellite communications. NTIA also coordinated with the Federal Communications Commission to temporarily authorize the use of private sector satellite, ultrawideband, and microwave communication services. In addition to these response efforts, NTIA also provided financial support to reestablish the communications infrastructure in Louisiana, helping the state to take an initial and important step toward recovery.[53]

Department of the Interior

The *Bureau of Indian Affairs* (BIA) of the Department of the Interior (DOI) focused their efforts on assisting tribes in the Gulf region to address their public safety, emergency access, and emergency services needs.[54] They maintained communications before hurricane landfall and coordinated directly with Tribal governments, such as the Mississippi Choctaw Tribal government.[55] BIA waited until Tribal governments made requests before sending assistance, but started preparing and moving assets ahead of time, so that when the requests for assistance did come, they were already responding.

BIA had responded to seven hurricanes previously and knew exactly what to do when the time and requests came. The Bureau arranged for fresh water to be delivered from other States, replaced spoiled food, cleared debris from roadways, brought in necessary supplies, ensured continuity of education for children attending BIA-funded schools, and improved public safety infrastructure by assigning Bureau law enforcement personnel to the area. The Bureau also correctly assumed that those Tribes near the affected regions would take in other members that were victims of the hurricane and flood, and worked to provide financial and other assistance, helping the Tribes take care of each other.[56]

Federal land-managing agencies, such as the *Bureau of Land Management* (BLM), as well as their state counterparts sent hundreds of employees to help restore public health and safety in the devastated region. They also deployed to the Mississippi-Louisiana border to clear roadways and power lines of damaged and fallen trees that had cut off those in the coastal communities, so that first responders could gain access to the victims and help restore power. BLM personnel also skillfully applied their experience with planning, logistical support and tracking (gained from years of managing wildland fires) to the situation in the Gulf region. [57]

Coordinating with FEMA, the U.S. Army Corps of Engineers and their sister organizations within the DOI, the **Bureau of Reclamation** mobilized equipment and staff in response to the hurricane and flood. Recognizing the need to purify drinking water, the Bureau of Reclamation sent an expeditionary water purification unit to Mississippi, purifying both contaminated and salt water to levels that not only met, but exceeded, EPA drinking water standards. The unit produced 100,000 to 200,000 gallons of purified water per day. The Bureau also deployed employees to assist with debris removal and install temporary roofing. They had equipment and trained personnel who were well acquainted with the rigors and requirements of water purification and other missions in contaminated and disaster-driven conditions.[58]

Scientists from the **Geological Survey** worked with the Louisiana Department of Environmental Quality to monitor water quality in the state following the hurricane and flood. Using a mobile laboratory, they collected and analyzed water samples from 22 sites in and around Lake Pontchartrain, a major recreational area and fishery, for three weeks to determine levels of contamination, and whether this contamination extended into the Mississippi Sound.[59] They applied sound scientific research practices and attention to detail to the problem of contaminated water in the region.

Volunteers from the DOI **Office of Surface Mining** (OSM) deployed to Texas and worked at 13 different debris-disposal sites, dealing with more than one million cubic yards of debris. Additionally, OSM personnel conducted safety training, handled equipment inventory, purchasing and other administrative requirements. They applied their vast experience with clearing large amounts of debris to the situation, moving debris out as efficiently and effectively after the disaster as they do for surface mining.[60]

Department of Labor

Recognizing that getting back to work and starting new jobs would be critical for those affected, whether they returned to their home states or chose to live elsewhere in the U.S., the Department of Labor established a "Pathways to Employment" initiative. Using the Department's network of over 3,500 career centers nationwide, the initiative helps evacuees and survivors find jobs. The Department sent numerous personnel directly to the affected region to provide job counseling to evacuees (including tailored assistance to the disabled looking for employment), and help all in need of jobs use the expanded resources provided by this initiative. Additionally, the Department expedited and increased its Job Corps offerings, providing over 4,000 scholarships to economically disadvantaged young adults (aged 16-24).[61]

Department of Education

The Department of Education established an innovative website to help provide assistance to those schools that had accepted students displaced by Hurricane Katrina and the flood. At this site schools list the needs of these students (e.g. books, clothes, school supplies, computers – even counseling) and donors list what they can provide. Schools and donors have access to one another's information, and are then encouraged to contact each other directly, and hundreds of matches have been made.[62] The Department of Education also worked with the **Defense Logistics Agency**, the **General Services Administration**, and the **Federal Emergency Management Agency** to pool federal resources and quickly provide thousands of pieces of furniture, computers and other equipment from the federal surplus to schools in need.[63]

Department of State

Using the recently developed Employee Profile Plus database, managers in the State Department rapidly located current and former employees with skills in about 300 specific areas. The web-based system was deployed during the Department's tsunami relief efforts in late 2004 and again following the hurricane and flood. They quickly found employees with required language, area and disaster relief expertise in a matter of minutes, rather than days or weeks.[64] These skilled personnel were critical in communicating information to those that primarily or solely spoke foreign languages.

Department of the Treasury

The ***Bureau of Public Debt*** immediately realized that there would be a great need for money in the devastated region, but that ordinary access to cash would be limited at the banks. The Bureau expedited both the replacement of savings bonds that had been destroyed, as well as the redemption of Series EE and I savings bonds that were less than one year old.[65] Other organizations in the Department of the Treasury, such as the ***Financial Management Service*** (FMS), immediately issued guidance to financial institutions to help them confirm the identify of people trying to redeem Treasury checks – to help the institutions prevent fraud and help the victims obtain needed funds.[66] The ***Internal Revenue Service*** also took action to advise taxpayers in the affected region of recent changes in tax law that under certain conditions would allow them to withdraw funds early from retirement plans, without the usual penalties.[67] Although Treasury checks, savings bonds, and of course, retirement plans, are often considered long-term investments, the Department of the Treasury allowed investors to turn them into sources of cash in this emergency, understanding that without the cash to address immediate needs, there would be no long-term future for these victims.

> The Administrative Resource Center within Treasury's Bureau of the Public Debt, provides administrative services to many Federal agencies. The Armed Forces Retirement Home, with residences for elderly veterans in Gulfport, MS and Washington, DC, is one of its customers. As soon as the Administrative Resource Center procurement staff was informed, late on August 29, 2005, of the decision to evacuate approximately 400 residents and essential staff from the flooded Gulfport home to the Washington, DC facility, they set about applying their procurement skills to orchestrate a safe and rapid evacuation and relocation. This included arranging for the rental of buses along with procuring necessary nursing services, lodging, and meals for the several-day journey. The frailest of residents were either redirected to Maxwell Air Force Base, for faster and less stressful transport to Washington, DC, or, in extreme cases, were found places in a nearby nursing home. While the Gulfport residents were in transit to Washington, the Center also quickly procured a host of goods and services to prepare the facilities at the Washington, DC campus for the huge and sudden influx of new residents. This included procuring beds, linens, furniture, air conditioners, and extra support services, such as medical, food, transportation and custodial services. Within eight days of Katrina making landfall, the last busload of Gulfport residents arrived safely at the Washington, DC campus.

> While working on the phones for FEMA, Dionne Lewis, a four-year IRS employee for Atlanta Accounts Management, received a call from a distressed person in Texas who was living in the Houston Astrodome. This person had been displaced by Hurricane Katrina and was in desperate need of help. Thrilled to have reached someone with such compassion, the person wanted to know if Ms. Lewis could also help the next person in line there at the Astrodome. She agreed, but little did she know that the call would last throughout her entire shift as one person after another came to the phone to find what help the IRS could offer. There was little time for breaks. Ms. Lewis did not let the magnitude of the calls or the prospect of being on the phone for nearly eight hours keep her from being professional, assuring that each person was informed of their Privacy Act rights, and then affording them an opportunity to tell their story and receive what assistance the IRS could offer. These and other all day long marathon calls occurred quite frequently and became known as the Delta calls. IRS employees answered well over 760,000 registration calls for FEMA and more than 30,000 calls on the special IRS toll-free line for affected taxpayers.

> Internal Revenue Service, Portland call site assistor Jon Fredericks, received a call from an eighty-one year-old woman outside of a New Orleans home needing urgent help. She was sitting in the sweltering heat, without power, waiting for someone to evacuate her. She had tried to call several help lines, but had not reached anyone so far except the IRS. Mr. Fredericks told her to stay on the line and with the help of coworker Jim McMahan, contacted city emergency services and alerted them to her situation and location. Within a short time, the rescue team arrived at her home.

The Department of Veterans Affairs

The Department of Veterans Affairs (VA) took a hard look at their resources, missions, assets and personnel, and redirected them to fill the needs of the victims of the hurricane and flood, while maintaining service to America's veterans. The VA not only provided medical services, hospital beds, and medications in accordance with its standing emergency health care mission,[68] it also removed VA properties for sale from the market in eleven states to use them instead to fill housing needs for those displaced,[69] and worked with veterans to replace their benefit checks.[70] The VA cared for many victims of the hurricane and flood, while also continuing to care for the soldiers who have borne the battle, and for their families.

Jack Myers, Maintenance and Repair Foreman, Wayne Brown, Air Conditioning Shop Foreman, and James Ware, Plumbing Shop Foreman, had taken shelter from Hurricane Katrina in a building on the north side of the Gulfport Veterans Affairs campus leaving their vehicles and their office on the more dangerous south side. That afternoon, the three men went to check on their vehicles. They found a five-year-old boy alone under a four-foot tall pile of debris that minutes before had been part of an apartment complex. The men took him back to their shelter. There, they dried him off, fed him and clothed him with an oversized uniform crudely tailored to fit his small frame. Fortunately, he suffered only minor cuts and scratches. "He's a very smart boy," said Brown. "He knew his name and his school and his teacher's name. He told us his momma had given him a Pop Tart and told him to go upstairs." The boy just continued to clutch that wet Pop Tart, remembered Brown, and was eventually reunited with his mother and brother.

By Friday, Sept. 2, all patients, employees, and family members had been safely evacuated from the VA in New Orleans using boats, military trucks, and military transport planes. Nine veterans, however, remained in the hospital morgue. Lynn Ryan, chief financial officer with the South Central VA Health Care Network, was determined to make sure everyone was evacuated. He searched and found a local company that had a refrigerated tractor-trailer and a willing driver. The following day, the truck driver, Ryan, co-worker Ceagus Reed, a human resources coordinator, and VA Police Officers Charlie Donelson and Reginald Finch, both with the G.V. (Sonny) Montgomery VA Medical Center in Jackson, Mississippi, made it through all the roadblocks and to the outskirts of downtown New Orleans. Four feet high floodwaters and the approaching evening hours forced them to take shelter for the night, sleeping in their vehicles at a toll plaza where law enforcement officers had set up a temporary station. On Sunday, two additional colleagues arrived to help—Steve Jones, an engineer, and Steve Morris, occupational safety and health manager. The team made it to downtown New Orleans but the refrigerated tractor-trailer couldn't make it through the flooded streets to the hospital's loading dock. Ryan flagged down a five-ton military transport truck that helped ferry the bodies from the hospital to the refrigerated trailer. At the loading dock, Ryan, Reed, Morris, and Jones donned biohazard gear and climbed the three flights of stairs to the hospital morgue. One at a time, they carried the bodies out. They returned to Jackson and notified the next of kin and made burial arrangements, including some at the VA's national cemetery in Natchez.

Phil Boogaerts, chief engineer at the New Orleans VA Medical Center, single-handedly kept the hospital supplied with necessary power and utilities to ensure adequate care for patients, employees and their families for four days prior to their evacuation. As a direct result of his actions, VA staff was able to provide adequate care to patients and successfully evacuate all patients, families, and employees, including nine ventilator-dependent patients. In addition, Mr. Boogaerts videotaped the facility before, during, and after the storm providing valuable documentation that assisted with the assessment of damages to the physical plant as a result of the storm. Finally, Boogaerts voluntarily remained at the hospital after it was evacuated to continue maintenance of the facility. For several days, Boogaerts lived at the hospital in isolation, without air conditioning, running water, or prepared meals.

After evacuating the VA Medical Center, employees donated all of their food, 300 cases of water, all their medical supplies, and needed medication to Charity Hospital, a neighboring hospital that was still operating and had yet to completely evacuate. Employees delivered the provisions by boat, making their way through the murky waters of flooded downtown New Orleans. Among the medicines Charity needed and donated by the VA, were medicines for ant bites and snake bites.

Environmental Protection Agency

The Environmental Protection Agency (EPA) worked with their partners in the Louisiana Department of Environmental Quality and other local officials to help remove hazardous household and other materials. They created a "curbside pickup" program to collect the materials from the houses, instead of making already overwhelmed victims deliver hazardous materials to another location.[71] They also identified the potential hazards returning victims would face, and distributed information to people in affected areas regarding a range of hazards, from asbestos to septic systems.[72] They collected and removed many hazardous materials, including electronics, batteries, computer hardware, paint, solvents, lawn and garden products. They enabled people to reestablish clean and safe environments in their houses and for their families. Without EPA assistance, this would not have occurred. Additionally, the EPA also waived national sulfur emissions standards for diesel fuel for a short period so that fuel produced for non-road uses could be legally used in highway vehicles.[73]

> The success of the Incident Command System (ICS) was clearly demonstrated in Hancock County, considered to be the most devastated area within Mississippi. Carter Williamson led a team during the early stages of EPA's response effort to protect the citizens of Hancock County from releases of hazardous materials. Under adverse conditions, working sixteen-hour days every day, Mr. Williamson motivated the team members who were living under severe conditions, where basic support services such as electricity, shelter, running water, and telephones were, if available, very limited. In a demonstration of leadership, Carter remained in a variety of primitive shelters throughout the entire hurricane response, embedded with the team in the impacted community. His efforts resulted in the team's ability to provide more effective service and helped his team to empathize with the plight of the community. Whereas most other EPA employees rotated in and out of the work area on a two week basis, Mr. Williamson chose to remain in the community, despite having a wife and children back home, because he believed the consistency of leadership would be beneficial to the response effort. Although the magnitude of the task was overwhelming and the working conditions were poor, the quality of the response effort lead by Mr. Williamson was outstanding.

> With Hurricane Katrina approaching, Nancy Jones was preparing to implement a Hurricane Debris Management Plan, like the one she had drafted for the US Army Corps of Engineers (USACE) while participating in the "Hurricane Pam" planning workshops. Because of this experience, the USACE specifically requested that Ms. Jones be deployed to assist the USACE in handling the debris collection and segregation of the hazardous materials resulting from Hurricane Katrina. She was instrumental in setting up the collection and debris management plan in many of the eastern Parishes including the City of New Orleans. Her coordination with the USACE made the response to the hurricane more efficient and effective. The Parish Officials and the City of New Orleans have developed trust and respect for the EPA because of her efforts. Ms. Veronica White with the City of New Orleans sums up Nancy's efforts well. "She is excellent and thorough. She has answered every question we (the City of New Orleans) have had. If she didn't know the answer right off, she got back to us with a response very quickly." Ms. White asked that the EPA keep Ms. Jones on the project through completion. She stated that they did not want to lose her.

Federal Energy Regulatory Commission

In another effort to get needed resources in the region freed up for use by the victims and responders there, as well by citizens throughout the Nation, the Federal Energy Regulatory Commission took immediate steps to reconstruct the natural gas infrastructure of the region, and reduce the disruption in the natural gas supply.[74] Because the Commission approved temporary waivers and expanded eligibility standards they were able to help natural gas companies restore service and deliver additional gas to the market.

Federal Communications Commission

The Commission acted quickly to facilitate the resumption of communications services in the affected areas and to authorize the use of temporary communications services for use by emergency personnel and evacuees in shelters. First, the Commission operated twenty-four hours a day every day of the week to assist industry efforts to restore communications. The Commission streamlined procedures to approve requests for special temporary authority (STA), which would in turn expedite industry recovery efforts. The Commission quickly granted more than ninety STA requests and 100 temporary frequency authorizations that telecommunications companies and broadcasters needed to get service restored. The Commission also contacted each segment of the communications industry to help match their needs with resources (such as such as emergency generators and fuel) around the nation. Additionally, the Commission used its High Frequency Direction Finding Capability Center to remotely assess the damage done to radio stations in the areas struck by Hurricane Katrina and to monitor the progress of restoration activity. Further, the Commission assisted telecommunication carriers by helping their repair crews to secure the transportation and credentials recognized by local authorities to gain access to damaged sites.

Office of Management and Budget

Recognizing that recipients of federal grants in those areas affected by Hurricane Katrina and its ensuing flood either would have to stop grant-related activities or be unable to perform as well as usual, the Office of Management and Budget (OMB) worked with the Federal agencies and the Office of Science and Technology Policy (OSTP) to assist these grantees in resuming operations. OMB directed federal agencies and OSTP to: (1) provide greater flexibility with grant application deadlines, (2) approve no-cost extensions on expiring awards for up to 12 months, (3) accept short written requests for project continuation, (4) allow grantees to continue to charge salaries and benefits to current grants, as well as costs to resume project activities, (5) waive some requirements for prior federal approval for re-budgeting and automatic carryover of unspent funds, (6) extend deadlines for reports, (7) continue already approved indirect cost rates for up to a year, (8) delay submitting financial and other reports to close out projects, and (9) help grantees reconstruct their records by allowing them to substitute copies for original records and providing copies of what had already been submitted.[75] OMB relieved short-term administrative and financial management requirements without compromising accountability.

APPENDIX C – LIST OF ACRONYMS

AAR	After Action Review
ABA	American Bus Association
AHRQ	Agency for Healthcare Research and Quality
APHIS	Animal and Plant Health Inspection Service
ARC	American Red Cross
ARS	Agricultural Research Service
ASD (HD)	Assistant Secretary of Defense, Homeland Defense
ATF	Bureau of Alcohol, Tobacco, Firearms and Explosives
ATF SRT	Bureau of Alcohol, Tobacco, Firearms and Explosives Special Response Team
AUSA	Assistant United States Attorney
BENS	Business Executives for National Security
BIA	Bureau of Indian Affairs
BLM	Bureau of Land Management
BRT	Business Round Table
C3I	Command, Control, Communications, Information
CDC	Centers for Disease Control and Prevention
CERT	Citizen Emergency Response Team
CIS	Catastrophic Incident Supplement
CLO	Chief Logistics Officer
CNGB	Chief of the National Guard Bureau
CONOPS	Concept of Operations
COOP	Continuity of Operations
CRWG	Hurricane Katrina Comprehensive Review Working Group
CSG	Counterterrorism Security Group
CST	Civil Support Team
BEA	Bureau of Economic Analysis
DART	Disaster Assistance Response Team
DHS	Department of Homeland Security
DMAT	Disaster Medical Assistance Team
DMORT	Disaster Mortuary Operational Response Team
DoD	Department of Defense
DOE	Department of Energy
DOEd	Department of Education
DOI	Department of the Interior
DOJ	Department of Justice
DOL	Department of Labor
DOL/OSHA	Department of Labor Occupational Safety and Health Administration
DOS	Department of State
DOT	Department of Transportation
DPMU	Disaster Portable Morgue Unit
DRC	Disaster Recovery Center

DRG	Disaster Response Group
DUSM	Deputy United States Marshal
EAS	Emergency Alert System
EBS	Emergency Broadcast System
EHR	Electronic Health Records
EOC	Emergency Operations Center
EPA	Environmental Protection Agency
EMAC	Emergency Management Assistance Compact
EMS	Emergency Medical Services
ERT	Emergency Response Team
ERT-A	Emergency Response Team-Advanced
ERT-N	Emergency Response Team-National
ESF	Emergency Support Function
FAA	Federal Aviation Administration
FBI	Federal Bureau of Investigation
FEMA	Federal Emergency Management Agency
FCO	Federal Coordinating Officer
FNS	Food and Nutrition Service
FPS	Federal Protection Service
FRP	Federal Response Plan
FSA	Farm Service Agency
HHS	Department of Health and Human Services
HHS SERT	Health and Human Services Secretary's Emergency Response Teams
HLT	Hurricane Liaison Team
HSC	Homeland Security Council
HSOC	Homeland Security Operations Center
HSPD	Homeland Security Presidential Directive
HUD	Department of Housing and Urban Development
ICE	Immigration and Customs Enforcement
ICS	Incident Command System
IIMG	Interagency Incident Management Group
IMT	Incident Management Team
INS	Incident of National Significance
IRA	Immediate Response Authority
IRS	Internal Revenue Services
JFHQ-State	Joint Force Headquarters-State
JFO	Joint Field Office
JIC	Joint Information Center
JTF-Katrina	Joint Task Force-Katrina
JTF-State	Joint Task Force-State
LECC	Law Enforcement Coordination Center
LSU	Louisiana State University
LTG	Lieutenant General
MERS	Mobile Emergency Response System
MOB center	Mobilization center
MRC	Medical Reserve Corps
MRE	Meals-Ready-To-Eat
NASAR	National Association of Search and Rescue
NCC	National Coordinating Center
NCS	National Communications System
NDMS	National Disaster Medical System
NEEP	National Exercise and Evaluation Program
NEMA	National Emergency Management Association
NEP	National Exercise Program
NGA	National Geospatial Intelligence Agency

NGB	National Guard Bureau
NGO	Non-Governmental Organization
NHC	National Hurricane Center
NHSU	National Homeland Security University
NICCL	National Incident Communications Conference Line
NIFC	National Interagency Fire Center
NIH	National Institutes of Health
NIMS	National Incident Management System
NIPP	National Infrastructure Protection Plan
NISAC	National Infrastructure Simulation & Analysis Center
NOAA	National Oceanic and Atmospheric Administration
NOC	National Operations Center
NOFD	New Orleans Fire Department
NOPD	New Orleans Police Department
NPG	National Preparedness Goal
NPS	National Park Service
NRCC	National Response Coordination Center
NRP	National Response Plan
NRP-CIS	National Response Plan Catastrophic Incident Supplement
NSA	National Security Agency
NSC	National Security Council
NS/EP	National Security and Emergency Preparedness
NTIA	National Telecommunications and Information Administration
NVOAD	National Volunteer Organizations Active in Disaster
NWR	NOAA Weather Radio
NWS	National Weather Services
OFDA	Office of Foreign Disaster Assistance
OMB	Office of Management and Budget
OSD-HD	Office of the Secretary of Defense for Homeland Defense
OSM	Office of Surface Mining
OSTP	Office of Science and Technology Policy
PAO	Public Affairs Office
PAO	Public Affairs Official
PFO	Principal Federal Officer
PHS	Public Health Service
RAMP	Remedial Action Management Program
RRCC	Regional Response Coordination Center
RSOI	Reception, Staging, Onward movement, and Integration
SAR	Search and Rescue
SCRAG	Senior Civilian Representative of the Attorney General
SES	Senior Executive Service
SFLEO	Senior Federal Law Enforcement Official
SIMCEN	National Exercise Simulation Center
SLO	State Liaison Officer
SNS	Strategic National Stockpile
SOE	Senior Official Exercise
SOP	Standard Operational Procedures
SSA	Social Security Administration
STA	Special Temporary Authority
SWAT	Special Weapons and Training
TAG	Adjutant General
TCC	Traffic Control Center
TCL	Target Capabilities List
TELL	Office of Training, Exercises, and Lessons Learned
TPC	Tropical Prediction Center

TSA	Transportation Security Administration
USACE	United States Army Corps of Engineers
USAID	United States Agency for International Development
USCG	United States Coast Guard
USDA	United States Department of Agriculture
USFS	United States Forest Service
USJFCOM	United States Joint Forces Command
USMS	Unites States Marshals Service
USNORTHCOM	United States Northern Command
USPACOM	United States Pacific Command
USSOUTHCOM	United States Southern Command
USSTRATCOM	United States Strategic Command
USTRANSCOM	United States Transportation Command
US&R	Urban Search and Rescue
VOAD	Volunteer Organizations Active in a Disaster
VA	Department of Veteran Affairs
VADM	Vice Admiral

APPENDIX D – STAFF PAGE

Hurricane Katrina Lessons Learned Staff

Special thanks go to the dedicated team of tireless professionals—working with colleagues across the country at all levels of government—who have contributed to this Report. For the past four months, they have reviewed the Federal government's role and performance in preparing for, responding to, and recovering from Hurricane Katrina.

White House Staff
Frances Fragos Townsend, Assistant to the President for Homeland Security
  and Counterterrorism
Kenneth P. Rapuano, Deputy Assistant to the President for Homeland Security
Joel B. Bagnal, Special Assistant to the President for Homeland Security
Michele L. Malvesti, Senior Director, National Security Council
Kirstjen M. Nielsen, Special Assistant to the President for Homeland Security
Thomas P. Bossert, Policy Director, Homeland Security Council
Daniel J. Kaniewski, Policy Director, Homeland Security Council
Marie O'Neill Sciarrone, Policy Director, Homeland Security Council
Joshua C. Dozor, Policy Director, Homeland Security Council
Michael J. Taylor, Executive Assistant, Homeland Security Council

Katrina Lessons Learned Review Group
Stuart G. Baker, Department of Homeland Security
Richard W. Brancato, Department of Transportation
Donovan E. Bryan, Department of Defense
Christopher Combs, Federal Bureau of Investigation
Theodore M. Cooperstein, Department of Justice
William T. Dolan, Colonel, United States Army
Michael O. Forgy, Department of Homeland Security
Douglas J. Morrison, Colonel, United States Army
Richard L. Mourey, Commander, United States Coast Guard
David C. Rutstein, Captain, United States Public Health Corps

APPENDIX E – ENDNOTES

FOREWORD

[1] President George W. Bush, Jackson Square, New Orleans, September 15, 2005.
[2] President George W. Bush, Jackson Square, New Orleans, September 15, 2005.
[3] The White House, *Homeland Security Presidential Directive-5: Management of Domestic Incidents* (Washington, D.C., February 28, 2003); see also, U.S. Department of Homeland Security, *National Response Plan* (Washington, D.C., December 2004), Preface.

CHAPTER ONE: KATRINA IN PERSPECTIVE

[1] The White House, "Proclamation by the President: National Day of Prayer and Remembrance for the Victims of Hurricane Katrina," news release, September 8, 2005, http://www.whitehouse.gov/news/releases/2005/09/print/20050908-12.html.
[2] As measured by damage to property. Measuring destructiveness in terms of damage to property rather than loss of life is a useful way to compare disasters. Loss of life reflects both the magnitude of the disaster, as well as the quality of the response, while property destruction correlates more directly to the magnitude of the disaster alone.
[3] In 1871, Chicago was the fifth largest city in the United States, with a population of almost 300,000. The fire killed 300 people, made one-third of the city homeless, and destroyed a third of the city's property. For Chicago Fire deaths and population displacement, see Lawrence J. Vale and Thomas J. Campanella, eds., *The Resilient City: How Modern Cities Recover from Disaster* ["*Resilient City*"] (New York: Oxford University Press, 2005), 28; U.S. Census Bureau, "Table 10. Population of the 100 Largest Urban Places: 1870," June 15, 1998, http://www.census.gov/population/ documentation/twps0027/tab10.txt. For all other Chicago Fire statistics, see Chicago Historical Society, "The Great Chicago Fire," http://www.chicagohs.org/fire/intro/gcf-index.html; *The Chicago Fire and the Fire Insurance Companies* (New York: J.H. and C.M. Goodsell, 1871); and *Insurance Year Book* (1874). (Note that statistics for disasters can vary significantly depending on the source consulted, both due to variances in how terms are defined and the lack of consistent historical records.)
For statistics on the San Francisco Earthquake/Fire and Hurricane Andrew, see Figure 1.1 and accompanying notes.
[4] Rebecca Watson, Assistant Secretary for Land and Minerals Management, U.S. Department of the Interior, written statement for a hearing on Global Oil Demand/Gasoline Prices, on September 6, 2005, submitted to the Senate Committee on Energy and Natural Resources, 109th Congress, 1st session.
[5] U.S. Department of Energy, Office of Electricity Delivery and Energy Reliability, "Hurricane Katrina Situation Report #6," August 28, 2005.
[6] Evidence suggests that Hurricane Katrina reached Category 3 intensity as it made second landfall, but that only winds to the east of the eye sustained Category 3 speeds. New Orleans probably experienced Category 2 wind speeds at most. See Richard D. Knabb, Jamie R. Rhome, and Daniel P. Brown, *Tropical Cyclone Report: Hurricane Katrina, August 23-30, 2005* ["*Katrina Tropical Cyclone Report*"], prepared for the National Hurricane Center (Miami, Florida, December 20, 2005), 8. Under the Saffir-Simpson scale, Category 3 hurricanes are characterized by winds of 111—130 miles per hour. For an explanation of the Saffir-Simpson scale, see U.S. Department of Commerce, National Oceanic and Atmospheric Administration, National Hurricane Center, "The Saffir-Simpson

Hurricane Scale," ["*NHC Saffir-Simpson Scale*"] http://www.nhc.noaa.gov/aboutsshs.shtml. During the same period (1851—2005), eighteen Category 4 and three Category 5 hurricanes hit the United States. For hurricane statistics through 2004, see Eric S. Blake et al., *The Deadliest, Costliest, and Most Intense United States Tropical Cyclones from 1851 to 2004 (And Other Frequently Requested Hurricane Facts)* ["*United States Tropical Cyclones*"], NOAA Technical Memorandum NWS TPC-4 (Miami, Florida, August 2005), 12, http://www.nhc.noaa.gov/Deadliest_Costliest.shtml. For 2005 hurricane data, see U.S. Department of Commerce, National Oceanic and Atmospheric Administration, National Hurricane Center, "2005 Atlantic Hurricane Season Tropical Cyclone Reports," http://www.nhc.noaa.gov/2005atlan.shtml; U.S. Department of Commerce, National Climatic Data Center and National Oceanic and Atmospheric Administration Satellite Information Service, "Climate of 2005 Atlantic Hurricane Season," http://www.ncdc.noaa.gov/oa/climate/research/2005/hurricanes05.html.

[7] Hurricane Camille is a useful point of comparison—until the 2005 hurricane season, it was the second most intense hurricane of record ever to strike the United States. U.S. Department of Commerce, National Oceanic and Atmospheric Administration, National Hurricane Center, "Hurricane History—Hurricane Camille, 1969," ["*Hurricane History—Hurricane Camille*"], http://www.nhc.noaa.gov/HAW2/english/history.shtml#camille. Under the Saffir-Simpson scale, Category 5 hurricanes are characterized by winds greater than 155 miles per hour. See *NHC Saffir-Simpson Scale*.

[8] Axel Graumann et al., *Hurricane Katrina: A Climatological Perspective: Preliminary Report* ["*Climatological Perspective*"], Technical Report 2005-01, prepared for the National Climatic Data Center, (Asheville, NC, January 2006), 21, http://www.ncdc.noaa.gov/oa/reports/tech-report-200501z.pdf. For Hurricane Camille's strength on landfall, see *Hurricane History—Hurricane Camille*.

[9] *Climatological Perspective*, 21. Hurricane force winds are defined as those 64 knots (74 miles per hour) or above lasting for one minute at ten meters above ground with unobstructed exposure. For Hurricane Katrina, the radius was 103.5 miles in the northeast and southeast quadrants, and 69 miles in the northwest and southwest quadrants. Northern moving systems like Katrina typically have stronger winds to the east, as the storm's clockwise rotation results in greater centrifugal force, and therefore force, in that direction. *Katrina Tropical Cyclone Report*, 3.

[10] *Katrina Tropical Cyclone Report*, 9. The report states: "Even though Hurricane Camille (1969) was more intense than Katrina at landfall while following a similar track, Camille was far more compact and produced comparably high storm surge values along a much narrower swath." See U.S. Department of Commerce, National Oceanic and Atmospheric Administration, National Hurricane Center, "Preliminary Report on Hurricane Camille: August 14-22, 1969," ftp://ftp.nhc.noaa.gov/pub/storm_archives/atlantic/prelimat/atl1969/camille/prelim06.gif. See U.S. Department of Commerce, National Oceanic and Atmospheric Administration, National Weather Service, "Preliminary Storm Report: Hurricane Katrina," September 6, 2005, http://www.srh.noaa.gov/tlh/tropical/PSHTAE_Katrina.txt.

[11] Estimates on the total affected area vary according to the criteria selected. The estimate of 93,000 square miles was derived by adding the areas of the 138 parishes and counties first declared Major Disaster areas and made eligible for Individual Assistance or Public Assistance, Categories C – G (31 in Louisiana, 74 in Mississippi, 22 in Alabama, and 11 in Florida). The exact sum is 92,930 square miles. See also U.S. Department of Homeland Security, "United States Government Response to the Aftermath of Hurricane Katrina," news release, September 1, 2005, http://www.dhs.gov/dhspublic/display?content=4777.

[12] *Katrina Tropical Cyclone Report*, 8-9.

[13] *Katrina Tropical Cyclone Report*, 8-9.

[14] Louisiana Department of Transportation and Development, "DOTD's 'Louisiana Team' to Collect Data on Levee Failures," news release, October 10, 2005, http://www.dotd.louisiana.gov/press/pressrelease .asp?nRelease=545. See also Dr. Ivor van Heerden, written statement for a hearing on Hurricane Katrina: Performance of the Flood Control System, on November 2, 2005, submitted to the Senate Committee on Homeland Security and Governmental Affairs, 109th Congress, 1st session.

[15] See *Katrina Tropical Cyclone Report*, 9.

[16] U.S. Census Bureau, "Annual Estimates of the Population for Incorporated Places over 100,000, Ranked by July 1, 2004 Population: April 1, 2000 to July 1, 2004," *Cities & Towns: Places over 1,000: 2000 to 2004*, http://www.census.gov/popest/cities/SUB-EST2004.html. The estimate of the population of New Orleans on July 1, 2004 was 462,269.

[17] The Galveston Hurricane was a tremendous human tragedy. At least 8,000 people lost their lives in this storm. See *United States Tropical Cyclones*, 12, http://www.nhc.noaa.gov/Deadliest_Costliest.shtml (estimating 8,000—12,000 deaths); U.S. Department of Commerce, National Oceanic and Atmospheric Administration, National Hurricane Center, "Hurricane History—Galveston Hurricane, 1900,"

http://www.nhc.noaa.gov/HAW2/english/history.shtml#galveston (estimating 6,000—12,000 deaths); Erik Larson, *Isaac's Storm: A Man, a Time, and the Deadliest Hurricane in History* (New York: Random House, 1999), 264-265 (estimating 6,000—10,000 deaths); and Galveston Historical Foundation, "Galveston History," http://www.galvestonhistory.org/history.htm (estimating over 6,000 deaths and stating that Galveston was the fourth largest city in Texas at the time).

[18] Haley Barbour, Governor of Mississippi, testimony before a hearing on Hurricane Katrina: Recovering from Hurricane Katrina, on September 7, 2005, House Committee on Energy and Commerce, 109th Congress, 1st session; Haley Barbour as quoted on the Public Broadcasting Service, "Storm-Ravaged Mississippi," *NewsHour with Jim Lehrer*, September 7, 2005, http://www.pbs.org/newshour/bb/weather/july-dec05/miss_9-7.html.

[19] See Dr. Robert C. Sheets, former Director of the National Hurricane Center, testimony before a hearing on Rebuilding FEMA: Preparing for the Next Disaster, on May 18, 1993, Senate Committee on Governmental Affairs, 103rd Congress, 1st session.

[20] Unless otherwise specified, all damage estimates in this chapter are in third-quarter 2005 dollars.

[21] Figure 1.1 includes both the most deadly and the most destructive natural disaster from each decade in the period 1900 to 2005. Often, these are the same disaster. The four major Atlantic hurricanes of 2004, while neither the most deadly nor most destructive of the decade, are also included to provide context on recent hurricane activity. They are grouped because they struck overlapping areas, in rapid succession, and together constituted the most damaging U.S. hurricane season on record until Hurricane Katrina struck in August 2005. The disasters included in the chart are discrete, violent natural disasters in the United States. They do not include terrorist events, technological failures (e.g., dams breaking or ferries sinking), or protracted, non-destructive natural events such as deadly heat waves or epidemics, which are difficult to compare to discrete, violent events. Where multiple death estimates are available, the highest credible estimate is shown, capturing deaths caused both directly and indirectly by the event. Where multiple damage estimates are available, the lowest credible estimate is shown, excluding local post-disaster inflation effects and effects on the national economy.

The chart does not reflect the enormous loss of life due to the pandemic influenza—sometimes known as the "Spanish Flu"—outbreak of 1918—1919, which claimed the lives of approximately 500,000 Americans and over 20 million people worldwide. U.S. Department of Health and Human Services, National Vaccine Program Office, "Pandemics and Pandemic Scares in the 20th Century," last revised February 12, 2004, http://www.hhs.gov/nvpo/pandemics/flu3.htm. See generally Alfred W. Crosby, *America's Forgotten Pandemic: The Influenza of 1918* (New York: Cambridge University Press, 2003).

Table 1.2, below, contains the data used in Figure 1.1

Table 1.2 Worst Natural Disasters in the United States, 1900-2005[21]
Damage in Third Quarter 2005 dollars

Top Disasters	Estimated deaths	Estimated damage
Galveston Hurricane (1900)	8,000	< $1 billion
San Francisco Earthquake and Fire (1906)	5,000	$6 billion
Atlantic-Gulf Hurricane (1919)	600	< $1 billion
Mississippi Floods (1927)	246	$2 billion
Hurricane San Felipe and the Okeechobee Flood (1928)	2,750	< $1 billion
New England Hurricane (1938)	600	$4 billion
Northeast Hurricane (1944)	390	< $1 billion
Hurricane Diane (1955)	184	$5 billion
Hurricane Audrey (1957)	390	< $1 billion
Hurricane Betsy (1965)	75	$7 billion
Hurricane Camille (1969)	335	$6 billion
Hurricane Agnes (1972)	122	$8 billion
Hurricane Hugo (1989)	86	$11 billion
Hurricane Andrew (1992)	61	$33 billion
East Coast Blizzard (1993)	270	$4 billion
Major 2004 Hurricanes (Charley, Frances, Ivan, Jeanne)	167	$46 billion
Hurricane Katrina (2005)	1,330	$96 billion

Note that statistics for disasters can vary significantly depending on the source consulted, both due to variances in how terms are defined and the lack of consistent historical records.

For statistics on those hurricanes not listed separately below, see *United States Tropical Cyclones*; U.S. Department of Commerce, National Oceanic and Atmospheric Administration, National Hurricane Center, "Hurricane History," http://www.nhc.noaa.gov/HAW2/english/history.shtml; U.S. Department of Commerce, National Oceanic and Atmospheric Administration, National Weather Service, "Memorial Web Page for the 1928 Okeechobee Hurricane," http://www.srh.noaa.gov/mfl/newpage/Okeechobee.html; Russell L. Pfost, "Reassessing the Impact of Two Historical Florida Hurricanes" (American Meteorological Society, Boston 2003), 1367; and U.S. Department of Commerce, National Oceanic and Atmospheric Administration, National Hurricane Center, "NHC/TPC Archive of Past Hurricane Seasons," http://www.nhc.noaa.gov/pastall.shtml.

For the Galveston Hurricane, see note 17.

For the 1906 San Francisco Earthquake and Fire, see *Resilient City*, 28 (estimating 5,000 deaths); Harry Chase Brearley, *Fifty Years of a Civilizing Force: An Historical and Critical Study of the Work of the National Board of Fire Underwriters* (New York: Frederick A. Stokes Company, 1916), 98-100 (estimating $6 billion in property damage); U.S. Geological Survey, "Casualties and damage after the 1906 Earthquake," http://quake.wr.usgs.gov/info/1906/casualties.html (estimating more than 3,000 deaths and $7 billion in property damage). See generally Rutherford H. Platt, "The Bay Area: One Disaster After Another," in Rutherford H. Platt, ed., *Disasters and Democracy: The Politics of Extreme Natural Events* (Washington, DC: Island Press, 1999), 245-247; Virtual Museum of the City of San Francisco, "The Great 1906 Earthquake And Fire," http://www.sfmuseum.org/1906/06.html.

For the 1927 Mississippi floods, see Paul S. Trotter et al., "Floods on the Lower Mississippi: An Historical Economic Overview," technical attachment prepared for the National Weather Service, http://www.srh.noaa.gov/topics/attach/html/ssd98-9.htm (estimating 246 deaths and $2 billion in property damage); Miriam Gradie Anderson and Rutherford H. Platt, "St. Charles County, Missouri: Federal Dollars and the 1993 Flood," in Platt, *Disasters and Democracy: The Politics of Extreme Natural Events* (Washington, DC: Island Press, 1999), 215-216 (estimating 245-500 deaths).

For Hurricane Camille, see Ernest Zebrowski and Judith A. Howard, *Category 5: The Story of Camille* ["*The Story of Camille*"] (Ann Arbor, MI: University of Michigan Press, 2005), 266 (reporting 335 deaths); Roger A. Pielke, Jr., Chantal Simonpietri, and Jennifer Oxelson, *Thirty Years After Hurricane Camille: Lessons Learned, Lessons Lost* (Boulder, Colorado, July 1999) (estimating more than 200 deaths); *Hurricane History—Hurricane Camille* (reporting 256 deaths and $6 billion in damage).

For Hurricanes Hugo and Andrew, the East Coast Blizzard, and the major 2004 hurricanes, see U.S. Department of Commerce, National Oceanic and Atmospheric Administration Satellite and Information Service and National Climatic Data Center, "1980-2003 Billion Dollar U.S. Disasters," in *A Climatology of 1980-2003 Extreme Weather and Climate Events*, Technical Report 2003-01 ["*Billion Dollar U.S. Disasters*"] (Asheville, NC, December 2003), http://www.ncdc.noaa.gov/oa/reports/billionz.html; Ed Rappaport, "Preliminary Report: Hurricane Andrew, 16 - 28 August, 1992, prepared for the National Hurricane Center" ["*Preliminary Report: Hurricane Andrew*"](Miami, Florida, December 1993), http://www.nhc.noaa.gov/1992andrew.html; U.S. Department of Commerce, National Oceanic and Atmospheric Administration, National Hurricane Center, "Hurricane History," http://www.nhc.noaa.gov/HAW2/english/history.shtml.

For Hurricane Katrina deaths, see Louisiana Department of Health and Hospitals, "Reports of Missing and Deceased" ["*Louisiana Missing and Deceased*"], February 17, 2006, http://www.dhh.louisiana.gov/offices/page.asp?ID=192&Detail=5248; *Katrina Tropical Cyclone Report*. For property damage, see U.S. Department of Commerce, Bureau of Economic Analysis, "Damages and Insurance Settlements from the Third-quarter Hurricanes," http://www.bea.gov/bea/faq/national/2005q3hurricanes.pdf (estimates reflect data as of December 21, 2005); U.S. Department of Commerce, Bureau of Economic Analysis, "Estimated Damage and Insurance Settlements Effects from Hurricanes Katrina, Rita, and Wilma on Monthly Personal Income," ["*Estimated Damage and Insurance Settlements Effects from Hurricanes Katrina, Rita, and Wilma*"] http://www.bea.gov/bea/faq/national/oct2005hurricane.pdf (accessed on January 20, 2006).

For GDP deflation, see U.S. Department of Commerce, Bureau of Economic Analysis, "Gross Domestic Product and Corporate Profits: Third Quarter 2005 'final' estimates," news release, December 21, 2005, http://www.bea.gov/bea/newsrelarchive/2005/gdp305f.htm; and Louis D. Johnston and Samuel H. Williamson, "The Annual Real and Nominal GDP for the United States, 1790—Present," *Economic History Services*, October 2005, http://www.eh.net/hmit/gdp.

[22] The three next most costly natural disasters are Hurricane Andrew, which hit south Florida in 1992 ($33 billion), the Midwest Floods of 1993 ($27 billion), and the Northridge Earthquake, which hit southern California in 1994 ($25 billion). By comparison, the direct damages caused by the 9/11 terrorist attacks totaled $18 billion. See Robert Looney, "Economic Costs to the United States Stemming From the 9/11 Attacks," *Strategic Insights* 1, no. 6 (Monterey, CA, August 2002), http://www.ccc.nps.navy.mil/si/aug02/homeland.asp. Damages are in 2005 dollars. For Hurricane Andrew, see note 21, above. For the Midwest Floods, see *Billion Dollar U.S. Disasters*. For the Northridge Earthquake, see U.S. Geological Survey, *USGS Response to an Urban Earthquake – Northridge '94* (n.d., ca. 1996), http://pubs.usgs.gov/of/1996/ofr-96-0263/introduc.htm#impacts.

[23] Numbers do not equal sum due to rounding. Estimate derived from the U.S. Department of Commerce, Bureau of Economic Analysis, "Damages and Insurance Settlements from the Third-quarter Hurricanes," http://www.bea.gov/bea/faq/national/2005q3hurricanes.pdf (estimates reflect data as of December 21, 2005); *Estimated Damage and Insurance Settlements Effects from Hurricanes Katrina, Rita, and Wilma.*

[24] Michael Chertoff, Secretary of the Department of Homeland Security, prepared written statement for a hearing on Hurricane Katrina: The Homeland Security Department's Preparation and Response, on February 15, 2006, submitted to the Senate Homeland Security and Governmental Affairs Committee, 109th Congress, 2nd session. Depending on the definition of "damaged and destroyed homes," this number could be considerably higher or lower than the figure cited.

[25] Damage to homes includes major but not minor damage. Stanley K. Smith and Christopher McCarty, *Demographic Effects of Natural Disasters: A Case Study of Hurricane Andrew* ["*Demographic Effects of Natural Disasters*"], Demography, Vol. 33, No. 2 (May, 1996), 266 (repeating results of American Red Cross survey). Note that the authors of the case study provide a higher estimate of 144,100 houses destroyed or suffering major damage.

[26] American Red Cross, "Hurricane Season 2004," http://www.redcross.org/sponsors/drf/h2004-stewardreport.html.

[27] Damage to homes includes major but not minor damage. For statistics on Hurricane Camille, see *The Story of Camille*, 226 (reporting 335 deaths); Roger A. Pielke, Jr., Chantal Simonpietri, and Jennifer Oxelson, *Thirty Years After Hurricane Camille: Lessons Learned, Lessons Lost* (Boulder, Colorado, July 1999) (estimating more than 200 deaths and 22,008 homes destroyed or damaged); *Hurricane History—Hurricane Camille* (reporting 256 deaths and $6 billion in damage). For statistics on Hurricane Andrew, see *Preliminary Report: Hurricane Andrew* (reporting 61 deaths and $25 billion in damage); *Demographic Effects of Natural Disasters* (reporting 15 deaths and $22 billion in damage). For statistics on Hurricane Ivan, see *Billion Dollar U.S. Disasters*, Technical Report 2003-01 (Asheville, NC, December 2003), http://www.ncdc.noaa.gov/oa/reports/billionz.html (reporting 57 deaths); American Red Cross, "Hurricane Season 2004," http://www.redcross.org/sponsors/drf/h2004-stewardreport.html (reporting 63 deaths). For statistics on Hurricane Katrina, see note 21.

[28] Michael Chertoff, Secretary of the Department of Homeland Security, written statement submitted for a hearing on Hurricane Katrina: The Homeland Security Department's Preparation and Response, on February 15, 2006, to the Senate Homeland Security and Governmental Affairs Committee, 109th Congress, 2nd session.

[29] Michael Chertoff, Secretary of the Department of Homeland Security, written statement for a hearing on "Hurricane Katrina: The Homeland Security Department's Preparation and Response," on February 15, 2006, submitted to the Senate Homeland Security and Governmental Affairs Committee, 109th Congress, 2nd session.

[30] A football field is 120 yards long by 53 yards wide. End-zones are included in this calculation. National Football League, "Beginner's Guide to Football," http://www.nfl.com/fans/rules/basics. Based upon this, the height of debris is calculated by finding the volume of the debris stacked on the football field. This is done by dividing 118,000,000 by the product of 120 and 53: 118,000,000 / 6360 = 18,553 yards. There are 1760 yards in a mile, so the number of miles high is then calculated by dividing 18,553 by 1760: 18,553 / 1760 = 10.5. So the debris, if stacked onto the space of a football field, would reach ten and a half miles high.

[31] The methodology and time period examined by the Bureau of Labor Statistics in developing these statistics for "most affected areas" differ from those used to develop the estimate of areas "impacted" by Hurricane Katrina included in note 11. First, the Bureau of Labor Statistics defines "most affected areas" as the thirty-four parishes in Louisiana and forty-seven counties in Mississippi that FEMA designated for both individual and public disaster assistance. This Report defines areas "impacted" by Hurricane Katrina as those parishes and counties designated for individual assistance and/or public assistance, categories C-G (reimbursement for rebuilding and/or replacing disaster-damaged public facilities such as roads, bridges, and public buildings). Second, the Bureau of Labor Statistics includes all counties designated for assistance as of September 30, 2005, thereby including the areas affected by Hurricane Rita in addition to those affected by Katrina. By contrast, this Report's methodology on this

point only includes those counties and parishes designated for assistance as of August 29, 2005, thereby counting only those counties that were affected by Katrina. U.S. Department of Labor, Bureau of Labor Statistics, "Labor Market Statistics for Areas Affected by Hurricanes Katrina and Rita: September and October 2005," http://www.bls.gov/katrina/data_after.htm; U.S. Department of Labor, Bureau of Labor Statistics, "Labor Market Statistics Prior to Disaster for Areas Affected by Hurricanes Katrina and Rita," http://www.bls.gov/katrina/data.htm#2.

[32] U.S. Department of Commerce, Bureau of Economic Analysis, "State Personal Income: Third Quarter 2005," news release, December 20, 2005, 4, http://www.bea.gov/bea/newsrelarchive/2005/spi1205.pdf.

[33] Nationwide all grade conventional retail prices increased from $2.28 per gallon on August 1 and $2.62 on August 29, to peak at $3.08 on September 5. U.S. Department of Energy, Energy Information Administration, "Retail Gasoline Historical Prices, Worksheet for U.S. All Grades Conventional Retail Gas Prices (Cent Per Gallon)," All Grades spreadsheet, http://www.eia.doe.gov/oil_gas/petroleum/data_publications/ wrgp/mogas_history.html. While gas prices had risen steadily throughout 2005 due to increasing global demand for crude oil, the temporary shutdown of major oil refineries and pipelines in the Gulf region as a direct result of Hurricane Katrina spurred a sharp and sudden drop in domestic supply that further exacerbated this price incline. See U.S. Department of Energy, Energy Information Administration, "A Primer on Gasoline Prices," http://www.eia.doe.gov/pub/oil_gas/petroleum/analysis_publications/primer_on_gasoline_prices/html/petbro.html (accessed February 6, 2006).

[34] U.S. Department of the Interior, Minerals Management Service, "Hurricane Katrina/Hurricane Rita Evacuation and Production Shut-in Statistics Report," news release, January 11, 2006, http://www.mms.gov/ooc/press/ 2006/press0111.htm.

[35] U.S. Department of Energy, Office of Electricity Delivery and Energy Reliability, "Hurricane Katrina Situation Report #10," August 30, 2005.

[36] Stacy R. Stewart, *Tropical Cyclone Report: Hurricane Ivan, 2-24 September 2004*, prepared for the National Hurricane Center (Miami, Florida, May 2005), http://www.nhc.noaa.gov/2004ivan.shtml.

[37] Kenneth Moran, Director of the Office of Homeland Security, Enforcement Bureau, Federal Communications Commission, testimony before a hearing on Ensuring Operability During Catastrophic Events, House Committee on Homeland Security, Subcommittee on Emergency Preparedness, Science, and Technology, October 26, 2005, 109th Congress, 1st session.

[38] Kenneth Moran, Director of the Office of Homeland Security, Enforcement Bureau, Federal Communications Commission, written statement for a hearing on Hurricane Katrina and Communications Interoperability, on September 29, 2005, submitted to the Senate Committee on Commerce, Science and Transportation, 109th Congress, 1st session.

[39] Kevin J. Martin, Chairman, Federal Communications Commission, written statement provided for a hearing on Public Safety Communications from 9/11 to Katrina: Critical Public Policy Lessons, submitted to Subcommittee on Telecommunications and the Internet, Committee on Energy and Commerce, U.S. House of Representatives September 29, 2005.

[40] Louisiana Hurricane Recovery Resources, "Energy, Oil, and Gas," http://www.laseagrant.org/hurricane/oil.htm (accessed January 11, 2006); U.S. Department of Energy, Office of Electricity Delivery and Energy Reliability, "Gulf Coast Hurricanes Situation Report #31," October 31, 2005.

[41] The ten major to medium spills caused by Katrina accounted for 7,359,990 gallons. Given that 134 spills of less than 10,000 gallons have not been assessed in detail, the actual oil spill figure for Hurricane Katrina is likely higher than 7.4 million gallons. Louisiana Hurricane Recovery Resource, "Energy, Oil, and Gas," http://www.laseagrant.org/hurricane/oil.htm (accessed January 11, 2006). The Exxon Valdez spilled about 10.8 million gallons into the waters off of Alaska. See Exxon Valdez Oil Spill Trustee Council, "Excerpt from the Official Report on the 1989 Exxon Valdez Oil Spill," http://www.evostc.state.ak.us/History/excerpt.htm (accessed January 11, 2006).

[42] *Gulf Coast Hurricane Emergency Environmental Protection Act of 2005*, H. Res. 4139, 109th Congress, 1st session (October 25, 2005).

[43] As of the time of writing, Louisiana has recovered 1,103 bodies, 23 of which were not storm related, for 1,080 storm related deaths. See *Louisiana Missing and Deceased*. There were 231 deaths in Mississippi, fifteen in Florida, two in Alabama, and two in Georgia. See *Katrina Tropical Cyclone Report*, 10. Since there are still at least 2,096 people from the Gulf Coast area missing, it is likely that the death toll numbers will increase.

[44] For the number of dead in other states, see *Katrina Tropical Cyclone Report*, 10. For the definition of the New Orleans metropolitan area, see The White House, Office of Management and Budget, "Updates of Statistical Area Definitions and Guidance on Their Uses," *OMB Bulletin 06 – 01*, December 5, 2005, 42, http://www.whitehouse.gov/omb/bulletins/fy2006/b06-01.pdf.

[45] These numbers were extrapolated from data on 754 released bodies of known age, of which 183 were between the ages of sixty-one and seventy-five and 355 were over the age of seventy-five. Louisiana Department of Health and Hospitals, "Vital Statistics of All Bodies at St. Gabriel Morgue," January 18, 2006, www.dhh.state.la.us/offices/publications/pubs-192/5796.pdf.

[46] Louisiana Department of Health and Hospitals, "Deceased Katrina Victims Released to Families 11-4-2005," news release, November 4, 2005, http://www.dhh.louisiana.gov/news.asp?ID=145&Detail=728&Arch=2005.

[47] As of February 17, 2006, 191 victims were unclaimed. *Louisiana Missing and Deceased.*

[48] *Louisiana Missing and Deceased.* In the immediate wake of the hurricane, the Department of Justice requested that the National Center for Missing and Exploited Children (NCMEC) establish a hotline to accept reports of missing children and adults related to both Hurricanes Katrina and Rita. As of February 13, 2006, 97 percent of the 5,071 missing children cases reported to the NCMEC for Hurricane Katrina had been resolved, with the majority of the unresolved cases in Louisiana. The NCMEC received 12,514 reports of missing adults, all of which were referred to the National Center for Missing Adults (NCMA). National Center for Missing and Exploited Children, "Katrina/Rita Missing Persons Hotline: Update on calls/cases," report through February 13, 2006, http://www.missingkids.com/en_US/documents/KatrinaHotlineUpdate.pdf.

[49] Michael Chertoff, Secretary of the Department of Homeland Security, testimony before a hearing on Hurricane Katrina: The Homeland Security Department's Preparation and Response, on February 15, 2006, Senate Homeland Security and Governmental Affairs Committee, 109th Congress, 2nd session. In the first half of the 1930s, almost one million people left the plains, and after 1935, 2.5 million left. Not all of this migration, however, was due to the Dust Bowl, as drought and changing economic conditions played a factor as well. Donald Worster, *Dust Bowl: The Southern Plains in the 1930s* (New York: Oxford University Press, 1979), 49.

[50] By January 13, only 82 individuals still resided in transient shelters in Louisiana, representing those few who were ineligible for housing programs or had refused other housing options. Scott Wells, Deputy Federal Coordinating Officer for Louisiana, testimony before a hearing on Housing Needs after Hurricanes Katrina and Rita, on January 13, 2006, House Financial Services Committee, Subcommittee on Housing and Community Opportunity, 109th Congress, 2nd session.

[51] U.S. Department of Health and Human Services, "Secretary Leavitt To Gulf Region: Announces Streamlines Access to Benefits for Hurricane Katrina Victims," news release, September 13, 2005. See also Arizona Department of Health Services, "Hurricane Evacuees Find Lost Records-And More-Through Arizona's Office of Vital Records," news release, September 23, 2005, http://www.azdhs.gov/news/2005all/katrina _vrecords.htm; District of Columbia Office of the Mayor, "Mayor Williams Introduces Legislation to Aid Katrina Victims," September 20, 2005, http://dc.gov/mayor/news/release.asp?id=763&mon=200509.

[52] HHS Secretary Mike Leavitt said that most of those displaced by Katrina did not have access to their medical records. Sarah A. Lister, *Hurricane Katrina: The Public Health and Medical Response*, Congressional Research Service Report for Congress RL33096 (Washington, DC, September 21, 2005).

[53] Bruce Katz, Matt Fellowes, and Mia Mabanta, *Katrina Index: Tracking Variables of Post-Katrina Reconstruction* (Washington, DC: Brookings Institute, February 2006,), 24, 38, 40, 44.

[54] U.S. Department of Commerce, Economics and Statistics Administration, "Addendum: Revisions/Updates to the Dec. 15 Katrina Economic Impact Report," December 2005. In total, Katrina, combined with Hurricanes Rita and Wilma, forced about 600,000 into unemployment. This is measured by the number of jobless claims benefits with the hurricanes listed as the primary reason.

[55] U.S. Department of Labor, Bureau of Labor Statistics, "Labor Market Statistics Prior to Disaster for Areas Affected by Hurricane Katrina," September and October 2005, http://www.bls.gov/katrina/data_archived.htm.

CHAPTER TWO: NATIONAL PREPAREDNESS — A PRIMER

[1] Homeland Security Presidential Directive 5, Domestic Incident Management, states "[t]he Federal Government recognizes the roles and responsibilities of State and local authorities in domestic incident management. Initial

responsibility for managing domestic incidents generally falls on State and local authorities. The Federal Government will assist State and local authorities when their resources are overwhelmed, or when Federal interests are involved. The Secretary will coordinate with State and local governments to ensure adequate planning, equipment, training, and exercise activities. The Secretary will also provide assistance to State and local governments to develop all-hazards plans and capabilities, including those of greatest importance to the security of the United States, and will ensure that State, local, and Federal plans are compatible." The White House, *Homeland Security Presidential Directive-5* ["*HSPD-5*"] (Washington, DC, February 2003), § 6.

[2] "The powers delegated by the proposed Constitution to the federal government, are few and defined. Those which are to remain in the State governments are numerous and indefinite." The Federalist No. 45.

[3] U.S. Constitution art. 1, sec. 10; U.S. Constitution art. 4, sec. 2; *United States v. Lopez*, 514 U.S. 549, 552 (1995) ("The Constitution creates a Federal Government of enumerated powers"); *McCulloch v. Maryland*, 17 U.S. 316 (1819); The Federalist No. 45. "It must never be forgotten that the Federal government is one of enumerated powers and that it does not possess a general police power," Ronald D. Rotunda and John E. Novak, *Treatise on Constitutional Law*, 3rd ed. (Minnesota: West Group Publishing, 1999), 346.

[4] U.S. Constitution, amend. 10.

[5] U.S. Constitution, art. 1, sec. 8; art. 2, sec. 2.

[6] U.S. Constitution, art. 4, sec. 4.

[7] 10 U.S.C. § 331 (2005). The other two sections of the Insurrection Act permit Presidential action independent of State requests. The President may send in Federal military forces or federalize a State's National Guard troops without a request from the Governor in those situations where the President finds it necessary to enforce Federal laws, judicial decisions, or protect Federal rights. 10 U.S.C. §§ 332, 333 (2005).

[8] See generally, Thomas E. Drabek and Gerard J. Hoetmer ["*Drabek & Hoetmer*"], *Emergency Management: Principles and Practice for Local Government* (Washington, DC: International City Management Association, 1991), 3-29.

[9] National Academy of Public Administration, *Coping With Catastrophe: Building an Emergency Management System to Meet People's Needs in Natural and Manmade Disasters* ["*NAPA Report*"] (Washington, DC: National Academy of Public Administration, 1993), 10.

[10] *NAPA Report*, 10.

[11] See *Drabek & Hoetmer*, 6-7; *NAPA Report*, 10-11.

The Federal Emergency Management Agency—a former independent agency that became part of the new Department of Homeland Security in March 2003—is tasked with responding to, planning for, recovering from and mitigating against disasters. FEMA can trace its beginnings to the Congressional Act of 1803, generally considered the first piece of disaster legislation. In the century that followed, *ad hoc* legislation was passed more than 100 times in response to hurricanes, earthquakes, floods and other natural disasters.

By the 1930s, when the Federal approach to problems became popular, the Reconstruction Finance Corporation was given authority to make disaster loans for repair and reconstruction of certain public facilities following an earthquake, and later, other types of disasters. In 1934, the Bureau of Public Roads was given authority to provide funding for highways and bridges damaged by natural disasters. The Flood Control Act, which gave the U.S. Army Corps of Engineers greater authority to implement flood control projects, was also passed. This piecemeal approach to disaster assistance was problematic and it prompted legislation that required greater cooperation between Federal agencies and authorized the President to coordinate these activities.

The 1960s and early 1970s brought massive disasters requiring major Federal response and recovery operations by the Federal Disaster Assistance Administration, established within the Department of Housing and Urban Development (HUD). Hurricane Carla struck in 1962, Hurricane Betsy in 1965, Hurricane Camille in 1969 and Hurricane Agnes in 1972. The Alaskan Earthquake hit in 1964 and the San Fernando Earthquake rocked Southern California in 1971. These events served to focus attention on the issue of natural disasters and brought about increased legislation. In 1968, the National Flood Insurance Act offered new flood protection to homeowners, and in 1974 the Disaster Relief Act firmly established the process of Presidential disaster declarations.

However, emergency and disaster activities were still fragmented. When hazards associated with nuclear power plants and the transportation of hazardous substances were added to natural disasters, more than 100 Federal agencies were involved in some aspect of disasters, hazards and emergencies. Many parallel programs and policies existed at the State and local level, compounding the complexity of Federal disaster relief efforts. The National Governor's Association sought to decrease the many agencies with whom State and local governments were forced to work. They asked President Jimmy Carter to centralize Federal emergency functions.

President Carter's 1979 executive order merged many of the separate disaster-related responsibilities into a new Federal Emergency Management Agency (FEMA). Among other agencies, FEMA absorbed: the Federal Insurance Administration, the National Fire Prevention and Control Administration, the National Weather Service Community Preparedness Program, the Federal Preparedness Agency of the General Services Administration and the Federal Disaster Assistance Administration activities from HUD. Civil defense responsibilities were also transferred to the new agency from the Defense Department's Defense Civil Preparedness Agency. See U.S. Department of Homeland Security, Federal Emergency Management Agency, "FEMA History," http://www.fema.gov/about/history.

[12] The Red Cross had originally been chartered in 1900, but its re-chartering in 1905 significantly expanded its role in responding to disasters. See Brien R. Williams, "The Federal Charter of the American Red Cross," American Red Cross Museum, April 2005, http://www.redcross.org/museum/history/charter.asp; and American Red Cross, "A Brief History of the American Red Cross 2001," http://www.redcross.org/museum/briefarc.html. In response to the San Francisco earthquake and fire of 1906, President Theodore Roosevelt announced that all Federal aid was to be channeled through the American Red Cross. Federal troops were sent to the city in order to provide security and the Federal government established tent camps where those affected by the disaster were provided with shelter and food. *NAPA Report*, 10.

[13] *NAPA Report*, 11.

[14] *NAPA Report*, 11; *Federal Civil Defense Act of 1950*, as amended, Public Law 920, 81st Congress, 2nd session (January 12, 1951).

[15] The order stated, "Federal disaster relief provided under the [Federal Civil Defense Act of 1950] shall be deemed to be supplementary to relief afforded by state, local, or private agencies and not in substitution therefor. . ." Executive Order no. 10427, 18 Fed. Reg. 407 (1953).

[16] *NAPA Report*, 11 (citing Message from the President of the United States transmitting a report on "New Approaches to Federal Disaster Preparedness and Assistance," May 14, 1973).

[17] *The Robert T. Stafford Disaster Relief and Emergency Assistance Act*, Pub. L. No. 100-707, § 5170, 102 Stat. 4689 (1988) (amended 2000) ["*Stafford Act*"].

[18] *Stafford Act*, 42 U.S.C. § 5170 and § 5191 (2005) require the Governor's request as a condition for Presidential declaration of a major disaster. Robert Theodore Stafford served in Congress as a Representative and a Senator from Vermont. Prior to his Congressional career, Stafford served in the United States Navy during both World War II and during the Korean conflict. He was the Governor of Vermont from 1959-1961. While in the Senate, he led the passage of the Stafford Act, which was the amended version of the 1974 Disaster Relief Act (*Disaster Relief Act of 1974*, Pub. L. No. 93-288, § 401, 88 Stat. 143). For additional information, "Stafford, Robert Theodore," *Biographical Directory of the United States Congress*, http://bioguide.congress.gov/scripts/ biodisplay.pl?index=S000776.

[19] This figure represents an average since the Disaster Relief Act was enacted in 1974. U.S. Department of Homeland Security, Federal Emergency Management Agency, "Annual Major Disaster Declaration Totals," http://www.fema.gov/news/disaster_totals_annual.fema. U.S. Department of Homeland Security, Federal Emergency Management Agency, "2004 Federal Disaster Declarations," http://www.fema.gov/news/disasters.fema?year=2004.

[20] "Discipline" refers to the various emergency response fields (e.g., police, medical, firefighters).

[21] The White House, Office of Homeland Security, *National Strategy for Homeland Security* (Washington, DC, July 2002), 42.

[22] 6 U.S.C. § 312 (2005) (requiring the Secretary to execute these responsibilities through the Under Secretary for Emergency Preparedness and Response).

[23] The White House, "President Bush signs Homeland Security Act," news release, November 25, 2002, http://www.whitehouse.gov/news/releases/2002/11/20021125-6.html.

[24] U.S. Department of Homeland Security, "Department of Homeland Security Facts for March 1, 2003," February 28, 2003, http://www.dhs.gov/dhspublic/display?content=817. See also The White House, "Ridge Sworn In as Secretary of Homeland Security," news release, January 24, 2003, http://www.whitehouse.gov/news/releases/2003/01/print/20030124-5.html. Before becoming Secretary of Homeland Security, Thomas Joseph Ridge was the first Homeland Security Advisor to the President of the United States and Director of the White House Office of Homeland Security, the precursor to the current Homeland Security Council. Prior to his service to the President, Secretary Ridge was the governor of Pennsylvania. The White House, "Biography of Secretary Tom Ridge," http://www.whitehouse.gov/homeland/ridgebio.html.

[25] *HSPD-5*, § 4.

[26] *HSPD-5*, § 18.

[27] U.S. Department of Homeland Security, *National Incident Management System* ["*National Incident Management System*"] (Washington, DC, 2004), ix.

[28] *National Incident Management System*, 2.

[29] U.S. Department of Homeland Security, Federal Emergency Management Agency, "NIMS and the Incident Command System," http://www.fema.gov/txt/nims/nims_ics_position_paper.txt. The 9/11 Commission found that the September 11, 2001, attacks demonstrated the need for nationwide adoption of the ICS. See National Commission on Terrorist Attacks Upon the United States, *The 9/11 Commission Report* (New York: WW Norton and Company), 397. After President Bush issued HSPD-5 on February 28, 2003, the Department of Homeland Security worked with State and local governments, the emergency management community, the private sector and other key stakeholders to develop the *National Incident Management System*.

[30] *National Incident Management System*, 7.

[31] *National Incident Management System*, 138.

[32] *National Incident Management System*, 11.

[33] *National Incident Management System*, 7.

[34] *National Incident Management System*, 14-16.

[35] The President directed the development of a National Response Plan to align Federal coordination structures, capabilities, and resources into a unified, all-discipline, and all-hazards approach to domestic incident management. See HSPD-5. The development of the NRP included extensive vetting and coordination with Federal, State, local, and tribal agencies, nongovernmental organizations, private-sector entities, and the first-responder and emergency management communities. For a list of the signatories of the NRP, see U.S. Department of Homeland Security, *National Response Plan* ["*National Response Plan*"] (Washington, DC, December 2004), iii-viii.

[36] *National Response Plan*, 15.

[37] States and locals, using mutual aid agreements, are frequently able to respond without Federal assistance. In addition, many requests by Governors for Federal assistance are made that do not result in a disaster declaration but are nevertheless significant.

[38] See generally, *National Response Plan*.

[39] The *Catastrophic Incident Annex* is an integral part of the *National Response Plan*. It lays out the "context and overarching strategy" for response to catastrophic incidents. It also presages the publication of the *Catastrophic Incident Supplement*—"a more detailed and operationally specific" plan for catastrophic incident response. U.S. Department of Homeland Security, "Catastrophic Incident Annex," in *National Response Plan*, pg. "CAT-1." As of February 2006, the *Catastrophic Incident Supplement* exists in draft form only, and has not been officially released. A *catastrophic incident* is defined as "Any natural or manmade incident, including terrorism, that results in extraordinary levels of mass casualties, damage, or disruption severely affecting the population, infrastructure, environment, economy, national morale, and/or government functions. . . ." *National Response Plan*, 63. Although the *National Response Plan* by virtue of the *Catastrophic Incident Annex* did anticipate the need for a more robust Federal response to a catastrophic incident, that is all it did. Without the *Catastrophic Incident Supplement*, that acknowledgement was not made operational and thus had no practical effect.

[40] *National Response Plan*, 3.

[41] *National Response Plan*, 3.

[42] *National Response Plan*, 1.

[43] *HSPD-5*, § 4.

[44] *National Response Plan*, 4.

[45] Governor Blanco's letter to the President requesting Federal assistance in the form of an emergency declaration seems to have satisfied the second criterion, while the substantial involvement of multiple Federal departments and agencies seems to have satisfied the third. On August 27, 2005, Governor Kathleen Blanco sent a letter to President Bush requesting an emergency declaration for the State of Louisiana. The letter stated, "I have determined that this incident is of such severity and magnitude that effective response is beyond the capabilities of the State and affected local governments, and that supplementary Federal assistance is necessary to save lives, protect property, public health, and safety, or to lessen or avert the threat of a disaster." Kathleen Blanco, Governor of Louisiana, "Letter to President Bush requesting that he declare an emergency for the State of Louisiana due to Hurricane Katrina" (Baton Rouge, August 27, 2005). That same day President Bush declared a state of emergency in Louisiana, stating, "I have determined that the emergency conditions in certain areas of the State of Louisiana, resulting from Hurricane

Katrina beginning on August 26, 2005, and continuing is of sufficient severity and magnitude to warrant an emergency declaration…" For complete text of declaration, see 70 Fed. Reg. 53238 (Sept. 7, 2005).

[46] *National Response Plan*, 4.

[47] *National Response Plan*, 7.

[48] Prior to Katrina's landfall on the Gulf Coast, all of the lead agencies responsible for various support activities had already deployed liaisons to FEMA headquarters or field locations, and the Federal and State coordinating officers had co-located in Baton Rouge to begin establishing a unified command. Upon declaring an INS, the Secretary designated a PFO. NRP actions that had not yet been taken at this time included standup of the Interagency Incident Management Group and establishment of a fully functional Joint Field Office. U.S. Department of Homeland Security, "Hurricane Katrina DHS SITREP #4," August 27, 2005, 11-15, indicates all ESFs have been activated. Former Federal Coordinating Officer of Louisiana, William Lokey, states, "On Saturday morning, August 27, 2005, I was assigned to respond with the ERT-N to Louisiana as FCO for Katrina Operations. I arrived in Baton Rouge late in the afternoon. After checking in with FEMA staff who had been working in New Orleans on a previously declared disaster and who had evacuated to Baton Rouge, I went to the Louisiana State Emergency Operations Center. There, I met with FEMA staff from Region VI that had responded as the Advance Emergency Response Team (ERT-A), other members of the ERT-N who were arriving, and Colonel Jeff Smith (State Coordinating Officer), my primary counterpart for State of Louisiana operations. My first priority was to work with Jeff Smith to identify the State's priorities, then to organize my staff to start planning and working with our State counterparts to identify tasks and objectives to meet those priorities. The State was heavily involved in the ongoing evacuation efforts but did begin working with us on such issues as search and rescue, commodity distribution, and medical needs. We worked late into the night and began again early on Sunday morning . . . Other ERT members from the Emergency Support Functions (ESF) had arrived and began discussions with their counterparts. These included but were not limited to people from ESF-1 Transportation, ESF-8 Health and Medical, and the Defense Coordinating Officer. We worked on identifying distribution sites; sending food and water to the Superdome; coordinating with health officials in New Orleans and the State; and planning with State and Federal agencies on potential search and rescue efforts." William Lokey, Federal Coordinating Officer for Louisiana, testimony before a hearing on Hurricane Katrina Preparedness and Response by the State of Louisiana, on December 14, 2005, House Select Bipartisan Committee to Investigate the Preparation for and Response to Hurricane Katrina, 109th Congress, 1st session.

[49] FEMA has used the NRP during all major disasters since the NRP was adopted. *National Response Plan*, Appendix 5. http://www.fema.gov/news/disasters.fema?year=2005.

[50] Operationally, the Federal government was utilizing the NRP before landfall and prior to the declaration of an INS.

[51] The Joint Field Office (JFO) structure and Principal Federal Official (PFO) position can be implemented without an INS declaration by the Secretary of Homeland Security. *National Response Plan*, 28-33. The NRP states, "During actual or *potential* Incidents of National Significance, the overall coordination of Federal incident management activities is executed through the Secretary of Homeland Security" (emphasis added). *National Response Plan*, 15. This suggests that the Secretary can create the structures found in the NRP, such as JFO and PFO, even if there is only the potential for an INS, and an INS has not yet been declared.

[52] *National Response Plan*, 28-33.

[53] *HSPD-5*, § 5.

[54] *National Response Plan*, 71.

[55] 42 U.S.C. § 5143 (2005) ; *National Response Plan*, 65. The delineation of roles and responsibilities between the statutorily empowered FCO and the policy constructed PFO are unclear. Section 5143 of the Stafford Act expressly requires the President, immediately upon his declaration of a major disaster or emergency, to appoint a FCO to conduct response and recovery operations in the affected area. The President has also formally delegated his response and recovery powers granted him in the Stafford Act to the Secretary of Homeland Security. The Stafford Act of 1974 gave this authority (to direct other departments) to the President; Executive Order 12148 delegated this authority in 1979 to the FEMA Director; and Executive Order 13286 subsequently transferred the authority in 2003 to the Secretary of Homeland Security. See Executive Order no. 12148, 44 Fed. Reg. 43239 (1979); Executive Order no. 13286, 68 Fed. Reg. 10619 (2003). This delegation of authority is consistent with the Secretary's designation as PFO for incident management in HSPD-5. However, the Secretary has delegated his Stafford Act authority to the FEMA Director and according to the NRP can name a third and separate individual PFO for an Incident of National Significance.

[56] *National Response Plan*, 16. See also note 65.

[57] *National Response Plan*, 15, 25.

[58] *National Response Plan*, 15.

[59] See "Emergency Support Function Annexes" in *National Response Plan,* pgs. "ESF-i" et seq.

[60] *Reorganization Plan no. 3 of 1978*, 43 Fed.. Reg. 41943 (June 19, 1978). The organization of FEMA was further defined in Executive Order no. 12,127, 44 Fed. Reg. 19367 (March 31,1979) and Executive Order no. 12148, 44 Fed. Reg. 43239 (July 20, 1979).

[61] *Homeland Security Act of 2002* ["*Homeland Security Act*"], Public Law 296, 107th Congress, 2nd session (November 25, 2002) § 501, codified at 6 U.S.C. § 312 (2005).

[62] *National Response Plan*, pg. "ESF 5-1." See also *Homeland Security Act*, § 507, codified at 6 U.S.C. § 317 (2005).

[63] U.S. Department of Homeland Security, Federal Emergency Management Agency, "Regional and Area Offices," http://www.fema.gov/regions.

[64] FEMA Disaster Assistance Employees (DAEs) are on-call personnel, not carried on the permanent payroll, activated to augment the full time employee pool when a surge capacity is required to respond to a disaster. Many have years of experience, while others may have little to no prior disaster or emergency response experience. These employees are only used to assist in the aftermath of specific disasters and emergencies. The reservists are trained to fulfill specific disaster response staffing needs, including key program, technical, and administrative functions.

[65] The RRCC is a standing facility operated by FEMA that is activated to coordinate regional response efforts, establish Federal priorities, and implement local Federal support until a JFO is established in the field and/or the PFO, FCO, or Federal Resource Coordinator (FRC) can assume their NRP coordination responsibilities. The RRCC establishes communications with the affected State emergency management agency and the National Response Coordination Center (NRCC) coordinates deployment of the Emergency Response Team–Advance Element (ERT-A) to field locations, assesses damage information, develops situation reports, and issues initial mission assignments. *National Response Plan*, 27.

[66] These regions have two of the largest regional staffs within FEMA: Region VI has 100 employees and over 300 reservists, and Region VI has 115 employees and over 550 reservists. See U.S. Department of Homeland Security, Federal Emergency Management Agency, "FEMA: Region VI – About Region VI," http://www.fema.gov/regions/vi/about.shtm (last updated March 3, 2005); U.S. Department of Homeland Security, Federal Emergency Management Agency, "FEMA: Region IV," http://www.fema.gov/regions/iv/index.shtm (last updated October 22, 2004). The NRCC and the RRCC in Region IV began monitoring Hurricane Katrina as early as Tuesday, August 23. On Thursday, August 25, the NRCC activated to Level 2—partial activation—at 7:00 am, and the Region IV RRCC activated to Level 2 at 12:30 pm. On Saturday, August 27, the NRCC went to Level 1—full activation—at 7:00 am, and Region IV and Region VI RRCCs went to Level 1 activation at 12:00 pm. U.S. Department of Homeland Security, Federal Emergency Management Agency, "Hurricane Katrina Response Timeline," September 10, 2005. FEMA employs more than 2,600 full-time staff, about 1,000 of them in its ten regional offices, and nearly 4,000 disaster reservists. FEMA disaster reservists, officially known as Disaster Assistance Employees, serve as a surge force for rapidly increasing the pool of Federal response personnel during a major disaster. The program recruits and trains citizen volunteers to become full Federal employees when a major disaster exceeds the capacity of FEMA's permanent staff. The agency has access to this collective pool of human resources, but does not have its own critical response assets, such as buses, trucks, and ambulances.

[67] *Stafford Act*, 42 U.S.C. § 5170 (2005).

[68] *Stafford Act*, 42 U.S.C. § 5191 (2005).

[69] *Stafford Act*, 42 U.S.C. § 5170 (2005).

[70] Louisiana Office of Homeland Security and Emergency Preparedness, *Emergency Operations Plan* (Baton Rouge, April 5, 2005), 3.

[71] The Constitution requires that "[n]o State shall, without the Consent of Congress, . . . enter into any Agreement or Compact with another State . . . ." U.S. Constitution, art.1, sec.10.

[72] EMAC was developed in the 1990s and officially ratified by Congress as an organization with thirteen member States in 1996. *Emergency Management Assistance Compact*, Public Law 104-321, 104th Congress, 2nd session, (October 19, 1996). As of October 2005, 49 States, the District of Columbia, the U.S. Virgin Islands, and Puerto Rico had enacted EMAC legislation. National Emergency Management Association, "EMAC Overview," December 2005, http://www.emacweb.org/?323. EMAC is administered by the National Emergency Management

Association (NEMA). During an emergency, NEMA's staff works with EMAC member states to coordinate the EMAC system.

[73] Louisiana Office of Homeland Security and Emergency Preparedness, *Emergency Operations Plan* (Baton Rouge, April 5, 2005), 3.

[74] U.S. Department of Homeland Security, *Catastrophic Incident Annex* ["*Catastrophic Incident Annex*"], in *National Response Plan*, pg. "CAT-1."

[75] *National Response Plan*, 63.

[76] *Catastrophic Incident Annex*, pg. "CAT-1."

[77] *National Response Plan*, 44.

[78] Given its draft status, the *Catastrophic Incident Supplement* has never been part of incident planning or exercises nor had it been widely disseminated, and as a result is not a part of current operational plans for incident management. Furthermore, our experience in Hurricane Katrina suggests it must now be reconsidered to make it more robust in ensuring that Federal assistance arrives as soon as possible.

[79] The White House, "President Discusses Hurricane Relief in Address to the Nation," news release, September 15, 2005, http://www.whitehouse.gov/news/releases/2005/09/20050915-8.html.

CHAPTER THREE: HURRICANE KATRINA — PRE-LANDFALL

[1] The White House, "President Discusses Hurricane Katrina, Congratulates Iraqis on Draft Constitution," news release, August 28, 2005.

[2] U.S. Department of Commerce, National Oceanic and Atmospheric Administration, Atlantic Oceanographic and Meteorological Laboratory, Hurricane Research Division, "Frequently Asked Questions," http://www.aoml.noaa.gov/hrd/tcfaq/A3.html. The National Hurricane Center defines "major hurricanes" as hurricanes that reach maximum sustained 1-minute surface winds of at least 111 mph.

[3] U.S. Department of Commerce, National Oceanic and Atmospheric Administration, "NOAA: 2005 Atlantic Hurricane Season Outlook," May 16, 2005. In 2004, the hurricane season had been particularly devastating. Twenty seven disasters were declared in fifteen States and two U.S. Territories. The season was especially difficult for Florida, which took a direct hit from four hurricanes and one tropical storm in six weeks. Together, Hurricanes Charlie, Frances, Ivan, and Jeanne, directly or indirectly resulted in over 150 U.S. deaths and approximately forty-six billion dollars in damage. Richard J. Pasch, Daniel P. Brown, and Eric S. Blake, *Tropical Cyclone Report: Hurricane Charlie*, prepared for the National Hurricane Center, National Oceanic and Atmospheric Administration (Miami, Florida, October 18, 2004), (updated January 5, 2005); Jack Beven II, *Tropical Cyclone Report: Hurricane Frances*, prepared for National Hurricane Center, National Oceanic and Atmospheric Administration (Miami, Florida, December 17, 2004); Stacy R. Stewart, *Tropical Cyclone Report: Hurricane Ivan*, prepared for the National Hurricane Center, National Oceanic and Atmospheric Administration (Miami, Florida, December 16, 2004), (updated May 27, 2005); Miles B. Lawrence and Hugh D. Cobb, *Tropical Cyclone Report: Hurricane Jeanne*, prepared for the National Hurricane Center, National Oceanic and Atmospheric Administration (Miami, Florida, November 22, 2004), (updated January 7, 2005).

[4] U.S. Department of Commerce, National Oceanic and Atmospheric Administration, "NOAA Issues 2005 Atlantic Hurricane Season Outlook: Another Above Normal Season Expected," news release, May 16, 2005.

[5] U.S. Department of Commerce, National Oceanic and Atmospheric Administration, National Weather Service, "New Weather Forecast Office in Key West Hoists Hurricane Flags for Wilma," news release, October 24, 2005: "Hurricane Wilma is part of a hurricane season replete with "firsts": . . . a record of seven named storms had formed by the end of July."

[6] Jack Beven II, *Tropical Cyclone Report: Hurricane Dennis*, prepared for the National Hurricane Center, National Oceanic and Atmospheric Administration (Miami, Florida, November 22, 2005) (updated December 16, 2005).

[7] Monroe County, Key West Florida, "Emergency News Hurricane Dennis," July 8, 2005, http://www.monroecounty-fl.gov/Pages/MonroeCoFL_EmerNews/EmergencyArchives/S00633CB7. Evacuations were ordered in the Florida Keys for "all non-residents" and "all residents west of the Seven Mile Bridge." For information on major disaster declarations, see *Federal Register*. U.S. Department of Homeland Security, "Alabama; Major Disaster and Related Determinations," July 10, 2005,

http://www.fema.gov/news/dfrn.fema?id=4284; U.S. Department of Homeland Security, "Mississippi; Major Disaster and Related Determinations," July 10, 2005, http://www.fema.gov/news/dfrn.fema?id=4285; U.S. Department of Homeland Security, "Florida; Major Disaster and Related Determinations," July 10, 2005, http://www.fema.gov/news/dfrn.fema?id=4286. In preparation for Hurricane Dennis, FEMA activated its Regional Response Coordination Center (RRCC) in Atlanta at the highest operational level. FEMA conducted coordination calls between Federal, State and local officials, positioned liaison officers at State Emergency Operations Centers, pre-staged emergency supplies and response teams at various locations, and requested the activation of the First U.S. Army's crisis action team. See U.S. Department of Homeland Security, Federal Emergency Management Agency, "FEMA Regional Center at Highest Level in Preparation for Hurricane Dennis," news release, July 9, 2005; Department of Defense, First U.S. Army, "First U.S. Army Stands up Crisis Action Team for Hurricane Dennis," news release, July 9, 2005. Other military preparations for Hurricane Dennis included the alert of National Guardsmen in Florida, Mississippi, Alabama, Louisiana and Georgia. See U.S. Department of Defense, "Military Taking Precautions as Hurricane Dennis Approaches," news release, July 8, 2005.

[8] State of Louisiana, Office of the Governor, "Governor Blanco Declares State of Emergency Regarding Hurricane Dennis," news release, July 8, 2005, http://gov.louisiana.gov/index.cfm?md=newsroom&tmp=detail&articleID=717.

[9] Jack Beven II, *Tropical Cyclone Report: Hurricane Dennis*, prepared for the National Hurricane Center, National Oceanic and Atmospheric Administration (Miami, Florida, November 22, 2005), (updated December 16, 2005).

[10] U.S. Department of Commerce, National Oceanic and Atmospheric Administration, *August 2005 Update to Atlantic Hurricane Season Outlook: Bulk of This Season's Storms Still to Come* (Washington, D.C, August 2, 2005).

[11] U.S. Department of Commerce, National Oceanic and Atmospheric Administration, "NOAA Raises the 2005 Atlantic Hurricane Season Outlook," August 2, 2005, http://www.noaanews.noaa.gov/stories2005/s2484.htm.

[12] Richard D. Knabb, Jamie R. Rhome, and Daniel Brown, *Tropical Cyclone Report: Hurricane Katrina, August 23-30, 2005*, prepared for the National Hurricane Center, National Oceanic and Atmospheric Administration (Miami, Florida, December 2005), 1. Excerpt from this text: "The complex genesis of Katrina involved the interaction of a tropical wave, the middle tropospheric remnants of Tropical Depression Ten, and an upper tropospheric trough. This trough, located over the western Atlantic and the Bahamas, produced strong westerly shear across Tropical Depression Ten, causing it to degenerate on 14 August approximately 825 n. mi. east of Barbados. The low-level circulation gradually weakened while continuing westward, and it eventually dissipated on 21 August in the vicinity of Cuba. Meanwhile, a middle tropospheric circulation originating from Tropical Depression Ten lagged behind and passed north of the Leeward Islands on 18-19 August. A tropical wave moved through the Leeward Islands and merged with the middle tropospheric remnants of Tropical Depression Ten on 19 August, forming a large area of showers and thunderstorms north of Puerto Rico. This activity continued to move slowly northwestward, passing north of Hispaniola and then consolidating just east of the Turks and Caicos during the afternoon of 22 August. Dvorak satellite classifications from the Tropical Analysis and Forecast Branch (TAFB) of the Tropical Prediction Center (TPC) began at 1800 UTC that day. The upper tropospheric trough weakened as it moved westward toward Florida, and the shear relaxed enough to allow the system to develop into a tropical depression by 1800 UTC 23 August over the southeastern Bahamas about 175 n. mi. southeast of Nassau. The depression was designated Tropical Depression Twelve rather than "Ten" because a separate tropical wave appeared to be partially responsible for the cyclogenesis, and, more importantly, the low-level circulation of Tropical Depression Ten was clearly not involved."

[13] U.S. Department of Commerce, National Oceanic and Atmospheric Administration, National Hurricane Center, *Hurricane Katrina Advisory #1* (Miami, Florida, August 23, 2005). National Hurricane Center Katrina Advisories were released every several hours beginning at 5:00 PM EDT on August 23 and ending at 10:00 AM CDT on August 30. Advisories were typically issued at 5:00 AM, 11:00 AM, 5:00 PM, and 11:00 PM EDT each day. The advisories are numbered sequentially from 1 to 31. Most of the advisories were updated with supplemental advisories—for example, Hurricane Katrina Advisory 1 was released at 5:00 PM EDT and Advisory 1a was released at 8:00 PM EDT. Advisory 2 was released at 11:00 PM EDT. The official publication time zone switched from Eastern Daylight Time to Central Daylight Time with Advisory #17, released at 10:00 AM CDT, August 27, 2005. All Hurricane Katrina Advisories are available from the National Hurricane Center. See U.S. Department of Commerce, National Oceanic and Atmospheric Administration, National Hurricane Center, "Hurricane Katrina Advisory Archive," http://www.nhc.noaa.gov/archive/2005/KATRINA.shtml?.

[14] Admiral Timothy J. Keating, Commander North American Aerospace Defense Command and U.S. Northern Command, written statement for a hearing on Hurricane Katrina: Preparedness and Response by the Department of Defense, the Coast Guard, and the National Guard of Louisiana, Mississippi, and Alabama, on October 27, 2005, submitted to the House Select Bipartisan Committee to Investigate the Preparation for and Response to Hurricane Katrina, 109th Congress, 1st session.

[15] "Based on aircraft reconnaissance flight-level wind data, the cyclone became Katrina, the 11th tropical storm of the 2005 Atlantic hurricane season, at 1200 UTC 24 August when it was centered over the central Bahamas about 65 n. mi. east-southeast of Nassau." Richard D. Knabb, Jamie R. Rhome, and Daniel Brown, *Tropical Cyclone Report: Hurricane Katrina, August 23-30, 2005*, prepared for the National Hurricane Center, National Oceanic and Atmospheric Administration (Miami, Florida, December 20, 2005), 1.

[16] FEMA's Hurricane Liaison Team became operational at 7:00 AM EDT on August 24, 2005. The HLT had begun monitoring the storm the previous evening. FEMA Tropical Storm Katrina Briefing, August 25, 2005.

[17] U.S. Department of Defense, OASD HD, Hurricane Katrina/Rita/Ophelia Interim Timeline (Aug. – Sept. 2005), November 2, 2005, 2.

[18] U.S. Department of Commerce, National Oceanic and Atmospheric Administration, National Hurricane Center, *Tropical Storm Katrina Advisory 4* (Washington, D.C., August 24, 2005).

[19] U.S. Department of Commerce, National Oceanic and Atmospheric Administration, National Weather Service Tropical Prediction Center and National Hurricane Center, "Hurricane Katrina Discussion Number 9," August 25, 2005; U.S. Department of Commerce, National Oceanic and Atmospheric Administration, National Weather Service Tropical Prediction Center and National Hurricane Center, "Tropical Storm Katrina Discussion Number 8," August 25, 2005.

[20] U.S. Department of Commerce, National Oceanic and Atmospheric Administration, National Weather Service, Miami-South Florida Forecast Office, "Hurricane Katrina Storm Report," September 1, 2005, http://www.srh.noaa.gov/mfl/events/?id=katrina.

[21] Richard D. Knabb, Jamie R. Rhome, and Daniel P. Brown, *Tropical Cyclone Report: Hurricane Katrina, 23-30 August 2005*, prepared for the National Hurricane Center (Miami, Florida, August 2005), 10.

[22] Florida Power & Light, Company, "FPL begins assessment process following Hurricane Katrina," news release, August 26, 2005, http://www.fpl.com/news/2005/contents/05101.shtml.

[23] National Aeronautics and Space Administration, Remote Sensing Tutorial, "Hurricanes Katrina, Rita, and Wilma," http://rst.gsfc.nasa.gov/Sect14/Sect14_10a.html.

[24] U.S. Department of Commerce, National Oceanic and Atmospheric Administration, National Weather Service, Miami-South Florida Forecast Office, "Hurricane Katrina Storm Report," September 1, 2005, http://www.srh.noaa.gov/mfl/events/?id=katrina; and Florida Department of Agriculture and Consumer Services, "Bronson to Assess Hurricane Katrina Damage to South Florida Agriculture," news release, August 29, 2005, http://www.doacs.state.fl.us/press/2005/08292005.html.

[25] U.S. Department of Homeland Security, "Hurricane Katrina DHS SITREP # 1," August 25, 2005. The Emergency Operations Center is the physical location at which the coordination of information and resources to support domestic incident management activities normally takes place. An EOC may be a temporary facility or may be located in a more central or permanently established facility. See U.S. Department of Homeland Security, *National Response Plan* (Washington, D.C., December 2004), 64.

[26] Hurricane Katrina DHS SITREP #1, August 25, 2005.

[27] "Despite all of our efforts and despite the fact that we pre-positioned more commodities and staged more rescue and medical teams than ever before in our agency's history, our initial response was overwhelmed." William Lokey, Federal Coordinating Officer, Baton Rouge, written statement for a hearing on Hurricane Katrina Response in Louisiana, on December 14, 2005, submitted to the House Select Bipartisan Committee to Investigate the Preparation for and Response to Hurricane Katrina, 109th Congress, 1st session.

[28] On August 25, FEMA began to identify ERT-A teams for deployment to Florida and Alabama. FEMA Tropical Storm Katrina Briefing, August 25, 2005. For definition of ERT-A, see U.S. Department of Homeland Security, Federal Emergency Management Agency, "Glossary," http://training.fema.gov/EMIWeb/IS/is14/glossary.htm#E.

[29] U.S. Department of Homeland Security, Federal Emergency Management Agency, "National Situation Update," August 26, 2005, http://www.fema.gov/emanagers/2005/nat082605.shtm. Throughout this Report, note that events were occurring in different time zones. Times referenced as Central Daylight Time (CDT) reflect the local time events took place in Louisiana. All Noon FEMA video teleconferences took place at 12:00 PM Eastern

Daylight Time (EDT), which was 11:00 AM in Louisiana and Mississippi. Throughout the report, times are referenced in accordance with the source material supporting the text.

[30] U.S. Department of Commerce, National Oceanic and Atmospheric Administration, National Hurricane Center, *Hurricane Katrina Advisory #11* (Washington, D.C., August 26, 2005).

[31] Richard D. Knabb, Jamie R. Rhome, and Daniel Brown, *Tropical Cyclone Report: Hurricane Katrina (23-30 August 2005)*, prepared for the National Hurricane Center, National Oceanic and Atmospheric Administration (Miami, Florida, December 2005), 2-3.

[32] U.S. Department of Commerce, National Oceanic and Atmospheric Administration, National Hurricane Center, *Hurricane Katrina Intermediate Advisory # 14* (Miami, Florida, August 26, 2005); U.S. Department of Homeland Security, Federal Emergency Management Agency, "National Situation Update," August 26, 2005.

[33] See National Weather Service Tropical Prediction Center and National Hurricane Center Hurricane Katrina Advisories 15 through 26, covering a period from August 26, 2005, 11:00 PM EDT to August 29, 2005, 6:00 AM CDT. These advisories are available at the U.S. Department of Commerce, National Oceanic and Atmospheric Administration, National Weather Service Tropical Prediction Center and National Hurricane Center, "Hurricane Katrina Advisory Archive," http://www.nhc.noaa.gov/archive/2005/KATRINA.shtml?.

[34] U.S. Department of Commerce, National Oceanic and Atmospheric Administration, National Hurricane Center, "Hurricane Katrina Forecast Timeline," n.d., ca. 2005.

[35] Brigadier General David L. Johnson (USAF, Ret.), Director of the National Weather Service, National Oceanic and Atmospheric Administration, U.S. Department of Commerce, written statement for a hearing on NOAA Hurricane Forecasting, on October 7, 2005, submitted to the House Committee on Science, 109th Congress, 1st session, 2.

[36] The last National Hurricane Center Advisory on August 26 was issued at 11:00 PM EDT. Katrina made landfall at 6:10 AM CDT on August 29, fifty-six hours later. U.S. Department of Commerce, National Oceanic and Atmospheric Administration, National Hurricane Center, *Hurricane Katrina Advisory # 15* (Miami, Florida, August 26, 2005).

[37] State of Louisiana, Exective Department, *Proclamation No. 48 KBB 2005: State of Emergency—Hurricane Katrina* (Baton Rouge, August 26, 2005); State of Alabama, Office of the Governor, *State of Emergency Proclamation* (Jackson, August 26, 2005).

[38] Brent Warr, Mayor of Gulfport, Mississippi, written statement for a hearing on Hurricane Katrina: Preparedness and Response by the State of Mississippi, on December 7, 2005, submitted to the Select Bipartisan Committee to Investigate the Preparation for and Response to Hurricane Katrina, 109th Congress, 1st session.

[39] Department of Homeland Security SITREP #4, August 27, 2005. See generally, Robert R. Latham Jr., Executive Director of the Mississippi Emergency Management Agency, written statement for a hearing on Hurricane Katrina: Preparedness and Response by the State of Mississippi, on December 7, 2005, submitted to the House Select Bipartisan Committee to Investigate the Preparation for and Response to Hurricane Katrina, 109th Congress, 1st session.

[40] Louisiana State Police, "LSP Timeline of Events," n.d., ca. 2005, 2.

[41] Louisiana National Guard, Task Force Pelican, "Hurricane Katrina Overview of Significant Events," November 28, 2005, 4.

[42] State of Alabama, Office of the Governor, *Executive Order No. 939* (Jackson, August 26, 2005).

[43] U.S. Department of Defense, "Mississippi Guard Provide Relief to State," *Armed Forces Press Service*, September 8, 2005, http://www.defenselink.mil/news/Sep2005/20050908_2648.html.

[44] "More than 8,000 people perished September 8, 1900 when the category 4 hurricane barreled into Galveston…," U.S. Department of Commerce, National Oceanic and Atmospheric Administration, "The Galveston Storm of 1900 – The Deadliest Disaster in History," http://www.noaa.gov/galveston1900/. See also Erik Larson, *Isaac's Storm: A Man, a Time, and the Deadliest Hurricane in History* (New York: Random House, 1999), 264-265. Note that statistics for disasters can vary significantly depending on the source consulted, due to both variances in how terms are defined and the difficulty of confirming specific data in the aftermath of a devastating event.

[45] The Saffir-Simpson scale for measuring hurricane strength had not been developed until 1969—four years after Hurricane Betsy made landfall on the Louisiana coast. The classification of Hurricane Betsy as a Category 3 storm was made retroactively based on wind speed readings. For general information on Hurricane Betsy, see U.S. Army Corps of Engineers, "Historical Records of the U.S. Army Corps of Engineers' Response to Recent Hurricanes," http://www.hq.usace.army.mil/history/Hurricane_files/ Hurricane.htm. For deaths, see Eric S. Blake et al., *The Deadliest, Costliest, and Most Intense United States Tropical Cyclones from 1851 to 2004 (And Other Frequently*

Requested Hurricane Facts), NOAA Technical Memorandum NWS TPC-4 (Miami, Florida, August 2005), 7, http://www.nhc.noaa.gov/Deadliest_Costliest.shtml; compare to U.S. Army Corps of Engineers, "How Safe is New Orleans from Flooding?" September 11, 2003, http://www.usace.army.mil/inet/functions/cw/hot_topics/11sep_msy.htm (reporting 81 deaths). For extent of flooding by parish see, Joseph A. Towers, former Attorney for the Army Corps of Engineers, testimony before the Task Force on Updating the National Environmental Policy Act, Congressional Resources Committee, 109th Congress, 1st session, 2005, http://resourcescommittee.house.gov/nepataskforce/archives/josephtowers.htm.

[46] "Damaged homes" include those with major damage, but not those with minor damage. For deaths, see Ernest Zebrowski and Judith A. Howard, *Category 5: The Story of Camille* (Ann Arbor, MI: University of Michigan Press, 2005); For homes damaged or destroyed, see Roger A. Pielke, Jr., Chantal Simonpietri, and Jennifer Oxelson, *Thirty Years After Hurricane Camille: Lessons Learned, Lessons Lost* (Boulder, Colorado, July 1999). For other information, see U.S. Department of Commerce, National Oceanic and Atmospheric Administration, National Hurricane Center, "Hurricane History – Hurricane Camille, 1969," http://www.nhc.noaa.gov/HAW2/english/history.shtml#camille.

[47] See Greg Brouwer "The Creeping Storm," *Civil Engineering Magazine*, June, 2003, http://www.pubs.asce.org/ceonline/ceonline03/0603feat.html. See also U.S. Army Corps of Engineers, "Morganza to the Gulf of Mexico Hurricane Protection Project," http://www.mvn.usace.army.mil/prj/mtog/. It is important to note that the levees protecting New Orleans were designed in advance of the Saffir-Simpson model. Although it is often reported that New Orleans levees were constructed to protect against a Category 3 storm, the levee system was actually designed to withstand a Standard Project Hurricane (SPH)—a theoretical hybrid of many different storms. The central pressure for an SPH is in the Category 4 range, the highest wind speed is that of a high strength Category 2, and the surge is similar to that of a Category 3. Al Naomi (Senior Project Manager, U.S. Army Corps of Engineers), "Talkback," *Riverside* (a publication of the U.S. Army Corps of Engineers), January, 2005, 8, http://www.mvn.usace.army.mil/pao/Riverside/ Jan_05_Riv.pdf.

[48] In 1999, the Senate of the State of Louisiana issued a resolution "to authorize and to urge the governor of … Louisiana to support the development of the 'Comprehensive Hurricane Protection Plan for Coastal Louisiana' by the U.S. Army Corps of Engineers to provide continuous hurricane protection from Morgan City to the Mississippi border." Senate of the State of Louisiana, *House Concurrent Resolution No. 142* (Baton Rouge, June 18, 1999). The Comprehensive Hurricane Protection Plan for Coastal Louisiana by the New Orleans District U.S. Army Corps of Engineers was released in June 2000. U.S. Army Corps of Engineers, *Comprehensive Hurricane Protection Plan for Coastal Louisiana* (New Orleans, June 2000).

[49] U.S. Army Corps of Engineers, *Comprehensive Hurricane Protection Plan for Coastal Louisiana* (New Orleans, June 2000).

[50] U.S. Department of Commerce, National Oceanic and Atmospheric Administration, National Weather Service, Southern Region headquarters, "Tropical Cyclone Hazards: Inland Flooding," July 27, 2004, http://www.srh.noaa.gov/srh/tropicalwx/awareness/flooding.htm: "It is common to think the stronger the storm the greater the potential for flooding. However, this is not always the case. A weak, slow moving tropical storm can cause more damage due to flooding than a more powerful fast moving hurricane." See also, U.S. Army Corps of Engineers, *Comprehensive Hurricane Protection Plan for Coastal Louisiana* (New Orleans, June 2000).

[51] Statement of Vice Admiral Conrad C. Lautenbacher, Jr (Undersecretary of Commerce for Oceans and Atmosphere.), before 31st AMS Broadcasters Conference 200-300 Broadcast Meteorologists/Private Sector and Industry, June 26, 2002, http://www.noaa.gov/lautenbacher/ams-broadcasters.htm

[52] The origins of the Southeast Louisiana Catastrophic Hurricane Planning Project can be traced back to 1998 when, in the wake of Hurricane Georges, the Louisiana Office of Homeland Security and Emergency Preparedness recognized the need for more comprehensive hurricane planning. After an initial period of development, the State of Louisiana submitted planning proposals to FEMA for approval. FEMA granted the State funding in 2001, but was forced to withdraw those funds a year later, due to budgetary constraints. Despite this setback, the need for catastrophic hurricane planning in Louisiana continued to be recognized at both the Federal and State level. On March 17, 2004, FEMA awarded funding to the State of Louisiana for what would become the Southeast Louisiana Catastrophic Hurricane Planning Project. See Sean E. Fontenot, Former Chief, Planning Division, Louisiana Office of Homeland Security and Emergency Preparedness, written statement submitted for a hearing on Preparing for Catastrophe: The Hurricane Pam Exercise, on January 24, 2006, before the Senate Committee on Homeland Security and Governmental Affairs, 109th Congress, 2nd session, 10.

---

[53] U.S. Department of Homeland Security, Federal Emergency Management Agency, "Hurricane PAM Exercise Concludes," July 23, 2004. The Hurricane PAM exercise included participants from thirteen southeast Louisiana Parishes: Ascension, Assumption, Jefferson, Lafourche, Orleans, Plaquemines, St. Bernard, St. Charles, St. James, St. John, St. Tammany, Tangipahoa, and Terrebonne. See also Senator Susan Collins (R-Maine), statement at a hearing on Preparing for a Catastrophe: The Hurricane Pam Exercise, on January 24, 2006, to the Senate Committee Homeland Security and Governmental Affairs, 109th Congress, 2nd session.

[54] Wayne Fairley, Chief, Response Operation Branch, Response and Recovery Division, FEMA Region IV, written statement submitted for a hearing on Preparing for Catastrophe: The Hurricane Pam Exercise, on January 24, 2006, before the Senate Committee on Homeland Security and Governmental Affairs, 109th Congress, 2nd session, 9.

[55] U.S. Department of Homeland Security, Federal Emergency Mangement Agency, National Response Coordination Center, video teleconference, August 27, 2005.

[56] Department of Commerce, National Oceanic and Atmospheric Administration, National Hurricane Center, *Hurricane Katrina Advisory # 15A* (Washington, D.C., August 27, 2005); Department of Commerce, National Oceanic and Atmospheric Administration, National Hurricane Center, *Hurricane Katrina Advisory # 19* (Washington, D.C., August 27, 2005). As noted previously, times are referenced in accordance with the time zone—Eastern Daylight Time or Central Daylight Time—listed on the source material supporting the text.

[57] U.S. Department of Commerce, National Oceanic and Atmospheric Administration, National Weather Service Tropical Prediction Center and National Hurricane Center, *Hurricane Katrina Advisory # 19* (Miami, Florida, August 27, 2005).

[58] NHC's Bill Reeve warned that the storm was headed toward "the worst possible locations for storm surge" and would produce a surge typical of a Category 4 or Category 5 hurricane. See U.S. Department of Homeland Security, Federal Emergency Mangement Agency, National Response Coordination Center, video teleconference, August 27, 2005.

[59] Richard D. Knabb, Jamie R. Rhome, and Daniel Brown, *Tropical Cyclone Report: Hurricane Katrina: August 23-30, 2005*, prepared for the National Hurricane Center, National Oceanic and Atmospheric Administration (Miami, Florida, December 2005). See also U.S. Department of Commerce, National Oceanic and Atmospheric Administration, National Weather Service Tropical Prediction Center and National Hurricane Center, *Hurricane Katrina Intermediate Advisory # 18A*, (Miami, Florida, August 27, 2005).

[60] Louisiana Office of the Governor, Response to U.S. Senate Committee on Homeland Security and Governmental Affairs and Information Request Dated October 7, 2005 (Baton Rouge, December 2005), 4. State Representative Cedric Richmond called Governor Blanco on Saturday afternoon after visiting a ballpark where hundreds were in attendance. Representative Richmond "learned that some people had not paid attention to the weekend news and did not realize the severity of the hurricane aiming at New Orleans. He worries that many may have thought that the hurricane was still targeting the Florida panhandle...."

[61] Louisiana Office of the Governor, Response to U.S. Senate Committee on Homeland Security and Governmental Affairs and Information Request Dated October 7, 2005 (Baton Rouge, December 2005), 4.

[62] Louisiana Department of Transportation and Development, "Timeline for Hurricane Katrina," n.d., ca. 2005, 2.

[63] In Phase I or the Precautionary Phase, "The Plan prescribes that during the Precautionary phase, the location of staging areas for people who need transportation will be announced and that public transportation will concentrate on moving people from the staging areas to safety in host parishes with priority given to people with special needs. Furthermore, during the Precautionary stage the Plan directs that nursing homes and other custodial care organizations in the risk areas should be contacted to ensure that they are prepared to evacuate their residents." Louisiana Office of Homeland Security and Emergency Preparedness, "Southeast Louisiana Hurricane Evacuation and Sheltering Plan," in *State of Louisiana Emergency Operations Plan Supplement 1A* (Baton Rouge, January 2000); Louisiana State Police, "LSP Timeline of Events," n.d., ca. 2005, 2. On Saturday August 27, 2005, representatives of the Louisiana Nursing Home Association (LNHA), sitting at the Louisiana State EOC, started calling and emailing all the at-risk nursing homes in Louisiana, checking on their preparedness for the storm and determining if they were planning to evacuate or shelter-in-place. They were able to reach most of the nursing homes. They learned that the State EOP was also calling nursing homes, as were the local parish sheriffs. By Sunday morning, some nursing homes that intended to shelter-in-place had decided to evacuate. They had previously been told that buses were available but, by the time they decided to evacuate, drivers were not available. At that point the LNHA made formal requests for bus drivers, but none materialized prior to landfall. In all, prior to the storm, twenty-one nursing homes evacuated and sixty-eight sheltered-in-place. See generally, Joseph A. Donchess, Executive Director of the Louisiana Nursing Home Association, written statement for a hearing on

---

Challenges in a Catastrophe: Evacuating New Orleans in Advance of Hurricane Katrina, on January 31, 2006, submitted to the Senate Committee on Homeland Security and Governmental Affairs, 109th Congress, 2nd session.

[64] Mississippi State officials estimated that approximately 400,000 people used U.S. 49 and Interstates 55 and 59 to evacuate during the 2004 hurricane season.

[65] The TCC received traffic reports from Louisiana State Police troops, LA DOTD traffic counters, and other sources. Louisiana State Police, "LSP Timeline of Events," n.d., ca. 2005, 2-4.

[66] Louisiana State Police, "LSP Timeline of Events," n.d., ca. 2005, 4; State of Mississippi, Mississippi Emergency Management Agency, "Highway Evacuation Advisory," news release, August 27, 2005.

[67] According to Robert Latham Jr., Executive Director of MEMA, "During the 2004 hurricane season, culminating with Hurricane Ivan on September 13, 2004, the contra-flow plan was never executed, but major congestion in and around Hattiesburg, Mississippi resulted in a comprehensive review of our evacuation plan . . . As a result of these problems, Governor Barbour asked Mississippi Public Safety Commissioner George Phillips to develop a plan that would provide additional law enforcement officers to support evacuations, especially in the Hattiesburg area. This plan was completed prior to this year's hurricane season and executed flawlessly for the evacuation, including execution of contra-flowing both Interstates 55 and 59 from Louisiana to Mississippi." Robert R. Latham Jr., Executive Director of the Mississippi Emergency Management Agency, written statement for a hearing on Hurricane Katrina: Preparedness and Response by the State of Mississippi, on December 7, 2005, submitted to the House Select Bipartisan Committee to Investigate the Preparation for and Response to Hurricane Katrina, 109th Congress, 1st session; Louisiana Office of the Governor, Response to U.S. Senate Committee on Homeland Security and Governmental Affairs and Information Request Dated October 7, 2005 (Baton Rouge, December 2005).

[68] City of New Orleans, Office of Emergency Preparedness, *Hurricanes Annex--Part Three: Sheltering* (New Orleans, n.d.).

[69] Erin Fowler of the Department of Health and Human Services Regional Emergency Coordination Program Office spoke with Dr. Roseanne Pratts, Director of Emergency Preparedness for the Louisiana Department of Health, on August 27, "and inquired if federal HHS assistance was needed for patient movement or evacuation, or anything else. [Dr. Pratts] responded no, that they do not require anything at this time, and they would be in touch if and when they needed assistance." Senators Susan Collins and Joseph Lieberman, statements during a hearing on Challenges in a Catastrophe: Evacuating New Orleans in Advance of Hurricane Katrina, on January 31, 2006, Senate Committee on Homeland Security and Governmental Affairs, 109th Congress, 2nd session. HHS also offered assistance to New Orleans health officials on August 27, 2005. See generally, Joseph A. Donchess, Executive Director of the Louisiana Nursing Home Association, written statement for a hearing on Challenges in a Catastrophe: Evacuating New Orleans in Advance of Hurricane Katrina, on January 31, 2006, submitted to the Senate Committee on Homeland Security and Governmental Affairs, 109th Congress, 2nd session.

[70] Louisiana Office of the Governor, Response to U.S. Senate Committee on Homeland Security and Governmental Affairs and Information Request Dated October 7, 2005 (Baton Rouge, December 2005).

[71] Liability concerns may have constrained the development of this program. Nicholas Riccardi and James Rainey, "Katrina's Aftermath," *Los Angeles Times*, September 13, 2005 ; Bruce Nolan, "In Storm, N.O. Wants No One Left Behind," *The Times-Picayune*, July 24, 2005.

[72] Louisiana Office of the Governor, Response to U.S. Senate Committee on Homeland Security and Governmental Affairs and Information Request Dated October 7, 2005 (Baton Rouge, December 2005).

[73] For the notice on recommended evacuations of Algiers, the Lower Ninth Ward, and low-lying areas, see City of New Orleans, "Mayor Nagin Urges Citizens to Prepare for Hurricane Katrina," news release, August 27, 2005. The Louisiana evacuation plan called for New Orleans to begin evacuations thirty hours prior to projected landfall. This delay was designed to enable residents of coastal areas to evacuate, see Mayor's Office of Communications, City of New Orleans, "Mayor Nagin Urges Citizens to Prepare for Hurricane Katrina," news release, August 27, 2005; "Mayor Urges Storm Preparations," *NOLA.com: Times Picayune Breaking News Weblog*, August 27, 2005

[74] Bruce Nolan, "Katrina Takes Aim," *The New Orleans Times-Picayune*, August 28, 2005: "New Orleans Mayor Ray Nagin followed at 5:00 PM, issuing a voluntary evacuation."

[75] City of New Orleans, Mayor's Office of Communications, "Mayor Nagin Urges Citizens to Prepare for Hurricane Katrina," news release, August 27, 2005.

[76] State of Mississippi, Mississippi Emergency Management Agency, "Evacuation Traffic Expected to Increase on Interstates," news release, August 27, 2005; U.S. Department of Commerce, National Oceanic and Atmospheric Administration, National Hurricane Center, "Hurricane Katrina Forecast Timeline," n.d., ca. 2005. See also U.S. Department of Homeland Security, Federal Emergency Mangement Agency, National Response Coordination

Center, video teleconference, August 27, 2005, (Mississippi EOC reporting voluntary evacuations being encouraged along coastal counties).

[77] In an interview with *Frontline*, New Orleans Mayor Ray Nagin described the difficulty completing a mandatory evacuation: "But keep in mind the last time a hurricane event happened is 1965. Most people ride out these storms—they're Category 2s or whatever, and it's no big deal. The storm before Katrina a couple of weeks earlier—another Parish official made this huge declaration to mandatorily evacuate in spite of what everyone else was saying. So public confidence was a little low at the time . . . I think regardless of what we do in this town, some people will stay." Ray Nagin, Mayor of New Orleans, interview by Public Broadcasting Service, *Frontline*, November 22, 2005.

[78] Louisiana Office of the Governor, Response to U.S. Senate Committee on Homeland Security and Governmental Affairs and Information Request Dated October 7, 2005 (Baton Rouge, December 2005).

[79] American Red Cross, "Gulf Coast States Prepare for Hurricane Katrina," news release, August 27, 2005, http://www.redcross.org/article/ 0,1072,0_332_4467,00.html

[80] State of Mississippi, Mississippi Emergency Management Agency, "Evacuation Traffic Expected to Increase on Interstates," news release, August 27, 2005.

[81] Louisiana Office of Emergency Preparedness, "Situation Report Executive Summary: Hurricane Katrina," August 27, 2005.

[82] The declaration of the Superdome as a "special needs shelter" was an element of the State's Emergency Operations Plan. According to the plan, the Superdome serves as the Category II special needs shelter for Jefferson, Plaquemines, Orleans, and St. Bernard parishes. "Category II" facilities are for patients whose conditions are "less serious and less likely to undergo a severe deterioration." State of Louisiana, *Emergency Operations Plan, Supplement 1C: Louisiana Shelter Operations Plan* (Baton Rouge, April 2005), Annex X "Special Needs Plan," 5, 10, Appendix 2. The Superdome had also been used as "a shelter of last resort" in previous hurricanes. The Superdome was first used in this capacity in 1998 when people sought refuge from Hurricane Georges. U.S. Department of Commerce, National Oceanic and Atmospheric Administration, National Weather Service Forecast Office, "Top Weather Events of the 20th Century within the NWSFO New Orleans/Baton Rouge Service Area," December 8, 2005, http://www.srh.noaa.gov/lix/html/top10.htm. The State of Louisiana Emergency Operations Plan defines a shelter of last resort as "a place for persons to be protected from the high winds and heavy rains from the storm. Unlike a shelter, there may be little or no water or food and possibly no utilities. A Last Resort Refuge is intended to provide best available survival protection for the duration of the hurricane only." Louisiana Office of Homeland Security and Emergency Preparedness, *State of Louisiana Emergency Operations Plan: Supplement 1A* (Baton Rouge, January 2000), 29.

[83] City of New Orleans, "Comprehensive Emergency Management Plan: Special Needs Shelter Plan," http://www.cityofno.com/portal.aspx?portal=46&tabid=28. The Plan states: "[I]t is not appropriate to admit individuals to this shelter who require constant care or who require constant electricity to support machines necessary to maintain their life. Dialysis will not be available. Persons who are acutely ill will be evaluated and referred to local hospitals for definitive care. On a daily basis, every person with a chronic medical problem should have a viable plan that has been discussed with their primary physician so that when a disaster occurs, they will have an action plan established which can be put into effect."

[84] State of Texas, Texas State Operations Center, "Situation Report #8," August 27, 2005.

[85] State of Mississippi, Mississippi Emergency Management Agency, "Mississippi to Reverse Lane Interstates 55 and 59," news release, August 27, 2005.

[86] Robert R. Latham Jr., Executive Director of the Mississippi Emergency Management Agency, written statement for a hearing on Hurricane Katrina: Preparedness and Response by the State of Mississippi, on December 7, 2005, submitted to the House Select Bipartisan Committee to Investigate the Preparation for and Response to Hurricane Katrina, 109th Congress, 1st session.

[87] Louisiana National Guard, Task Force Pelican, "Hurricane Katrina Overview of Significant Events," November 28, 2005, 5.

[88] State of Alabama, Office of the Governor, "Governor Riley Says Supplies Ready to Assist Hurricane Victims," news release, August 28, 2005: "Alabama has pre-positioned supplies . . . Governor Riley said the state already has 290,000 bags of ice, more than 250,000 gallons of water, 652,000 MREs (meals ready to eat), and 110,000 tarps measuring 20 feet by 25 feet."

[89] Office of the Governor of Alabama, "Governor Riley Briefed on State's Hurricane Preparations," news release, August 27, 2005; State of Alabama, Office of the Governor, "Governor Riley Says Supplies Ready to Assist Hurricane Victims," news release, August 28, 2005.

[90] State of Texas, State Operations Center, "Situation Report #8," August 27, 2005.

[91] Level 1 operations began at 7:00 AM EDT. U.S. Department of Homeland Security, "Hurricane Katrina DHS SITREP # 4," August 27, 2005, 11.

[92] Hurricane Katrina DHS Situation Report #4, 27 Aug 05, 1800 hrs.

[93] See U.S. Department of Homeland Security, Federal Emergency Mangement Agency, National Response Coordination Center, video teleconference, August 27, 2005, 16.

[94] See U.S. Department of Homeland Security, Federal Emergency Mangement Agency, National Response Coordination Center, video teleconference, August 27, 2005, 16 – 17.

[95] See U.S. Department of Homeland Security, Federal Emergency Mangement Agency, National Response Coordination Center, video teleconference, August 27, 2005, 16-18. The figures for liters of water, pounds of ice, and number of MREs and tarps were converted using FEMA conversion factors of 18,000 liters of water, 40,000 pounds of ice, 2,520 tarps, and 21,888 MREs per truckload. FEMA Office of Legislative Affairs, Hurricane Katrina Response Fact Sheet.

[96] U.S. Department of Homeland Security, "Hurricane Katrina DHS SITREP # 4," August 27, 2005.

[97] See U.S. Department of Homeland Security, Federal Emergency Mangement Agency, National Response Coordination Center, video teleconference, August 27, 2005, 22.

[98] Colonel Jeff Smith, Acting Deputy Director, Louisiana Office of Homeland Security and Emergency Preparedness, testimony at hearing on the Hurricane Katrina Response in Louisiana, on December 14, 2005, before the House Select Committee to Investigate the Preparation and Response to Hurricane Katrina, 109th Congress, 2nd session. See also transcript of August 27, 2005, NRCC Video Teleconference. The Emergency Response Team-National is a national "on-call" team that is ready to deploy to large disasters such as Category 3 or 4 hurricanes. See also, U.S. Department of Homeland Security, "Hurricane Katrina DHS SITREP # 4," August 27, 2005. For definition of ERT-N, see U.S. Department of Homeland Security, Federal Emergency Management Agency. See also FEMA National Situation Update, August 28, 2005, http://www.fema.gov/emanagers/2005/nat082805.shtm. "Glossary," http://training.fema.gov/EMIWeb/IS/is14/glossary.htm#E.

[99] U.S. Department of Homeland Security, National Response Plan (Washington, DC, December 2004), 40. See also Dan Bement, "FEMA Operations," prepared for the U.S. Department of Transportation, Federal Highway Administration, http://www.fhwa.dot.gov/modiv/fema.htm.

[100] U.S. Department of Defense, "Hurricane Katrina Timeline," August 29, 2005..

[101] U.S. Department of Defense, "Hurricane Katrina Timeline," August 29, 2005.

[102] See U.S. Department of Homeland Security, "Hurricane Katrina DHS SITREP #4," August 27, 2005.

[103] The emergency declaration for Mississippi was requested by Governor Barbour on Saturday, August, 27, 2005; the emergency declaration for Alabama was requested by Governor Riley on Sunday, August 28, 2005. Presidential states of emergency were declared for both States on August 28. 70 Fed. Reg. 53239 (Aug. 28, 2005) (Mississippi); 70 Fed. Reg. 54061-62 (Aug. 28, 2005) (Alabama).

[104] President Bush authorized FEMA ". . . to identify, mobilize, and provide at its discretion, equipment and resources necessary to alleviate the impacts of the emergency" for the parishes of Allen, Avoyelles, Beauregard, Bienville, Bossier, Caddo, Caldwell, Claiborne, Catahoula, Concordia, De Soto, East Baton Rouge, East Carroll, East Feliciana, Evangeline, Franklin, Grant, Jackson, LaSalle, Lincoln, Livingston, Madison, Morehouse, Natchitoches, Pointe Coupee, Ouachita, Rapides, Red River, Richland, Sabine, St. Helena, St. Landry, Tensas, Union, Vernon, Webster, West Carroll, West Feliciana, and Winn. The White House, "Statement on Emergency Assistance for Louisiana," news release, August 27, 2005. See also, Robert T. Stafford Disaster Relief and Emergency Assistance Act, Public Law 93-288, as amended ["Stafford Act"], § 502(a)(b).

[105] Data on pre-landfall disaster declarations compiled from: Department of Homeland Security, Federal Emergency Management Agency, "Federally Declared Disasters by Calendar Year," Library, http://www.fema.gov/library/drcys.shtm. Hurricane Floyd did not make landfall until 6:30 AM on September 16, 1999, but the storm caused significant coastal damage as it passed offshore Florida, Georgia, and the Carolinas; as a result, President Clinton issued emergency declarations for Florida and Georgia on September 14. He did the same for the Carolinas the following day. For more information, see: U.S. Department of Homeland Security, Federal Emergency Management Agency, "Emergency Aid Ordered For Florida Hurricane Response," news release, September 14, 1999, http://www.fema.gov/news/newsrelease.fema?id=8554; U.S. Department of Homeland

Security, Federal Emergency Management Agency, "Emergency Aid Ordered For Georgia Hurricane Response," news release, September 14, 1999, http://www.fema.gov/news/newsrelease.fema?id=8553; U.S. Department of Homeland Security, Federal Emergency Management Agency, "Emergency Aid Ordered For South Carolina Hurricane Response," news release, September 15, 1999, http://www.fema.gov/news/newsrelease.fema?id=8552 and U.S. Department of Homeland Security, Federal Emergency Management Agency, "Emergency Aid Ordered For North Carolina Hurricane Response," news release, September 15, 1999, http://www.fema.gov/news/newsrelease.fema?id=8551.

[106] On August 27, 2005, Governor Kathleen Blanco sent a letter to President Bush requesting an emergency declaration for the State of Louisiana. The letter stated, "I have determined that this incident is of such severity and magnitude that effective response is beyond the capabilities of the State and affected local governments, and that supplementary Federal assistance is necessary to save lives, protect property, public health, and safety, or to lessen or avert the threat of a disaster." The letter contained a list of "State and local resources that have been or will be used to alleviate the conditions of this emergency." It also certified that "the State and local governments will assume all applicable non-Federal share of costs required by the Stafford Act." Governor Blanco specifically requested "emergency protective measures, direct Federal Assistance, Individual and Household Program (IHP) assistance, Special Needs Program assistance, and debris removal" for all affected areas. She defined the affected areas as "all the southeastern parishes including the New Orleans Metropolitan area and the mid-state Interstate I-49 corridor and northern parishes along the I-20 corridor that are accepting the thousands of citizens evacuating . . . .," Kathleen Blanco, Governor of Louisiana, Letter to President Bush requesting that he declare an emergency for the State of Louisiana due to Hurricane Katrina (Baton Rouge, August 27, 2005). That same day President Bush declared a state of emergency in Louisiana. 70 Fed. Reg. 53238 (August 27, 2005).

[107] William Lokey, Federal Coordinating Officer for Baton Rouge, written statement for a hearing on Louisiana Hurricane Katrina Response and Recovery, on December 14, 2005, submitted to the House Select Committee to Investigate the Preparation for and Response to Hurricane Katrina, 109th Congress, 1st session.

[108] Louisiana Office of the Governor, Response to U.S. Senate Committee on Homeland Security and Governmental Affairs and Information Request Dated October 7, 2005 (Baton Rouge, December 2005); U.S. Department of Commerce, National Oceanic and Atmospheric Administration, National Hurricane Center, "Hurricane Katrina Forecast Timeline," n.d., ca. 2005.

[109] Max Mayfield, testimony before a hearing on "The Lifesaving Role of Accurate Hurricane Prediction," Disaster Prevention and Prediction Hearing, U.S. Senate Committee on Commerce, Science, and Transportation, on September 20, 2005, 109th Congress, 1st session, 11. Mayfield said: "Yes Sir, I called. I don't do that very often. But I—in fact, I have only done that only one other time for Hurricane Lili in the— when it was a Category 4 Hurricane in the Gulf of Mexico. I called the former Governor of Louisiana in 2002. And this was Saturday night around 8:30 or 9 o'clock eastern time and I called the—I got hold of the Governor of Louisiana, the Governor of Mississippi and Governor Blanco in Louisiana suggested I call Mayor Nagin in New Orleans. I called him and left a message and he called me right back and I have—a lot of people have asked me what I said and I, you know, with the hundreds of briefings that we did, I don't remember exactly. But the whole purpose of that was just to be absolutely sure that they understood the severity of the situation and I do remember telling all three of them that I want to leave the National Hurricane Center that night and be able to go home and sleep knowing that I had done everything that I could do."

[110] Max Mayfield, testimony before a hearing on "The Lifesaving Role of Accurate Hurricane Prediction," Disaster Prevention and Prediction , U.S. Senate Committee on Commerce, Science, and Transportation, on September 20, 2005, 109th Congress, 1st session, 11.

[111] See U.S. Department of Homeland Security, Federal Emergency Mangement Agency, National Response Coordination Center, video teleconference, August 27, 2005.

[112] Brigadier General David L. Johnson, Director, National Oceanographic and Atmospheric Administration, National Weather Service, testimony before a hearing on "Predicting Hurricanes: What We Knew About Katrina," U.S. House Select Committee on Hurricane Katrina, on September 22, 2005, 109th Congress, 1st session, 43 (testifying that Hurricane Katrina became a Category 4 storm at 12:40 AM on Sunday, August 28, and became a Category 5 storm at 6:15 AM that same day).

[113] Richard D. Knabb, Jamie R. Rhome, and Daniel Brown, *Tropical Cyclone Report: Hurricane Katrina: August 23-30, 2005*, National Hurricane Center, National Oceanic and Atmospheric Administration (Miami, Florida, December 2005), 3.

[114] U.S. Department of Commerce, National Oceanic and Atmospheric Administration, National Weather Service, New Orleans/Baton Rouge Forecast Office, Slidell, Louisiana, "Urgent Weather Message," August 28, 2005.

[115] U.S. Department of Commerce, National Oceanic and Atmospheric Administration, National Hurricane Center, *Hurricane Katrina Advisory # 25*, (Miami, Florida, August 28, 2005).

[116] U.S. Department of Commerce, U.S. Department of Commerce, National Oceanic and Atmospheric Administration, National Weather Service, New Orleans/Baton Rouge Forecast Office, Slidell, LA, "Urgent Weather Message," August 28, 2005.

[117] The Emergency Alert System (EAS) is a mechanism for public officials—Federal, State, and local—to communicate disaster information and instructions rapidly and widely. The system aims to reach the broadest possible audience by disseminating emergency updates on existing radio and television stations, including via digital and satellite networks. Federal Communications Commission, FCC Consumer Facts: The Emergency Alert System (Washington, DC, 2005), 1. See also State of California, "What Is EAS?," http://eas.oes.ca.gov/Pages/whatseas.htm. The new EAS system is the direct descendent of the Emergency Broadcast System (EBS), the Nation's alert system from 1963 until the advent of EAS. EAS was officially launched on January 1, 1997 (for radio stations) and December 31, 1998 (for television). Federal Emergency Management Agency, "Background on the Emergency Alert System," October 23, 2004, http://www.fema.gov/rrr/rep/easrep.shtm. While EAS fulfills the same function as EBS, it differs in that it takes advantage of digital technology to permit automation of transmission. Federal Emergency Management Agency, "Background on the Emergency Alert System," October 23, 2004, http://www.fema.gov/rrr/rep/easrep.shtm. The Emergency Broadcast System and its EAS successor were originally designed for the President to speak to the Nation during an emergency, particularly following catastrophic nuclear attacks. But the system was made available to State and local officials in 1963, and since then has been used primarily for weather emergencies. "There are two contexts in which the EAS will be used—Presidentially-initiated alerts and messages and those initiated by State and local governments in concert with the broadcast industry." Federal Emergency Management Agency, "Background on the Emergency Alert System," October 23, 2004, http://www.fema.gov/rrr/rep/easrep.shtm. See also, Federal Communications Commission, *FCC Consumer Facts: The Emergency Alert System* (Washington, DC, 2005), 2. The document states: "a state emergency manager may use the system to send out a public warning by broadcasting that warning from one or more major radio stations in a particular state." EAS was not activated prior to landfall aside from NOAA hurricane warnings and advisories. "The Emergency Alert System was never activated by the White House or by State or local governments during Katrina." Ken Kerschbaumer, "Broadcasters Seek Better Emergency Alert System," *Broadcasting and Cable*, September 12, 2005.

[118] National Oceanic and Atmospheric Administration, National Weather Service, "NOAA Weather Radio All Hazards," January 31, 2006, http://www.weather.gov/nwr/. The Federal Communication Commission's EAS Primary Entry Point (PEP) station in New Orleans (station WWL) was one of the few radio stations in the area to provide continuous service to the New Orleans area. The NOAA Weather Radio (NWR) is a national network of radio stations that continuously broadcast weather and hazard information from local Weather Service offices. Operating in close conjunction with EAS, NOAA Weather Radio comprises an "all hazards" radio network that acts as a "single source for comprehensive weather and emergency information." National Oceanic and Atmospheric Administration, National Weather Service, "NOAA Weather Radio All Hazards," January 31, 2006, http://www.weather.gov/nwr.

[119] Transcript of August 27, 2005, NRCC Video Teleconference.

[120] U.S. Department of Homeland Security, Coast Guard, *Hurricane Katrina: The U.S. Coast Guard at its Best* (Washington, D.C., 2005), 15.

[121] "New Orleans Mayor, Louisiana Governor Hold Press Conference," *CNN*, August 28, 2005, http://transcripts.cnn.com/TRANSCRIPTS/0508/28/bn.04.html.

[122] "New Orleans Mayor, Louisiana Governor Hold Press Conference," *CNN*, August 28, 2005, http://transcripts.cnn.com/TRANSCRIPTS/0508/28/bn.04.html . Louisiana law provides the parish presidents with the authority to issue mandatory evacuation orders. The law allows the Parish President to "Direct and compel the evacuation of all or part of the population from any stricken or threatened area within the boundaries of the parish if he deems this action necessary for mitigation, response, or recovery measures." The law declares the penalty for violating such an order to be a fine not more than five hundred dollars, or confinement in the parish jail for not more than six months, or both. *Louisiana Homeland Security and Emergency Assistance and Disaster Act,* La. Rev. Stat. 29-727. Although a State responsibility, it is unclear how the State or Parish law enforcement authorities intended to enforce this order. The Mayor ordered a mandatory evacuation for the entire Parish of Orleans, with the

exceptions of essential personnel of the Federal government, State of Louisiana and City of New Orleans, as well as essential personnel of regulated utilities and mass transportation services, hospitals and their patients, essential media, Orleans Parish Criminal Sheriff's office and its inmates, and the essential personnel of operating hotels and their patrons. The Mayor ordered every person not exempt to immediately evacuate the City of New Orleans, or if no other alternative was available, to immediately move to one of the facilities within the City that would be designated a refuge of last resort.

[123] U.S. Department of Homeland Security, National Response Coordination Center, video teleconference, August 28, 2005.

[124] Frances Fragos Townsend, Assistant to the President for Homeland Security and Counterterrorism, remarks to the National Emergency Management Association's 2006 mid-year conference, February 13, 2006.

[125] See U.S. Department of Homeland Security, National Response Coordination Center, video teleconference, August 28, 2005.

[126] See U.S. Department of Homeland Security, National Response Coordination Center, video teleconference, August 28, 2005.

[127] Secretary Chertoff asked, "…are there any DOD assets that might be available. Have we reached out to them, and have we I guess made any kind of arrangement in case we need some additional help from them?" Director Brown responded, "We have DOD assets over here at the EOC. They are fully engaged, and we are having those discussions with them now." U.S. Department of Homeland Security, Federal Emergency Mangement Agency, National Response Coordination Center, video teleconference, August 28, 2005.

[128] Michael Chertoff, Secretary, Department of Homeland Security, testimony on the Department of Homeland Security Relief Response, on October 19, 2005, before the House Select Bipartisan Committee to Investigate the Preparation for and Response to Hurricane Katrina, 109th Congress 1st session, 48. Secretary Chertoff testified, "it is correct that under the declaration there's an FCO appointed. It was Lokey in Louisiana and Carwile in Mississippi. But Brown went down as their supervisor with direct authority over them to be on the ground in charge of the entire Gulf Coast response. In other words, he went down on Sunday. He was—on Saturday he was in FEMA in Washington running the operation with each of the support function representatives, including DOD literally sitting at the table with him at FEMA headquarters. He then moved himself—after the Sunday VTC, down to Baton Rouge and operated using his authority over the FCOs as the head of the whole agency. He was in charge of this thing on the ground from his arrival on Sunday through the end. The designation as a PFO, I guess, was a kind of formal recognition of that."

[129] Michael Chertoff, Secretary of the Department of Homeland Security, written statement for a hearing on the Department of Homeland Security's Hurricane Relief Response, on October 19, 2005, submitted to the House Select Bipartisan Committee to Investigate the Preparation for and Response to Hurricane Katrina, 109th Congress, 1st session, 14.

[130] TheWhite House, "President Discusses Hurricane Katrina, Congratulates Iraqis on Draft Constitution," news release, August 28, 2005.

[131] By Sunday afternoon, Mississippi ordered mandatory or voluntary evacuation orders for six counties. Alabama Governor Bob Riley issued evacuation orders for Mobile and Baldwin counties. State of Mississippi, Mississippi Emergency Management Agency, "Mississippians Urged to Take Precautions for Hurricane Katrina," news release, August 28, 2005; State of Alabama, Office of the Governor, "Governor Riley Orders Evacuation of Parts of Mobile and Baldwin Counties," news release, August 28, 2005; Leigh Ann Ryals, Director of the Baldwin County Emergency Management Agency, testimony before a hearing on Hurricane Katrina: Preparedness and Response by the State of Alabama, on November 9, 2005, House Committee on Government Reform on the State of Alabama's Preparation for and Response to Hurricane Katrina,109th Congress, 1st session.

[132] "Before Katrina came, I developed a new evacuation plan that includes contra-flow, where both sides of the interstates are used for outbound traffic. I am proud that we rapidly moved over 1.2 million people - some 92% of the population - to safety without gridlock or undue delay prior to Katrina." Governor Kathleen Blanco, written statement for a hearing on Hurricane Katrina: Preparedness and Response by the State of Louisiana, on December 14, 2005, submitted to the U.S. House Select Committee to Investigate the Preparation for and Response to Hurricane Katrina, 109th Congress, 1st session. See also, Johnny Bradberry, Secretary of the Louisiana Department of Transportation and Development, testimony before a hearing on the Evacuation of New Orleans, Senate Homeland Security and Governmental Affairs Committee, January 31, 2006, 109th Congress, 2nd session.

[133] U.S. Department of Transportation, "Hurricane Katrina - Situation Report Five," August 29, 2005; Louis Armstrong New Orleans International Airport, "Hurricane Katrina from the Airport's Point of View," http://www.flymsy.com/.

[134] Governor Kathleen Blanco, written statement for a hearing on Hurricane Katrina: Preparedness and Response by the State of Louisiana, on December 14, 2005, submitted to the U.S. House Select Committee to Investigate the Preparation for and Response to Hurricane Katrina, 109th Congress, 1st session. The Louisiana DOTD estimated that 500,000 vehicles evacuated during Phase 3 operations, see Louisiana State Police, "LSP Timeline of Events," n.d., ca. 2005, 5.

[135] U.S. Department of Homeland Security, "Hurricane Katrina DHS SITREP #6," August 29, 2005, 12.

[136] State of Texas, State Operations Center, "Situation Report #9," August 28, 2005.

[137] Ray Nagin, Mayor of New Orleans, testimony before a hearing on Hurricane Katrina: Preparedness and Response by the State of Louisiana, on December 14, 2005, U.S. House Select Committee to Investigate the Preparation for and Response to Hurricane Katrina, 109th Congress, 1st session, "After a Sunday morning statewide conference call, I announced the first ever in our almost 300-year history a citywide mandatory evacuation order, which followed the evacuation orders, I might add, of some of the other low-lying parishes that also were encouraging their citizens to evacuate post haste. We opened the Superdome as our refuge of last resort, and we staged buses throughout the city to transport people to the Superdome, and set a curfew for dusk. The city also evacuated 400 special needs residents to the state shelter and then opened the Superdome at 8 a.m. that morning for the remaining special needs populations. There were thousands of residents that did not leave, including those with means who would choose to ride out the storm like their parents had done during Hurricane Betsy. When reality set in for many of them on Sunday, they made their way to the refuge of last resort, the Superdome." Louisiana National Guard personnel on-scene reported no evacuees at the Superdome until after noon. Louisiana National Guard, Task Force Pelican, "Hurricane Katrina Overview of Significant Events," November 28, 2005, 5-6.

[138] Major General Bennett Landreneau, Louisiana National Guard, testimony before a hearing on Hurricane Katrina: Preparedness and Response by the Department of Defense, the Coast Guard, and the National Guard of Louisiana, Mississippi, and Alabma, on October 27, 2005, House Select Bipartisan Committee to Investigate the Preparation for and Response to Hurricane Katrina, 109th Congress, 1st session. A shelter of last resort is intended to serve only as a location to ride out the winds of a storm. Under the State of Louisiana Emergency Operations Plan, it could "be located either inside or outside of the Hurricane Risk" and did not have to meet American Red Cross shelter standards. It is required to be "wind resistant" and "located outside of the flood zone or [provide the] ability to locate on floors." Louisiana Office of Emergency Preparedness, *State of Louisiana Emergency Operations Plan Supplement 1C: Louisiana Shelter Operations Plan* (Baton Rouge, as revised July 2000), Annex M.

[139] Marty Bahamonde, Regional Director for External Affairs, Region One, FEMA, written statement for a hearing on Hurricane Katrina in New Orleans, A Flooded City, A Chaotic Response, on October 20, 2005, submitted to the Senate Committee on Homeland Security and Governmental Affairs, 109th Cong., 1st session, 2, stating, "Later that night after most of the 12,000 evacuees entered the Superdome, I returned to the EOC around midnight to ride out the storm." Although estimates put the Superdome population at between 20,000 and 40,000 by Friday, September 2, when evacuations of the Superdome began, Louisiana officials have stated that this increase took place after landfall on the Gulf Coast. Colonel Jeff Smith, Acting Deputy Director, Louisiana Office of Homeland Security and Emergency Preparedness, testimony before a hearing on the Hurricane Katrina Response in Louisiana, on December 14, 2005, House Select Committee to Investigate the Preparation and Response to Hurricane Katrina, 109th Congress, 2nd session. Jeff Smith had recently taken the job of Acting Deputy Director of the Louisiana Office of Homeland Security and Emergency Preparedness. On November 29, 2004, a Federal grand jury had indicted Michael L. Brown, the former Deputy Director of the Louisiana Office of Homeland Security and Emergency Preparedness (LOHSEP) and the State official responsible for overall management of Louisiana's Hazardous Mitigation Grants from FEMA, on charges of obstructing a Federal audit. This grant program funds mitigation projects to prevent flood loses or flood claims made upon the National Flood Insurance Program. Two other LOHSEP officials were indicted with him. U.S. Department of Justice, Three State Officials Indicted for Obstructing Federal Audit, press release, November 29, 2004, http://www.usdoj.gov/usao/law/news/wdl20041129.html; Ken Silverstein and Josh Meyer, "Katrina's Aftermath: Louisiana Officials Indicted Before Katrina Hit," Los Angeles Times, September 17, 2005, 17.

[140] For example, the State of Alabama made a request on August 28 for shuttle trucks and tarps to be delivered to Maxwell Air Force Base. Alabama also requested the transport and delivery of two 50-man Joint Field Office kits

to Montgomery. Mississippi requested the pre-positioning of 30 trucks of water with tractors at Meridian NAS and two helicopters to transport response personnel.

[141] FEMA Office of Legislative Affairs, Hurricane Katrina Response Fact Sheet.

[142] Speaking before before the House Ways and Means Committee, Joseph C. Becke, Senior Vice President, American Red Cross, stated "It has been the policy of the Red Cross that there are no safe areas south of the I-10/I-12 corridor for a large-scale hurricane . . . We do not establish shelters in facilities that do not meet our criteria for safety during landfall." In saying this, Mr. Becke clearly implies that the Superdome is considered by the Red Cross to be an "unsafe" shelter. See Joseph C. Becke, Senior Vice President of Preparedness and Response, American Red Cross, written statement for a hearing on the Response of Charities to Hurricane Katrina, on December 13, 2005, before the House Ways and Means Committee, 109th Congress 1st session. However, the Red Cross was not against the use of the Superdome as a shelter of last resort. In a "frequently asked questions" portion of the official Red Cross website the organization states, "the original plan was to evacuate all the residents of New Orleans to safe places outside the city. With the hurricane bearing down, the city government decided to open a shelter of last resort in the Superdome downtown. *We applaud this decision and believe it saved a significant number of lives.*" See American Red Cross, "Frequently Asked Questions," http://www.redcross.org/faq/ 0,1096,0_682_4524,00.html (emphasis added). Thus, the Superdome, while it did not meet the Red Cross' safety requirements, served a valuable purpose as a shelter of last resort. Although the Red Cross's own policies prevented it from directly staffing the Superdome, the organization claims that it was willing to supply the shelter with essential commodities after Katrina made landfall. According to the "Frequently Asked Questions" statement on its website, the organization was prevented from carrying out this mission by the National Guard and local authorities.

[143] "New Orleans Mayor, Louisiana Governor Hold Press Conference," *CNN Breaking News,* August 28, 2005, http://transcripts.cnn.com/transcripts/0508/28/bn.04.html.

[144] Major General Bennett Landreneau, Adjutant General, State of Louisiana, testimony before a hearing on Military Disaster Relief, on October 27, 2005, House Select Bipartisan Committee to Investigate the Preparation for and response to Hurricane Katrina, 109th Congress, 1st session.

[145] Louisiana National Guard, Task Force Pelican, "Hurricane Katrina Overview of Significant Events," November 28, 2005, 3, 5.

[146] Louisiana National Guard, Task Force Pelican, "Hurricane Katrina Overview of Significant Events," November 28, 2005, 6.

[147] Louisiana National Guard, Task Force Pelican, "Hurricane Katrina Overview of Significant Events," November 28, 2005, 6.

[148] Louisiana National Guard, Task Force Pelican, "Hurricane Katrina Overview of Significant Events," November 28, 2005, 7.

[149] Louisiana National Guard, Task Force Pelican, "Hurricane Katrina Overview of Significant Events," November 28, 2005, 7.

[150] Louisiana National Guard, Task Force Pelican, "Hurricane Katrina Overview of Significant Events," November 28, 2005, 7-8. U.S. Department of Health and Human Services (HHS) contacted the Director of Emergency Preparedness for the Louisiana Health Department. The State declined assistance.

[151] "New Orleans Mayor, Louisiana Governor Hold Press Conference*,*" *CNN,* August 28, 2005, http://transcripts.cnn.com/TRANSCRIPTS/0508/28/bn.04.html.

[152] Louisiana State Police, "LSP Timeline of Events," n.d., ca. 2005. 5. The storm forced Troop B of the Louisiana State Police to relocate from their barracks to the Kenner Police Department's headquarters.

[153] Parish officials declared mandatory evacuations for Lafourche, Orleans, Plaquemines, St. Bernard, St. Charles and St. John the Baptist parishes. Officials declared mandatory evacuations for limited geographical or flood-prone areas of the following parishes: Jefferson, St. James, Livingston, Tangipahoa, St. Tammany and Terrebone. Parish officials recommended evacuations in Ascension, Assumption and Washington parishes. See Louisiana State Police, "Southeast Louisiana Evacuations Continue," news release, August 28, 2005; Louisiana State Police, "Hurricane Evacuations: Livingston Parish,"news release, August 28, 2005; Louisiana State Police, "Hurricane Evacuations: St. Tammany Parish," news release, August 28, 2005; Louisiana State Police, "Hurricane Evacuations: Washington Parish," news release, August 28, 2005.

[154] U.S. Department of Homeland Security, Federal Emergency Management Agency, Tropical Storm Katrina Briefing, August 25, 2005.

[155] Mobile Emergency Response Support (MERS) detachments consist of trained personnel and mobile response assets. FEMA has five MERS detachments strategically placed across the country. MERS detachments

are designed to provide communications capabilities and operational and logistical support to first responders. Each MERS detachment has a suite of vehicle assets to provide support. Because its diverse asserts are housed on a number of different trucks, a single MERS detachment "can concurrently support a large Disaster Field Office and multiple field operating sites within the disaster area." Thus, the deployment of one MERS unit is not married to a single location. The communications component of MERS capabilities consists of Ku-band satellite, International Maritime Satellite (INMARSAT) and American Mobile Satellite Corporation (AMSC) satellite terminals, line of sight microwave transmission, and high frequency, very high frequency, and ultra high frequency radio. MERS logistics support includes power, heating, ventilation, and cooling (HVAC), fuel, and [potable] water." A MERS detachment can provide "generators to supply the power generation requirements of one or more facilities or locations within the disaster area," and "heating, ventilation, and cooling requirements for a large office building." A MERS detachment also provides personnel experienced in facility management, acquisition support, warehouse operation, transportation management, and property accountability." Further, "the MERS Detachments have resources that can provide temporary office or operational space." The Denton, Texas MERS team operates FEMA's *Emergency Operations Vehicle* (EOV), an "82 foot long expandable trailer providing office workstations and conference space for 20-25 people." The EOV also has kitchen, power generation, and communications facilities. MERS detachments also have rapid response teams to provide initial support immediately following a disaster. The Quick Reaction System (QRS) consists of "13 people with 4-wheel drive vehicles and support equipment for 72 hours that provide the initial damage assessment." This unit also has "an INMARSAT and AMSC satellite terminal, cellular telephones and laptop computers, VHF and HF radios, life support (water, food, batteries, etc.), and generators." Finally, ERTA and ERTS units are "preloaded trucks with food, water, clothing, first aid items, safety equipment, sleeping bags, hygiene items, office equipment, tools, and lumber." These trucks can support "100 people for 10 days." For a detailed assessment of MERS capabilities, see U.S. Department of Homeland Security, Federal Emergency Management Agency, *Response and Recovery: Mobile Operations Capability Guide for Emergency Managers and Planners,* October 23, 2004, http://www.fema.gov/rrr/mers01.shtm.

[156] U.S. Department of Homeland Security, Federal Emergency Management Agency, "FEMA National Situation Update," August 29, 2005, 3.

[157] U.S. Department of Homeland Security, Federal Emergency Management Agency, Office of Legislative Affairs, *Hurricane Katrina Response Fact Sheet.*

[158] National Aeronautics and Space Administration, Goddard Space Flight Center, "Hurricane Katrina from TRMM: August 28, 2005," http://svs.gsfc.nasa.gov/vis/a000000/a003200/a003218/ (data from NASA spacecraft).

[159] "New Orleans Mayor, Louisiana Governor Hold Press Conference," *CNN,* August 28, 2005, http://transcripts.cnn.com/TRANSCRIPTS/0508/28/bn.04.html.

CHAPTER FOUR: A WEEK OF CRISIS — AUGUST 29 – SEPTEMBER 5

[1] The White House, "President Discusses Hurricane Relief in Address to the Nation," news release, September 15, 2005, http://www.whitehouse.gov/news/releases/2005/09/20050915-8.html.

[2] These wind gusts were reported in Poplarville, Mississippi, at the Pearl River County Emergency Operations Center. See Richard D. Knabb, Jamie R. Rhome, and Daniel P. Brown, *Tropical Cyclone Report: Hurricane Katrina, 23-30 August 2005*, prepared for the National Hurricane Center (Miami, Florida, December 20, 2005), 3, 8.

[3] Hurricane Katrina was downgraded to Category 1 on the Saffir-Simpson scale at 6:00 PM UTC on August 29. Richard D. Knabb, Jamie R. Rhome, and Daniel P. Brown, *Tropical Cyclone Report: Hurricane Katrina, 23-30 August 2005*, prepared for the National Hurricane Center (Miami, Florida, December 20, 2005), 4.

[4] Richard D. Knabb, Jamie R. Rhome, and Daniel P. Brown, *Tropical Cyclone Report: Hurricane Katrina, 23-30 August 2005*, prepared for the National Hurricane Center (Miami, Florida, December 20, 2005), 4.

[5] Richard D. Knabb, Jamie R. Rhome, and Daniel P. Brown, *Tropical Cyclone Report: Hurricane Katrina, 23-30 August 2005*, prepared for the National Hurricane Center (Miami, Florida, December 20, 2005). A National Data Buoy Center (NDBC) buoy located 64 nautical miles south of Dauphin Island, Alabama, measured a peak significant wave height of 55 feet on August 28, matching the record for "the largest significant wave height ever measured by a NDBC buoy."

[6] Richard D. Knabb, Jamie R. Rhome, and Daniel P. Brown, *Tropical Cyclone Report: Hurricane Katrina, 23-30 August 2005*, prepared for the National Hurricane Center (Miami, Florida, December 20, 2005), 8-9.

[7] As of the time of this writing, Louisiana had counted 1,103 deaths, twenty-three of which were not storm related, for 1,080 storm related deaths. See Louisiana Department of Health and Hospitals, "Reports of Missing and Deceased," February 17, 2006, http://www.dhh.louisiana.gov/offices/page.asp?ID=192&Detail=5248 (accessed February 17, 2006). There were 231 deaths in Mississippi, fifteen in Florida, two in Alabama, and two in Georgia. See Richard D. Knabb, Jamie R. Rhome, and Daniel P. Brown, *Tropical Cyclone Report: Hurricane Katrina, 23-30 August 2005,* prepared for the National Hurricane Center (Miami, Florida, December 20, 2005), 10. Since there are still 2,096 people from the Gulf Coast area missing, it is likely that the death toll numbers will increase. See also U.S. Department of Commerce, National Oceanic and Atmospheric Administration Satellite and Information Service and National Climatic Data Center, *2005 Annual Climate Review: U.S. Summary* (Asheville, NC, January 2006), http://www.ncdc.noaa.gov/oa/climate/research/2005/ann/us-summary.html; and Ray Nagin, Mayor of New Orleans, testimony before a hearing on Hurricane Katrina: Managing the Crisis and Evacuating New Orleans, on February 1, 2006, Senate Committee on Homeland Security and Governmental Affairs, 109th Congress, 2nd session.

[8] The White House, "President Outlines Hurricane Katrina Relief Efforts," news release, August 31, 2005.

[9] Richard D. Knabb, Jamie R. Rhome, and Daniel P. Brown, *Tropical Cyclone Report: Hurricane Katrina, 23-30 August 2005*, prepared for the National Hurricane Center (Miami, Florida, December 20, 2005), 11.

[10] Brett Martel, "'What Hiroshima looked like' - Katrina's full wrath still being felt, death toll soars past 100," Associated Press, August 31, 2005.

[11] U.S. Department of Homeland Security, "Hurricane Katrina DHS SITREP #8," August 30, 2005. See also American Red Cross, "Hurricane Katrina Damage Assessments," http://www.msema.org/redcrossassessments.htm (accessed February 13, 2006).

[12] Guy Gugliotta and Peter Whoriskey, "Floods Ravage New Orleans; Two Levees Give Way; in Mississippi, Death Toll Estimated at 110," *Washington Post*, August 31, 2005.

[13] "The eastbound lanes of Interstate 10 between Gulfport and Biloxi were impassable because of storm debris." "Katrina kills 50 in one Mississippi county," *CNN.com*, August 30, 2005, http://www.cnn.com/2005/WEATHER/08/29/hurricane.katrina.

[14] "Katrina kills 50 in one Mississippi county," *CNN.com*, August 30, 2005, http://www.cnn.com/2005/WEATHER/08/29/hurricane.katrina. See also U.S. Department of Homeland Security, "Hurricane Katrina DHS SITREP #8," August 30, 2005, 3 ("Widespread flooding has also been reported across coastal Mississippi and Alabama").

[15] U.S. Department of Commerce, National Oceanic and Atmospheric Administration Satellite and Information Service and National Climatic Data Center, "Hazards/Climate Extremes," http://www.ncdc.noaa.gov/oa/climate/research/2005/aug/hazards.html; and Richard D. Knabb, Jamie R. Rhome, and Daniel P. Brown, *Tropical Cyclone Report: Hurricane Katrina, 23-30 August 2005*, prepared for the National Hurricane Center (Miami, Florida, December 20, 2005), 8-9, 10.

[16] U.S. Department of Homeland Security, "Hurricane Katrina DHS SITREP #14," September 2, 2005.

[17] Norman Mineta, Secretary of the Department of Transportation, written statement for a hearing on the Department of Transportation (Hurricane Katrina), on October 6, 2005, submitted to the House Committee on Appropriations, Subcommittee on Transportation, Treasury, Housing and Urban Development, the Judiciary, District of Columbia, and Independent Agencies, 109th Congress, 1st session.

[18] Tommy Longo, Mayor of Waveland, Mississippi, testimony before a hearing on Hurricane Katrina: Preparedness and Response by the State of Mississippi, on December 7, 2005, House Select Bipartisan Committee to Investigate the Preparation for and Response to Hurricane Katrina, 109th Congress, 1st session, 51.

[19] Tommy Longo, Mayor of Waveland, Mississippi, testimony before a hearing on Hurricane Katrina: Preparedness and Response by the State of Mississippi, on December 7, 2005, House Select Bipartisan Committee to Investigate the Preparation for and Response to Hurricane Katrina, 109th Congress, 1st session. See also U.S. Department of the Interior, U.S. Geological Survey, Coastal & Marine Geology Program, "Before and After Photo Comparisons: Mainland Mississippi," *Hurricane Katrina Impact Studies*, August 31, 2005, http://coastal.er.usgs.gov/hurricanes/katrina/photo-comparisons/mainmississippi.html.

[20] Haley Barbour, Governor of Mississippi, testimony via video teleconference before a hearing on Hurricane Katrina: Recovering from Hurricane Katrina, on September 7, 2005, House Committee on Energy and Commerce, 109th Congress, 1st session.

---

[21] U.S. Department of Homeland Security, Homeland Security Operations Center, "Hurricane Katrina Update," August 30, 2005, 12.

[22] U.S. Department of Energy, "Department of Energy's Hurricane Response Chronology, as Referred to by Secretary Bodman at Today's Senate Energy and Natural Resources Committee Hearing," news release, October 27, 2005, http://energy.gov/news/2404.htm.

[23] U.S. Department of Energy, Office of Electricity Delivery and Energy Reliability, "Hurricane Katrina Situation Report #10," August 30, 2005, 1; and U.S. Department of Energy, "Department of Energy's Hurricane Response Chronology, as Referred to by Secretary Bodman at Today's Senate Energy and Natural Resources Committee Hearing," news release, October 27, 2005, http://energy.gov/news/2404.htm.

[24] U.S. Department of Homeland Security, "Hurricane Katrina DHS SITREP #36," September 13, 2005, 7. "The wireline telecommunications network sustained enormous damage both to the switching centers that route calls and to the lines used to connect buildings and customers to the network." Kenneth Moran, Director of the Office of Homeland Security, Enforcement Bureau, Federal Communications Commission, written statement for a hearing on Hurricane Katrina and Communications Interoperability, on September 29, 2005, submitted to the Senate Committee on Commerce, Science and Transportation, 109th Congress, 1st session.

[25] Nearly one hundred radio and television stations remained off the air a month after Hurricane Katrina's landfall. Kenneth Moran, Director of the Office of Homeland Security, Enforcement Bureau, Federal Communications Commission, written statement for a hearing on Hurricane Katrina and Communications Interoperability, on September 29, 2005, submitted to the Senate Committee on Commerce, Science, and Transportation, 109th Congress, 1st session.

[26] Paul McHale, Assistant Secretary of Defense for Homeland Defense, testimony before a hearing on Hurricane Katrina: Preparedness and Response by the Department of Defense, the Coast Guard, and the National Guard of Louisiana, Mississippi, and Alabama, on October 27, 2005, House Select Bipartisan Committee to Investigate the Preparation for and Response to Hurricane Katrina, 109th Congress, 1st session, 74.

[27] "The public health and health care delivery infrastructures have been either completely destroyed or have sustained significant damage across the affected Gulf Coast. Existing facilities that are operational are under extreme stress as they assume even greater responsibilities to fill the gaps created by the loss of so many facilities. Physician offices, cancer, imaging, dialysis and rehabilitation centers, hospitals, clinics, long-term care facilities, pharmacies, laboratories, etc., need to be rebuilt or repaired, not to mention re-supplied, with information technology systems, equipment and inventory." Ardis D. Hoven, Member of the American Medical Association Board of Trustees, written statement for a hearing on Assessing Public Health and the Delivery of Care in the Wake of Hurricane Katrina, on September 22, 2005, submitted to the House Energy and Commerce Committee, Subcommittees on Health and Oversight and Investigations, 109th Congress, 1st session.

[28] "Nursing homes and hospitals were not a priority during the rescue process. For the first two days, [the Louisiana Nursing Home Association] was on its own to improvise and find ways to rescue the elderly in nursing homes." Joseph A. Donchess, Executive Director of the Louisiana Nursing Home Association, written statement for a hearing on Challenges in a Catastrophe: Evacuating New Orleans in Advance of Hurricane Katrina, on January 31, 2006, submitted to the Senate Committee on Homeland Security and Governmental Affairs, 109th Congress, 2nd session. "Only a third of nursing homes in the New Orleans area evacuated before Katrina, according to state and industry officials. In hard-hit Orleans and Jefferson parishes, eight of forty-one nursing homes removed residents before the storm." Roma Khanna, "Katrina's toll on the sick, elderly emerges," *Houston Chronicle*, November 28, 2005. Fatality statistics illustrate Hurricane Katrina's heavy toll on older Louisiana residents. For example, 71% of the dead at St. Gabriel Morgue whose age could be determined were more than sixty years old. See Louisiana Department of Health and Hospitals, "Vital Statistics of All Bodies at St. Gabriel Morgue," January 4, 2006, http://www.dhh.louisiana.gov/publications .asp?ID=192&Detail=878.

[29] For example, Dr. Mark Peters of East Jefferson General Hospital in Metairie, Louisiana, stated that, "A day or two after the storm, we ran low on food. We always were able to feed our patients, and there were only two days when the staff had to eat once a day, and in small amounts. After that, we were able to contact various businesses and vendors to replenish our supplies and food." Dr. Mark Peters, President and Chief Executive Officer of East Jefferson General Hospital, written statement for a hearing on Assessing Public Health and Delivery of Care in the Wake of Hurricane Katrina, on September 22, 2005, submitted to the House Committee on Energy and Commerce, Subcommittee on Health and Subcommittee on Oversight and Investigations, 109th Congress, 1st session. Also see U.S. Department of Health and Human Services, "Secretary's Operations Center Flash Report #8--Hurricane

---

Katrina," August 31, 2005, 1-2; and U.S. Department of Health and Human Services, "Secretary's Operations Center Flash Report #9--Hurricane Katrina," August 31, 2005, 1.

[30] For example, six or seven patients at the Bethany Home, a nursing facility in New Orleans, succumbed to the conditions as they awaited evacuation. See Joseph A. Donchess, Executive Director of the Louisiana Nursing Home Association, testimony before a hearing on Challenges in a Catastrophe: Evacuating New Orleans in Advance of Hurricane Katrina, on January 31, 2006, Senate Committee on Homeland Security and Governmental Affairs, 109th Congress, 2nd session. See also Roma Khanna, "Katrina's Aftermath," *Houston Chronicle*, November 27, 2005.

[31] The Louisiana State Attorney General subsequently charged the nursing home's owners with thirty-four counts of negligent homicide. Louisiana Office of the Attorney General, "Nursing Home Owners Surrender to Medicaid Fraud Control Unit Investigators," news release, September 14, 2005, http://www.ag.state.la.us/ViewPressRel.aspx ?RelID=420.

[32] Ray Nagin, Mayor of New Orleans, testimony before a hearing on Hurricane Katrina: Preparedness and Response by the State of Louisiana, on December 14, 2005, House Select Committee to Investigate the Preparation for and Response to Hurricane Katrina, 109th Congress, 1st session, 3.

[33] Richard D. Knabb, Jamie R. Rhome, and Daniel P. Brown, *Tropical Cyclone Report: Hurricane Katrina, 23-30 August 2005,* prepared for the National Hurricane Center (Miami, Florida, December 20, 2005), 9.

[34] U.S. Department of Homeland Security, "Hurricane Katrina SITREP #6," August 29, 2005.

[35] R.B. Seed, P.G. Nicholson, R.A. Dalrymple, et al., *Preliminary Report on the Performance of the New Orleans Levee Systems in Hurricane Katrina on August 29, 2005,* November 17, 2005.

[36] U.S. Department of Homeland Security, Federal Emergency Management Agency, "Urban Search and Rescue Operations Completed: Hurricane Katrina Urban Search and Rescue Teams Are Due to Return Home," news release, September 30, 2005, http://www.fema.gov/news/newsrelease.fema?id=19320.html

[37] Governor Kathleen Blanco, Michael Brown, Senator Mary Landrieu, Bill Lokey, and Senator David Vitter, "Governor Kathleen Blanco (D-LA) Hold a News Conference Regarding Hurricane Katrina," Congressional Quarterly Transcription, August 30, 2005.

[38] FEMA Urban Search and Rescue teams "helped 6,582 people reach safety in the hours and days immediately following Hurricane Katrina. U.S. Department of Homeland Security, Federal Emergency Management Agency, "Urban Search and Rescue Operations Completed: Hurricane Katrina Urban Search and Rescue Teams Are Due to Return Home," September 30, 2005, http://www.fema.gov/news/newsrelease.fema?id=19320.html. National Guard forces were engaged in search and rescue operations within four hours after landfall. Lieutenant General H. Steven Blum, written statement for a hearing on Responding to Catastrophic Events: The Role of the Military and National Guard in Disaster Response, on October 20, 2005, submitted to the House Committee on Government Reform, 109th Congress, 1st session. Early search and rescue actions of local first responders: Ray Nagin, Mayor of New Orleans, written statement submitted for a hearing on Hurricane Katrina: Preparedness and Response by the State of Louisiana, on December 14, 2005, to the House Select Committee to Investigate the Preparation for and Response to Hurricane Katrina, 109th Congress, 1st session, 1.

[39] U.S. Department of Commerce, National Oceanic and Atmospheric Administration, National Weather Service, *Flash Flood Warning for Louisiana, August 29, 2005* (New Orleans, LA, August 2005).

[40] U.S. Department of Homeland Security, "Hurricane Katrina DHS SITREP #7," August 29, 2005.

[41] U.S. Department of Homeland Security, Homeland Security Operations Center, "FEMA National Sitrep 2005 Aug 29," August 29, 2005.

[42] U.S. Department of Homeland Security, Homeland Security Operations Center, "HSOC#4317-05: HC Katrina Update- 11:30hrs," August 29, 2005.

[43] U.S. Department of Homeland Security, Homeland Security Operations Center, "HSOC#4317-05: VTC NOTES 29 AUG 05."

[44] It was not until 7:30 PM that the HSOC developed a spot report that described the USACE report, but it is unclear if this spot report was distributed outside of the HSOC.

[45] Marty Bahamonde, Regional Director for External Affairs, Region One, Federal Emergency Management Agency, testimony before a hearing on Hurricane Katrina in New Orleans, A Flooded City, A Chaotic Response, on October 20, 2005, Senate Committee on Homeland Security and Governmental Affairs, 109th Congress, 1st session.

[46] Marty Bahamonde, Regional Director for External Affairs, Region One, Federal Emergency Management Agency, testimony before a hearing on Hurricane Katrina in New Orleans, A Flooded City, A Chaotic Response, on October 20, 2005, Senate Committee on Homeland Security and Governmental Affairs, 109th Congress, 1st session.

[47] Michael Brown, former Director of the Federal Emergency Management Agency, testimony before a hearing on Hurricane Katrina: Hurricane Preparedness, on February 10, 2006, Senate Committee on Homeland Security and Governmental Affairs, 109th Congress, 2nd session.

[48] Marty Bahamonde, Regional Director for External Affairs, Region One, Federal Emergency Management Agency, testimony before a hearing on Hurricane Katrina in New Orleans, A Flooded City, A Chaotic Response, on October 20, 2005, Senate Committee on Homeland Security and Governmental Affairs, 109th Congress, 1st session.

[49] U.S. Department of Homeland Security, Homeland Security Operations Center, "HSOC Spot Rep #13," August 29, 2005).

[50] U.S. Department of Homeland Security, "Hurricane Katrina DHS Sit Rep #8," August 30, 2005.

[51] U.S. Department of Homeland Security, Homeland Security Operations Center, "HSOC #4217-05: HC Katrina—NO 200 Ft Breached Levee Update," August 30, 2005; U.S. Department of Homeland Security, Homeland Security Operations Center, "HSOC #4317-05: HC Katrina – NO 200 Ft of Levee Breached," August 30, 2005; and U.S. Department of Homeland Security, Homeland Security Operations Center, "HSOC Spot Rep FW: US Army Corps of Engineers Spot Rep," August 30, 2005.

[52] Governor Kathleen Blanco, Michael Brown, Senator Mary Landrieu, Bill Lokey, and Senator David Vitter, "Governor Kathleen Blanco (D-LA) Hold a News Conference Regarding Hurricane Katrina," Congressional Quarterly Transcription, August 30, 2005.

[53] Richard D. Knabb, Jamie R. Rhome, and Daniel P. Brown, *Tropical Cyclone Report: Hurricane Katrina, 23-30 August 2005*, prepared for the National Hurricane Center (Miami, Florida, December 20, 2005); and Ray Nagin, Mayor of New Orleans, testimony before a hearing on Hurricane Katrina: Preparedness and Response by the State of Louisiana, on December 14, 2005, House Select Committee to Investigate the Preparation for and Response to Hurricane Katrina, 109th Congress, 1st session. In contrast, Raymond B. Seed, prepared statement for a hearing on Hurricane Katrina: Performance of the Flood Control System, on November 2, 2005, submitted to the Senate Committee on Homeland Security and Government Affairs, 109th Congress, 1st session, 2, http://hsgac.senate.gov/_files/110205Seed.pdf. Both sources report that eighty percent of New Orleans experienced some amount of flooding.

[54] Michael Brown, former Director of the Federal Emergency Management Agency, testimony before a hearing on Hurricane Katrina: Hurricane Preparedness, on February 10, 2006, Senate Committee on Homeland Security and Governmental Affairs, 109th Congress, 2nd session.

[55] International Association of Firefighters, "Reports from the Hurricane Frontlines: Katrina (August 29-September 6)," August 30, 2005, http://daily.iaff.org/Katrina/Katrina.htm?c=report1.

[56] International Association of Firefighters, "Reports from the Hurricane Frontlines: Katrina (September 7-September 13)," September 10, 2005, http://daily.iaff.org/Katrina/Katrina.htm?c=report2.

[57] Warren J. Riley, Superintendent of the New Orleans Police Department, written statement for a hearing on Hurricane Katrina: Managing Law Enforcement and Communications in a Catastrophe, on February 6, 2006, submitted to the Senate Committee on Homeland Security and Governmental Affairs, 109th Congress, 2nd session. In contrast, see Ray Nagin, Mayor of New Orleans, testimony before a hearing on Hurricane Katrina: Preparedness and Response by the State of Louisiana, on December 14, 2005, House Select Committee to Investigate the Preparation for and Response to Hurricane Katrina, 109th Congress, 1st session ("Pre-Katrina, we had 1,668 officers. Post-Katrina, we're at 1,506 -- so we're down 162 officers. We've had about 133 officers that have either been terminated, resigned, you know, are under investigation or resigned for personal reasons.").

[58] Louisiana State Police, "Hurricane Katrina Timeline of Events," n.d.,ca. 2005.

[59] Christopher Rhoads, "Cut Off: At Center of Crisis, City Officials faced struggle to keep in touch," *Wall Street Journal*, September 9, 2005.

[60] Willis Carter, Chief of Communications, Shreveport, Louisiana Fire Department, written statement for a hearing on Communications Interoperability, on September 29, 2005, submitted to the Senate Committee on Commerce, Science and Transportation, 109th Congress, 1st session.

[61] Louisiana State Police, "Hurricane Katrina Timeline of Events," n.d., ca. 2005.

[62] Senator Robert Barham, quoted in Joby Warrick, "Crisis Communications Remain Flawed," *Washington Post*, December 10, 2005.

[63] Nick Felton, New Orleans Local 632 President, quoted in International Association of Firefighters, "Reports from the Hurricane Frontlines: Katrina (September 7-September 13)," September 13, 2005, http://daily.iaff.org/Katrina/Katrina.htm?c=report2.

[64] Lieutenant Colonel Keith LaCaze, Louisiana Department of Wildlife and Fisheries, Enforcement Division, *Activity Report on Hurricane Katrina* (Baton Rouge, 2005), 2; Massachusetts Urban Search and Rescue Task Force One, *Hurricane Katrina: National Urban Search and Rescue Response System Issue Statements and Recommendations* (Beverly, MA, 2005), 7; and Ceci Connolly, "'I Don't Think I've Ever Had a More Surreal Experience'; Veteran Rescue Workers Surprised by Challenges in Louisiana," *Washington Post*, September 12, 2005.

[65] Juliet Eilperin, "Flooded Toxic Waste Sites Are Potential Health Threat," *Washington Post*, September 10, 2005. "A Superfund site is any land in the United States that has been contaminated by hazardous waste and identified by the Environmental Protection Agency (EPA) as a candidate for cleanup because it poses a risk to human health and/or the environment." See U.S. Environmental Protection Agency, "About Superfund," http://www.epa.gov/superfund/about.htm (accessed January 28, 2005).

[66] *Gulf Coast Hurricane Emergency Environmental Protection Act of 2005*, HR Res. 4139, section 102 (c), 109th Congress, 1st session (October 25, 2005). See also U.S. Department of Homeland Security, "Hurricane Katrina: What Government is Doing," http://www.dhs.gov/interweb/assetlibrary/katrina.htm (accessed February 10, 2006).

[67] For first-hand accounts of these conditions, see Lieutenant Colonel Keith LaCaze, Louisiana Department of Wildlife and Fisheries, Enforcement Division, *Activity Report on Hurricane Katrina* (Baton Rouge, 2005), 2; Massachusetts Urban Search and Rescue Task Force One, *Hurricane Katrina: National Urban Search and Rescue Response System Issue Statements and Recommendations* (Beverly, MA, 2005), 7; and Ceci Connolly, "'I Don't Think I've Ever Had a More Surreal Experience'; Veteran Rescue Workers Surprised by Challenges in Louisiana," *Washington Post*, September 12, 2005. For details on the contaminants found in tested floodwaters, see U.S. Environmental Protection Agency, "Environmental Assessment Summary for Areas of Jefferson, Orleans, St. Bernard, and Plaquemines Parishes Flooded as a Result of Hurricane Katrina," December 6, 2005, http://www.epa.gov/katrina/testresults/katrina_env_assessment_summary.htm.

[68] For example, see Governor Kathleen Babineaux Blanco, letter to Governor Bill Owens, entitled "Calling Certain Elements of the Colorado National Guard to Active Duty to Assist with Emergency Response Efforts Related to Hurricane Katrina," September 1, 2005. Governor Blanco signed similar memoranda with fifteen other States on the same date. EMAC was established to provide form and structure to interstate mutual aid. Approved by Congress in 1996 (Public Law 104-321), the EMAC membership has since grown to include 49 States, the District of Columbia, Puerto Rico and the Virgin Islands. Through EMAC, a disaster-struck member State may request and receive assistance from other member States quickly and efficiently, facilitated by the Compact's legal foundation. Once the conditions for providing assistance to a requesting State have been set, the terms constitute a legally binding contractual agreement that obligates States for reimbursement. See Emergency Management Assistance Compact, "About EMAC," http://www.emacweb.org.

[69] U.S. Department of Defense, National Guard Bureau, *After Action Review: Hurricane Response September 2005,* December 21, 2005, 57.

[70] Ray Nagin, Mayor of New Orleans, written statement for a hearing on Hurricane Katrina: Preparedness and Response by the State of Louisiana, on December 14, 2005, submitted to the House Select Committee to Investigate the Preparation for and Response to Hurricane Katrina, 109th Congress, 1st session, 1.

[71] U.S. Department of Homeland Security, Federal Emergency Management Agency, "Urban Search and Rescue Operations Completed: Hurricane Katrina Urban Search and Rescue Teams Are Due to Return Home," news release, September 30, 2005, http://www.fema.gov/news/newsrelease.fema?id=19320.html. FEMA pre-positioned US&R teams to the region and eventually deployed all twenty-eight National US&R teams within the first week after Hurricane Katrina's second landfall. FEMA US&R Task Forces, in conjunction with USCG, DOD, other Federal agencies, and State and local first responders, rescued over 6,500 people.

[72] Donna Miles, "Military Support to Katrina Relief Effort Continues to Grow," American Forces Information Service, August 31, 2005, http://www.defenselink.mil/news/Aug2005/20050831_2576.html.

[73] U.S. Department of Homeland Security, Coast Guard, *Hurricane Katrina: The U.S. Coast Guard at its Best* (Washington, D.C., 2005), 7, 47. See also U.S. Department of Homeland Security, Coast Guard, "Coast Guard Response to Hurricane Katrina," *Coast Guard Fact File*, http://www.uscg.mil/hq/g-cp/comrel/factfile/index.htm (accessed February 10, 2006); and U.S. Department of Homeland Security, "Hurricane Katrina: What Government is Doing," http://www.dhs.gov/interweb/assetlibrary/katrina.htm (accessed February 10, 2006).

[74] John Sherffius, cartoon, reproduced by the U.S. Department of Homeland Security, Coast Guard Aviation Association, September 2005, http://www.aoptero.org/images/nola%20st.gif (accessed February 7, 2006).

[75] Haley Barbour, Governor of Mississippi, written statement for a hearing on Hurricane Katrina: Preparedness and Response by the State of Mississippi, on December 7, 2005, submitted to the House Select Bipartisan Committee to Investigate the Preparation and Response to Hurricane Katrina, 109th Congress, 1st session, 2-3.

[76] U.S. Department of Homeland Security, Federal Emergency Management Agency, "Urban Search and Rescue Operations Completed: Hurricane Katrina Urban Search and Rescue Teams Are Due to Return Home," September 30, 2005, http://www.fema.gov/news/newsrelease.fema?id=19320.html.

[77] Lieutenant General H. Steven Blum, written statement for a hearing on Responding to Catastrophic Events: The Role of the Military and National Guard in Disaster Response, on October 20, 2005, submitted to the House Committee on Government Reform, 109th Congress, 1st session.

[78] "US&R activities include locating, extricating, and providing onsite medical treatment to victims trapped in collapsed structures." U.S. Department of Homeland Security, National Response Plan (Washington, D.C., December 2004), ESF #9-1.

[79] National Search and Rescue Committee, National Search and Rescue Plan (Washington, D.C., 1999), 8-9.

[80] East Baton Rouge Parish, Draft After-Action Report for Hurricanes Katrina and Rita (Baton Rouge, 2005), 37-38.

[81] Louisiana Office of the Governor, Response to U.S Senate Committee on Homeland Security and Governmental Affairs Document and Information Request Dated October 7, 2005 and to the U.S House of Representatives Select Committee to Investigate the Preparation for and Response to Hurricane Katrina (Baton Rouge, December 2, 2005), 11; and Lieutenant Colonel Keith LaCaze, Louisiana Department of Wildlife and Fisheries, Enforcement Division, Activity Report on Hurricane Katrina (Baton Rouge, 2005).

[82] U.S. Department of Homeland Security, National Response Plan (Washington, D.C., December 2004), ESF #9-1.

[83] Louisiana Office of Emergency Preparedness, Emergency Operations Plan Supplement 1A: Southeast Louisiana Hurricane Evacuation and Sheltering Plan (Baton Rouge, January 2000), Parts I, II, VI. The City of New Orleans had drafted a hurricane annex to its emergency management plan that outlined the responsibilities of municipal organizations for executing the City's evacuation. See New Orleans Office of Emergency Preparedness, City of New Orleans Comprehensive Emergency Management Plan: Hurricanes Annex (New Orleans, n.d.).

[84] William Lokey, Federal Coordinating Officer for Louisiana, written statement for a hearing on Hurricane Katrina: Preparedness and Response by the State of Louisiana, on December 14, 2005, submitted to the House Select Committee to Investigate the Preparation for and Response to Hurricane Katrina, 109th Congress, 1st session, 93 ; Brigadier General Mark Graham, Deputy Commanding General, Fifth U.S. Army, written statement for a hearing on Hurricane Katrina: Managing the Crisis and Evacuating New Orleans, on February 1, 2006, submitted to the Senate Homeland Security and Governmental Affairs Committee, 109th Congress, 2nd session; and Vince Pearce, National Response Program Manager, Department of Transportation, written statement for a hearing on Hurricane Katrina: Managing the Crisis and Evacuating New Orleans, on February 1, 2006, submitted to the Senate Committee on Homeland Security and Government Affairs, 109th Congress, 2nd session, 1-2.

[85] On August 29, the population of evacuees at the facility was estimated to be between 10,000 and 12,000. Marty J. Bahamonde, Office of Public Affairs, Federal Emergency Management Agency, testimony before the Senate Homeland Security Committee and Governmental Affairs, October 20, 2005, 2; Louisiana Office of the Governor, Response to U.S. Senate Committee on Homeland Security and Governmental Affairs and Information Request Dated October 7, 2005 and to the U.S. House of Representatives Select Committee to Investigate the Preparation for and Response to Hurricane Katrina, (Baton Rouge, December 2, 2005), 7; and Louisiana National Guard, Task Force Pelican, "Hurricane Katrina: Overview of Significant Events," November 28, 2005, 14. An inaccurate estimate of 25,000 general population evacuees at the Superdome was reported by DHS on August 29. U.S. Department of Homeland Security, "Hurricane Katrina DHS SITREP #6," August 29, 2005, 13.

FEMA estimated the Superdome population at 20,000 people on August 29. The Louisiana National Guard estimates that the crowd grew to 35,000 over the course of the next three days. See Louisiana National Guard, Task Force Pelican, "Hurricane Katrina: Overview of Significant Events," November 28, 2005, 13, 15-17.

[86] Louisiana National Guard, Task Force Pelican, "Hurricane Katrina: Overview of Significant Events," November 28, 2005, 16, 17.

[87] Major General Bennett Landreneau, Adjutant General for the State of Louisiana, testimony before a hearing on Hurricane Katrina: Preparedness and Response by the Department of Defense, on October 27, 2005, House Select Bipartisan Committee to Investigate the Preparation for and Response to Hurricane Katrina, 109th Congress, 1st session.

[88] Louisiana National Guard, Task Force Pelican, "Hurricane Katrina: Overview of Significant Events," November 28, 2005, 17.

[89] Louisiana National Guard, Task Force Pelican, "Hurricane Katrina: Overview of Significant Events," November 28, 2005, 15-17; Marty Bahamonde, Regional Director for External Affairs, Region One, Federal Emergency Management Agency, written statement for a hearing on Hurricane Katrina in New Orleans: A Flooded City, a Chaotic Response, on October 20, 2005, submitted to the Senate Committee on Homeland Security and Governmental Affairs, 109th Congress, 1st session.

[90] U.S. Department of Health and Human Services, "Secretary's Operations Center Flash Report #6,"August 30, 2005.

[91] Louisiana Office of the Governor, *Response to U.S Senate Committee on Homeland Security and Governmental Affairs Document and Information Request Dated October 7, 2005 and to the U.S House of Representatives Select Committee to Investigate the Preparation for and Response to Hurricane Katrina* (Baton Rouge, December 2, 2005), 9.

[92] FEMA requested of the Governors of a number of States that their States accept and temporarily house evacuees. See, e.g., Arizona Department of Housing, "Arizona to Accept Evacuees from Gulf Coast," news release, n.d., ca. 2005, http://www.housingaz.com/evacuees.asp.; Oregon Office of the Governor, "Questions and Answers on Relief Efforts," http://governor.oregon.gov/Gov/hurricane_qa.shtml. The Governor of Louisiana and her staff also made direct requests to States. See Louisiana Office of the Governor, *Response to U.S Senate Committee on Homeland Security and Governmental Affairs Document and Information Request Dated October 7, 2005 and to the U.S House of Representatives Select Committee to Investigate the Preparation for and Response to Hurricane Katrina* (Baton Rouge, December 2, 2005), 9-10.

[93] Louisiana Office of the Governor, *Response to U.S Senate Committee on Homeland Security and Governmental Affairs Document and Information Request Dated October 7, 2005 and to the U.S House of Representatives Select Committee to Investigate the Preparation for and Response to Hurricane Katrina* (Baton Rouge, December 2, 2005), 10.

[94] The provision of buses occurred through ESF-1, which is led by the Department of Transportation. Vincent Pearce, National Response Program Manager for the Department of Transportation, written statement submitted for a hearing on Hurricane Katrina: Managing the Crisis and Evacuating New Orleans, on February 1, 2006, to the Senate Homeland Security and Governmental Affairs Committee; and U.S. Department of Transportation, "Actions for Hurricane Katrina: Annotated Chronology of Significant Events," October 6, 2005, 4.

[95] FEMA directly requested that several States receive and house evacuees. For examples, see Arizona Department of Housing, "Arizona to Accept Evacuees from Gulf Coast," news release, n.d., ca. 2005, http://www.housingaz.com/evacuees.asp.; and Oregon Office of the Governor, "Questions and Answers on Relief Efforts," http://governor.oregon.gov/Gov/hurricane_qa.shtml. In other cases, such requests were made by one State's governor to another. For example, see District of Columbia Office of the Mayor, "Mayor Williams Announces Airlift of Several Hundred Hurricane Evacuees to DC Armory," news release, September 5, 2005, http://dc.gov/mayor/news/release.asp?id=758&mon=200509; and New York Office of the Governor, "Governor: NY Stands Ready to Welcome Hurricane Katrina Evacuees, news release, September 7, 2005, http://www.ny.gov/governor/press/05/sep7_05.htm.

[96] I-10 is a major interstate cutting east-west through New Orleans. Near the Superdome, I-10 features an elevated four-way interchange, called a cloverleaf due to its distinctive shape. Evacuees gathered atop this interchange to escape Hurricane Katrina's floodwaters. Brigadier General Mark A. Graham, Deputy Commanding General, Fifth U.S. Army, written statement for a hearing on Hurricane Katrina: Managing the Crisis and Evacuating New Orleans, on February 1, 2006, submitted to the Senate Homeland Security and Government Affairs Committee, 109th Congress, 2nd session, 2, 3-4; and William Lokey, Federal Coordinating Officer for Louisiana, written statement for a hearing on Hurricane Katrina: Preparedness and Response by the State of Louisiana, on December 14, 2005, submitted to the House Select Committee to Investigate the Preparation for and Response to Hurricane Katrina, 109th Congress, 1st session, 5, 7, 92.

[97] Louisiana Office of the Governor, *Response to U.S Senate Committee on Homeland Security and Governmental Affairs Document and Information Request Dated October 7, 2005 and to the U.S House of Representatives Select Committee to Investigate the Preparation for and Response to Hurricane Katrina* (Baton Rouge, December 2, 2005), 10.

[98] Louisiana National Guard, Task Force Pelican, "Hurricane Katrina: Overview of Significant Events," November 28, 2005, 23, 24. Ray Nagin, Mayor of New Orleans, written statement for a hearing on Hurricane Katrina: Preparedness and Response by the State of Louisiana, on December 14, 2005, submitted to the House Select Committee to Investigate the Preparation for and Response to Hurricane Katrina, 109th Congress, 1st session.

[99] Louisiana National Guard, Task Force Pelican, "Hurricane Katrina: Overview of Significant Events," November 28, 2005, 23.

[100] Louisiana National Guard, Task Force Pelican, "Hurricane Katrina: Overview of Significant Events," November 28, 2005, 23; Ray Nagin, Mayor of New Orleans, written statement for a hearing on Managing the Crisis: Evacuating New Orleans, on February 1, 2006, submitted to the Senate Homeland Security and Governmental Affairs Committee, 109th Congress, 2nd session; and Louisiana Office of the Governor, *Response to U.S Senate Committee on Homeland Security and Governmental Affairs Document and Information Request Dated October 7, 2005 and to the U.S House of Representatives Select Committee to Investigate the Preparation for and Response to Hurricane Katrina* (Baton Rouge, December 2, 2005), 10.

[101] Louisiana Office of the Governor, *Response to U.S Senate Committee on Homeland Security and Governmental Affairs Document and Information Request Dated October 7, 2005 and to the U.S House of Representatives Select Committee to Investigate the Preparation for and Response to Hurricane Katrina* (Baton Rouge, December 2, 2005), 11. Also see Kathleen Blanco, written statement for a hearing on Hurricane Katrina: Preparedness and Response by the State of Louisiana, on December 14, 2005, submitted to the House Select Committee to Investigate the Preparation for and Response to Hurricane Katrina, 109th Congress, 1st session, 68.

[102] "The buses that the city of New Orleans controls are basically Regional Transit Authority. And those buses were always staged, or has been staged in an area that has been high and dry throughout every storm that has ever hit the city of New Orleans. And we expected the same for this event. Unfortunately, those buses flooded also because 80 percent of the city went underwater." Ray Nagin, Mayor of New Orleans, written statement for a hearing on Hurricane Katrina: Preparedness and Response by the State of Louisiana, on December 14, 2005, submitted to the House Select Committee to Investigate the Preparation for and Response to Hurricane Katrina, 109th Congress, 1st session, 99.

[103] Louisiana Office of the Governor, *Response to U.S Senate Committee on Homeland Security and Governmental Affairs Document and Information Request Dated October 7, 2005 and to the U.S House of Representatives Select Committee to Investigate the Preparation for and Response to Hurricane Katrina* (Baton Rouge, December 2, 2005), 11.

[104] "About 20,000 people were in the dome when efforts began, and that number swelled as people poured in to get a ride out of town, Capt. John Pollard said." The Associated Press, "Superdome Evacuation Completed," September 3, 2005. http://www.msnbc.msn.com/id/9175611/

[105] Medical evacuations from the Convention Center began on September 2, as well. U.S. Department of Homeland Security, "Hurricane Katrina DHS SITREP #14," September 2, 2005, 1; and Louisiana National Guard, Task Force Pelican, "Hurricane Katrina: Overview of Significant Events," November 28, 2005, 23-24. Louisiana National Guard, Task Force Pelican, "Hurricane Katrina: Overview of Significant Events," November 28, 2005, 23-24. U.S. Department of Homeland Security, "Hurricane Katrina DHS SITREP #16," September 3, 2005, 1.

[106] U.S. Department of Homeland Security, "Hurricane Katrina DHS SITREP #17," September 3, 2005, 1.

[107] U.S. Department of Homeland Security, "Hurricane Katrina DHS SITREP #16," September 3, 2005, 1.

[108] U.S. Department of Homeland Security, "Hurricane Katrina DHS SITREP #18," September 4, 2005, 1.

[109] The next three largest U.S. domestic airlifts were: Hurricane Andrew in 1992 (13,500 people), the Mariel Boatlift (12,000 people by helicopter), and Hurricane Rita (9,000 people). U.S. Department of Transportation, "Largest Airlift in U.S. History to Get Over 10,000 People Out of New Orleans by End of Today," news release, September 3, 2005, http://www.dot.gov/affairs/dot12005.htm; National Museum of the U.S. Air Force, "Year by Year Events: 1990-1997," http://www.pafb.af.mil/museum/50th/event90.htm.

[110] In addition, the U.S. Army provided ground support at the airport, including physically assisting in loading passengers up airplane stairs and into aircraft. See also U.S. Department of Transportation, "Hurricane Katrina – Situation Report Fifteen," September 3, 2005, 2; U.S. Department of Homeland Security, "Hurricane Katrina DHS SITREP #14," September 2, 2005 ("Coordinated major airlift of evacuees to begin 8:00 AM CDT, September 2, 2005. Evacuees will depart New Orleans Superdome by bus, and be flown at a rate of 4-5 planes per hour from New Orleans Airport to Lackland Air Force Base, TX for reception and housing at Kelly AFB"); U.S. Department of Transportation, *In re: Foreign Air Carriers: Facilitation of Air Services in Support of Hurricane Katrina Relief Efforts,* Docket OST-2005-22395 (September 2, 2005), 3; and James C. May, President and Chief Executive Officer of Air Transport Association of America, testimony before a hearing on Review of the Impact of Hurricane Katrina on the Aviation Industry, on September 14, 2005, Senate Committee on Commerce, Science, and Transportation, Subcommittee on Aviation, 109th Congress, 1st session, 8.

[111] U.S. Department of Homeland Security, Federal Emergency Management Agency, "FEMA VIP Briefing," slide presentation, September 2, 2005.

[112] U.S. Department of Defense, "Hurricane Katrina Update," September 8, 2005, 4; U.S. Department of Homeland Security, Federal Emergency Management Agency, Region VI Regional Response Coordinating Center, "SITREP #10," September 4, 2005, 1; and Bryon Okada, "Screeners kept flights moving," *Dallas Fort-Worth Star Telegram*, September 12, 2005, as reprinted by the Transportation Security Administration, *What Others Are Saying About TSA,* http://www.tsa.gov/public/display?theme=204&content=090005198016ab96.

[113] The Department of Transportation had arranged for Amtrak to transport evacuees from New Orleans to Lafayette on a twice-daily run. The trains had enough food and water to sustain the passengers during the two to four hour ride. The first Amtrak train arrived at Avondale Station in New Orleans at 4:30 AM on September 3. The train could have accommodated 600 passengers, but only ninety-six were at the station because of a bus problem in New Orleans. See U.S. Department of Transportation, "Hurricane Katrina – Situation Report Fifteen," September 3, 2005, 10. In contrast, however, see Ray Nagin, Mayor of New Orleans, testimony before a hearing on Hurricane Katrina: Managing the Crisis and Evacuating New Orleans, on February 1, 2006, Senate Homeland Security and Governmental Affairs Committee, 109th Congress, 2nd session.

[114] CNN, "Rita Now a Monster Category-Five Storm," transcript, September 22, 2005. http://transcripts.cnn.com/TRANSCRIPTS/0509/22/lad.04.html

[115] For examples, see Mississippi Emergency Management Agency, "Hurricane Katrina Situation Report 24," September 1, 2005, 11; For examples of media reports on the looting, see Walt Philbin, "Widespread looting hits abandoned businesses; Lack of police after storm leaves stores vulnerable," *New Orleans Times-Picayune*, August 30, 2005; "Katrina kills 50 in one Mississippi county," *CNN.com*, August 30, 2005, http://www.cnn.com/2005/WEATHER/08/29/hurricane.katrina.

[116] In one notable example, on August 30, a New Orleans Police officer was shot in the head by looters. See Louisiana State Police, "Hurricane Katrina Timeline of Events," n.d., ca. 2005, 8. Also in New Orleans, a man was arrested by Federal agents for firing at a U.S. military helicopter on a search and rescue mission. U.S. Attorney's Office for the Eastern District of Louisiana, news release, October 8, 2005. The reported target of the gunfire was a U.S. military helicopter on a search and rescue mission. While the gunfire did not hit the helicopter, the incident was widely reported and contributed to the perception of lawlessness in New Orleans. See, e.g., "ATF Makes First Federal Arrest in New Orleans," *US Fed News,* September 6, 2005; "US authorities arrest New Orleans man accused of firing on helicopter," *Agence France Presse,* September 7, 2005; "Federal agents start post-storm arrests; Algiers man accused of shooting at copter," *New Orleans Times-Picayune,* September 7, 2005.

[117] For examples, see U.S. Department of Homeland Security, "Hurricane Katrina DHS SITREP #7," August 29, 2005, 5; U.S. Department of Homeland Security, "Hurricane Katrina DHS SITREP #11," August 31, 2005, 4. Additionally, without functioning jails in New Orleans, law enforcement officers initially had no choice but to release those that they arrested for minor crimes.

[118] Reports on general lawlessness in New Orleans, were later found to be embellished or completely false. Brian Thevenot and Gordon Russel, "Rape. Murder. Gunfights," *New Orleans Times-Picayune*, September 26, 2005; Robert E. Pierre and Ann Gerhart, "News of Pandemonium May Have Slowed Aid," *Washington Post*, October 5, 2005; and Michelle Roberts, "Reports of rape, murder at Katrina shelters were probably exaggerated, officials now say," Associated Press, September 27, 2005.

[119] U.S. Department of Homeland Security, Federal Emergency Management Agency, "Hurricane Katrina Response Brief," September 1, 2005. The brief reported that security and lawlessness were becoming a "very critical concern" and were hindering relief efforts. See also U.S. Department of Homeland Security, Federal Emergency Management Agency, "VIP Katrina Briefing," slide presentation, September 1, 2005.

[120] U.S. Department of Homeland Security, Coast Guard District Eight, internal message from August 31, 2005; U.S. Department of Homeland Security, Homeland Security Operations Center, "HSOC SPOT REP #53," September 1, 2005; and U.S. Department of Homeland Security, "Hurricane Katrina DHS SITREP #13," September 1, 2005.

[121] U.S. Department of Homeland Security, Federal Emergency Management Agency, Region VI Regional Response Coordination Center, "1603-DR-LA SitRep #7," September 1, 2005; U.S. Department of Homeland Security, "Hurricane Katrina DHS SITREP #13," September 13, 2005; and U.S. Department of Defense, "CJCS Katrina Update," draft, September 6, 2005.

[122] U.S. Department of Health and Human Services, "Secretary's Operations Center Flash Report #10 – Hurricane Katrina," September 1, 2005; and U.S. Department of Health and Human Services, "Secretary's Operations Center Flash Report #12 – Hurricane Katrina," September 2, 2005.

[123] U.S. Department of Homeland Security, "Hurricane Katrina DHS SITREP #15," September 2, 2005; U.S. Department of Homeland Security, "Hurricane Katrina DHS SITREP #19," September 4, 2005; U.S. Department of Homeland Security, "Hurricane Katrina DHS SITREP #18," September 4, 2005; U.S. Department of Homeland Security, "Hurricane Katrina DHS SITREP #29," September 9, 2005.

[124] U.S. Department of Homeland Security, "Hurricane Katrina DHS SITREP #13," September 1, 2005, 4, 10, 12; U.S. Department of Homeland Security, "Hurricane Katrina DHS SITREP #15," September 2, 2005, 5, 13, 14; U.S. Department of Homeland Security, "Hurricane Katrina DHS SITREP #16," September 3, 2005, 10; U.S. Department of Homeland Security, "Hurricane Katrina DHS SITREP #18," September 4, 2005, 1; U.S. Department of Homeland Security, "Hurricane Katrina DHS SITREP #19," September 4, 2005, 11; U.S. Department of Homeland Security, "Hurricane Katrina DHS SITREP #21," September 5, 2005, 11; U.S. Department of Homeland Security, "Hurricane Katrina DHS SITREP #22," September 6, 2005, 9.

[125] The Department of Homeland Security's law enforcement response began on August 29, when Immigration and Customs Enforcement (ICE) deployed officers from the Federal Protective Service to protect critical Federal facilities and to assist FEMA where needed. From August 30 to September 1, DHS deployed additional ICE personnel to the region to perform public safety and security missions. The U.S. Coast Guard also deployed personnel to conduct security and law enforcement missions. By August 30, Customs & Border Protection (CBP) deployed a site survey team and Special Operations Division agents to the hurricane area; CBP air and maritime assets also joined in conducting law enforcement operations. On August 31, the Secret Service deployed personnel to implement its Continuity of Operations Plan (COOP) and Restoration of Operations, Personnel and Equipment (ROPE) mission assignments.

On September 1, the Office of the Attorney General directed ATF, DEA, FBI, and the U.S. Marshals Service to identify personnel, assets, and other resource for immediate deployment to areas impacted by Hurricane Katrina. On September 2, having received the inventory of assets and personnel available for deployment, the Attorney General issued a memorandum to the same agencies directing the Federal Bureau of Investigation to continue to deploy agents (including SWAT agents) and tactical assets (including helicopters, boats, and technical/communications assets) to the affected area; the Drug Enforcement Administration to prepare to deploy Mobile Enforcement Teams, special agents, and tactical assets (including helicopters and other aircraft) to the affected area; the Bureau of Alcohol, Tobacco, Firearms, and Explosives to establish a Violent Crime Impact Team (VCIT) in Baton Rouge, Louisiana, with related VCIT personnel and assets, to address any rise in criminal activity in that city; and the United States Marshals Service to continue to deploy Deputy U.S. Marshals and Court Security Officers to conduct prisoner transport operations and provide additional court security and to prepare to utilize the Justice Prisoner and Alien Transportation (JPATS) to deploy law enforcement personnel to airports around the country as needed.

[126] In the first week following Hurricane Katrina's landfall, DHS and DOJ deployed the following numbers of law enforcement personnel to New Orleans to assist in restoring order. Other departments contributed significant numbers of law enforcement personnel as well.

Date	DHS	DOJ
Aug 29	66	268
Aug 30	74	292
Aug 31	196	326
Sep 1	162	443
Sep 2	381	547
Sep 3	1033	645
Sep 4	1230	690

[127] 42 U.S.C. § 10501 *et seq.* See also letter from Governor Kathleen Babineaux Blanco to Attorney General Alberto Gonzales, dated September 3, 2005 [letter is dated September 3, 2005, but was received via facsimile on the following day]; letter from Attorney General Gonzales to Governor Blanco, dated September 4, 2005 (approving request); letter from Governor Blanco to Attorney General Gonzales and Secretary Chertoff, dated September 6, 2005 (requesting additional support); letter from Attorney General Gonzales to Governor Blanco, dated September 7, 2005 (approving request); letter from Secretary Chertoff to Governor Blanco, dated September 7, 2005

(approving request). Governor Barbour of Mississippi made a similar request on September 3, which was granted pursuant to an order by the Attorney General on that date.

[128] DHS deployed law enforcement officers from Customs and Border Protection, the Federal Air Marshals Service, the Federal Protective Service, and Immigration and Customs Enforcement. DOJ deployed officers from the Bureau of Alcohol, Tobacco, Firearms, and Explosives, the Drug Enforcement Agency, the Federal Bureau of Investigation, and the U.S. Marshals Service. U.S. Department of Homeland Security, "Hurricane Katrina DHS SITREP #21," September 5, 2005.

[129] By September 8, the Department of Interior deployed 175 law enforcement officers from the U.S. Fish and Wildlife Service, the National Park Service, the Bureau of Indian Affairs, and the Tribal Police. The Department of the Treasury and the Department of Veteran Affairs deployed thirty-four and thirty-three law enforcement officers, respectively. The Environmental Protection Agency sent seventeen officers to the region, and the U.S. Postal Inspection Service deployed a total of 117 law enforcement personnel. U.S. Department of Homeland Security, "Federal Law Enforcement Deployed to Region," September 8, 2005. In addition, USDA's Forest Service deployed approximately 300-350 law enforcement officers to the affected area as members of ESF-4 Incident Management Teams. Eventually, over 3,500 Federal law enforcement officers were deployed to the region.

[130] In Louisiana, for example, a State Police attorney had to physically be present to swear in Federal agents. Additionally, law enforcement personnel from the Department of the Interior (DOI) had to be sworn in as Deputy U.S. Marshals to give them Federal law enforcement authority beyond their statutory DOI jurisdiction.

[131] For additional information on the disarray of the New Orleans criminal justice system in Hurricane Katrina's aftermath, see Melinda Deslatte, "Prisons in New Orleans empty as temporary booking facility up and running," Associated Press, September 3, 2005; Ann Woolner, "A Legal System in Chaos: New Orleans Struggles," Fulton County Daily Report, October 4, 2005; and Chuck Crumbo, "Evacuation leaves Louisiana prison system in chaos," The State (Columbia, SC), October 5, 2005.

[132] On September 3, the Associated Press reported that "computer logs still hadn't been retrieved from the criminal district court in New Orleans…[and] tracking down witnesses, finding court records and trial transcripts and organizing a temporary court" would remain challenges to the reestablishment of the city's criminal justice system. Melinda Deslatte, "Prisons in New Orleans empty as temporary booking facility up and running," Associated Press, September 3, 2005; Ann Woolner, "A Legal System in Chaos: New Orleans Struggles," Fulton County Daily Report, October 4, 2005; and Chuck Crumbo, "Evacuation leaves Louisiana prison system in chaos," The State (Columbia, SC), October 5, 2005. Both State and Federal courts closed their doors. Supreme Court of Louisiana, Order by Justice Catherine D. Kimball, September 2, 2005, Baton Rouge, Louisiana; Supreme Court of Mississippi, Order by Justice James W. Smith, Jr., September 7, 2005; U.S. District Court for the Eastern District of Louisiana, Order by Chief Judge Helen G. Berrigan, September 4, 2005, accessed from http://katrinalaw.org/dokuphp?id=louisiana_eastern_district_court on February 17, 2006; U.S. Bankruptcy Court for the Eastern District of Louisiana, September 2, 2005, accessed from http://katrinalaw.org/dokuphp?id=louisiana_eastern_bankruptcy_court on February 17, 2006; Fourth Circuit Court of Appeal, State of Louisiana, Order by Justice Max N. Tobias, Jr., September 2, 2005, accesed from http://katrinalaw.org/dokuphp?id=fourth_circuit_court_of_appeal on February 17, 2006; Fifth Circuit Court of Appeal, State of Louisiana, Order by Justice Walter J. Rothschild, September 2, 2005, accessed from: http://katrinalaw.org/dokuphp?id= fifth_circuit_court_of_appeal, accessed on February 17, 2006; Civil District Court, Parish of Orleans, State of Louisiana, Order by Chief Justice Robin M. Giarrusso, September 2, 2005, accessed from http://katrinalaw.org/dokuphp?id= orleans_parish_civil_district_court, accessed on February 17, 2006.

[133] The DOJ's Bureau of Prisons moved or facilitated movement of a large number of prisoners incarcerated in Louisiana facilities during the first week of the disaster. The Bureau noted that no major difficulties or issues were encountered during the actual transport of the prisoners, though both the Bureau and the U.S. Marshals Service noted flaws in the decision making process and a general failure on the part of State and local prison authorities to be proactive in evacuating their incarcerated populations.

[134] Scott Wells, Deputy Federal Coordinating Officer for Louisiana, written statement for a hearing on Hurricane Katrina: Perspectives of FEMA's Operations Professionals, on December 8, 2005, submitted to the Senate Committee on Homeland Security and Governmental Affairs, 109th Congress, 1st session.

[135] Michael Chertoff, Secretary of the Department of Homeland Security, memorandum for distribution entitled "Designation of Principal Federal Official for Hurricane Katrina," August 30, 2005, 1.

An INS was arguably in effect since President Bush earlier issued his Emergency Declarations and Major Disaster Declarations. See the *National Preparedness—A Primer* chapter for a detailed discussion of this issue, as well as U.S. Government Accountability Office, *Preliminary Observations on Hurricane Response* (Washington, DC, February 2006, 4).

[136] Though Secretary Chertoff subsequently testified that Director Brown had the authority to manage the incident even prior to his formal designation as PFO, "…when he went down on Sunday it was with the understanding that he was going to manage this thing as the battlefield commander, you know, with the authority he had as the director of FEMA, which put him in supervisory authority over the federal coordinating officers." Secretary Chertoff added, "When I actually formally designated him the PFO, it was essentially formalizing something that had occurred in practice." Michael Chertoff, testimony before a hearing on "Hurricane Katrina: The Role of the Department of Homeland Security," on October 19, 2005, House Select Committee to Investigate the Preparation for and Response to Hurricane Katrina, 109th Congress, 1st session.

[137] U.S. Department of Homeland Security, *National Response Plan* (Washington, D.C., December 2004), 33.

[138] According to the NRP, the FCO is "The Federal officer who is appointed to manage Federal resource support activities related to Stafford Act disasters and emergencies. The FCO is responsible for coordinating the timely delivery of Federal disaster assistance resources and programs to the affected State and local governments, individual victims, and the private sector." *National Response Plan*, p. 65.

[139] "[Director Brown] was going to manage this thing as the battlefield commander, you know, with the authority he had as the director of FEMA, which put him in supervisory authority over the federal coordinating officers." Michael Chertoff, testimony before a hearing on Hurricane Katrina: The Role of the Department of Homeland Security, on October 19, 2005, House Select Committee to Investigate the Preparation for and Response to Hurricane Katrina, 109th Congress, 1st session. See also *Robert T. Stafford Disaster Relief and Emergency Assistance Act ["Stafford Act"]*, as amended by Public Law 106-390 (October 30, 2000).

[140] Colonel Jeff Smith, Deputy Director of the Louisiana Office of Homeland Security and Emergency Preparedness, written statement for a hearing on Hurricane Katrina: Preparedness and Response by the State of Louisiana, on December 14, 2005, submitted to the House Select Committee to Investigate the Preparation and Response to Hurricane Katrina, 109th Congress, 1st session.

[141] A virtual National JIC "links all participants through technological means (secure or nonsecure) when geographical restrictions, incident management requirements, and other limitations preclude physical attendance by public affairs leadership at a central location." U.S. Department of Homeland Security, *National Response Plan* (Washington, D.C., December 2004), PUB-3.

[142] U.S. Department of Homeland Security, *National Response Plan* (Washington, D.C., December 2004), 28.

[143] Some of this lack of planning can be attributed to the failure to finalize the JFO Standing Operating Procedures prior to Katrina, as required by the National Response Plan.

[144] U.S. Department of Homeland Security, "Hurricane Katrina DHS Sitrep #20," September 5, 2005, 1; U.S. Department of Homeland Security, "Hurricane Katrina DHS Sitrep #23," September 6, 2005, 1; U.S. Department of Homeland Security, Federal Emergency Management Agency, Daily Conference Call on Hurricane Katrina, September 7, 2005, 1; U.S. Department of Homeland Security, "Hurricane Katrina DHS Sitrep #27," September 8, 2005, 1; U.S. Department of Homeland Security, Federal Emergency Management Agency, "Region VI Regional Response Coordinating Center Sitrep #15," September 9, 2005, 1; U.S. Department of Homeland Security, "Hurricane Katrina DHS Sitrep #20," September 5, 2005, 1; U.S. Department of Health and Human Services, "Secretary's Operations Center Flash Report #32—Hurricane Katrina," September 12, 2005, 2, 3; U.S. Department of Health and Human Services, "Secretary's Operations Center Flash Report #32—Hurricane Katrina," September 12, 2005, 2; U.S. Department of Homeland Security, "Emergency Response Issues," September 11, 2005, 10; Robert B. Stephan, Assistant Secretary for Infrastructure Protection, U.S. Department of Homeland Security, prepared statement for a hearing on "Hurricane Katrina: The Roles of DHS and FEMA Leadership," on February 10, 2006, submitted to the Committee on Homeland Security and Governmental Affairs, U.S. Senate, 109th Congress, 2nd session, pgs. 7-8.

[145] Federal officials recognized the need for a presence in New Orleans to effectively coordinate the efforts to stabilize the City, so a "forward PFO" in New Orleans was eventually established. The JFO remained in Baton Rouge.

[146] Although the JFO in Baton Rouge was located in close proximity to the Louisiana State Emergency Operations Center, the vast majority of the response operations in the early stages of the incident occurred in the greater New Orleans area. It quickly became apparent that the JFO was too far away to coordinate operational activities in New

Orleans. For this reason, the Law Enforcement Coordination Center (LECC) was initially established in Baton Rouge and then moved to New Orleans to coordinate law enforcement activities. The Department of Defense (DOD) set up its Katrina Task Force HQ in Mississippi. New Orleans officials established the New Orleans Emergency Operations Center downtown, with no connectivity to the JFO.

[147] U.S. Department of Defense, National Guard Bureau, Office of Legislative Liaison, "National Guard Status Comparison Chart," n.d., http://www.ngb.army.mil/ll/statuscomparison.asp. State active duty and Title 32 forces are not subject to *posse comitatus* restrictions, see 18 U.S.C. § 1385 (Military forces generally may not perform domestic law enforcement), which bar Federal military forces from enforcing civil law. Thus, while serving in State active duty status or Title 32 status (which allows for Federal pay while under state command and control), the Army National Guard and the Air National Guard can directly assist civil authorities in maintaining peace and order. Lieutenant General Steven H. Blum, "A Vision for the National Guard," *Joint Force Quarterly*, December 2004, 36.

[148] U.S. Department of Defense, Under Secretary of Defense for Policy, *Manual 3025.1-M, Manual for Civil Emergencies* (Washington, D.C., June 1994), para. C2.2. Active duty forces are authorized to perform critical functions such as rescue, evacuation, and emergency treatment of casualties; emergency restoration of power; debris removal; food distribution; roadway control, and emergency communications.

[149] Chairman of the Joint Chiefs of Staff, Execution Order, August 30, 2005.

[150] JTF-Katrina was established at Camp Shelby on August 28 and activated three days later on August 31. It served as U.S. Northern Command's forward joint command element for integrating the military component of the Federal response.

[151] Donald H. Rumsfeld, Secretary of the Department of Defense, and General Richard Myers, Chairman of the Joint Chiefs of Staff, "Defense Department Operational Update Briefing," Tuesday, September 6, 2005. http://www.defenselink.mil/news/Sep2005/d20050906slide.pdf

[152] Department of Defense, *DOD Support to Hurricane Katrina, Executive Summary OASD(HD)*, September 5, 2005.

[153] "DOD aircraft have flown mosquito abatement aerial spraying missions covering more than two million acres." Paul McHale, Assistant Secretary of Defense for Homeland Defense, written statement for a hearing on Responding to Catastrophic Events: The Role of the Military and National Guard in Disaster Response, on November 9, 2005, submitted to the House Committee on Armed Services, Subcommittee on Terrorism, Unconventional Threats, and Capabilities jointly with the House Committee on Homeland Security, Subcommittee on Emergency Preparedness, Science, and Technology, 109th Congress, 1st session.

[154] U.S. Department of Defense, National Guard Bureau, "After Action Review: Hurricane Response September 2005," December 21, 2005, 6.

[155] U.S. Department of Defense, National Guard Bureau, "After Action Review: Hurricane Response September 2005," December 21, 2005, 14.

[156] U.S. Department of Defense, National Guard Bureau, "After Action Review: Hurricane Response September 2005," December 21, 2005.

[157] U.S. Department of Defense, National Guard Bureau, "After Action Review: Hurricane Response September 2005," December 21, 2005, 57.

[158] President George W. Bush, "President Discusses Progress in War on Terror to National Guard," February 9, 2006.

[159] U.S. Department of Defense, National Guard Bureau, "After Action Review: Hurricane Response September 2005," December 21, 2005, 57.

[160] U.S. Department of Defense, National Guard Bureau, "After Action Review: Hurricane Response September 2005," December 21, 2005, 20; Lieutenant General H. Steven Blum, Chief of the National Guard Bureau, written statement submitted for a hearing on Responding to Catastrophic Events: The Role of the Military and National Guard in Disaster Response, on October 20, 2005, for the House Committee on Government Reform, 109th Congress, 1st session.

[161] 16,599 National Guard forces were deployed in 1989-90 following the San Francisco Loma Prieta earthquake. U.S. Department of Defense, National Guard Bureau, "After Action Review: Hurricane Response September 2005," December 21, 2005.

[162] U.S. Department of Defense, Office of the Assistant Secretary of Defense for Homeland Defense, "DoD Support to Hurricane Katrina, OASD(HD) Executive Summary," September 5, 2005; U.S. Department of Defense, National Guard Bureau, "After Action Review: Hurricane Response September 2005," NGB J7, December 21, 2005; Lieutenant General H. Steven Blum, testimony on Hurricane Katrina: Preparedness and Response by the

Department of Defense, the Coast Guard, and the National Guard of Louisiana, Mississippi, and Alabama, before the House Bipartisan Select Committee on Hurricane Katrina, United States House of Representatives, 109th Congress,1st Session, October 27, 2005.

[163] U.S. Department of Defense, National Guard Bureau, "After Action Review: Hurricane Response September 2005," NGB J7, December 21, 2005, 146.

[164] U.S. Department of Defense, National Guard Bureau, "After Action Review: Hurricane Response September 2005," NGB J7, December 21, 2005, 6.

[165] Paul McHale, Assistant Secretary of Defense for Homeland Defense, testimony before a hearing on Responding to Catastrophic Events: The Role of the Military and National Guard in Disaster Response, on November 9, 2005, Emergency Preparedness, Science, and Technology Subcommittee, House Homeland Security Committee, 109th Congress, 1st session, 14. According to Assistant Secretary McHale, a police officer is likely to be carrying a handheld Motorola while an active duty military officer is likely to use a secure SINCGARS radio; these two radios cannot easily talk to one another.

[166] The two deployed MERS detachments were the Region IV detachment from Thomasville, Georgia and the Region VI detachment from Denton, Texas. U.S. Department of Homeland Security, Federal Emergency Management Agency, "FEMA National Situation Report," August 29, 2005, 3; and Michael Brown, former Director of the Federal Emergency Management Agency, testimony before a hearing on Hurricane Katrina: The Role of the Federal Emergency Management Agency, on September 27, 2005, House Select Bipartisan Committee to Investigate the Preparation for and Response to Hurricane Katrina, 109th Congress, 1st session.

Each MERS detachment has a suite of assets that were also deployed to Florida, Georgia, and Texas. U.S. Department of Homeland Security, Federal Emergency Management Agency, "FEMA National Situation Report," August 29, 2005, 3.

[167] U.S. Department of Homeland Security, *National Response Plan* (Washington, D.C., December 2004), ESF #15-5.

[168] U.S. Department of Homeland Security, Federal Emergency Management Agency, "Response and Recovery: Available Support," October 23, 2004, http://www.fema.gov/rrr/mers02.shtm.

[169] Rear Admiral Joe Kilkenny, Joint Force Maritime Component Commander and Commander of Carrier Strike Group Ten, U.S. Fleet Forces, Joint Task Force Katrina, *Hurricanes Katrina and Rita: Providing Rescue and Civil Support Relief from the Sea, Air, and Land,* (November 1, 2005). The DJC2 is a standardized, integrated, rapidly deployable, modular, scaleable, command and control (C2) capability that provides a military commander with a planning, operating, and collaborating capability. Lt. Col. Roarke Anderson, JS J6, *Deployable Joint Command and Control (DJC2): DJC2 Program Overview,* (n.d.), 2.

[170] U.S. Department of Defense, Office of the Assistant Secretary of Defense, "Defense Department Briefing on DoD Response to Hurricane Katrina," news release on briefing by Lieutenant General H. Steven Blum, August 31, 2005.

[171] The National Coordinating Center (NCC) for Telecommunications is defined in the NRP as "A joint telecommunications industry–Federal Government operation established to assist in the initiation, coordination, restoration, and reconstitution of [National Security/Emergency Preparedness] telecommunications services and facilities." U.S. Department of Homeland Security, *National Response Plan* (Washington, D.C., December 2004), 69. For a discussion on NCC, see Dr. Peter M. Fonash, Deputy Manager of the National Communications System, Preparedness Directorate, U.S. Department of Homeland Security, written statement for a hearing on Ensuring Operability during Catastrophic Events, on October 26, 2005, submitted to the House Committee on Homeland Security, Subcommittee on Emergency Preparedness, Science and Technology, 109th Congress, 1st session, 2.

[172] Dr. Peter M. Fonash, Deputy Manager of the National Communications System, Preparedness Directorate, U.S. Department of Homeland Security, written statement for a hearing on Ensuring Operability during Catastrophic Events, on October 26, 2005, submitted to the House Committee on Homeland Security, Subcommittee on Emergency Preparedness, Science and Technology, 109th Congress, 1st session.

[173] Dr. Peter M. Fonash, Deputy Manager of the National Communications System, Preparedness Directorate, U.S. Department of Homeland Security, written statement for a hearing on Ensuring Operability during Catastrophic Events, on October 26, 2005, submitted to the House Committee on Homeland Security, Subcommittee on Emergency Preparedness, Science and Technology, 109th Congress, 1st session; and Chad Hart, *A Research Note On: Land Mobile Radio and Public Safety Communications*, prepared for the Venture Development Corporation, Datacom and Telecom Practice (Natick, MA, November 2005), http://www.vdc-corp.com/telecom/research/05_lmr_rn.pdf.

[174] U.S. Department of Homeland Security, "Hurricane Katrina DHS SITREP #13," September 1, 2005.

[175] U.S. Department of Homeland Security, "Hurricane Katrina DHS SITREP #21," September 5, 2005.

[176] For examples, see Ardis D. Hoven, Member of the American Medical Association Board of Trustees, testimony before a hearing on Assessing Public Health and the Delivery of Care in the Wake of Katrina, on September 22, 2005, House Energy and Commerce Committee, Subcommittees on Health and Oversight and Investigations, 109th Congress, 1st session, 3; and Robert Latham, Director, Mississippi Emergency Management Agency, testimony before a hearing on Hurricane Katrina: Preparedness and Response by the State of Mississippi, on December 7, 2005, House Select Bipartisan Committee to Investigate the Preparation for and Response to Hurricane Katrina, 109th Congress, 1st session.

[177] William Lokey, Federal Coordinating Officer for Louisiana, written statement for a hearing on Hurricane Katrina: Preparedness and Response by the State of Louisiana, on December 14, 2005, submitted to the House Select Committee to Investigate the Preparation for and Response to Hurricane Katrina, 109th Congress, 1st session, 51.

[178] In an interview with CNN, FEMA Director Michael Brown stated "we've got enough people and commodities in place right now for a three to five day surge capacity. But what I've ordered my folks to do is to jam that supply line as far back as Fort Worth and as far back as Atlanta so as those supplies begin to run out, we can continue to feed those in here as long as it takes." "Hurricane Katrina," *CNN Breaking News*, August 29, 2005.

[179] Michael Brown, former Director of the Federal Emergency Management Agency, testimony before a hearing on Hurricane Katrina: The Role of the Federal Emergency Management Agency, on September 27, 2005, House Select Committee to Investigate the Preparation for and Response to Hurricane Katrina, 109th Congress, 1st session, 49-50.

[180] Congressman Tom Davis (R-VA), written opening statement for a hearing on Hurricane Katrina: Preparedness and Response by the State of Mississippi, on December 7, 2005, House Select Bipartisan Committee to Investigate the Preparation for and Response to Hurricane Katrina, 109th Congress, 1st session; and William Carwile, Federal Coordinating Officer for Mississippi, testimony before a hearing on Hurricane Katrina: Preparedness and Response by the State of Mississippi, on December 7, 2005, House Select Bipartisan Committee to Investigate the Preparation for and Response to Hurricane Katrina, 109th Congress, 1st session.

[181] William Carwile, Federal Coordinating Officer for Mississippi, testimony before a hearing on Hurricane Katrina: Preparedness and Response by the State of Mississippi, on December 7, 2005, House Select Committee to Investigate the Preparation for and Response to Hurricane Katrina, 109th Congress, 1st session, 45.

[182] Tommy Longo, Mayor of Waveland, Mississippi, testimony before a hearing on Hurricane Katrina: Preparedness and Response by the State of Mississippi, on December 7, 2005, House Select Bipartisan Committee to Investigate the Preparation for and Response to Hurricane Katrina, 109th Congress, 1st session, 51; and Ray Nagin, Mayor of New Orleans, written statement for a hearing on Hurricane Katrina: Managing the Crisis and Evacuating New Orleans, on February 1, 2006, submitted to the Senate Committee on Homeland Security, 109th Congress, 2nd session, 3-5.

[183] Congressman William Jefferson (D-LA), during a hearing on Hurricane Katrina: The Role of the Federal Emergency Management Agency, on September 27, 2005, House Select Committee to Investigate the Preparation for and Response to Hurricane Katrina, 109th Congress, 1st session, 93.

[184] U.S. Department of Commerce, "Gutierrez Announces Hurricane Contracting Information Center: One-Stop Shop to Help U.S. Businesses Participate in Hurricane Rebuilding Efforts," news release, October 11, 2005. Also see U.S. Department of Commerce, "Hurricane Contracting Information Center," http://www.rebuildingthegulfcoast.gov.

[185] "Under Title I of the Defense Production Act of 1950, as amended (DPA), the President is authorized to require preferential acceptance and performance of contracts or orders supporting certain approved national defense and energy programs, and to allocate materials, services, and facilities in such a manner as to promote these approved programs. Additional priorities authority is found in Section 18 of the Selective Service Act of 1948, in 10 U.S.C. § 2538, and in 50 U.S.C. § 82. The DPA priorities and allocations authority has also been extended to support emergency preparedness activities under Title VI of the Robert T. Stafford Disaster Relief and Emergency Assistance Act (Stafford Act)." […] "The Department of Commerce is delegated authority to implement these priorities and allocations provisions for industrial resources. The Bureau of Industry and Security's Office of Strategic Industries and Economic Security (SIES) administers this authority through the Defense Priorities and Allocations System (DPAS) regulation (15 CFR Part 700). The purpose of the DPAS is to (1) assure the timely availability of industrial resources to meet current national defense and emergency preparedness program requirements; and (2) provide an operating system to support rapid industrial response in a national emergency."

U.S. Department of Commerce, Bureau of Industry and Security, "Defense Priorities and Allocations System Program (DPAS)," https://www.bis.doc.gov/defenseindustrialbaseprograms/OSIES/DPAS/Default.htm. As an example of how this authority was used in the response to Hurricane Katrina, Norfolk Southern Railway used a DPAS rated contract to procure switch equipment and generators so that it could repair railway automated signals.

[186] FEMA issued a mission assignment on the morning of September 3 that stated "FEMA requests that DOD provide planning and execution for transportation and distribution of ice, water, food and medical supplies in support of the Katrina disaster in Louisiana and Mississippi." U.S. Department of Homeland Security, Federal Emergency Management Agency, "1604DR-MS-DOD-19, Amendment 1," September 3, 2005.

[187] Paul McHale, Assistant Secretary of Defense for Homeland Defense, testimony before a hearing on Hurricane Katrina: Preparedness and Response by the Department of Defense, the Coast Guard, and the National Guard of Louisiana, Mississippi, and Alabama, on October 27, 2005, House Select Bipartisan Committee to Investigate the Preparation for and Response to Hurricane Katrina, 109th Congress, 1st session, 70-71.

[188] In developing the NRP, it was envisioned that additional and specific planning would be needed for logistics, international coordination, private sector coordination and donations management. In fact, each issue has its own support annex in the NRP. The annexes, however, provide little detail or operational direction and do not provide clear responsibility for the various roles and tasks referred to in the annexes.

[189] The Swiss offer was received September 5, 2005 and not fully vetted by FEMA until September 14. As another example, a C-130 aircraft traveling from Sweden with a water purification system and a cellular network waited four days for flight clearance from the U.S.

[190] An estimated $854.5 million in donations have been pledged to the U.S.

[191] USAID Liaisons were sent throughout the region: FEMA RRCCs – Atlanta, GA, Denton, TX, Tucker, AL; JFOs – Baton Rouge, LA, Montgomery, AL, Jackson, MS, New Orleans, LA; JTF – Shreveport, LA, JTF Camp Shelby – Hattiesburg, MS; JTF Forward – USS Iwo Jima, National Guard Forward Deployment – New Orleans, LA, Dobbins AFB – GA; FEMA Disaster Recovery Center – Mobile, AL; NORTHCOM – Colorado Springs, CO; Dobbins AFB – Little Rock, AK. The first four were deployed on September 2 – two went to FEMA HQ and two went to the State Task Force. On September 3, the State Department started sending people to the FEMA call-center, and on September 4 to the RRCC in Atlanta, the JTF at Camp Shelby, and Dobbins AFB in Georgia. On September 5, personnel were deployed to Shreveport, Little Rock, and Denton.

[192] U.S Department of Homeland Security, "Hurricane Katrina DHS SITREP #21," September 5, 2005; and United States Agency for International Development, "Agency Channels Foreign Aid for Hurricane Katrina Victims," *Front Lines*, October 2005.

[193] It applied to Alabama, Louisiana, and Mississippi since August 29 and to Florida since August 24—after Hurricane Katrina's first landfall. U.S. Department of Health and Human Services, "HHS Designates First Medical Shelters and Provides Vital Medical Supplies and Medical Assistance," news release, September 2, 2005, http://www.hhs.gov/news/press/2005pres/20050902.html.

[194] Sarah A. Lister, *Hurricane Katrina: The Public Health and Medical Response*, Congressional Research Service Report for Congress RL33096 (Washington, D.C., September 2005), summary and CRS-11.

[195] "19 NDMS DMATs and other NDMS teams were pre-staged for Katrina, and as the storm passed, they along with the US&R Task Forces, began moving, into the impact areas. By the day after the storm, teams were providing medical care and continue to do so today. The mission is still ongoing, with personnel staffing hospitals and clinics destroyed or rendered inoperable by the storms as we speak." Dr. Roy L. Alson, Associate Professor of Emergency Medicine at Wake Forest University School of Medicine and Commander of Disaster Medical Assistance Team NC-1, written statement for a hearing on Mitigating Catastrophic Events Through Effective Medical Response, on October 20, 2005, submitted to the House Committee on Homeland Security, Subcommittee on Prevention of Nuclear and Biological Attack, 109th Congress, 1st session. According to an attachment Dr. Alson provided with his testimony, 16,477 patients were treated by NDMS personnel in FEMA region IV through 13 October 2005, and 40,995 patients were treated and 59,917 individuals immunized by NDMS personnel in FEMA region VI through 13 October 2005.

[196] Hilarie H. Cranmer, "Hurricane Katrina: Volunteer Work – Logistics First," *New England Journal of Medicine* 353(15), no. 13, October, 2005. Dr. Cranmer was a member of the American Red Cross team that had been deployed "to perform the critical-needs assessments that would help define the public health response to Hurricane Katrina." Dr. Thomas Kirsch, Medical Director for Disaster Health Services for the American Red Cross, written statement for a hearing on Assessing Public Health and the Delivery of Care in the Wake of Katrina, on September 22, 2005, submitted to the House Energy and Commerce Committee, Subcommittees on Health and Oversight and

Investigations, 109th Congress, 1st session. See Ardis D. Hoven, Member of the American Medical Association Board of Trustees, written statement for a hearing on Assessing Public Health and the Delivery of Care in the Wake of Katrina, on September 22, 2005, submitted to the House Energy and Commerce Committee, Subcommittees on Health and Oversight and Investigations, 109th Congress, 1st session. Dr. Kirsch said he took a team to Louisiana to assess nineteen Red Cross shelters and three very large state shelters: "Every shelter had good access to medical care either through local physicians providing care in the shelter, visiting medical teams, DMAT teams or relationships with local hospitals." Moreover, "[w]ith flooding widespread across the region and power and communications networks out, physicians and other health care professionals in hospitals desperately tried to keep patients alive, and appear to have mostly succeeded, even when their back-up generators failed."

[197] Louisiana Nursing Home Association staff lacked means to communicate with key decision makers early in the crisis. The Association "set up our own rescue missions." Joseph A. Donchess, Executive Director of the Louisiana Nursing Home Association, written statement for a hearing on Challenges in a Catastrophe: Evacuating New Orleans in Advance of Hurricane Katrina, on January 31, 2006, submitted to the Senate Committee on Homeland Security and Governmental Affairs, 109th Congress, 2nd session. Dr. Clyde Martin told *Government Executive* magazine that he joined a private relief effort in Louisiana after waiting for several days for Federal or State agencies to deploy him in their medical response. Justin Rood, "Medical Catastrophe," *GOVEXEC.com*, November 1, 2005, http://www.govexec.com/features/1105-01/1105-01s1.htm (accessed February 6, 2006).

[198] Louisiana State University, Office of University Relations, "LSU is Site of Largest Acute-Care Field Hospital in U.S. History," news release, September 6, 2005; and Elizabeth M. Duke, Health Resources Services Administrator, Department of Health and Human Services, "Remarks to the National Association of Community Health Centers' 2005 Annual Convention and Community Health Institute," September 19, 2005, http://newsroom.hrsa.gov/speeches/2005/NACHC-Sept.htm (accessed Febuary 10, 2006).

[199] Separate JFOs were set up and became fully operational in: Mobile, Alabama on September 1; Denver, Colorado on September 6; Montgomery, Alabama (supplanting the Mobile facility) and Oklahoma (State) on September 10; Austin, Texas on September 11; Baton Rouge and New Orleans, Louisiana on September 12; Little Rock, Arkansas on September 13; and Jackson, Mississippi on September 16. U.S. Department of Homeland Security, Federal Emergency Management Agency, "Federal Concept of Operations Matrix," September 18, 2005; U.S. Department of Homeland Security, Federal Emergency Management Agency, Region IV Regional Response Coordinating Center, "Situation Report 9," September 11, 2005; U.S. Department of Health and Human Services, "Secretary's Operations Center Flash Report #32 – Hurricane Katrina," September 12, 2005; U.S. Department of Homeland Security, Federal Emergency Management Agency/Arkansas Joint Field Office, "Situation Report 11," September 13, 2005; U.S. Department of Homeland Security, Federal Emergency Management Agency, "Executive Briefing," slide presentation, September 17, 2005.

[200] Preliminary steps were taken toward establishing the JTF-Forward on September 6, but the facility was not fully established until later on the 7th. U.S. Department of Defense, Office of the Assistant Secretary of Defense for Homeland Defense, "Hurricane Katrina Timeline," October 16, 2005, 13; and U.S. Department of Health and Human Services, "Secretary's Operations Center Flash Report #23—Hurricane Katrina," September 7, 2005. This temporary site was supplanted by the physical facility established on September 12, as referenced above.

[201] Regarding the timing of the appointment of VADM Allen, Secretary Chertoff testified that on "Saturday [September 3] I identified Admiral Allen as a person that I wanted to consider putting into place. I spoke to the Commandant over the weekend, made sure that Admiral Allen was free to come down, had him come down with the intention of having him take over at least the Louisiana piece of this in order to make sure we had that under control. And then ultimately on Friday [September 9] I made the determination that I would put Admiral Allen in control of the entire operation." Michael Chertoff, testimony before a hearing on Hurricane Katrina: The Role of the Department of Homeland Security, on October 19, 2005, House Select Committee to Investigate the Preparation for and Response to Hurricane Katrina, 109th Congress, 1st session.

[202] U.S. Department of Homeland Security, "Statement by Homeland Security Secretary Michael Chertoff," news release, September 9, 2005.

[203] The FCO "is appointed to manage Federal resource support activities ... [and] is responsible for coordinating the timely delivery of Federal disaster assistance resources and programs to the affected State and local governments, individual victims, and the private sector." Whereas the PFO is an invention of HSPD-5 and the NRP, the FCO position was created by the Stafford Act, and empowered with statutory authority to perform assigned responsibilities. U.S. Department of Homeland Security, *National Response Plan* (Washington, D.C., December

2004), 65. VADM Allen's appointments: 70 Fed. Reg. 56929 (Sep. 29, 2005) (Louisiana); 70 Fed. Reg. 57308 (Sep. 30, 2005) (Alabama); 70 Fed. Reg. 57309 (Sep. 30, 2005) (Mississippi).

[204] When Secretary Chertoff designated VADM Allen as the FCO (in addition to his earlier appointment as PFO), Allen gained statutory authority that enabled him to more efficiently coordinate Federal disaster assistance.

[205] "The SFLEO is the senior law enforcement official from the agency with primary jurisdictional responsibility as directed by statute, Presidential directive, existing Federal policies, and/or the Attorney General. The SFLEO directs intelligence/investigative law enforcement operations related to the incident and supports the law enforcement component of the Unified Command on-scene. In the event of a terrorist incident, this official will normally be the FBI SAC." U.S. Department of Homeland Security, *National Response Plan* (Washington, D.C., December 2004), 35.

[206] U.S. Department of Justice, Federal Bureau of Investigation, "FBI Hurricane Timeline," October 21, 2005, 3. The LECC is a construct familiar to law enforcement personnel, integrating the Federal, State, and local law enforcement communities, but is not a term currently incorporated into the NRP.

[207] The LECC was built on a modified FBI Joint Operations Center construct. It coordinated a plan to answer thousands of 911 calls in New Orleans that had gone unresolved and provided the conduit for coordination between civilian law enforcement and the National Guard and Title 10 U.S. Army forces operating in New Orleans. The LECC not only provided a facility for all Federal law enforcement, but built a separate headquarters for the New Orleans Police adjacent to it since the NOPD's headquarters had been destroyed.

[208] U.S. Department of Defense, "CJCS Hurricane Katrina Update," September 12, 2005.

[209] New Orleans Mayor's Office of Communications, "Updated Situation Report for New Orleans," September 13, 2005.

[210] Search and rescue teams in New Orleans carried out primary and secondary searches. Primary searches were visual, with hailing calls as searchers moved through a certain area. Forced entry into a building was not conducted without probable cause. Secondary searches were conducted door to door in areas where flooding had occurred higher than 5.5 feet above the floor. Damage incurred by access into a building was kept to a minimum and the building was re-secured after the search. New Orleans Police Department officers were on site for all the searches conducted. U.S. Department of Homeland Security, Federal Emergency Management Agency, "Urban Search and Rescue Operations Completed: Hurricane Katrina Urban Search and Rescue Teams are due to Return Home," news release, September 30, 2005.

[211] Mike Tamillow, Section Chief, Federal Emergency Management Agency Urban Search and Rescue, to Ed Buikema, Director, Region V, Federal Emergency Management Agency, memorandum on "US&R Section – Hurricane Katrina Update," September 10, 2005. Also see U.S. Department of Homeland Security, Federal Emergency Management Agency, "Urban Search and Rescue Operations Completed: Hurricane Katrina Urban Search and Rescue Teams Are Due to Return Home," news release, September 30, 2005, http://www.fema.gov/news/newsrelease.fema?id=19320.

[212] U.S. Department of Homeland Security, "Hurricane Katrina DHS SITREP #23," September 6, 2005; and U.S. Department of Homeland Security, "Hurricane Katrina DHS SITREP #29," September 9, 2005.

[213] HHS serves as the coordinator of NRP Emergency Support Function #8 ("Public Health and Medical Services"), which includes mortuary affairs. However, FEMA's NDMS has responsibilities for victim identification and mortuary services through its DMORTs. Consequently, HHS must request assistance from FEMA NDMS to deploy Disaster Mortuary Operational Response Teams to an incident site. U.S. Department of Homeland Security, *National Response Plan* (Washington, D.C., December 2004), ESF #8-6.

[214] U.S. Department of Homeland Security, "Hurricane Katrina DHS SITREP #18," September 4, 2005; and U.S. Department of Defense, "Hurricane Katrina Update," September 8, 2005, 20.

[215] Louisiana requested DMORT and DPMU support on August 29. Mississippi requested a DMORT assessment team on August 30. The first DMORT team was reported as engaged in Louisiana on August 31. By September 4, DMORT 1, DMORT 2, DMORT 4, DMORT 5, and DMORT Family Assistance Center (east), along with one DPMU, were deployed to Gulfport-Biloxi Municipal Airport. DMORT 6, DMORT 7, DMORT 8, DMORT WMD, and DMORT Family Assistance Center (west), along with one DPMU, were deployed to St. Gabriel, Louisiana. U.S. Department of Health and Human Services, "Secretary's Operations Center Flash Report #5—Hurricane Katrina," August 29, 2005, 2; U.S. Department of Health and Human Services, "Secretary's Operations Center: Flash Report # 6—Hurricane Katrina," August 30, 2005, 2; U.S. Department of Health and Human Services, "Secretary's Operations Center: Flash Report #8—Hurricane Katrina," August 31, 2005, 5-7; U.S. Department of

Health and Human Services, "Secretary's Operations Center Flash Report #17—Hurricane Katrina," September 4, 2005, 7-9.

[216] Kenyon International Management Services, "Hurricane Katrina Update: Kenyon International Activates Emergency Team for Hurricane Katrina Response," news release, http://www.kenyoninternational.com; Thomas Fitzgerald and Joyce Tsai, "Louisiana Governor Blasts FEMA Over Recovery of Bodies," Knight Ridder News Service, September 14, 2005; and Mark Hosenball and Keith Naughton, "Cash and 'Cat 5' Chaos," Newsweek, September 26, 2005.

[217] As Louisiana Governor Kathleen Blanco described it, "While Kenyon International of Houston has been and still is on the ground, working each day along with DMORT teams, they have not added enough personnel to do the work because of the lack of proper support or a contract." Louisiana Office of the Governor, "Statement by Governor Kathleen Babineaux Blanco on Body Removal Process in Southeast Louisiana," news release, September 13, 2005, http://www.gov.state.la.us/index.cfm?md=newsroom&tmp=detail&articleID=832.

[218] On September 9, the U.S. Department of Health and Human Services reported: "It is unclear as to the future resources for this mission as we heard the contractor Kenyon International may be in default of their verbal contract." U.S. Department of Defense, "Hurricane Katrina Update," slide presentation, September 8, 2005, 20; and U.S. Department of Homeland Security, "Hurricane Katrina DHS SITREP #37," September 13, 2005, 18.

[219] On September 9, White House spokesman Scott McClellan stated: "Mortuary affairs efforts on the ground – the State has the responsibility for overseeing the plan, implementing the plan and the federal government through the military and other ways, we're supporting those efforts with teams in the region, as well." The White House, "Press Briefing by Scott McClellan," news release, September 9, 2005, http://www.whitehouse.gov/news/releases/2005/09/print/20050909-3.html. FEMA spokeswoman Nicol Andrews made the same point in October, arguing that "Body retrieval is a state responsibility." Renae Merle and Griff Witte, "Lack of Contracts Hampered FEMA: Dealing With Disaster on the Fly Proved Costly," *Washington Post*, October 10, 2005.

[220] Louisiana Office of the Governor, "Statement by Governor Kathleen Babineaux Blanco on Body Removal Process in Southeast Louisiana" news release, September 13, 2005, http://www.gov.state.la.us/index.cfm?md=newsroom&tmp=detail&articleID=832.

[221] Bush-Clinton Katrina Fund, "Bush-Clinton Katrina Fund Announces Allocations for Louisiana, Mississippi and Alabama," news release, January 19, 2006, http://www.bushclintonkatrinafund.org/index.php?src=news&submenu=Media&prid=20&category=Press%20Releases.

[222] The National Book Festival is an annual event organized and sponsored by the Library of Congress and hosted by First Lady Laura Bush. White House website, "Mrs. Bush's Remarks at the National Book Festival Author's Breakfast," September 24, 2005, http://www.whitehouse.gov/news/releases/2005/09/20050924-2.html.

[223] "Despite the massive migration of evacuees and their subsequent placement in evacuation centers, only one known outbreak of communicable disease (norovirus) requiring unusual mobilization of public health resources had been reported as of September 23." U.S. Centers for Disease Control, "Infectious Disease and Dermatologic Conditions in Evacuees and Rescue Workers After Hurricane Katrina – Multiple States, August-September, 2005," as reprinted in the *Journal of the American Medical Association* 294, no. 17, November 2, 2005, 2159.

[224] U.S. Department of Health and Human Services, "Estimates Show More Than 40% of Hurricane Evacuees Now Receiving HHS Benefits or Services," news release, September 29, 2005.

[225] Expedited Assistance is FEMA's program to provide $2,000 in "an initial emergency first installment" of assistance, prior to a completed inspection of a victim's home, to help pay for food, shelter, clothing, personal necessities and medical needs. Eligible evacuees could also get additional FEMA assistance for a total up to $26,500 per household. U.S. Department of Homeland Security, Federal Emergency Management Agency, "Emergency Assistance Flowing to Gulf Coast," news release, September 9, 2005; and U.S. Department of Homeland Security, Federal Emergency Management Agency, "Disaster Assistance Frequently Asked Questions," http://www.fema.gov/rrr/dafaq.shtm (accessed February 3, 2006).

[226] U.S. Department of Homeland Security, "Hurricane Katrina DHS SITREP #21," September 5, 2005; and U.S. Department of Homeland Security, "Hurricane Katrina DHS SITREP #41," September 15, 2005.

[227] U.S. Department of Homeland Security, Federal Emergency Management Agency, "FEMA VIP Briefing," slide presentation, September 12, 2005, 6:00 PM; U.S. Department of Homeland Security, "Hurricane Katrina DHS SITREP #44," September 17, 2005; U.S. Department of Homeland Security, Federal Emergency Management Agency, "Nearly $690 Million in Assistance Helping More Than 330,000 Families Displaced by Katrina," news release, September 10, 2005.

[228] However, the NRP inconsistently describes the role and purpose of DRCs. The NRP states a DRC "is a central facility where individuals affected by a disaster can *obtain information* on disaster recovery assistance programs from various Federal, State, local, tribal, private-sector, and voluntary organizations." However, the NRP also states the DRC is "[a] facility established in a centralized location within or near the disaster area at which disaster victims (individuals, families, or businesses) *apply for* disaster aid." NRP, p.64. (Emphasis added).

[229] U.S. Department of Homeland Security, Federal Emergency Management Agency, "Disaster Assistance Frequently Asked Questions," news release, September 13, 2005. FEMA's "Disaster Assistance Frequently Asked Questions" stated, "You cannot register for assistance at a DRC, you must register by calling 1-800-621-FEMA ... or apply on line at www.FEMA.gov."

[230] U.S. Department of Homeland Security, "Hurricane Katrina DHS SITREP #34," September 12, 2005, 3. Approximately one-third of Louisiana households were without power or telephone service as of September 12.

[231] U.S. Department of Homeland Security, Federal Emergency Management Agency/State of Alabama Joint Field Office, "FEMA-1605-DR-AL-SITREP #08," September 4, 2005. On September 4, the FEMA/State of Alabama JFO reported, "The Helpline number is currently unavailable. Due to the large number of teleregistration calls, all lines are being made available for registration." This is an indication that the FEMA phone system lacked the capacity to sustain the demand for service on both the teleregistration line and Helpline, at least at that time for some customers.

[232] U.S. Department of Homeland Security, Federal Emergency Management Agency, "FEMA Getting Assistance to Individuals," news release, September 7, 2005; U.S. Department of Homeland Security, Federal Emergency Management Agency, "FEMA VIP Briefing," slide presentation, September 7, 2005, 6:00 PM, 7; U.S. Department of Homeland Security, Federal Emergency Management Agency, "FEMA VIP Briefing," slide presentation, September 9, 2005, 6:00 PM, 2; and U.S. Department of Homeland Security, Federal Emergency Management Agency, "FEMA VIP Briefing," slide presentation, September 10, 2005, 6:00 AM, 3. "Currently, the amount of money being distributed through the expedited assistance program is $2,000 per household. ... This emergency assistance is provided to help with disaster needs such as transportation, clothing, rental housing, other housing accommodations, and food, and is included in the calculation of total benefits for which victims are eligible."

[233] Government Accountability Office, *Expedited Assistance for Victims of Hurricanes Katrina and Rita: FEMA's Control Weaknesses Exposed the Government to Significant Fraud and Abuse*, GAO-06-403T, February 13, 2006, 18-19, http://www.gao.gov/new.items/d06403t.pdf.

[234] U.S. Department of Homeland Security, Federal Emergency Management Agency, "FEMA VIP Briefing," slide presentation, September 8, 2005; and Lisa Rein and Christopher Lee, "Debit Card Giveaway Goes Awry in Houston," *Washington Post*, September 9, 2005. FEMA individual assistance programs suffered from other problems. Accounting and verification problems prompted an investigation by the DHS Office of the Inspector General. "In a November 1, 2005, report on expedited assistance overpayment, DHS OIG attempted to identify the events that resulted in a married couple receiving duplicate payments for expedited assistance and determine why internal controls did not prevent the duplicate payment from being issued and why the applicants were not provided adequate information to return the excess funds. It was found that for a short time, the National Emergency Management Information System was not configured with system controls to prevent more than one payment per household. FEMA officials ... have identified more than 5,000 potentially duplicated payments." Executive Council on Integrity and Efficiency, *Oversight of Gulf Coast Hurricane Recovery: A 90-Day Progress Report to Congress* (Washington, D.C., December 2005), 33.

[235] U.S. Department of Homeland Security, "Good Story: Harris County, Texas Citizen Corps' Response to Hurricane Katrina," *Lessons Learned Information Sharing (LLIS.gov) database*, November 17, 2005, http://www.llis.gov; Harris County Joint Information Center, "Mission Fulfilled, Command stands Down," news release, September 20, 2005, http://www.hcjic.org/news_release.asp?p=62&intRelease_ID=2078&intAcc_ID=62.

[236] Harris County Joint Information Center, "Mission Fulfilled, Command stands Down," news release, September 20, 2005, http://www.hcjic.org/news_release.asp?p=62&intRelease_ID=2078&intAcc_ID=62.

[237] T. Yarbrough, "'Baptists' 10.5 Million Meals shatters Prior Disaster Relief Record," *North American Mission Board*, http://www.namb.net/site/apps/nl/content2.asp?c=9qKILUOzEpH&b=227361&ct=1568907 (accessed January 13, 2006). For other examples, see Liz Szabo, "Grass-roots groups pitch in to find shelter for evacuees," *USA Today*, September 8, 2005.

[238] This despite the NRP Volunteer and Donations Management Support Annex, which describes this process.

[239] The NRP Volunteer and Donations Management Support Annex focuses on managing unaffiliated volunteers and unsolicited donated goods. It does not provide guidelines for coordinating private sector and NGO relief efforts. U.S. Department of Homeland Security, *National Response Plan* (Washington, D.C., December 2004), VOL-1.

[240] Major Todd Hawks, Public Affairs Secretary for the Salvation Army of America, testimony before a hearing on the Response of Charities to Hurricane Katrina, on December 13, 2005, House Committee on Ways and Means, Subcommittee on Oversight, 109th Congress, 1st session.

[241] David Roberson, President and CEO of Cavalier Homes, Inc., testimony before a hearing on Emergency Housing Needs in the Aftermath of Hurricane Katrina, on September 15, 2005, House Committee on Financial Services, Subcommittee on Housing and Community Opportunity, 109th Congress, 1st session. Also see Laura Maggi, "Hotel Rooms Sought For Shelter Occupants; Other Housing Options Appear Slow To Arrive," *New Orleans Times-Picayune*, September 21, 2005; and Shankar Vedantam and Dean Starkman, "Lack of Cohesion Bedevils Recovery," *Washington Post*, September 18, 2005.

[242] James N. Russo, Federal Coordinating Officer for Mississippi Recovery Operations, Federal Emergency Management Agency, testimony before a hearing on Housing Options in the Aftermath of Hurricanes Katrina and Rita, on January 14, 2006, House Committee on Financial Services, Subcommittee on Housing and Community Opportunity, 109th Congress, 2nd session; David Roberson, representing the Manufactured Housing Institute and the Manufactured Housing Association for Regulatory Reform, testimony before a hearing on Emergency Housing Needs Following Hurricane Katrina, on September 15, 2005, House Committee on Financial Services, Subcommittee on Housing and Community Opportunity, 109th Congress, 1st session.

[243] U.S. Department of Homeland Security, "Hurricane Katrina DHS SITREP #20," September 5, 2005; and U.S. Department of Homeland Security, "Hurricane Katrina DHS SITREP #31," September 10, 2005.

[244] U.S. Department of Homeland Security, Federal Emergency Management Agency, "FEMA Executive Briefing," slide presentation, September 14, 2005, 6:00 AM.

[245] A complicating factor was that as Hurricane Rita approached the Gulf Coast, individuals in shelters from Hurricane Katrina had to be evacuated from their original shelter sites and moved to new ones. U.S. Department of Homeland Security, "Gulf Coast Hurricane Katrina (85) and Rita (37) Response and Recovery DHS SITREP," October 14, 2005.

[246] U.S. Department of Homeland Security, "U.S. Government Announces a Comprehensive Transitional Housing Assistance Program for Katrina Evacuees," news release, September 23, 2005; U.S. Department of Homeland Security, "Fact Sheet: Transitional Housing Assistance for Hurricane Katrina Evacuees," September 23, 2005; and U.S. Department of Homeland Security, "Press Briefing by Homeland Security Secretary Michael Chertoff and Secretary of Housing and Urban Development Alphonso Jackson," news release, September 24, 2005.

[247] Mr. Powell serves as the primary Federal contact for Congress, State, local and private leaders in supporting "mid and long term recovery and rebuilding plans." U.S. Department of Homeland Security, "Coordinator Named to Lead Federal Recovery and Rebuilding Activities in the Gulf Coast Region," news release, November 1, 2005.

[248] U.S. Department of Homeland Security, Federal Emergency Management Agency, "Federally Declared Disasters By Calendar Year," http://www.fema.gov/library/drcys.shtm. Forty emergency declarations were issued in the period from January 20, 2001 to Hurricane Katrina.

CHAPTER FIVE: LESSONS LEARNED

[1] The White House, "President Discusses Hurricane Relief in Address to the Nation," news release, September 15, 2005, http://www.whitehouse.gov/news/releases/2005/09/20050915-8.html.

[2] The critical challenges described here include and go beyond those identified in other evaluations of the national response to Hurricane Katrina. See, for example, David M. Walker, Comptroller General, *Statement by Comptroller General David M. Walker on GAO's Preliminary Observations Regarding Preparedness and Response to Hurricanes Katrina and Rita*, prepared for the U.S. Government Accountability Office, GAO-06-365R, (Washington, D.C., February 1, 2006).

[3] Though State and local preparedness is critical to the success of overall National preparedness and response efforts, this Report is not intended to assess State and local efforts.

[4] Melvin "Kip" Holden, Mayor-President of Baton Rouge, Louisiana, written statement for a hearing on Recovering from Hurricane Katrina: Responding to the Immediate Needs of Its Victims, on September 28, 2005, submitted to the Senate Homeland Security and Governmental Affairs Committee, 109th Congress, 1st session.

[5] The DHS Secretary designates a Principal Federal Official (PFO). See U.S. Department of Homeland Security, *National Response Plan* (Washington, D.C., December 2004), 71. The Federal Coordinating Officer (FCO) "is appointed to manage Federal resource support activities ... [and] is responsible for coordinating the timely delivery of Federal disaster assistance resources and programs to the affected State and local governments, individual victims, and the private sector." Whereas the PFO derives from HSPD-5 and the NRP, the FCO position was created by the Stafford Act (*Robert T. Stafford Disaster Relief and Emergency Assistance Act* ["*Stafford Act*"], as amended by Public Law 106-390, October 30, 2000). U.S. Department of Homeland Security, *National Response Plan* (Washington, D.C., December 2004), 65.

[6] U.S. Department of Homeland Security, "Hurricane Katrina DHS SITREP #20," September 5, 2005, 1; U.S. Department of Homeland Security, "Hurricane Katrina DHS SITREP #23," September 6, 2005, 1; U.S. Department of Homeland Security, Federal Emergency Management Agency, "FEMA Daily Conference Call on Hurricane Katrina," September 7, 2005, 1; U.S. Department of Homeland Security, "Hurricane Katrina DHS SITREP #27," September 8, 2005, 1; U.S. Department of Homeland Security, Federal Emergency Management Agency, "Region VI Regional Response Coordinating Center SitRep #15," September 9, 2005, 1; U.S. Department of Health and Human Services, "Secretary's Operations Center Flash Report #32—Hurricane Katrina," September 12, 2005, 2, 3; U.S. Department of Homeland Security, "Emergency Response Issues," September 11, 2005, 10; Robert B. Stephan, Assistant Secretary for Infrastructure Protection, U.S. Department of Homeland Security, prepared statement for a hearing on "Hurricane Katrina: The Roles of DHS and FEMA Leadership," on February 10, 2006, submitted to the Senate Committee on Homeland Security and Governmental Affairs, 109th Congress, 2nd session, 7-8.

[7] Federal officials recognized the need for a presence in New Orleans to effectively coordinate the efforts to stabilize the City, so a "forward PFO" in New Orleans was eventually established. The JFO remained in Baton Rouge. U.S. Department of Health and Human Services, "Secretary's Operations Center Flash Report #23," September 7, 2005; U.S. Department of Homeland Security, Federal Emergency Mangement Agency, "FEMA Executive Briefing," slide presentation, September 17, 2005, 6 AM.

[8] Only eight months had elapsed between the unveiling of the NRP and its implementation for the worst natural disaster in U.S. history. U.S. Department of Homeland Security, *National Response Plan* (Washington, DC: December 2004).

[9] The NRP requires all of the supporting Federal Departments and Agencies to modify existing interagency incident management and emergency response plans and protocols to incorporate linkages to and be consistent with NIMS, the NRP and its coordinating mechanisms. The NRP also requires that detailed standard operational procedures be developed for the HSOC, NRCC, IIMG, the JFO and each ESF Annex. These plans are meant to clearly define the functions of each organization and describe how the organization interfaces with the rest of the emergency response effort. See U.S. Department of Homeland Security, *National Response Plan* (Washington, D.C., December 2004), Letter of Instruction, ix.

[10] Starting after the 2002 Salt Lake City Olympics, money and resources that were once dedicated to training and exercising the National Emergency Response Teams (ERT-N) have been diverted from the ERT program to other programs. See William Carwile, Federal Coordinating Officer for Mississippi, Federal Emergency Management Agency, testimony before a hearing on the Preparation for and Response to Hurricane Katrina, on December 8, 2005, Senate Committee on Homeland Security and Governmental Affairs. ERT-N deploys for large-scale, high impact events, to coordinate the plans with other Federal agencies within FEMA regions. See U.S. Department of Homeland Security, *National Response Plan* (Washington, D.C., December 2004), 40. ERT-Ns also provide assistance to the smaller ERT deployed by the FEMA regions. The loss of funding has resulted in ERT-N teams that are not fully equipped nor train or exercise together. William Carwile, Federal Coordinating Officer for Mississippi, Federal Emergency Management Agency, testimony before a hearing on the Preparation for and Response to Hurricane Katrina, on December 8, 2005, Senate Committee on Homeland Security and Governmental Affairs. Scott Wells, the Deputy Federal Coordinating Officer for Louisiana, stated that FEMA lacked "the people, we did not have the expertise; we did not have the operational training folks that we needed to do our missions." He also stated generally that the staff level in the regional office is "woefully inadequate" to set up a Regional Response Coordination Center (RRCC) required for a disaster, and staff an ERT to go to the scene of a disaster. Wells describes FEMA staffing in disasters as robbing "Peter to pay Paul." Scott Wells, Deputy Federal Coordinating Officer for Louisiana, testimony before a hearing on Hurricane Katrina: Perspectives of FEMA's Operation

Professionals, on December 8, 2005, Senate Committee on Homeland Security and Governmental Affairs, 109th Congress, 1st session.

[11] A DHS request to DOD on September 2 that "DOD provide the support, planning, and execution of the full logistical support to the Katrina disaster in all declared states in coordination with FEMA" was initially denied because the request did not come from the Secretary of DHS to the Secretary of Defense. The Secretary of DHS immediately resubmitted the request to the Secretary of Defense which was then granted. Ultimately, DOD (OSD & Joint Staff) worked with the FEMA Response Division to meet this requirement. The Joint Staff and the Office of the Secretary of Defense (OSD) worked throughout the weekend of September 3-5 to meet this Mission Assignment. U.S. Department of Homeland Security, Federal Emergency Management Agency, "Mission Assignment, Program Code/Event #: 1604DR-MS: HURRICANE KATRINA, Action Request #:1509-32760," September 3, 2005; U.S. Department of Defense, "Hurricane Katrina/Rita/Ophelia Interim Timeline (August – September 2005)," November 2, 2005, 1, 8, 10-11; and "Hurricane Katrina: Preparedness and Response by the Department of Defense, the Coast Guard, and the National Guard of Louisiana, Mississippi and Alabama, October 27, 2005, hearing before the Select Bipartisan Committee to Investigate the Preparation fo and Response to Hurricane Katrina, 109th Congress, 1st session (Congressman Tom Davis, quoting from Ken Burris, email to Mathew Broderick et al., Subject: request, September 2, 2005.)

[12] U.S. Department of Homeland Security, *National Response Plan* (Washington, D.C., December 2004), p. 41. According to the NRP, the Local Chief Executive Officer "Requests State and, if necessary, Federal assistance through the Governor of the State when the jurisdiction's capabilities have been exceeded or exhausted" and the Governor "Requests Federal assistance when it becomes clear that State or tribal capabilities will be insufficient or have been exceeded or exhausted." According to the Louisiana *Emergency Operations Plan*, "The initial actions . . . are conducted by local government. Local authorities will exhaust their resources, and then use mutual aid agreements with volunteer groups, the private sector and/or neighboring parishes." The plan also states that "State assistance will supplement local efforts and Federal assistance will supplement State and local efforts when it is clearly demonstrated that it is beyond local and State capability to cope with the emergency/disaster." Louisiana Office of Homeland Security and Emergency Preparedness, *Emergency Operations Plan* (Baton Rouge, April 2005).

[13] U.S. Department of Defense, Joint Center for Operational Analysis, "Incident Command Request Briefing," November 1, 2005. However, Secretary of Defense Donald Rumsfeld verbally approved some requests. See also Paul McHale, Assistant Secretary of Defense for Homeland Defense, testimony before a hearing on Hurricane Katrina: The Defense Department's Role in the Response, on February 9, 2006, Senate Homeland Security and Governmental Affairs Committee, 109th Congress, 2nd session.

[14] Melvin "Kip" Holden, Mayor-President of Baton Rouge, Louisiana, noted that requirements for paperwork and form completions hindered immediate action and deployment of people and material to assist in rescue and recovery efforts. Melvin "Kip" Holden, written statement submitted for a hearing on Recovering from Hurricane Katrina: Responding to the Immediate Needs of Its Victims, on September 28, 2005, Senate Homeland Security and Governmental Affairs Committee, 109th Congress, 1st session.

[15] As noted in U.S. Department of Defense, National Guard Bureau (NGB J7), *After Action Review: Hurricane Response September 2005* (December 21, 2005), 146, 168.

[16] U.S. Department of Defense, *Hurricane Katrina Initial Observations and Lessons Learned* (n.d., ca. 2005). These deployments occurred under the EMAC system.

[17] U.S. Department of Defense, National Guard Bureau (NGB J7), After Action Review: Hurricane Katrina Response September 2005 (December 21, 2005).

[18] If chartered as a joint DOD activity, the NGB would become a member of the Joint Staff, rather than only having a reporting relationship with the Secretary of the Army and the Secretary of the Air Force. Lieutenant General H. Steven Blum, "A Vision for the National Guard," *Joint Forces Quarterly*, issue 36 (December 2004), 24-29.

[19] U.S. Department of Defense, National Guard Bureau (NGB J5), *Draft Baseline Capabilities for Joint Task Force-State (JTF-State)*, n.d., ca. 2005. The National Guard Bureau can provide overarching situational awareness and an integrated common, relevant operating picture regarding the employment of Army and Air Guard troops in each of the 54 States, Territories and the District of Columbia. This demonstrates the essential role of the National Guard Bureau as the channel of communications between the several States and the combatant commanders, the Joint Staff and the Departments of Defense, Army and Air Force. Given the current national security environment, the necessity to continue providing this kind of data will continue to grow. Capabilities include Joint Force Joint Operations Centers (JF JOC). This is a network composed of the NGB Joint Operations Center and a Joint

Operations Center in each of the States, Territories, and the District of Columbia. Each JF JOC has redundant communications connectivity to include: DOD unclassified (NIPR) and classified (SIPR) computer networks; a High Frequency network with high and low-side voice and data information; and commercial systems. The network provides DOD and interagency connectivity and situational awareness to deliberate planning and to emerging and on-going contingency operations in any State or Territory. The National Guard has successfully established a Joint CONUS Communications Support Environment (JCCSE) nationwide. Each JFHQ has established Homeland Security Information Network (HSIN) linkages. The HSIN is an unsecured collection of Department of Homeland Security systems designed to facilitate information sharing and collaboration.

[20] Colonel F. G. Dowden, Regional Liaison, New Orleans Department of Homeland Security and Public Safety, written statement for a hearing on Hurricane Katrina: Managing Law Enforcement and Communications in a Catastrophe, on February 6, 2006, submitted to the Senate Committee on Homeland Security and Governmental Affairs, 109th Congress, 2nd session.

[21] Kevin J. Martin, Chairman, Federal Communications Commission, written statement for a hearing on Public Safety Communications from 9/11 to Katrina: Critical Public Policy Lessons, submitted to Subcommittee on Telecommunications and the Internet, House Committee on Energy and Commerce, on September 29, 2005, 109th Congress, 1st session.

[22] U.S. Department of Energy, Office of Electricity Delivery and Energy Reliability, "Hurricane Katrina Situation Report #20," September 4, 2005.

[23] Communications "operability" refers to whether a basic communications network is functioning at all. Operability will fail when the underlying infrastructure is destroyed or otherwise fails (e.g. through loss of power).

[24] Communications "interoperability" refers to the ability to communicate across different, operable communication systems.

[25] Congressman Bill Pascrell, Jr., hearing on Government Operability during Catastrophic Events, on October 26, 2005, House Committee on Homeland Security, Subcommittee on Emergency Preparedness, Science and Technology, 109th Congress, 1st session.

[26] For example, FEMA had pre-positioned two of their five Mobile Emergency Response Support (MERS) detachments in the Gulf and quickly moved them to the affected areas in Louisiana and Mississippi soon after landfall, but additional MERS support should have been deployed to the Gulf when it became apparent that those pre-positioned were insufficient for an incident of Katrina's magnitude. U.S. Department of Homeland Security, Federal Emergency Management Agency, "FEMA National Situation Report," August 29, 2005, 3; and Michael Brown, former Director of the Federal Emergency Management Agency, testimony before a hearing on Hurricane Katrina: The Role of the Federal Emergency Management Agency, on September 27, 2005, to House Select Bipartisan Committee to Investigate the Preparation for and Response to Hurricane Katrina, 109th Congress, 1st session.

[27] Mark Rey, Under Secretary for Natural Resources and Environment, U.S Department of Agriculture, testimony before a hearing on Ensuring Operability during Catastrophic Events, on October 26, 2005, House Committee on Homeland Security, Subcommittee on Emergency Preparedness, Science and Technology, 109th Congress, 1st session.

[28] Dr. David G. Boyd, Director of the Office for Interoperability and Compatibility, Department of Homeland Security, written statement for a hearing on Ensuring Operability during Catastrophic Events, on October 26, 2005, House Committee on Homeland Security, Subcommittee on Emergency Preparedness, Science and Technology, 109th Congress, 1st session. As a first step, as required by the Fiscal Year 2005 and 2006 homeland security grant guidance, States and urban areas are to develop Tactical Interoperable Communication Plans to address means of improving communications operability and interoperability. See U.S. Department of Homeland Security, *Fiscal Year 2006 Homeland Security Grant Program Guidance: Program Guidance and Application Kit* (Washington, D.C., December 2005). Although not an issue during Hurricane Katrina, first responders still require more radio spectrum to effectively communicate during their missions. Public Law 109-171, enacted recently, provides first responders with more radio spectrum in the 700 megahertz band, starting April 7, 2009. The bill calls for auctioning off some of the radio spectrum relinquished by broadcasters. Some of that revenue would pay for upgrades to first responders' equipment. This transition for the 700 megahertz radio spectrum is considered a critical component in improving communications between police, fire, and other emergency agencies.

[29] Dr. David G. Boyd, Director of the Office for Interoperability and Compatibility, Department of Homeland Security, written statement for a hearing on Ensuring Operability during Catastrophic Events, on October 26, 2005, to House Committee on Homeland Security, Subcommittee on Emergency Preparedness, Science and Technology, House Homeland Security Committee, 109th Congress, 1st session.

[30] Private sector companies manage sophisticated supply and delivery chains using the most efficient means available to handle goods as few times as possible between the supplier and the customer.

[31] Vincent Pearce, National Response Program Manager for the Department of Transportation, testimony before a hearing on Hurricane Katrina: Managing the Crisis and Evacuating New Orleans, on February 1, 2006, Senate Homeland Security and Governmental Affairs Committee, 109th Congress, 2nd session.

[32] For example, a contractor arrived at an evacuation staging site at Zephyr Field stadium in New Orleans with 37,500 meals, as requested, only to discover that the evacuees had already left.

[33] FEMA US&R Task Forces, in conjunction with USCG, DOD, other federal agencies, and State and local first responders, rescued over 6,500 people. See U.S. Department of Homeland Security, Federal Emergency Management Agency, "Urban Search and Rescue Operations Completed: Hurricane Katrina Urban Search and Rescue Teams Are Due to Return Home," news release, September 30, 2005, http://www.fema.gov/news/newsrelease.fema?id=19320.html.

[34] Donna Miles, "Military Providing Full-Scale Response to Hurricane Relief Effort," American Forces Press Service, August 31, 2005, http://www.defenselink.mil/news/Aug2005/20050831_2576.html.

[35] "Some of the problems we encountered were low visibility at night, a lot of downed power lines, a lot of underwater obstructions, vehicles that were underwater, debris that was everywhere, and large numbers of people shouting for help from the house." Louisiana Department of Wildlife and Fisheries, "Department Timelines Chronology 3," *Activity Report on Hurricane Katrina* (Baton Rouge, 2005), 2.

[36] East Baton Rouge Parish, *Draft After-Action Report for Hurricanes Katrina and Rita* (Baton Rouge, 2005), 38.

[37] Scott Wells, testimony before a hearing on Hurricane Katrina: Perspectives of FEMA's Operations Professionals, on December 8, 2005, Senate Committee on Homeland Security and Governmental Affairs, 109th Congress, 1st session.

[38] Massachusetts Urban Search and Rescue Task Force-1, *Hurricane Katrina After-Action Report: August 30, 2005 through September 8, 2005* (Beverly, MA, 2005), 6.

[39] East Baton Rouge Parish, *Draft After-Action Report for Hurricanes Katrina and Rita* (Baton Rouge, 2005), 38.

[40] Louisiana Office of the Governor, *Response to U.S. Senate Committee on Homeland Security and Governmental Affairs* (Baton Rouge, December 2005), 11. See also Kathleen Babineaux Blanco, testimony before a hearing on Hurricane Katrina: Preparedness and Response by the State of Louisiana, on December 14, 2005, to the House Select Committee to Investigate the Preparation for and Response to Hurricane Katrina, 109th Congress, 1st session, 68. Louisiana Department of Wildlife and Fisheries, "Department Timelines Chronology 3," *Activity Report on Hurricane Katrina* (Baton Rouge, 2005), 7. http://www.nola.com/katrina/view.ssf.html; Newsweek, "The Lost City", September 12, 2005.

[41] U.S. Department of Homeland Security, *National Response Plan* (Washington, D.C., December 2004), 8, 43; and *National Response Plan ESF #13 Annex*, pg. 13-1.

[42] On August 31, most of the New Orleans police force was redirected from search and rescue missions to respond to the looting, detracting from the priority mission of saving lives. Homeland Security Operations Center Spot Report #33, 31 Aug 05, 1123 hrs. (recording that "on August 31, CEO Akerman of Bell South contacted [a DHS official] and requests immediate security assistance, relating that the Bell South Main Central Office was being overrun by mob during attempted evacuation of site and that its employees may be in physical danger"); U.S. Department of Homeland Security, "Hurricane Katrina DHS SITREP #15," September 2, 2005 (reporting that security concerns were prohibiting all operations in many grain industry facilities); U.S. Department of Homeland Security, "Hurricane Katrina DHS SITREP #18," September 4, 2005 (reporting that fuel and security for deliveries are a concern); U.S. Department of Homeland Security, "Hurricane Katrina DHS SITREP #19," September 4, 2005 (reporting that security remained a major concern for agriculture, food processing, distribution, services, and retail; access to service and retail facilities for re-stocking remains restricted in many areas; security for all infrastructures remained a major concern, with employers reluctant to restart businesses; safety of their employees is a priority); U.S. Department of Homeland Security, "Hurricane Katrina DHS SITREP #29," September 9, 2005 (reporting that security remained the top priority for the industry; contract security and other security sources were being coordinated with other Emergency Support Functions).

[43] Both the Department of the Interior and the Department of Commerce reported that their organic law enforcement assets were available for use in the Gulf Coast region and attempted to lend their assistance by contacting the Interagency Incident Management Group in Washington, D.C., but received no response. The Department of the Interior has 4,400 law enforcement officers—including hundreds of officers immediately deployable in the Gulf Coast area—trained to work in harsh environments, conduct search and rescue, emergency

medical services, and evacuation, yet these assets were not called upon to assist under the NRP until late September, when DOI contacted the LECC in New Orleans. The Department of Commerce's National Oceanic and Atmospheric Administration (NOAA) Office of Law Enforcement (OLE) also attempted to lend its law enforcement assistance to the Federal response effort, but received no response through the ESF-13 process.

[44] For example, the Department of Interior law enforcement personnel had to be sworn in as Deputy U.S. Marshals to give them Federal law enforcement authority beyond their statutory DOI jurisdiction.

[45] While some law enforcement officers provided by States under the EMAC readily accepted direction from Louisiana and Federal law enforcement officials, others operated in New Orleans with little coordination or supervision.

[46] According to the U.S. Marshals Service, this was "a critical issue" in both New Orleans and Southern Mississippi. The Marshals Service and the DOJ Office of Legal Policy have offered recommendations for more comprehensive monitoring of persons under law enforcement supervision. For additional information on the disarray of the New Orleans criminal justice system in Hurricane Katrina's aftermath, see Melinda Deslatte, "Prisons in New Orleans empty as temporary booking facility up and running," Associated Press, September 3, 2005; Ann Woolner, "A Legal System in Chaos: New Orleans Struggles," *Fulton County Daily Report*, October 4, 2005; and Chuck Crumbo, "Evacuation leaves Louisiana prison system in chaos," *The State (Columbia, SC)*, October 5, 2005.

[47] On September 3, the Associated Press reported that "computer logs still hadn't been retrieved from the criminal district court in New Orleans…[and] tracking down witnesses, finding court records and trial transcripts and organizing a temporary court" would remain challenges to the reestablishment of the city's criminal justice system. Melinda Deslatte, "Prisons in New Orleans empty as temporary booking facility up and running," Associated Press, September 3, 2005; Ann Woolner, "A Legal System in Chaos: New Orleans Struggles," *Fulton County Daily Report*, October 4, 2005; and Chuck Crumbo, "Evacuation leaves Louisiana prison system in chaos," *The State (Columbia, SC)*, October 5, 2005.

Both State and Federal courts closed their doors. Supreme Court of Louisiana, Order by Justice Catherine D. Kimball, September 2, 2005, Baton Rouge, Louisiana; Supreme Court of Mississippi, Order by Justice James W. Smith, Jr., September 7, 2005; U.S. District Court for the Eastern District of Louisiana, Order by Chief Judge Helen G. Berrigan, September 4, 2005, accessed from http://katrinalaw.org/dokuphp?id=louisiana_eastern_district_court on February 17, 2006; U.S. Bankruptcy Court for the Eastern District of Louisiana, September 2, 2005, accessed from http://katrinalaw.org/dokuphp?id=louisiana_eastern_bankruptcy_court on February 17, 2006; Fourth Circuit Court of Appeal, State of Louisiana, Order by Justice Max N. Tobias, Jr., September 2, 2005, accesed from http://katrinalaw.org/dokuphp?id=fourth_circuit_court_of_appeal on February 17, 2006; Fifth Circuit Court of Appeal, State of Louisiana, Order by Justice Walter J. Rothschild, September 2, 2005, accessed from: http://katrinalaw.org/dokuphp?id= fifth_circuit_court_of_appeal, accessed on February 17, 2006; Civil District Court, Parish of Orleans, State of Louisiana, Order by Chief Justice Robin M. Giarrusso, September 2, 2005, accessed from http://katrinalaw.org/dokuphp?id= orleans_parish_civil_district_court, accessed on February 17, 2006.

[48] The DOJ's Bureau of Prisons moved, or facilitated movement of, a large number of prisoners incarcerated in Louisiana facilities during the first week of the disaster. Though there were no major difficulties or issues encountered during the actual transport of the prisoners, there were flaws in the decision making process and a general failure on the part of State and local prison authorities to be proactive in evacuating their incarcerated populations.

[49] United Health Foundation, *America's Health Rankings--2005 Edition* (St. Paul, MN: Arundel Street Consulting, Inc., 2005), http://www.unitedhealthfoundation.org/shr2005/survey.asp (accessed January 25, 2006), 13.

[50] "The public health and health care delivery infrastructures have been either completely destroyed or have sustained significant damage across the affected Gulf Coast. Existing facilities that are operational are under extreme stress as they assume even greater responsibilities to fill the gaps created by the loss of so many facilities. Physician offices, cancer, imaging, dialysis and rehabilitation centers, hospitals, clinics, long-term care facilities, pharmacies, laboratories, etc., need to be rebuilt or repaired, not to mention re-supplied, with information technology systems, equipment and inventory." Dr. Ardis D. Hoven, Member of the American Medical Association Board of Trustees, written statement for a hearing on Assessing Public Health and the Delivery of Care in the Wake of Hurricane Katrina, on September 22, 2005, submitted to the House Committee on Energy and Commerce, Subcommittees on Health and Oversight and Investigations, 109th Congress, 1st session.

[51] Sarah A. Lister, *Hurricane Katrina: The Public Health and Medical Response*, Congressional Research Service Report for Congress RL33096, (Washington, D.C., September 21, 2005), Summary, CRS 1, CRS 6-7, CRS 11.

[52] "Our situations are urgent. Unless we find financial relief within the next seven to ten days, we will be forced to make some very tough decisions. We are committed to our patients, our hospital staff and our community. However, we can't continue to care for our patients and community – many of whom hopefully will return soon from the evacuation – unless we have immediate financial assistance. ... The Centers for Medicare & Medicaid Services already has eased some of its regulations governing Medicare and Medicaid. There are, however, additional measures that can be taken. The AHA suggests immediate federal coverage for the uninsured people affected by the hurricane. So that access can be granted as quickly as possible, additional relief from Medicare and Medicaid red tape is needed. ... The AHA also asks that [FEMA] funds be available for all types of community hospitals affected by the storm." Dr. Mark Peters, President & CEO, East Jefferson Memorial Hospital, Metairie, Louisiana, on behalf of the American Hospital Association, written statement for a hearing on Assessing Public Health and the Delivery of Care in the Wake of Katrina, on September 22, 2005, submitted to the House Committee on Energy and Commerce, Subcommittees on Health and Oversight and Investigations, 109th Congress, 1st session.

[53] In several instances, HHS had pre-positioned medical, public health and pharmaceutical assets in Louisiana and had them ready to deploy where needed as soon as they received a go-ahead from State decision-makers. In some cases, security and logistics may have been issues, but delays in 'on the ground' decision-making by local and State officials resulted in delays in the delivery of assets and services when and where they were needed.

[54] One key example: "Dr. Laurence Grummer-Strawn, a Centers for Disease Control and Prevention researcher and an HHS Public Health Service member, was deployed to central Louisiana with a team of 125 medical personnel to construct a temporary 1,000-bed hospital. The plan, Grummer-Strawn understood, was for that facility to treat 'overflow patients' transferred from hospitals in the southern part of the state. Arriving Saturday, Sept. 3, six days after Katrina hit, his team spent two days setting up the hospital before they were told they weren't needed there. The team left Alexandria, La., Wednesday - it took a day to pack up the beds and equipment - and fanned out to conduct needs assessments at shelters across the state." Justin Rood, "Medical Catastrophe,"*Government Executive Magazine*, November 1, 2005, http://www.govexec.com/features/1105-01/1105-01s1.htm.

[55] "Almost 34,000 volunteer health professionals registered through HHS's toll-free telephone number or through the website established for this purpose. Of these, only 1,400 were deployed, based on the tasking requirements from FEMA. By the end of the first week following Katrina's landfall, it became clear that the majority of the volunteers would not be urgently needed in the Gulf Coast. Though HHS announced this fact, this message did not reach many volunteers, who expressed frustration that their services were not being accepted or efficiently utilized. [M]any well-intentioned clinicians and health care organizations simply self-deployed and traveled to Louisiana, where their arrival compounded the overall disorganization of the effort to provide health care ... Lacking an assigned role within a properly planned framework, many found themselves sitting on their hands, doing nothing for which they had been trained." Hilarie H. Cranmer, "Hurricane Katrina: Volunteer Work – Logistics First," *New England Journal of Medicine* 353(15), no. (October 13, 2005).

[56] Irwin Redlener, Dennis Johnson, David A. Berman and Roy Grant, "Follow-Up 2005: Where the American Public Stands on Terrorism and Preparedness after Hurricanes Katrina and Rita," http://www.ncdp.mailman.columbia.edu/research.htm (accessed January 25, 2006).

[57] Sarah A. Lister, *Hurricane Katrina: The Public Health and Medical Response*, Congressional Research Service for Congress RL33096, (Washington, D.C., September 21, 2005), 22.

[58] As of September 11, 2005, 14 days after Katrina made landfall, FEMA had received 699,207 Louisiana, Alabama and Mississippi household registrations for assistance under the Individuals and Households Program (IHP); 393,294 had been approved for assistance; 366,370 households had been funded; and $818,939,600 in assistance had been released. U.S. Department of Homeland Security, "Hurricane Katrina DHS SITREP #35," September 12, 2005, 11. By late September, "an estimated more than 20 percent of all those affected by the storms and who have filed for FEMA assistance are now receiving HHS benefits and services. Furthermore, 41 percent of the 857,000 evacuees living in a different zip code from the damaged areas are receiving help from HHS." U.S. Department of Health and Human Services, "Estimates Show More Than 40 Percent of Hurricane Evacuees Now Receiving HHS Benefits or Services," news release, September 29, 2005.

[59] Examples include: health insurance for elderly and disabled Americans (Medicare) and health insurance for low-income people (Medicaid); financial assistance for low-income families; pre-school education and services (Head Start); Social Security benefits; veterans benefits; and unemployment benefits.

[60] U.S. Department of Homeland Security, *National Response Plan* (Washington, D.C., December 2004), ESF #6-1.

[61] U.S. Department of Homeland Security, *National Response Plan* (Washington, D.C., December 2004), ESF #6-5. "Mass care" includes overall coordination of the shelter, feeding and other activities to support the emergency needs of victims.

[62] U.S. Department of Homeland Security, *National Response Plan* (Washington, D.C., December 2004), ESF #6-3. "Human services" refer to the provision of resources, the processing of new Federal benefit claims, compensation claims and other supportive services.

[63] U.S. Department of Homeland Security, *National Response Plan* (Washington, D.C., December 2004), ESF #6-2.

[64] Based on the locations reported by those who applied for FEMA assistance as a result of the impact of Hurricanes Katrina and Rita. U.S. Department of Homeland Security, Federal Emergency Management Agency, "Reported Locations of Katrina/Rita Applicants," January 20, 2006, http://www.fema.gov/pdf/press/katrina_after/metro_stats.pdf (accessed January 25, 2006).

[65] Michael Chertoff, Secretary of the Department of Homeland Security, written statement for a hearing on Hurricane Katrina: The Homeland Security Department's Preparation and Response, on February 15, 2006, submitted to the Senate Homeland Security and Governmental Affairs Committee, 109th Congress, 2nd session.

Governor Kathleen Blanco estimates that 8 percent of the New Orleans population stayed behind. Governor Kathleen Babineaux Blanco, written statement for a hearing on Hurricane Katrina: Preparedness and Response by the State of Louisiana, on December 14, 2005, submitted to the U.S. House Select Committee to Investigate the Preparation for and Response to Hurricane Katrina, 109th Congress, 1st session.

Mayor Nagin testified to Congress that "thousands of residents" did not leave, even after he issued the mandatory evacuation order. Ray Nagin, Mayor of New Orleans, written statement for a hearing on Hurricane Katrina: Preparedness and Response by the State of Louisiana, on December 14, 2005, submitted to the House Select Bipartisan Committee to Investigate the Preparation for and Response to Hurricane Katrina, 109th Congress, 1st session.

[66] Ronald D. Utt, "After Weeks of Confusion, the Right Course for Evacuee Housing Assistance," *WebMemo #866*, prepared for The Heritage Foundation, September 28, 2005.

[67] "Had HUD staff been more closely involved in FEMA planning, the cost and delay of relearning 50 years of lessons could have been avoided." Ronald D. Utt, "After Weeks of Confusion, the Right Course for Evacuee Housing Assistance," *WebMemo #866*, prepared for The Heritage Foundation, September 28, 2005. HUD played a key role facilitating the identification of available housing resources and placement of Katrina evacuees in housing.

[68] National Oceanic and Atmospheric Administration, National Weather Service, "NOAA Weather Radio All Hazards," January 31, 2006, http://www.weather.gov/nwr/. The Federal Communication Commission's EAS Primary Entry Point (PEP) station in New Orleans (station WWL) was one of the few radio stations in the area to provide continuous service to the New Orleans area. The NOAA Weather Radio (NWR) is a national network of radio stations that continuously broadcast weather and hazard information from local Weather Service offices. Operating in close conjunction with EAS, NOAA Weather Radio comprises an "all hazards" radio network that acts as a "single source for comprehensive weather and emergency information." National Oceanic and Atmospheric Administration, National Weather Service, "NOAA Weather Radio All Hazards," January 31, 2006, http://www.weather.gov/nwr/.

[69] The Emergency Alert System (EAS) is a mechanism for public officials—Federal, State, and local—to communicate disaster information and instructions rapidly and widely. The system aims to reach the broadest possible audience by disseminating emergency updates on existing radio and television stations, including via digital and satellite networks. Federal Communications Commission, *FCC Consumer Facts: The Emergency Alert System* (Washington, DC, 2005), 1. See also State of California, "What Is EAS?," http://eas.oes.ca.gov/Pages/whatseas.htm. The new EAS system is the direct descendant of the Emergency Broadcast System (EBS), the Nation's alert system from 1963 until the advent of EAS. EAS was officially launched on January 1, 1997 (for radio stations) and December 31, 1998 (for television). Federal Emergency Management Agency, "Background on the Emergency Alert System," October 23, 2004, http://www.fema.gov/rrr/rep/easrep.shtm. While EAS fulfills the same function as EBS, it differs in that it takes advantage of digital technology to permit automation of transmission. Federal Emergency Management Agency, "Background on the Emergency Alert System," October 23, 2004, http://www.fema.gov/rrr/rep/easrep.shtm. The Emergency Broadcast System and its EAS successor were originally designed for the President to speak to the Nation during an emergency, particularly following catastrophic nuclear attacks. But the system was made available to State and local officials in 1963, and since then has been used primarily for weather emergencies. "There are two contexts in which the EAS will be used—Presidentially-initiated alerts and messages and those initiated by State and

local governments in concert with the broadcast industry." Federal Emergency Management Agency, "Background on the Emergency Alert System," October 23, 2004, http://www.fema.gov/rrr/rep/easrep.shtm. See also, Federal Communications Commission, *FCC Consumer Facts: The Emergency Alert System* (Washington, DC, 2005), 2. The document states: "a state emergency manager may use the system to send out a public warning by broadcasting that warning from one or more major radio stations in a particular state." EAS was not activated prior to landfall aside from NOAA hurricane warnings and advisories. "The Emergency Alert System was never activated by the White House or by State or local governments during Katrina." Ken Kerschbaumer, "Broadcasters Seek Better Emergency Alert System," *Broadcasting and Cable*, September 12, 2005.

[70] "The Big Disconnect on New Orleans," *CNN.com*, September 2, 2005, http://www.cnn.com/2005/US/09/02/katrina.response.

[71] In testimony before the House Select Bipartisan Committee to Investigate the Preparation and Response to Hurricane Katrina, Mr. Phil Parr, Deputy Federal Coordinating Officer, FEMA, and Mr. Terry Ebert, Director of the Louisiana Office of Homeland Security, of the City of New Orleans, both testified that exaggerated media reports impeded rescue efforts (December 14, 2005).

[72] The Nation relies on interdependent systems known as "critical infrastructure" to maintain its defense, continuity of government, economic prosperity, and quality of life. The term critical infrastructure means "systems and assets, whether physical or virtual, so vital to the United States that the incapacity or destruction of such systems and assets would have a debilitating impact on security, national economic security, national public health or safety, or any combination of those matters." See, e.g., *USA Patriot Act of 2001*, Section 1016(e), Public Law 107-56, 107th Congress, 1st session (October 26, 2001), 115 Stat. 401; *Critical Infrastructure Protection Act of 2001*, 42 U.S.C. § 5195c(e).

Transportation, electricity, banking, telecommunications, food supply, and clean water are examples of critical infrastructure services that have become basic aspects of our daily lives. These services are often only noticed when they are disrupted, and the American public expects speedy restoration of them. Private sector companies own and operate 85 percent of our Nation's critical infrastructure and are responsible for protecting their facilities and restoring operations following an incident. U.S. Department of Homeland Security, *Interim National Infrastructure Protection Plan* (Washington, DC). Response planning must also recognize the unique Federal responsibility to support private sector efforts and assist in the restoration of critical infrastructures imperative to the National economy or integral to larger cascading systems or supply chains.

[73] U.S. Department of Energy, Energy Information Administration, *Hurricane Katrina's Impact on the U.S. Oil and Natural Gas Markets*, September 6, 2005.

[74] Samuel Bodman, Secretary of the Department of Energy, written statement for a hearing on Hurricane Recovery Efforts, on October 27, 2005, submitted to the Senate Committee on Energy and Natural Resources, 109th Congress, 1st session.

[75] U.S. Department of Energy, Office of Electricity Delivery and Energy Reliability, "Hurricane Katrina Situation Report #10," August 30, 2005.

[76] U.S. Department of Homeland Security, *National Response Plan* (Washington, D.C., December 2004), 12.

[77] Sectors include: Agriculture and Food, Banking and Finance, Chemical, Commercial Facilities, Dams, Defense Industrial Base, Emergency Services, Energy, Government Facilities, Information Technology, National Monuments and Icons, Nuclear Reactors, Material and Waste, Postal and Shipping, Public Health and Healthcare, Telecommunications, Transportation, Water. The White House, *The National Strategy for the Physical Protection of Critical Infrastructures and Key Assets* (Washington, D.C., February 2003), 9.

[78] Industries with critical infrastructure contacted various Federal departments and agencies and requested assistance to protect or to restore their facilities. These requests were inconsistently coordinated across sectors and responded to in an ad hoc fashion.

[79] "The Regional Response Coordination Center (RRCC) initially deploys a DHS/Emergency Preparedness & Response (EPR)/FEMA-led Emergency Response Team Advance (ERT-A), including rapid needs assessment personnel and appropriate ESF representatives, to State operating facilities and incident sites to assess the impact of the situation, collect damage information, gauge immediate Federal support requirements, and make preliminary arrangements to set up Federal field facilities." U.S. Department of Homeland Security, *National Response Plan* (Washington, D.C. December 2004), 51. "Infrastructure Specialist (representing ESF #3)-assesses the status of transportation." In addition, they did not have expertise in the critical infrastructure in the region. U.S. Department of Homeland Security, Federal Emergency Management Agency, "FEMA Rapid Needs Assessment Form," April

2001, http://www.fema.gov/preparednesss/resources/em_mgt/rapid_needs_assessment_team.htm (accessed on January 17, 2005).[79]

[80] U.S. Department of Homeland Security, *Interim National Infrastructure Protection Plan* (Washington, D.C.).

[81] A Superfund site is a hazardous waste site that is part of the U.S. Environmental Protection Agency's (EPA's) Superfund Program. Years ago, before people became aware of the public health and environmental dangers of dumping chemical wastes, thousands of properties became uncontrolled or abandoned hazardous waste sites. Examples include abandoned warehouses or landfills. Concern about this problem led Congress to establish in 1980 the Superfund Program to locate, investigate and clean up the worst sites nationwide. The EPA administers the Superfund Program in cooperation with individual states and tribal governments. EPA, "About Superfund," http://www.epa.gov/superfund/about.htm, accessed February 15, 2006.

[82] *Gulf Coast Hurricane Emergency Environmental Protection Act of 2005*, HR 4139, 109th Congress, 1st session, (October 25, 2005), 3.

[83] U.S. Environmental Protection Agency, "Environmental Assessment Summary," December 6, 2005, http://www.epa.gov/katrina/testresults/katrina_env _assessment_summary.htm, (accessed January 18, 2006).

[84] "As of Oct. 4, 22 multi-agency environmental assessment and recovery teams had: conducted shoreline and waterway assessments throughout Mississippi and Alabama; resolved 2,315 of 2,380 cases reported to the Coast Guard and EPA; assessed a total of 504 vessels grounded or deposited inland along coastal areas for potential oil discharges; collected more than 10,000 hazardous materials such as drums, tanks, cylinders, containers and batteries throughout the Mississippi counties of Hancock, Harrison and Jackson as well as the Alabama counties of Baldwin and Mobile; recovered about 43,000 gallons of fuel; and assessed more than 200 facilities." U.S. Department of Homeland Security, Coast Guard, "Coast Guard Response to Hurricane Katrina," U.S. Coast Guard Fact File, September 11, 2005, http://www.uscg.mil/hq/g-cp/comrel/factfile/Factcards/Hurricane_Katrina.htm.

[85] The graph shown on the referenced website displays the estimated volume and surface area of the flood waters at one foot increments. Note that the volume and area estimates are only for the areas shown as inundated on the above graphic. The depths are relative to the water surface as of the afternoon of Friday, September 2, 2005. U.S. Geological Survey, "Hurricane Katrina: Science," http://eros.usgs.gov/katrina/science.html (accessed January 23, 2006). "The affected area was home to 2.3 million people, (0.8 percent of the U.S. population), and covers 90,000 square miles, (2.5 percent of the U.S. surface area). At the time Katrina hit, New Orleans was the 35th largest U.S. city by population." See House Committee on Ways and Means, "Economic Update: Hurricane Katrina," news release, September 8, 2005, http://waysandmeans.house .gov/media/pdf/taxdocs/090805katrina.pdf.

[86] Even after assessments were conducted, a number of Federal agencies reported that their personnel did not receive information or warnings concerning environmental hazards.

[87] *Stafford Act,* 42 U.S.C. § 5173.

[88] Michael Chertoff, Secretary of the Department of Homeland Security, written statement for a hearing on "Hurricane Katrina: The Homeland Security Department's Preparation and Response," on February 15, 2006, submitted to the Senate Homeland Security and Governmental Affairs Committee, 109th Congress, 2nd session.

[89] Debris on private property can only be removed with the owner's consent or with a State or local government request to the Federal government that must meet several conditions. This was a difficult process because many owners had evacuated the area and could not be located. U.S. Department of Homeland Security, Federal Emergency Management Agency; and Eric Cramer, "Waveland: A Case Study in Community Restoration," *Mississippi Valley Division News,* http://www.mvd.usace.army.mil/hurricane/mvk/news/waveland.pdf.

[90] The Department of State lists 151 countries, political entities and international organizations that offered assistance. Two additional countries offered assistance but wished no public recognition, for a total of 153. Of those, 139 were countries and the balance (14) was either political entities or international organizations. Note that of the fourteen, five different United Nations organizations are included. Pledges totaled $854 million. Of the $854 million pledged, $400 million was in commodity for cash assistance (oil to be sold and then cash value considered). Of the remaining $454 million, $126.4 million has been received so far. The other $328 million plus the $400 million in oil, has not been received, for a total of $728 million. (As of October 12, the foreign countries had pledged $854 million in financial contributions, and of this amount the USG had received $118.9 million (the latter figure had increased to $126.4 million by January 9). On October 20, 2005, after interagency consensus, $66 million of the foreign funds received by the U.S. was transferred to FEMA for a case management program. The

Federal government expects the balance of the foreign funds received to be allocated shortly. This accounts for all $854 million pledged.

[91] A German company offering a $3 million integrated satellite and cellular telephone system capable of handling 5,000 calls at once waited five days for a written deployment order from USNORTHCOM.

[92] Joel Brinkley and Craig S. Smith, "Score of nations offer their help," *International Herald Tribune*, September 8, 2005; and Sean McCormack, "Daily Press Briefing," US Department of State, September 7, 2005.

[93] The State Department made contact with all New Orleans-based consulates, facilitated visits by various consular officials, as well as monitored the arrival and distribution of in-kind assistance and held regular press briefings. There is no tracking of Green Card holders or tourists.

[94] U.S. Department of Homeland Security, "Emergencies and Disasters," http://www.dhs.gov/interweb/assetlibrary/katrina.html (accessed January 13, 2006).

[95] U.S. Citizen Corps, "Citizen Corps Support for Hurricane Katrina Response & Recovery Efforts," http://www.citizencorps.gov/doc/cc_Support_Katrina_1005.doc (accessed January 13, 2006).

[96] Long before Hurricane Katrina ever made landfall, the Harris County Citizen Corps laid the groundwork for success with its pre-incident organization and its partnerships with local volunteer groups and area businesses. These two factors allowed the Harris County Citizen Corps to mobilize and organize its resources quickly and efficiently to serve the thousands of evacuees sheltered in Houston-area sites. According to emergency responders on the scene, Citizen Corps members previously trained in the National Incident Management System (NIMS) and the Incident Command System (ICS) were of great value to the hurricane response. Due to their pre-incident training, many Citizen Corps volunteers were already familiar with NIMS/ICS terminology (e.g., Joint Information Center, Joint Operations Center, IC, etc.) and understood the responsibilities of emergency responders at the incident site. Information available at U.S. Department of Homeland Security, *Lessons Learned Information Sharing (LLIS.gov) website*, https://www.llis.dhs.gov/member/secure/detail.cfm?content_id=14990.

[97] Tim Yarbrough, "Baptists' 10.5 Million Meals shatters Prior Disaster Relief Record," *North American Mission Board*, http://www.namb.net/site/apps/nl/content2.asp?c=9qKILUOzEpH&b=227361&ct=1568907 (accessed January 13, 2006).

[98] The White House, Office of National Drug Control Policy, "Director Walters visits Baton Rouge, LA," September 30, 2005, http://www.pushingback.com/archives/05sep.html (accessed January 13, 2006). See also, Set Free Indeed Ministry, "Hurricane Katrina: Set Free Indeed Offering Recovery & Relief," http://www.setfreeindeedministry.com/katrina.html (accessed February 15, 2005).

[99] Melvin "Kip" Holden, Mayor of Baton Rouge, interview by Wolf Blitzer, *CNN Late Edition with Wolf Blitzer*, September 11, 2005, http://transcripts.cnn.com/TRANSCRIPTS/0509/11/le.01.html.

CHAPTER SIX: TRANSFORMING NATIONAL PREPAREDNESS

[1] The National Security Act of 1947 mandated a major reorganization of the foreign policy and military establishments of the U.S. Government. The act created many of the institutions that Presidents found useful when formulating and implementing foreign policy, including the National Security Council (NSC). The Council itself included the President, Vice President, Secretary of State, Secretary of Defense, and other members (such as the Director of Central Intelligence), who met at the White House to discuss both long-term problems and more immediate national security crises. A small NSC staff was hired to coordinate foreign policy materials from other agencies for the President. Beginning in 1953, the President's Assistant for National Security Affairs directed this staff.

The act also established the Central Intelligence Agency (CIA), which grew out of World War II era Office of Strategic Services and small post-war intelligence organizations. The CIA served as the primary civilian intelligence-gathering organization in the government. Later, the Defense Intelligence Agency became the main military intelligence body. The 1947 law also caused far-reaching changes in the military establishment. The War Department and Navy Department merged into a single Department of Defense under the Secretary of Defense, who also directed the newly created Department of the Air Force. However, each of the three branches maintained their own service secretaries. In 1949 the act was amended to give the Secretary of Defense more power over the individual services and their secretaries.

See generally *National Security Act of 1947*, 61 Stat. 495, codified at 50 U.S.C. §§ 401—403-3 (2005).

[2] The White House, *The National Security Strategy of the United States of America* (Washington, DC, September 2002); The White House, Office of Homeland Security, *National Strategy for Homeland Security* (Washington, DC, July 2002); and The White House, *National Strategy for Combating Terrorism* (Washington, DC, February 2003).

[3] See U.S. Department of Homeland Security, *National Response Plan* (Washington, DC, December 2004); U.S. Department of Homeland Security, *National Incident Management System* (Washington, DC, March 1, 2004); U.S. Department of Homeland Security, *Interim National Preparedness Goal* (Washington, DC, March 31, 2005); and U.S. Department of Homeland Security, *Interim National Infrastructure Protection Plan* (Washington, DC, February 2005).

[4] *Interim National Preparedness Goal*, 3.

[5] Homeland Security Presidential Directive-8 (HSPD-8) establishes policy that all Federal departments and agencies will cooperate to issue relevant State and local financial assistance, program announcements, solicitations, application instructions, and other guidance documents in a manner that is consistent with the National Preparedness Goal. The White House, *Homeland Security Presidential Directive-8: National Preparedness* [*"HSPD-8"*] (Washington, DC, December 17, 2003).

[6] Congress requires the Secretary of Defense to conduct a comprehensive examination every four years (known as the "Quadrennial Defense Review") of the national defense strategy, force structure, force modernization plans, infrastructure, budget plan, and other elements of the defense program and policies of the United States with a view toward determining and expressing the defense strategy of the United States and establishing a defense program for the next twenty years. See 10 U.S.C. § 118 (2005).

[7] See note 2.

[8] Among other reforms, the *Goldwater-Nichols* legislation clarified the chain of command from the President to the Secretary of Defense to the Combatant Commander. It also elevated the Chairman of the Joint Chiefs of Staff to be the President's principal military adviser and strengthened the Joint Staff as a truly "Joint" organization that works for the Chairman, not the armed services. *Goldwater-Nichols Act of 1986*, Public Law 99-433, 99th Congress, 2nd session, 101 Stat. 992 (October 1, 1986).

[9] Eligibility to receive State Homeland Security Grant Program funding is dependent upon DHS approval of statewide, territory, or regional homeland security strategies that adopt capability-based planning and a prioritization of assets based on risks and need in conformance with the National Preparedness Goal. The Urban Area Security Initiative is a subset of the State Homeland Security Grant Program, providing funds to address the unique planning, equipment, training, and exercise needs of high threat, high-density urban areas, and assist them in building an enhanced and sustainable capacity to prevent, protect against, respond to, and recover from acts of terrorism. U.S. Department of Homeland Security, FY 2006 Homeland Security Grant Program (Washington, DC, December 2005).

[10] *HSPD-8*, § 1.

[11] See generally *Interim National Preparedness Goal*.

[12] In particular, DHS would benefit from sufficient funds to permit the Department to deploy additional assets and resources upon warning of a catastrophic event. Furthermore, we as a Nation must not penalize DHS and other Federal responders when they undertake anticipatory actions for false alarms. To use medical terms, a *false negative* is unacceptable while we should be willing to accept some *false positives*.

[13] As described in the *National Incident Management System*, the command function may be exercised in two general ways: 1) through a "Single Command" structure led by an Incident Commander (IC), or through a "Unified Command." In a Single Command structure, the IC is solely responsible for establishing incident management objectives and strategies and for ensuring that all functional area activities are directed toward accomplishment of the strategy. In a Unified Command structure, the individuals designated by their jurisdictional authorities jointly determine objectives, strategies, plans, and priorities and work together to execute integrated incident operations and maximize the use of assigned resources. *National Incident Management System*, 12-16.

[14] The White House, *Homeland Security Presidential Directive-5: Management of Domestic Incidents* (Washington, DC, February 28, 2003). See also *Homeland Security Act of 2002* [*"Homeland Security Act"*], Public Law 296, 107th Congress, 2nd session (November 22, 2005), § 101, codified at 6 U.S.C. § 111 (2002).

[15] *HSPD-5*, § 14.

[16] There is no reason to eliminate the FCO role in the Stafford Act as there is a wide-range of incidents that are not nationally significant—such as most wildfires—where an FCO is essential to coordinate the Federal response, but a PFO is not necessary.

[17] *HSPD-5*, § 5.

---

[18] First issued in 1992, the *Federal Response Plan* (FRP) outlined how the Federal Government implemented the Stafford Act to assist State and local governments when a major disaster or emergency overwhelmed their ability to respond effectively to save lives; protect public health, safety, and property; and restore communities. The FRP outlined policies, planning assumptions, concept of operations, response and recovery actions, and responsibilities of twenty-five Federal departments and agencies and the American Red Cross, that guided Federal operations following a Presidential declaration of a major disaster or emergency. An interim edition of the FRP was released in 2003 to reflect the passage of the Homeland Security Act of 2002 and the establishment of DHS. *Federal Response Plan (Interim)*, January 2003.

[19] See generally *National Response Plan*, pg. ESF-i et seq. Under current arrangements, the *NRP* Emergency Support Functions (ESF) do not cleanly connect to the ICS structure required by *NIMS*, thus causing at time dueling systems or organizations to be created—one based on the ESF structure and one based on the ICS system. The Incident Command System (ICS) adopted by *NIMS* has five major sections (Command, Operations, Planning, Logistics, and Finance/Administration), each with their own subordinate groups that are modular and scalable to account for situations of various size and nature. See *National Incident Management System*, 7.

[20] An eligibility requirement for States, territories, and regions to receive State Homeland Security Grant Program and Urban Areas Security Initiative grant funds is compliance with the phased implementation of *NIMS*. U.S. Department of Homeland Security, *FY 2006 Homeland Security Grant Program* ["*FY 2006 Homeland Security Grant Program*"] (Washington, DC, December 2005). The implementation of the *National Incident Management System* is also one of seven priorities for spending Federal homeland security assistance as outlined in the NPG. *Interim National Preparedness Goal*, 10.

[21] The National Defense University, located at Fort McNair in Washington, DC, prepares military and civilian leaders from the United States and other countries to address national and international security challenges, through multi-disciplinary educational programs, research, professional exchanges, and outreach. For additional information, see www.ndu.edu.

[22] See *Goldwater-Nichols Act of 1986*, Public Law 99-433, 99th Congress, 2nd session (October 1, 1986), § 401-406.

[23] HSPD-8 directs the Secretary of Homeland Security to establish a national program and a multi-year planning system to conduct homeland security preparedness-related exercises in coordination with other appropriate Federal departments and agencies. See generally *HSPD-8*.

[24] The *National Strategy for Homeland Security* directed the establishment of a National Exercise Strategy. *HSPD-8* directed Secretary Tom Ridge to establish a "National Exercise Program" (NEP). Secretary Ridge charged the DHS Office of Domestic Preparedness to develop a program that identifies and integrates national level exercise activities to ensure those activities serve the broadest community of learning. In addition to full scale, integrated National level exercises—the NEP provides for tailored exercise activities that serve as the Department's primary vehicle for training national leaders and staff. The NEP enhances the collaboration among partners at all levels of government for assigned homeland security missions. National-level exercises provide the means to conduct "full-scale, full system tests" of collective preparedness, interoperability, and collaboration across all levels of government and the private sector. The program also incorporates elements to allow us to identify the implications of changes to homeland security strategies, plans, technologies, policies, and procedures. The cornerstone of national performance-based exercises is the Top Officials (TOPOFF), biennial exercise series. TOPOFF included a functional exercise in 2000 (TOPOFF I) and a full-scale exercise in 2003 (TOPOFF II). For additional information, see http://www.ojp.usdoj.gov/odp. The "Homeland Security Exercise and Evaluation Program" (HSEEP) is both doctrine and policy for designing, developing, conducting and evaluating exercises. HSEEP is a threat- and performance-based exercise program that includes a cycle, mix and range of exercise activities of varying degrees of complexity and interaction.
HSEEP includes a series of four reference manuals to help states and local jurisdictions establish exercise programs and design, develop, conduct, and evaluate exercises. For additional information, see http://www.ojp.usdoj.gov/odp/docs/hseep.htm.http://www.hseep.dhs.gov

[25] Office of Management and Budget, *The President's Management Agenda* (Washington, DC, 2001). See also *FY 2006 Homeland Security Grant Program*.

[26] U.S. Commission on the Intelligence Capabilities of the United States Regarding Weapons of Mass Destruction, *Report to the President of the United States* ["*WMD Report*"](Washington, DC, March 31, 2005), 337-341; National Commission on Terrorist Attacks Upon the United States, *The 9/11 Commission Report: Final Report of the National Commission on Terrorist Attacks Upon the United States* ["*9/11 Report*"] (New York: WW Norton and Company, July 22, 2004), 420-421.

---

[27] Prior to the 109th Congress, the Department was subject to the oversight of eighty-eight different Congressional committees and sub-committees. See 9/11 Public Discourse project, "Fact Sheet on Congressional Reform" (Washington, DC, July 11, 2005), http://www.9-11pdp.org/ua/2005-07-11_factsheet.pdf. Subsequently, the committee structure has been changed to attempt a consolidation of homeland security oversight through the formation of a Senate Committee on Homeland Security and Government Affairs and a House Committee on Homeland Security.

[28] For example, using a risk-based formula, the Urban Area Security Initiative is funded for FY06 at $765 million. This compares to the $950 million of FY06 funding allocated in both equal distributions and risk-based justifications across the States and territories through the State Homeland Security Grant Program and the Law Enforcement Terrorism Prevention Program. Moreover, when other "all-hazards" grant programs (e.g., Firefighter Assistance Grants and Emergency Management Performance Grants) are added to the equation, risk-based grants account for less than 30 percent of homeland security grants for preparedness and other responder needs. *Department of Homeland Security Appropriations Act of 2006,* Public Law 90, 109th Congress, 1st session (October 18, 2005). See also Shawn Reese, "Risk-Based Funding in Homeland Security Grant Legislation: Analysis of Issues for the 109th Congress," CRS Report # 33050, August 29, 2005.

[29] The *Interim National Preparedness Goal* defines capabilities-based planning as "planning, under uncertainty, to provide capabilities suitable for a wide range of threats and hazards while working within an economic framework that necessitates prioritization and choice." *Interim National Preparedness Goal,* 4.

[30] U.S. Department of Homeland Security, *National Planning Scenarios, Draft Version 20.1* ["*National Planning Scenarios*"] (Washington, DC, April 2005).

[31] Figure 2 duplicates Figure 1.1 in the previous "Katrina in Perspective" chapter, with the addition of the September 11th terrorist attacks and National Planning Scenarios 1, 3, and 9. For sources for these additions, see *9/11 Report,* Executive Summary, 1-2; Robert Looney, "Economic Costs to the United States Stemming From the 9/11 Attacks," *Strategic Insights* 1, no. 6 (Monterey, CA, August 2002), http://www.ccc.nps.navy.mil/si/aug02/homeland.asp; and *National Planning Scenarios.* Table 4, below, contains the data used in Figure 2.

Table 1. Worst Natural Disasters in the United States, 1900-2005, with September 11th Terrorist Attacks and Selected National Planning Scenarios
Damage in Third Quarter 2005 dollars

Top Disasters	Estimated deaths	Estimated damage
Galveston Hurricane (1900)	8,000	< $1 billion
San Francisco Earthquake and Fire (1906)	5,000	$6 billion
Atlantic-Gulf Hurricane (1919)	600	< $1 billion
Mississippi Floods (1927)	246	$2 billion
Hurricane San Felipe and the Okeechobee Flood (1928)	2,750	< $1 billion
New England Hurricane (1938)	600	$4 billion
Northeast Hurricane (1944)	390	< $1 billion
Hurricane Diane (1955)	184	$5 billion
Hurricane Audrey (1957)	390	< $1 billion
Hurricane Betsy (1965)	75	$7 billion
Hurricane Camille (1969)	335	$6 billion
Hurricane Agnes (1972)	122	$8 billion
Hurricane Hugo (1989)	86	$11 billion
Hurricane Andrew (1992)	61	$33 billion
East Coast Blizzard (1993)	270	$4 billion
September 11, 2001	2981	$18 billion
Major 2004 Hurricanes (Charley, Frances, Ivan, Jeanne)	167	$46 billion
Hurricane Katrina (2005)	1,330	$96 billion
National Planning Scenarios		

#1. 10-kt Improvised Nuclear Device	Hundreds of thousands	Hundreds of billions of dollars
#3. Pandemic Influenza	87,000	$87 billion (low estimate)
#9. Major Earthquake	1,400	Hundreds of billions of dollars

[32] Governor Kathleen Blanco estimates that 8 percent of the New Orleans population stayed behind: "Hurricane Ivan threatened us last year. Our evacuation looked like Houston's—not very pretty. Before Katrina came, I developed a new evacuation plan that includes contra-flow, where both sides of the interstates are used for outbound traffic. I am proud that we rapidly moved over 1.2 million people—some 92% of the population—to safety without gridlock or undue delay prior to Katrina." Governor Kathleen Babineaux Blanco, written statement for a hearing on Hurricane Katrina: Preparedness and Response by the State of Louisiana, on December 14, 2005, submitted to the U.S. House Select Committee to Investigate the Preparation for and Response to Hurricane Katrina, 109th Congress, 1st session.

[33] 9/11 Report, 336 (quoting then-Deputy Secretary of Defense Paul Wolfowitz).

[34] "1984: Tory Cabinet in Brighton bomb blast," BBC.co.uk, October 12, 1984, http://newssearch.bbc.co.uk/onthisday/hi/dates/stories/october/12/newsid_2531000/2531583.stm.

[35] The 9/11 Commission report describes the 9/11 attacks resulting partly from a failure in imagination. In particular, the Commission report highlights the importance of institutionalizing imagination in our methods for detecting and warning of surprise attacks. See 9/11 Report, 336, 339-348.

[36] National Response Plan, 5.

[37] See also Frances Fragos Townsend, Remarks at the National Emergency Management Association's 2006 Mid-Year Conference, February 13, 2006, available at www.lexis.com.

[38] Current programs aimed at increasing the preparedness of individual citizens and communities include Citizen Corps, the Community Emergency Response Team (CERT) program, the Fire Corps, the Neighborhood Watch Program, the Medical Reserve Corps Program, as well as Volunteers in Police Service. For summaries of these programs, see U.S. Citizen Corps, "Partners and Programs," http://www.citizencorps.gov/programs/.

[39] U.S. Department of Homeland Security, "Good Story: Harris County, Texas Citizen Corps' Response to Hurricane Katrina," Lessons Learned Information Sharing (LLIS.gov) database, November 17, 2005, http://www.llis.gov.

[40] 9/11 Report, 318.

[41] "The Ad Council has declared Ready one of the most successful campaigns in its more than 60-year history. Since its launch the Ready campaign has generated more than $466 million in donated media support and its website has received more than 1.9 billion hits and 22 million unique visitors. The U.S. Department of Homeland Security promotes individual emergency preparedness through the Ready campaign and Citizen Corps as part of a broader national effort conducted by the Department's Preparedness Directorate. Ready is a national public service advertising campaign produced by The Advertising Council in partnership with Homeland Security. The Ready campaign is designed to educate and empower Americans to prepare for and respond to emergencies, including natural disasters and potential terrorist attacks." U.S. Department of Homeland Security, "Homeland Security and the Advertising Council Provide Parents and Teachers with Resources to Educate Children about Emergency Preparedness," news release, February 2, 2006, http://www.dhs.gov/dhspublic/interapp/press_release/ press_release_0848.xml. See also www.ready.gov.

[42] The "Learn Not to Burn" curriculum, first released in 1979, teaches twenty-two key fire safety behaviors and is organized in three learning levels. The curriculum is intended for use by teachers in planning classroom activities and can be re-used from year to year. "Learn Not to Burn" incorporates fire safety behaviors into regular school subjects, so children absorb life-saving information while developing skills in reading, math, art, history, and science. National Fire Protection Association, "Learn Not to Burn," http://www.nfpa.org

[43] A 2004 study by the National Highway Traffic Safety Administration reported a record 80 percent of Americans wear their safety belts while driving or riding in their vehicles. Transportation Secretary Norman Y. Mineta said the 80 percent safety belt usage will save 15,200 lives and $50 billion in economic costs associated with traffic related crashes, injuries, and deaths every year. Donna Glassbrenner, "Safety Belt Use in 2004—Overall Results, Traffic Safety Facts," prepared for the National Center for Statistics and Analysis (September 2004). See

also U.S. Department of Transportation, National Highway Traffic Safety Administration, "Safety belt use jumps to record 80%," news release, September 16, 2004.

[44] Additional advertising campaigns that were successful in helping to change citizen behavior include efforts to stop the use of drugs through the 'Just Say No' message created by First Lady Nancy Reagan and 'Drug Abuse Resistance Education' (D.A.R.E.); prevent drunk driving originating with Mothers Against Drunk Driving (MADD); help quit smoking through the Surgeon General's campaign to educate people on health risks and the American Cancer Society's Great 'American Smoke Out'; and stop littering through the 'Keep America Beautiful' message promoted by First Lady Claudia 'Lady Bird' Johnson.

[45] For example, the development of the *Interim National Infrastructure Protection Plan* has developed upon a close partnership between governments at all levels and the private sector owners of the Nation's Critical Infrastructure and Key Resources. Our national efforts to improve air transportation security, furthermore, have depended upon unprecedented partnership between DHS's Transportation Security Administration and the airline industry. See generally, *Interim National Infrastructure Protection Plan* (Washington, DC, February 2005).

[46] *National Strategy for Homeland Security*, viii.

[47] For information on BRT, see Business Round Table letter to President George W. Bush, January 31, 2006, and http://www.businessroundtable.org/. For information on BENS, see www.bens.org. The BENS "Business Force" project partnerships of regional, State, and local officials, together with businesses and NGOs, have been successful in emergency response planning and using private sector resources and volunteers to fill gaps in preparedness and response capabilities.

[48] "A basic premise of the *NRP* is that incidents are generally handled at the lowest jurisdictional level possible. Police, fire, public health and medical, emergency management, and other personnel are responsible for incident management at the local level . . . In the vast majority of incidents, State and local resources and interstate mutual aid normally provide the first line of emergency response and incident management support. When an incident or potential incident is of such severity, magnitude, and/or complexity that it is considered an Incident of National Significance according to the criteria established in this plan, the Secretary of Homeland Security, in coordination with other Federal departments and agencies, initiates actions to prevent, prepare for, respond to, and recover from the incident." *National Response Plan*, 15.

[49] EMAC was developed in the 1990s and officially ratified by Congress as an organization with thirteen member States in 1996. *Emergency Management Assistance Compact*, Public Law 104-321, 104th Congress, 2nd session, (October 19, 1996). As of October 2005, 49 States, the District of Columbia, the U.S. Virgin Islands, and Puerto Rico had enacted EMAC legislation. National Emergency Management Association, "EMAC Overview," December 2005, http://www.emacweb.org/?323. EMAC is administered by the National Emergency Management Association (NEMA). During an emergency, NEMA staff works with EMAC member states to coordinate ensure information passes easily through the EMAC system.

APPENDIX B – WHAT WENT RIGHT

[1] The White House, "President Visits Mississippi, Discusses Gulf Coast Reconstruction," January 12, 2006, http://www.whitehouse.gov/news/releases/2006/01/20060112-3.html.

[2] U.S. Department of Homeland Security, "Hurricane Katrina: What Government is Doing," http://www.dhs.gov/katrina.htm.

[3] U.S. Department of Homeland Security, "Good Story: Harris County, Texas Citizen Corps' Response to Hurricane Katrina," *Lessons Learned Information Sharing (LLIS.gov) database*, November 17, 2005, http://www.LLIS.gov.

[4] North American Mission Board, Southern Baptist Convention, "Disaster Relief: Generosity Fatigue Nowhere in Sight," news release, September 23, 2005.

[5] Kip Holden, Mayor of Baton Rouge, Louisiana, interview by Wolf Blitzer, *CNN Late Edition with Wolf Blitzer*, September 11, 2005, http://transcripts.cnn.com/TRANSCRIPTS/0509/11/le.01.html; Set Free Indeed Ministry, "Hurricane Katrina Set Free Indeed Offering Recovery and Relief," http://setfreeindeedministry.com/katrina.html (accessed February 8, 2006); and Bethany World Prayer Center website, "Hurricane Relief. Hurricane Katrina (Timeline)," http://www.bethany.com/katrina_relief.php (accessed February 8, 2006).

[6] Operation Blessing, "Hurricane Relief: Hurricane Relief by State," http://www.ob.org/projects/hurricane_relief/

index.asp.

[7] Operation Blessing, "Hurricane Relief Activities in the Gulf Coast," http://www.ob.org/projects/hurricane_relief/relief_log.asp?NP_ID=1772.

[8] The Salvation Army, "Across the Nation the Salvation Army is Providing Aid to Survivors of Hurricane Katrina," news release, September 13, 2005.

[9] The Salvation Army, "Katrina Update 1-20-06," January 20, 2006, http://www.satern.org/response.html.

[10] Livingston Parish, "After Action Report," February 2006.

[11] Gary Krakow, "Ham Radio Operators to the Rescue after Katrina: Amateur Radio Networks Help Victims of the Hurricane," *MSNBC*, September 6, 2005, http://www.msnbc.msn.com/id/9228945/; American Radio Relay League (ARRL), "Amateur Radio Volunteers Involved in Katrina Recovery," news release, August 31, 2005, http://www.arrl.org/news/stories/2005/08/30/1/?nc=1; Ben Joplin, interview by National Public Radio, *All Things Considered*, August 30, 2005, http://www.npr.org/templates/story/story.php?storyId=4824598.

[12] American Radio Relay League (ARRL), "President Urges Orderly Amateur Radio Response in Katrina Recovery," news release, September 1, 2005, http://www.arrl.org/news/stories/2005/09/01/2/; American Radio Relay League (ARRL), "Amateur Radio Volunteers Involved in Katrina Recovery," news release, August 31, 2005, http://www.arrl.org/news/stories/2005/08/30/1/.

[13] Association of State Public Health Laboratories, "APHL Response to Hurricane Katrina 2005," http://www.aphl.org/article.cfm?ArticleID=98; U.S. Environmental Protection Agency, Region 4, "Response to Hurricane Katrina," September 5, 2005, http://epa.gov/region4/Katrina/response_20050905.htm; University of Iowa, "UI Hurricane Katrina Relief Includes Expertise, Enrollment, Supplies, Space," news release, September 2, 2005, http://www.uiowa.edu/~ournews/2005/september/090205katrina-relief.html; Iowa Office of the Governor, "Iowans continue to aid survivors of Hurricane Katrina: State agencies stand ready to aid victims of Hurricane Rita," news release, September 22, 2005, http://www.iowahomelandsecurity.org/asp/hurricane_katrina/IA_efforts_update.doc; and email from Association of State Public Health Laboratories.

[14] New York City Fire Department, "Update on FDNY Hurricane Katrina Relief Efforts," news release, September 26, 2005, http://www.nyc.gov/html/fdny/html/pr/2005/092605_alert_01.shtml.

[15] Federal Express, "FedEx Support of Relief Efforts in Areas Affected by Hurricane Katrina," news release, September 7, 2005, http://www.fedex.com/us/about/responsibility/katrina.html?link=4.

[16] Rich Karlgaard, "Wonderful Wealth," *Forbes* 176, no. 7 (October 10, 2005), 43; Dell USA, "Helping Those in Need," http://www1.us.dell.com/content/topics/segtopic.aspx/brand/katrina_relief?c=us&cs=19&l=en&s=gen (accessed February 8, 2006); Home Depot, "Hurricane Katrina: Relief and Rebuilding Efforts," http://www.homedepot.com (accessed February 8, 2006); IBM, "IBM Response Gains Ground in Aftermath of Katrina," http://www.ibm.com/news/us/en/2005/09/2005_09_06.html (accessed February 8, 2006); Lenovo, "Lenovo Responds to Hurricane Katrina Tragedy," September 2, 2006, http://www.pc.ibm.com/us/lenovo/about/hurricane.html (accessed February 8, 2006); Pfizer, "Pfizer Expands Hurricane Katrina Relief Effort," September 21, 2006, http://www.pfizer.com/pfizer/are/news_releases/2005pr/mn_2005_0921a.jsp (accessed February 8, 2006); and Wal-Mart, "Wal-Mart Commits Additional $15 Million to Katrina Relief," September 1, 2006, http://walmartstores.com/GlobalWMStoresWeb/navigate.do?catg=26&contId=4856 (accessed February 8, 2006).

[17] Gary P. LaGrange, President and Chief Executive Officer of the Port of New Orleans, testimony before a hearing on Revitalizing the Economy of South Louisiana, on November 7, 2005, to the Senate Committee on Commerce, Science, and Transportation, 109th Congress, 1st session.

[18] U.S. Department of Homeland Security, Customs and Border Protection, "U.S. Customs and Border Protection Donates More Than 100,000 Pieces of Seized Goods for Hurricane Katrina Evacuees in Mississippi," news release, September 12, 2005.

[19] U.S. Department of Homeland Security, Federal Emergency Management Agency, "Hurricane Katrina Information," news release, February 1, 2006, http://www.fema.gov/press/2005/resources_katrina.

[20] U.S. Department of Homeland Security, Federal Emergency Management Agency, National Disaster Medical System Section, FloridaOne Disaster Medical Assistance Team, "Hurricane Katrina Deployment," http://dev.floridaonedmat.com/index.cfm/m/1/m/88.

[21] U.S. Department of Homeland Security, "Hurricane Katrina DHS SITREP #18," September 4, 2005, 2.

[22] U.S. Department of Homeland Security, Federal Emergency Management Agency, "Executive Briefing," (September 17, 2005), 9.

[23] Paul McHale, Assistant Defense Secretary for Homeland Defense, testimony before a hearing on Hurricane Katrina: Preparedness and Response by the Department of Defense, the Coast Guard, and the National Guard of Louisiana, Mississippi, and Alabama, on October 27, 2005, House Select Bipartisan Committee to Investigate the Preparation for and Response to Hurricane Katrina, 109th Congress, 1st session; Lieutenant Colonel Richard Chavez, Chief of the Homeland Security Readiness Branch, testimony before a hearing on Hurricane Katrina: Preparedness and Response by the Department of Defense, the Coast Guard, and the National Guard of Louisiana, Mississippi, and Alabama, on October 27, 2005, to the House Select Bipartisan Committee to Investigate the Preparation for and Response to Hurricane Katrina, 109th Congress, 1st session.

[24] U.S. Department of Defense, Army Corps of Engineers, Mississippi Valley Division, Louisiana Recovery Field Office, "New Orleans: Unwatered," news release, October 11, 2005.

[25] Donna Miles, "Military Hurricane Relief Focuses on Saving Lives, Reducing Suffering," American Forces Press Service, September 1, 2005, http://www.defenselink.mil/news/Sep2005/20050901_2590.html.

[26] U.S. Marine Corps, "Beirut Battalion Concludes Contribution to Hurricane Relief," *Marine Corps News*, October 1, 2005.

[27] U.S. Marine Corps, "Marine Recruiters Save 150 Lives after Hurricane Katrina," *Marine Corps News*, September 28, 2005.

[28] William Carwile, Federal Coordinating Officer for Mississippi, Federal Emergency Management Agency, written statement for a hearing on Hurricane Katrina: Perspectives on FEMA's Operations Professionals, on December 8, 2005, submitted to the Senate Committee on Homeland Security and Governmental Affairs, 109th Congress, 1st session.

[29] Katy Glassborow, "US Navy joins disaster-relief effort in wake of Hurricane Katrina," *Jane's Navy International*, September 9, 2005. See also Paul McHale, Assistant Secretary of Defense for Homeland Defense, testimony before a hearing on the Role of the Military and National Guard in Disaster Response, on November 9, 2005, House Committee on Homeland Security, Subcommittee on Emergency Preparedness, Science, and Technology, 109th Congress, 1st session.

[30] U.S. Department of Defense, Navy, Commander of the 2nd Fleet Public Affairs, "Norfolk Ships Deploy to Support Hurricane Katrina Relief Efforts," *Navy Newsstand*, August 31, 2005.

[31] U.S. Department of Defense, Air Force Reserve, 53rd Weather Reconnaissance Squadron, "The Hurricane Hunters," http://www.hurricanehunters.com/welcome.htm (accessed February 2, 2006) ; U.S. Department of Defense, Air Force Reserve, 53rd Weather Reconnaissance Squadron, "Eye to Eye with Hurricane Katrina," http://www.hurricanehunters.com/katrina.htm (accessed January 25, 2006).

[32] U.S. Department of Commerce, National Oceanic and Atmospheric Administration, National Hurricane Center, "NHC/TPC Hurricane Reconnaissance Data Archive," ftp://ftp.nhc.noaa.gov/pub/products/nhc/recon; and U.S. Department of Defense, Air Force Reserve, 53rd Weather Reconnaissance Squadron, "Eye to Eye with Hurricane Katrina," http://www.hurricanehunters.com/katrina.htm (accessed January 25, 2006).

[33] U.S. Department of Defense, Air Force, "Air Force Support of Hurricane Katrina Continues," *Air Force Link*, September 4, 2005.

[34] U.S. National Geospatial Intelligence Agency, "Geospatial Intelligence Aids Hurricane Recovery Efforts," news release, September 7, 2005.

[35] The LECC is DOJ construct integrating the Federal, State, and local law enforcement communities, but is not a term currently incorporated into the NRP. See, e.g., U.S. Department of Justice, United States Attorney's Office, Northern District of Georgia, "LECC," http://www.usdoj.gov/usao/gan/lecc.html (accessed January 31, 2006).

[36] The LECC was built on a modified FBI Joint Operations Center construct. The LECC coordinated a plan to answer thousands of 911 calls in New Orleans that had gone unresolved. The LECC provided the conduit for coordination between civilian law enforcement and the National Guard and Title 10 U.S. Army forces operating in New Orleans. The LECC not only provided a facility for all Federal law enforcement, but built a separate headquarters for the New Orleans Police adjacent to the LECC, since their headquarters had been destroyed.

[37] Agency for Healthcare Research and Quality, *Use of Former("Shuttered") Hospitals to Expand Surge Capacity* (Gaithersburg, MD, August 2005).

[38] U.S. Department of Health and Human Services, Centers for Disease Control and Prevention, "Update on CDC's Response to Hurricane Katrina," September 16, 2005, http://www.cdc.gov/od/katrina/09-16-05.htm.

[39] Jennifer Thew and Phyllis Class, "Shelter from the Storm," *Nursing Spectrum*, October 1, 2005, http://www.nursingspectrum.com/Katrina/ShelterFromTheStorm.cfm; and U.S. Department of Health and Human

Services, Centers for Disease Control, "Update on CDC's Response to Hurricane Katrina," September 6, 2005, http://www.cdc.gov/od/katrina/09-06-05.htm.

[40] U.S. Department of Health and Human Services, National Institutes of Health, "NIH Opens Up Medical Consultation Line to Patients Affected by Hurricane Katrina," news release, September 14, 2005.

[41] U.S. Department of Transportation, "DOT Activities in Support of Federal Response to Hurricane Katrina," news release, September 5, 2005.

[42] U.S. Department of Housing and Urban Development, "HUD's Response to Hurricanes Katrina and Rita." http://www.hud.gov/news/katrina05response.cfm (accessed December 14, 2005).

[43] Ann Westling, "Tahoe National Forest Service Employees – Some Back from Hurricane Katrina," *YubaNet*, October 15, 2005, http://yubanet.com/artman/publish/article_26436.shtml; U.S. Department of Agriculture, "USDA Assists with Hurricane Katrina Relief Efforts," news release, September 5, 2005.

[44] U.S. Department of Agriculture, National Resources Conservation Service, Emergency Watershed Program, "Digital Data Provides Maps for Hurricane Relief," news release, September 23, 2005.

[45] U.S. Department of Agriculture, "USDA Prepares for Hurricane Rita: USDA Highlights Assistance to Regions Affected by Hurricane Katrina," news release, September 22, 2005, http://www.usda.gov/wps.

[46] U.S. Department of Agriculture, Farm Service Agency, "100% Cost Share Assistance Available to Farmers in FSA's Emergency Conservation Program," news release, *FSA Online*, September 15, 2005, http://www.fsa.usda.gov/ms/news0101.htm.

[47] U.S. Department of Agriculture, Rural Development, "Hurricane Katrina Recovery Resources from Rural Development," http://www.rurdev.usda.gov/rd/disasters/katrina.html.

[48] U.S. Department of Agriculture, Agricultural Research Service, "Plant Protection Research Unit News and Events," news release, November 14, 2005.

[49] U.S. Department of Energy, Office of Science, "DOE's Office of Science Responds to Hurricane Katrina," news release, September 8, 2005, http://www.sc.doe.gov/Sub/Newsroom/News_Releases/DOE-SC/2005/Hurricane/Hurricane.htm.

[50] U.S. Department of Commerce, Minority Business Development Agency, "MBDA to Assist with Rebuilding Minority Business Enterprises Hit by Hurricane Katrina," news release, September 9, 2005.

[51] Max Mayfield, Director of the National Hurricane Center, written statement for a hearing on the Lifesaving Role of Accurate Hurricane Prediction, on September 20, 2005, submitted to the U.S. Senate Committee on Commerce, Science, and Transportation, Subcommittee on Disaster Prevention and Prediction, 109th Congress, 1st session.

[52] U.S. Department of Commerce, National Oceanic and Atmospheric Administration, National Weather Service, *Flash Flood Warning*, (New Orleans, LA, August 29, 2005, 8:14 AM).

[53] U.S. Department of Commerce, National Telecommunications and Information Administration, "Commerce Department Awards $283,320 to Louisiana Educational Television Authority," news release, September 27, 2005.

[54] U.S. Department of the Interior, "Cason Announces Initial BIA Response to Aid Tribal Victims of Hurricane Katrina," news release, September 1, 2005.

[55] U.S. Department of the Interior, "Ragsdale Tours Mississippi Choctaw Reservation Impacted by Hurricane Katrina," news release, September 9, 2005.

[56] U.S. Department of the Interior, "Ragsdale Tours Mississippi Choctaw reservation Impacted by Hurricane Katrina," news release, September 9, 2005.

[57] U.S. Department of the Interior, Bureau of Land Management, "BLM, Other Federal Agencies Send Employees to Help with Katrina Relief Effort," news release, September 2, 2005.

[58] U.S. Department of the Interior, Bureau of Reclamation, "Reclamation Continues to Mobilize Response for Hurricane Katrina Disaster," news release, September 2, 2005.

[59] Donald M. Stoeckel et al., *Bacteriological Water Quality in the Lake Pontchartrain Basin, Louisiana, Following Hurricanes Katrina and Rita*, data series 143, prepared for the U.S. Department of the Interior and U.S. Geological Survey (September 2005).

[60] U.S. Department of the Interior, Office of Surface Mining, "OSM Volunteers Aid Hurricane Recovery," news release, December 19, 2005.

[61] U.S. Department of Labor, "U.S. Department of Labor Launches 'Pathways to Employment' Initiative, Expanding Employment Services for Hurricane Survivors," news release, September 30, 2005.

[62] U.S. Department of Education, "Hurricane Help for Schools," http://hurricanehelpforschools.gov/thanksto.html (accessed February 10, 2006).

[63] U.S. Department of Education, "Hurricane-Affected Schools Receive Federal Surplus Property," news release, November 1, 2005.

[64] Jenny Mandel, "Three Agencies Honored with Top Management Awards," *Government Executive Magazine*, December 14, 2005, http://govexec.com/dailyfed/1205/121405m1.htm; and Ambassador W. Robert Pearson, "Accomplishments and Challenges," *State Magazine*, January 2006, 2.

[65] U.S. Department of the Treasury, Bureau of the Public Debt, "Bureau of the Public Debt Aids Savings Bonds Owners Battered by Hurricane Katrina," news release, August 29, 2005.

[66] U.S. Department of the Treasury, Financial Management Service, *Special Notice for Depository Institutions: Update to U.S. Treasury Guidance on Cashing FEMA Disaster Assistance Checks and Government Benefit Checks Issued by the U.S. Treasury* (Washington, D.C., September 14, 2005).

[67] U.S. Department of the Treasury, Internal Revenue Service, "Tax Favored Treatment for Early Distributions from IRAs and other Retirement Plans for Victims of Hurricane Katrina," news release, October 17, 2005.

[68] U.S. Department of Veterans Affairs, Veterans Integrated Service Network, "Hurricanes: VA/VISN 4 Update #2," September 27, 2005.

[69] U.S. Department of Veterans Affairs, "web site bulletin," http://www.vba.va.gov/ro/central/stpau/Pages/Katrina.html.

[70] U.S. Department of Veterans Affairs, "VA Creates Procedures for Benefits in Wake of Hurricane Katrina," news release, September 14, 2005.

[71] U.S. Environmental Protection Agency, "Curbside Pickup of Household Hazardous Waste Planned in Plaquemines Parish," news release, September 25, 2005.

[72] U.S. Environmental Protection Agency, "Hurricane Response 2005: Public Outreach Materials," http://www.epa.gov/katrina/outreach; U.S. Environmental Protection Agency, "EPA and Federal Partners Warn of Potential Environmental Health Hazards When Returning to Homes and Businesses after Hurricane Katrina," news release, September 14, 2004.

[73] Lawrence Kumins and Robert Bamberger, *Oil and Gas Disruption from Hurricanes Katrina and Rita*, Congressional Research Service Report for Congress RL33124 (Washington, D.C., October 21, 2005), 7-8.

[74] Federal Energy Regulatory Commission, "Commission Temporarily Eases Natural Gas Construction Rules to Speed Recovery from Hurricanes," news release, November 17, 2005.

[75] White House Office of Management and Budget to the Chief Financial Officers and Grant Policy Officials, memorandum entitled "Administrative Relief for Grantees Impacted by Hurricanes Katrina and Rita," September 30, 2005.